NEW FASHION **PHOTOGRAPHY**

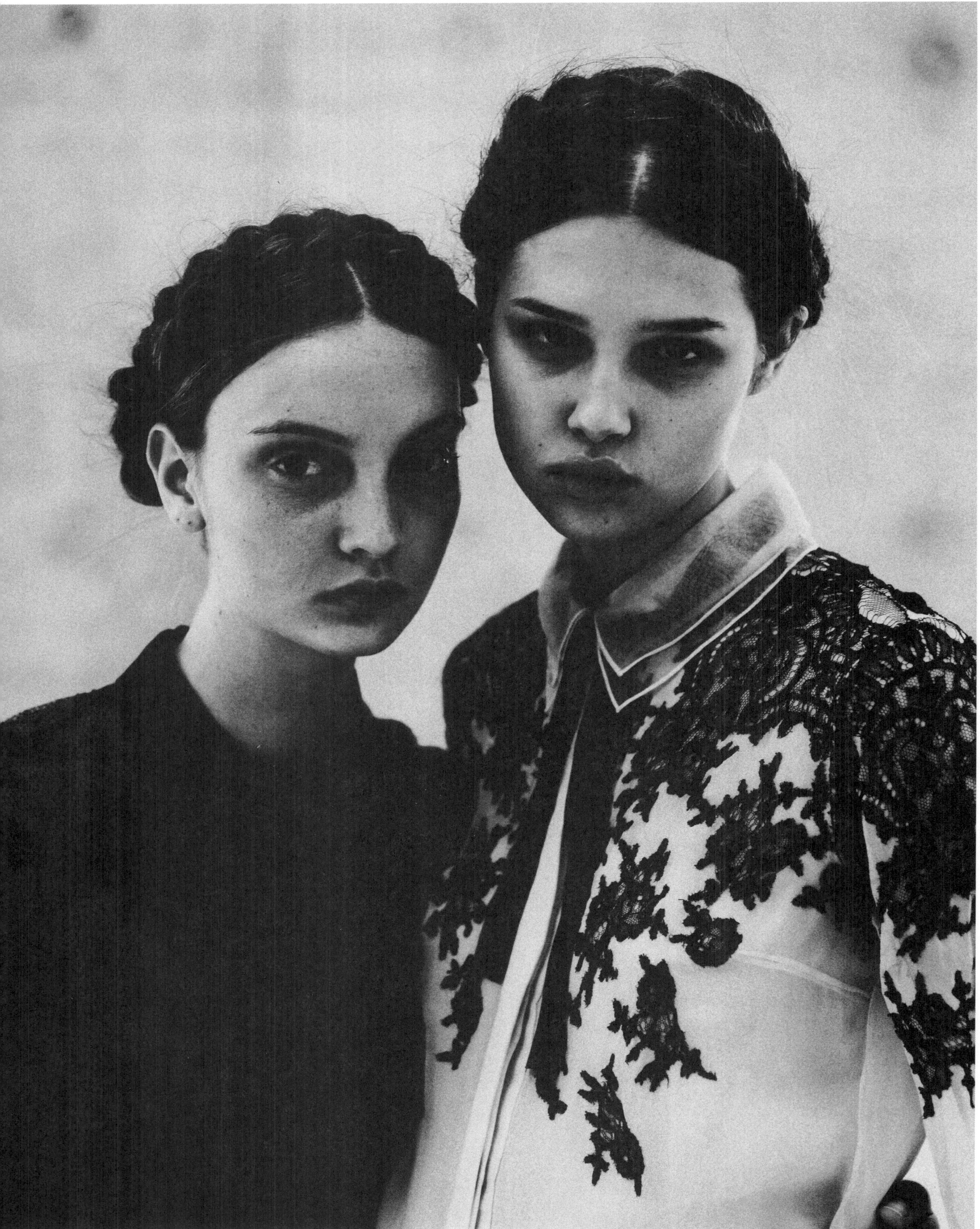

NEW FASHION **PHOTOGRAPHY**

compiled by paul sloman / introduction by tim blanks

PRESTEL

munich · london · new york

© Prestel Verlag, Munich · London · New York, 2013
© for the photographs resides with the individual photographers, 2013
© for the texts by Tim Blanks and Paul Sloman, 2013

Front cover: LaRoache Brothers, 'Obscurité' for *Schön*, 2010, courtesy Factory 311
Back cover: Yasunari Kikuma, Antonia Wesseloh for *Vision* China, 2012

page 2: Chadwick Tyler, Codi Young and Anaïs Pouliot for Mercedes Benz/Grey V 2011
pages 6–7: Tim Richardson, 'Diesel White Out' for *Commons & Sense Man*, styled by Shun Watanabe

Prestel, a member of Verlagsgruppe Random House GmbH

Prestel Verlag
Neumarkter Strasse 28
81673 Munich
Tel. +49 (0)89 4136-0
Fax +49 (0)89 4136-2335

www.prestel.de

Prestel Publishing Ltd.
4 Bloomsbury Place
London WC1A 2QA
Tel. +44 (0)20 7323-5004
Fax +44 (0)20 7636-8004

Prestel Publishing
900 Broadway, Suite 603
New York, NY 10003
Tel. +1 (212) 995-2720
Fax +1 (212) 995-2733

www.prestel.com

Library of Congress Control Number: 2012952514

British Library Cataloguing-in-Publication Data: a catalogue record for this book is available from the British Library. The Deutsche Bibliothek holds a record of this publication in the Deutsche Nationalbibliografie; detailed bibliographical data can be found under: http://dnb.d-nb.de

Prestel books are available worldwide. Please contact your nearest bookseller or one of the above addresses for information concerning your local distributor.

Editorial direction: Paul Sloman
Copyediting by: Ali Gitlow and Marcelo dos Santos Pereira
Proofreading by: Ali Gitlow
Production: Friederike Schirge and Paul Sloman
Design and layout: Paul Sloman / +SUBTRACT

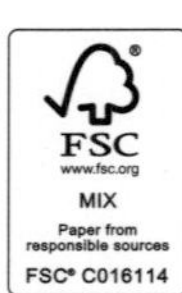

Origination: Altaimage
Printing and binding: Conti Tipocolor
Printed in Italy
Verlagsgrupe Random House FSC-DEU-0100
The FSC-certified paper Garda Matt has been supplied by Garda Cartiere
ISBN 978-3-7913-4791-2

CONTENTS /

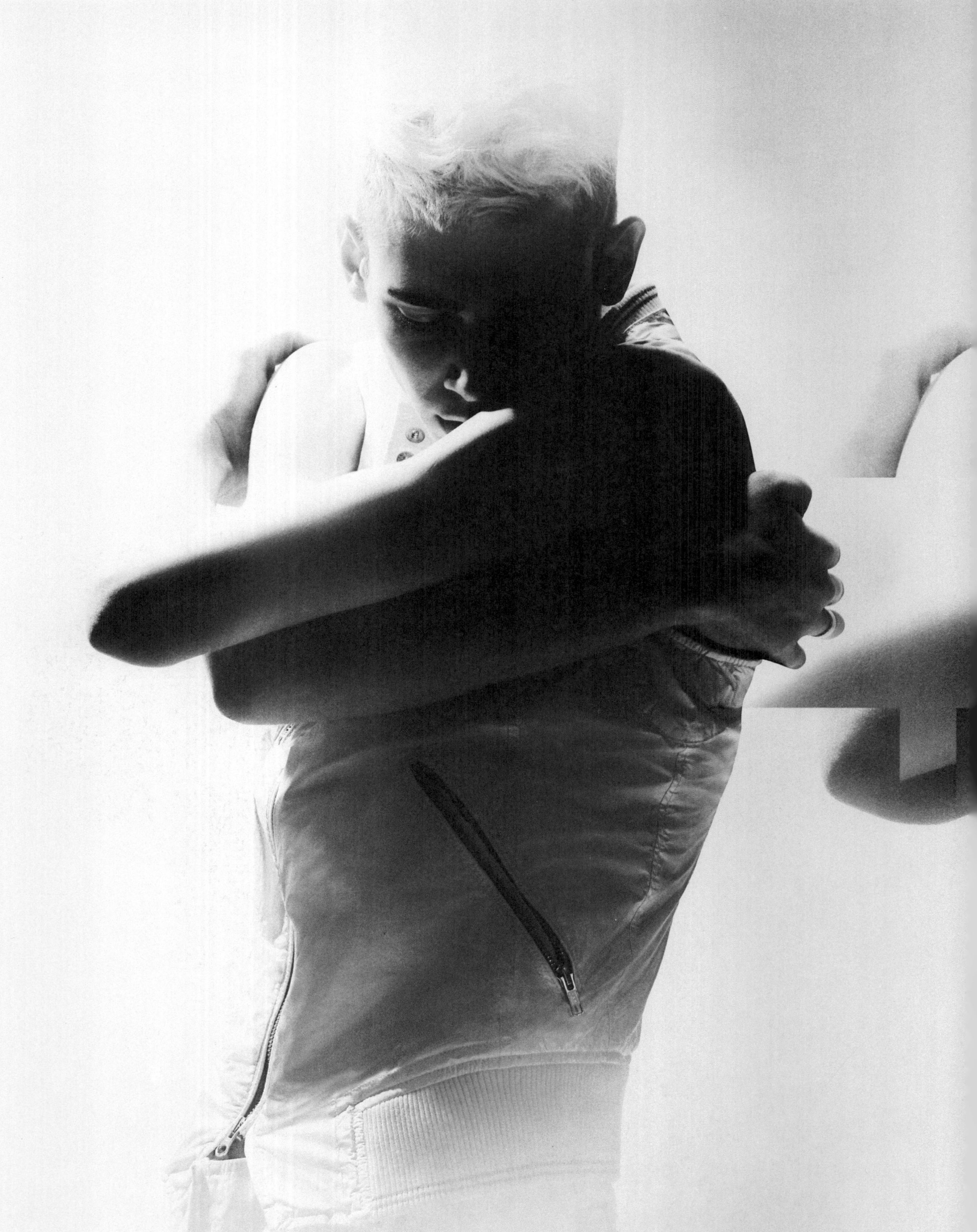

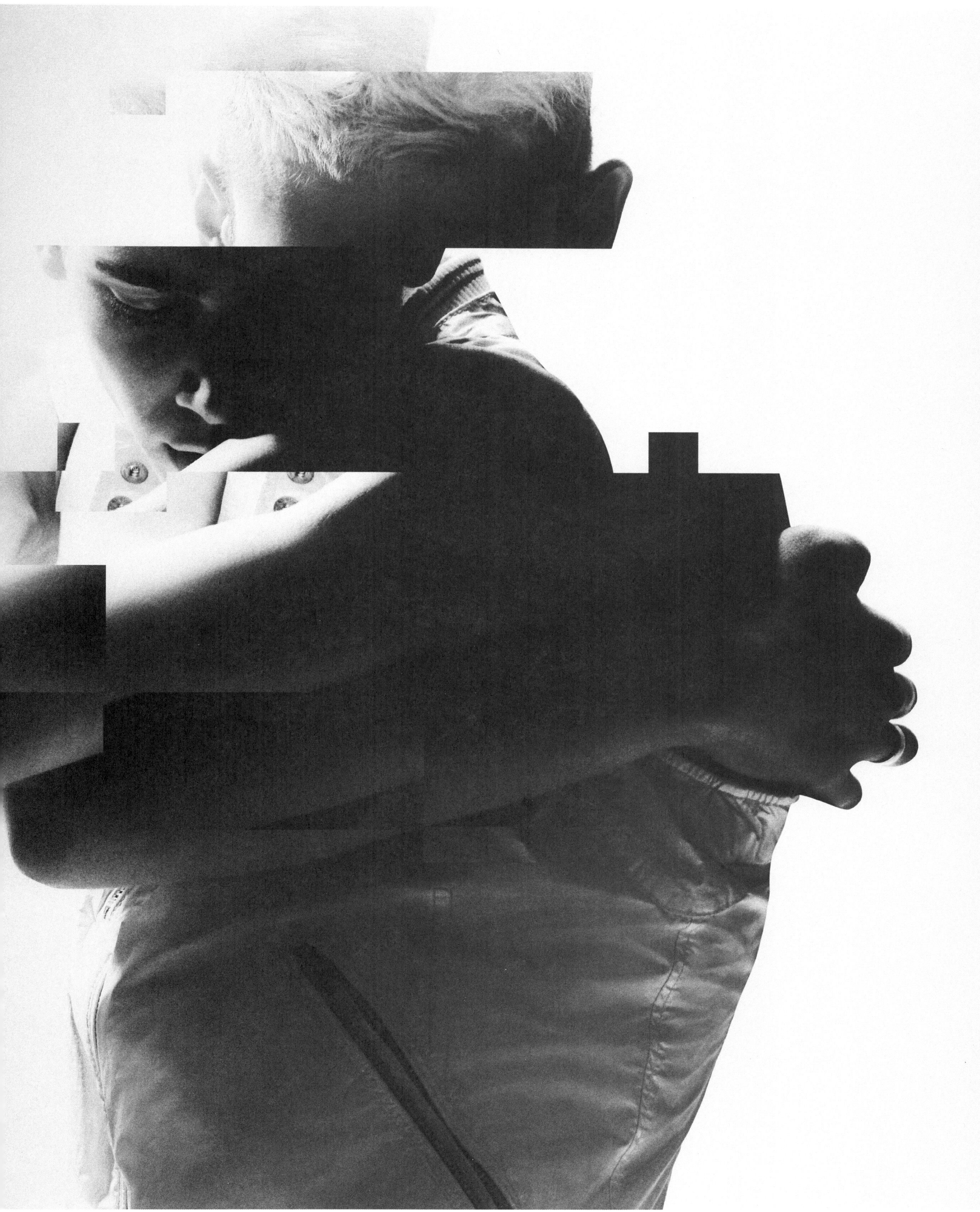

The relationship between photography and fashion dates from the earliest years of the medium. Louis Daguerre announced the first complete practical photographic process in 1839. The calotype of Lady Mary Ruthven made five years later by David Octavius Hill and Robert Adamson is generally considered to be ground zero for the fashion photograph. But the relationship was never one of equals. If the camera went on to capture epochal moments in the course of human history, its application in fashion was accorded rather less respect.

'The history of fashion photography is, quite simply, a record of those photographs made to show or sell clothing or accessories.'[1] That is the first line of Nancy Hall-Duncan's introduction to her 1979 overview, also called *The History of Fashion Photography*. The definite article is telling. It suggests that Duncan was confident she was producing a *definitive* something on the genre. And maybe, at that particular point in time, her confidence wasn't so misplaced. There weren't many other chroniclers stepping up to the fashion plate. Fashion photography had barely attained legitimacy as anything other than the fashion industry's shop window. Read the august critics of the time – the *New York Times*' Hilton Kramer, say, in his review of a 1975 exhibition of six decades of fashion snapping – and you can't miss the slightly sniffy sense that he thought it a dubious proposition at best, and an entirely unsavoury one, bordering on pornography, at worst. On that last point, by the way, Kramer's particular beef was with Helmut Newton, whose position in fashion photography's Olympian pantheon is now unassailable.

The reductive nature of Duncan's statement could also be excused by the fact that she was, after all, looking back over a century or so. Excuse? No, *j'accuse*, with one single piece of evidence for fashion photography's defence: a ten-page spread from the September 1962 issue of *Harper's Bazaar* featuring proto-supermodel Suzy Parker and director Mike Nichols photographed by Richard Avedon as they re-enacted paparazzi-hounded vignettes

from Elizabeth Taylor and Richard Burton's very public *amour fou*. Savagely funny, wildly topical and ridiculously glamorous, this was fashion photography as the fiercest comment on its social and cultural context, and I'll always come back to it as a moment of white-light vindication.

Around the same time that Kramer was feeling queasy over Newton (and waxing *way* less than enthusiastic over Richard Avedon), Susan Sontag was rhapsodising that the greatest fashion photography is more than the photography of fashion. This was always true, but it's a point that has been made with particular intensity since Sontag gave it voice more than thirty years ago. And it's being made again in this book which, in its curation of fashion-based work from the past few years, most of it from an innovative new generation of photographers, underscores the peculiar maturity-in-diversity of the medium. No longer in search of – let alone in need of – legitimacy, fashion photography has become a reference for and an influence on the culture at large. So insidious is it, in fact, that the image has become all: the dream, the desire, even a surrogate for the clothes themselves. Can't afford a new outfit? Buy a magazine. The medium has become the message. This has been most succinctly expressed as a shift from imitation (the image instructing you in how to duplicate its content) to identification (the image offering a more abstract pointer in how to actually *be*).

It's tempting to analyse that shift in the broad strokes of the same inevitable cultural dialectic which transforms every other creative endeavour: hypothesis/antithesis/synthesis. Take as the original hypothesis the formalism, elegance and elitism that characterised fashion photography's practice throughout much of the twentieth century. The influential French semiotician and dialectical wizard Roland Barthes scornfully observed that fashion itself was forbidden to offer 'anything aesthetically or morally unpleasant',[2] although what Barthes saw as abject failure was equally an accurate reflection of the world on which photographers trained their

1 Nancy Hall-Duncan
The History of Fashion Photography
Alpine Book Company, 1979, p. 9

2 Roland Barthes
Système de la mode
Paris, 1967

lenses. As that world changed, so did the photography. The salon surrendered to the street. The rise of ready-to-wear introduced the democracy of choice as opposed to the dictatorship of demagogic couture. It inspired the emergence of an egalitarian antithesis, with an attendant emphasis on surreal, provocative or confrontational elements which Barthes, who died in 1980, would surely have found more pleasing. In the representation of fashion, the clothes became less important than the attitude of the people wearing them. Capturing that attitude took fashion photography into the 'real' world, culminating in the everyday intimacy of the snapshot aesthetic.

If the consummation of any dialectic is the synthesis of hypothesis and antithesis, that ought to add up to a tidy union of elitism and egalitarianism in contemporary photography's approach to fashion. One key instrument of synthesis does in fact make that union quite graphic. It is the old-school house organ of the fashion industry, the glossy monthly magazine, although its most effective contemporary manifestation is more likely to be biannual. There has been a global proliferation of such publications. First up were *i-D* and *The Face*, kick-started in the DIY ferment of the post-punk years. Their early commitment to edgy, idiosyncratic/artistic self-expression was mutated over the years by the expensive production values we're now familiar with, particularly in those biannuals. They are usually underwritten by substantial advertising content, which turns them into perfect paradigms of art and commerce. In that, they are like outriders of the contemporary art world: small, mobile galleries with endlessly revolving exhibitions curated by editors, art directors and stylists, meaning that there have never been so many opportunities for young and/or new talents to display their work. The authority that editorial vision gives the best of these magazines ensures that their content becomes part of the broad cultural continuum that weaves through art, music, movies and design. Fashion comes all the way round to influence its influences.

That is one element of the 'newness' in fashion photography that this book seeks to communicate. Another is the role of technology. The digital revolution has made the medium faster and younger, which is evident in these pages. Digital innovation has stretched the limits of photography, fostering a technical facility that allows a head-spinning mix of media. The amount of sensory information that can be compressed into one single image has been stretched. Guy Bourdin's assistants once had to dye the sea bluer, paint the grass greener. Now, anything the artist's mind conceives is within reach of his or her fingertips. Look at the way an image can be transmogrified with digital brushstrokes. The photographic and the painterly co-join. Flesh itself becomes entirely mutable.

Still, what I find most intriguing is the way that the essence of *New Fashion Photography* suggests what the future might ultimately construe as the medium's eternal verities. Surprisingly, they look, on the whole, like a return to that original elegant, formal hypothesis. Icon-making in the classic tradition — going back to look forward, as it were. There is a chill composure in the images here. The extravagant mess of life is as distant as it was in the pictures of Adolph de Meyer, Cecil Beaton, Irving Penn, even Avedon. Actually, *why* should this be so surprising? It's the same urge that has impelled Steven Meisel through what may be the most durably dazzling career in fashion photography. Meisel would probably deny that his work is about anything more than the photography of fashion, but that shouldn't stop us taking a cue from Sontag and wondering what broader state of mind such image-making might reflect.

The work curated here may be diverse in appearance, but the connective thread is an open engagement with artifice. Innovation practically encourages it. After all, if technology makes anything possible for you, what better way to test it than with a carefully constructed irreality? But here, even the digital counter-revolutionaries — the anti-Photoshoppers and post-post-prodders — are channeling visions of artificiality. Would it be safe to assume that reality bites?

Artifice as an escape – or a refuge – has traditionally been symptomatic of a culture's decadence. The overt historicism of some of these images at least indicates an awareness of such a thing. But more striking is the reliance on hidden or masked features, from delicate veiling to complete obliteration. Identity – cultural, religious, gender – is one of the great social issues of the age. Fashion is an industry which trades in image as an expression of identity. The mask is an obvious comment on role-playing. Your choice of mask can reveal as much as it conceals. That much is evident here. Digital technology also allows a literal fluidity to reflect shifts in identity. But it seems to me there is another dynamic in the work in this collection. The notion of identification gains more traction. It reinforces a feeling that times are so uncertain it might be preferable to withdraw, maybe even to hide away, in the familiarity of the past or the unimaginability of the future. This hermetic sensibility is reflected in the hermetic nature of the images themselves and their worlds within worlds. After years of being invited to participate in the lives of Juergen Teller, Terry Richardson et al., not to mention the increasingly deadening weight of street style coverage, we are once again outside looking in.

It's not a bad place to be. There is, after all, something a little audacious at work here. Photography's Holy Grail has always been the decisive moment, legendary lensman Henri Cartier-Bresson's code for the illuminating flash of photographic truth. Maybe one of fashion photography's 'news' flashes is that the *indecisive* moment is closer to the truth, a tentative, transient instance which underscores the illusory nature of reality. The pursuit of beauty is a crash course in transience. It may be timeless in the abstract, but it is over in seeming seconds in the here and now. The melancholic tension between timelessness and transience made ideal fodder for centuries of painters, playwrights and poets. Now, it's manna from heaven for fashion photographers too.

The timeless-versus-transient debate is just one of the conversations that keeps this present volume humming along. There are others: realism versus surrealism; Freud versus Jung; innocence versus desecration; beauty versus horror. In fact, the lingering impression as you come to the end of the collection is that you could have been at the side-event of a symposium on the movies of Alfred Hitchcock, David Lynch and Roman Polanski. Alexander Liberman, who helped define the concept of the art director in his two decades at *Vogue*, once said the role of fashion was to seduce. Over the past twenty years that role has widened, as fashion has become an adjunct of the entertainment industry. Now it enthralls, and appalls as well. It tells stories too, fantastic fairy stories. The fantasy of fashion was often a stick with which its detractors beat it. Here, the fantasy is unabashedly all-powerful.

New Fashion Photography is a sequence of interrupted narratives, whose characters are captured in mid-flux. Like Lynch's *Blue Velvet* or Hitchcock's *Vertigo*, they have a passing acquaintance with real life, but their substance is dream-like disorientation. Just like those directors, the photographers are auteurs who orchestrate their visions with a team of dedicated collaborators. I'm thinking about how those two movies transcended time, place and medium to become cultural totems – dark, shiny fetish objects, in fact, which is perfect because their subject matter was so embedded in fetish. But so is fashion. And that acknowledgement is right at the heart of *New Fashion Photography*.

The soft contours of a portrait segue into a schism in 'Diesel White Out' by Tim Richardson for Commons & Sense Man *(pages 6–7). A digital fracturing creates a disruption of the image and a destabilisation of the real. The relationship between reality and artifice has always been at the crux of fashion, but this is something new. In the post-millenial flux of new technologies, the illusions that lie beneath the surface of the image are worn on the outside. Fashion photography has become self-conscious; instead of containing itself within specific rules of engagement, its apparent contradictions have begun to explode out in a kaleidoscopic, cross-format haze.*

Multi-disciplinary photographer René Habermacher says 'Fashion photography is an expression of momentum'.[1] In the twenty-first century, this hinges on the perpetual motion of new electronic and social structures. For some time, fashion photography has appeared to sidestep a clear aspirational ideal as a solution to modern identity, but now it goes further. Nick Knight refuses to let his camera tie his subjects down to a fixed image, choosing instead to immerse them in amorphous fluids and powders, the substances of an unstable moment. Pierre Debusschere unstitches the fabric of reality in his photographs using the very technology that produces them. His images frequently break down into stuttering animated GIFs that exist in an uncertain hinterland between film and photography. Richardson's disruptions of the image build a world from the visual scratches and glitches in digital material, illuminating the hidden moments within the immediately visible. Taking a blade to his portraits for *Harper's Bazaar* China in 2010, Daniel Sannwald cuts into the surface of his images to reveal conflicting scenes beneath.

The explicit destabilisation of the image has done the same thing to time and place. As the instability of the digitised moment ignites a return to formal classicism, fundamental disturbances in the image upset the balance of explicitly traditional compositions. Eugenio Recuenco pits contemporary decadence against timeless domesticity in his reworked visions of classical paintings; Daniel Jackson throws Victorian society parties with Nietzschean undertones; Daniele + Iango apply twenty-first century gender subversions to the traditions and rituals of Japanese sumo and the Edo-period pleasure district.

Historical returns, here, evoke continuity in a present that seems immersed in the chaos of its own multiplicity. Parallels of capitalism and excess exist at one end; restraint and austerity at the other. Fashion photography has often begged, borrowed and stolen from history. In *Fashion at The Edge*, theorist Caroline Evans describes fashion's 'particularly promiscuous historical behaviour, its brief life span and its incessant trawling through the old to fabricate the new.'[2] Photography, however, increasingly borrows from its own past as well as the history of the arts to make sense of the present. It is not so much a revisitation of history as the history of image-making itself. Formal association in Sannwald's series 'Looking for a Certain Ratio' for *Vogue Homme +* in 2011, in which a warped tripod matches the contours of its subject, echoes Manuel Vilariño's 1985 photograph *Sula Bassana*, which pairs a hammer with the neck and beak of a bird. Sean and Seng's comical pairing of Liyá Kebede with a flamingo uses the same idea but, abandoning any clear reference point between the two, it playfully rejects the formal relationship. This animal absurdity also reaches further back into the history of fashion photography, and indeed fashion itself, recalling the Surrealist fantasies of Grete Stern and the conceptual fashion symbolism of Elsa Schiaparelli in the 1930s.

The call of the Surreal, a 'cry of the mind turning back on itself',[3] echoes loudly. A Lynchian version of it is channeled in the images of Miles Aldridge; magic realist tangents come through in those of Ruven Afanador, Yelena Yemchuk, and Sanchez and Mongiello, who draw on the experimental writing of authors such as Gabriel García Márquez, Jorge Luis Borges and Mikhail Bulgakov. The multiple layers of these photographs embrace fluidity of meaning and the power of association, but the associations are complex and convoluted. Images are piled high with layer upon layer of symbols and signifiers. In a sea of psycho-symbolism and cross-cultural references, there are illusions and delusions, twists and turns, as images lurch backwards into the past and reach forward into imagined futures. This looks like the spectacle of fashion in its highest gear – so high that it might seem to be hyperventilating. Evans relates the overwhelming performance of fashion to Theodor Adorno's concept of the phantasmagoria, in which 'the tricks, deceits and illusions of nineteenth-century commodity culture, with its sleights of hand, peddled false desires.'[4] The mechanics of capitalism, Adorno argues, are hiding behind the greatest of spectacles – a majestic delusion. This is a wall of misdirection ultimately designed to bury the working methods of capitalist production behind a false surface of marketing and retail. And on this subject, fashion photography does carry a weight on its shoulders. 'In fashion, the phantasmagoria of commodities presses closest to the skin,' Susan Buck-Morss reiterates in *The Dialiectics of Seeing*.[5] Fashion appears inextricably linked to something from which it attempts to hide through the outward diversion of its own performance.

The essential yet turbulent relationship between fashion and commerce shares an alignment with art. Evoking the factory treadmill of Andy Warhol half a century before, Damien Hirst's provocative diamond-encrusted skull, labelled *For the Love of God*, brazenly exploits a driving force that most artists might prefer to ignore. Hirst's commercial and creative relationship with fashion – he has designed shoes with Manolo Blahnik using his marketable spot designs, and has produced conceptual photography in collaboration with Rankin – reinforces this parallel. It is nothing new; even the great portrait painters of the eighteenth century responded to market forces, dressing their subject in the latest fashions, symbols of wealth and social standing. And in the same way, in the pages of magazines, the fashion photographer is tied to a fashion product. Certainly the escapist fantasy inherent in many of these photographs offers an aspirational thrill that goes back to the birth of fashion. But there is a slight difference in the selective incisions into history that are being made today. These photographs are, more often than not, explicitly self-referential; the deceit of their

illusions and sleights of hand is undone by the overt nature of their own artifice. The relationship between fashion and commerce may remain uncomfortable, but in this new, more self-aware photography, if there is a deceptive merging of the real and the imagined, then the viewer is complicit. The relationship between the constructed nature of fashion and the everyday reality to which it speaks is no longer disguised.

In many ways, this is a continuation. The discordant complexities of these photographs are an extension of, and answer to, an aesthetic rupture of another kind that occured at the end of the previous millennium. As the close of the twentieth century approached, fashion and photography were giving way to pre-millenial anxiety. In the wake of postmodernism, structures of narrative, time and hierarchy had been pulled apart, fed back into each other and spewed out half-masticated in a soupy blend of contradictory paradigms. It was the manifestation of an ever diminishing faith in established pillars of authority, in the face of rapid globalisation and technological proliferation. And if the present seemed hard to get to grips with, the rules of the future looked even more volatile and unpredictable. Fashion itself responded with a strange brew of paranoia, fantasy and self-deconstruction. It pillaged the past with a sense of abandon that undermined the periods from which it drew. Styles were taken out of context, rendered meaningless, then slammed together to create new, relativist statements about the postmodern condition. The threat of social, global and even media fragmentation was visualised as decay; the deathly echoes of the spectacle were being played out on the catwalks of designers such as Alexander McQueen, Viktor & Rolf, and Junya Watanabe.

Fashion had a statement to make, but it oscillated between dangerous glamour and a courageous new tendency towards self-analysis. In his Autumn/Winter 1999–2000 catwalk show for Givenchy, McQueen favoured mannequins over living models; they rose out of the floor and descended again, like spectres lifted from the grave. Fashion was looking at itself and what it saw was an

1 René Habermacher
interview with Filep Motwary
Un Nouveau Ideal, 2009

2 Caroline Evans
Fashion at the Edge
Yale University Press, 2003, p. 89

3 André Breton
Declaration of January 27, 1925
Bureau de Recherches Surréalistes
15 Rue de Grenelle

4 Evans, p. 89

5 Susan Buck-Morss
*The Dialectics of Seeing:
Walter Benjamin and the Arcades Project*
1991, quoted in ibid., p. 92

6 Charlotte Cotton
Imperfect Beauty
V&A Publications, 2000, p. 6

objectification that sucked the life out of its victims. A strain of photography embraced the swell of the dark. Photographers began to plough a morbid path into subjects previously the preserve of artists – sex, death and mortality. Photographer Sean Ellis pioneered a sultry gothicism which mastered the message that came from the fashion designers. Ellis's 'The Clinic' for *The Face* suspended models on hooks; 'A Taste of Arsenic' let children loose in a menacing vision of liberation that inverted the hierarchy of age. In the hands of photographers, this deathly fixation was closely intertwined with the fantasy that was being pursued by fashion itself. Heavy makeup, theatre and spectacle made for a mortal coil that was, contrarily, darkly seductive.

The deathly pallor of the end of the century represented the face of the catwalk as critic of fashion in an alienated moment, but another response looked for a solution. The raw, unprocessed shoots that emerged from the pages of Terry Jones and Nick Knight at *i-D*, Rankin and Jefferson Hack at *Dazed & Confused*, and under the editorship of Phil Bicker at *The Face* all represented a loosening of the parameters of control for fashion photography. It was the next step in a style known as the 'straight-up', pioneered by *i-D* founder Jones, who shot punk photographs against a white background and packaged them as *Not Another Punk Book*, and Knight, who did the same thing for skinheads shortly after. Realist experiments represented a yearning for authenticity in the face of the increasing chasm that came between the individual and fashion. At *Dazed* in the 1990s, sensing a disconnect between the everyday buyer of fashion and the darkening spectacle of high-end couture, Rankin and Hack set about returning the magazine's photography to those who actually wore the fashion it depicted. 'Blow-Up', a series of photographs of ordinary people photographed in booths set up in clubs, took the lessons of Jones' technique and those of *Interview* magazine in Europe to reunite fashion with the fashion scene itself. *Dazed* ran club nights in London and fed off the results in a two-way interaction, sweeping away the conventions of unattainable fashion imagery and reasserting the individual. Simultaneously, Knight was commissioning

Juergen Teller for *i-D*, and Bicker was giving photographers and stylists complete freedom to express themselves in the pages of *The Face*. Stylists such as Corinne Day introduced secondhand clothes and personal items to modify editorials in a provocative exercise in customisation and casual realism that would capture a generation. As Charlotte Cotton explains in *Imperfect Beauty*, fashion image-makers were 'constructing narratives around characters that spoke of the aspirations and realities of contemporary youth culture'.[6] It was as if the photograph promised a window onto a very private interaction, shot at random, an archive from a private piece of film. The images felt grungy, real and gloriously untroubled. It was an emancipation of the photograph that established a new optimism for the art.

If the unrefined realism of these magazines has altered the foundations of contemporary photography, it is worth first noting, as Tim Blanks does, how little its raw visual aesthetic appears to have translated into the highly stylised fantasies of today. Authenticity appears to have visibly ebbed away from the frontline. Echoes of the dark, crepuscular glamour of the end of the millenium, on the other hand, carry on like ghosts of the previous century at the hands of photographers such as the LaRoache Brothers and Chadwick Tyler, although the message appears to have shifted. Reacting to the flat polish of a digital world, the clunky machinery of the LaRoache Brothers' 'Mechanical' has the nostalgic appeal of the Japanese steampunk aesthetic that draws on the era of British Victorian industry. This is a curious form of nostalgia written in petrol-black ink. Fashion and history materialise as more gloriously extravagant escapism in shoots such as Aram Bedrossian's 'Bonnie and Clyde' and Markus + Indrani's mythical 'Lady and the White Snake'. Cinematic framing suggests thrilling stories of lust and longing in the photographs of Wing Shya. They are a delicious indulgence; they seem at first to promise moments of complete escape from the real, rather than any expression of it. Their reference points are two steps removed from reality; the starting point for their narratives are already fictionalised stories themselves.

In the twenty-first century, the intense focus on the fashion photograph as authentic document has become troubled by the very technology that is democratising photography. Documentary fashion photographs have become ubiquitous; home-grown style guides articulate the voice of the street from day to day. Meanwhile, the mass-media photograph, with the emergence of the Internet and digital software, has become increasingly unreliable; it can all too easily be manufactured. The false authenticity of the photographic image has emerged in propaganda wars between nations in games of global politics. It has threatened to become the illusion it tried to reject.

Ellis, in his 2006 shoot 'Paths of Glory', enjoys indulging in the ambiguities of the document and our diminishing faith in it. His images have the jerky realism of photography on the edge of a warzone; the shots are blurred moments taken from beneath shattered brickwork and shards of metal. Yet, amidst the chaos of the front line, the subject that strides through the detritus has the elegance and assurance of the fashion model. This 'authentic moment' is explicitly constructed. Chadwick Tyler creates false authenticity through the prism of history; his portraits recall the pioneering Depression-era photography of Dorothea Lange. A portrait of Lily Cole by the LaRoache Brothers marries gloomy fantasy with the false authenticity of the Victorian-era *carte-de-visite* family album. These photographs problematise the real in the fashion photograph again, just as it appeared to be growing comfortable with itself.

Kourtney Roy's explicitly artificial backdrops in her 'Ideal Woman' portraits are a reminder of the early artifice of photographs such as Vittorio Alinari's *Cyclists* of 1895, an image in which men posed on bikes are suspended by cables to create the illusion of movement. Roy's images question the surface and let the viewer in on the constructed nature of portraiture. This is self-conscious artifice, and the question that follows is where the real becomes situated, if it is present at all. If fashion photography, in its return to conjured spectacle, is not encouraging us to wrap ourselves up in a cloak of falsehood and misdirection, what positive message is coming out of such self-consciously inauthentic imagery?

An intimation of an answer can be found in the work of artist Jeff Wall, who recreates authentic moments as staged reconstructions, disrupting our sense of the photograph as reliable source. His image *Dead Troops Talk* enacts the impossible. The authority of the image as capturing a genuine moment is broken down, but in its place the potential for the image itself to speak is opened. The imagined idea brings the dead to life, and gives voice to something beneath the surface. Looking again at Roy's 'ideal women', they may be posed against false backdrops, but the power of the image comes from the conflict between this and the emotional reality of the women themselves. Miles Aldridge, in his 2006 image 'First Impression' for *Vogue* Japan, creates a similar disconnect between the outer surface and the glassy eyes of the society women he depicts, as does Wing Shya in his portrayal of the distant gazes of men and women as they attempt to contain lustful and escapist yearnings. This is the lesson of Cindy Sherman's charade, embraced by the industry it serves to critique. It draws attention to something on the inside. In doing so it responds both to the troubles of the twentieth-century catwalk and the optimistic emancipation of the 'straight-up' revolution.

With the cracked surface of fashion worn shamelessly on the outside, the potential for a more meaningful relationship with a subliminal narrative gains weight. The acceptance of the complex interaction between identity and economy pushes the pursuit of reality in photography into a space that focuses on an intimate, dream-like realm. Fashion returns as a signifier of interior identity and consciousness. Just as science fiction addresses the present through the abstract parallels of imagined worlds, so the emphasis on fantasy reflects on a reality situated in the present moment; a reality that echoes Breton's 'mind turning back in on itself'. This is a return to a more more open engagement with something

7 Walter Benjamin
'The Work of Art in the Age of
Mechanical Reproduction', 1936

8 Susan Bright
Art Photography Now
Thames & Hudson, 2005, p. 10

9 'Reputations:
An Interview with Terry Jones'
Eye, Winter 1998

located at the very beginning of photography; something that Walter Benjamin identified in his 1936 essay 'The Work of Art in the Age of Mechanical Reproduction'. 'The camera,' Benjamin explains, 'introduces us to unconscious optics as does psychoanalysis to unconscious impulses'.[7] In a world where image surface is increasingly insecure, Benjamin's 'optical unconscious' offers a location for meaning.

The levitation in the LaRoache Brothers' 2011 editorial 'Holy Rollers', or the euphoric reverie of Chadwick Tyler's 2009 portrait of Constance Jablonski for *Grey II* are a reminder of the power of raw spectacle, but they also direct us towards Benjamin's unseen plane. The visualisation of these internal spaces, as Susan Bright explains in *Art Photography Now*, gives rise to things that before the photograph 'existed only in dreams — things that had never consciously been seen, let alone produced'.[8] It draws photographers towards a blurred boundary where meaning is immersed in mystery and the ephemeral, and the only concrete reality is the raw emotion of the subject. It is evoked in different ways in different hands — in the kaleidoscopic lens flare of Serge Leblon, the slow shutter speeds of Bruno Dayan, or the delicate symbolism of Paola Kudacki. Fashion photography has returned as an emotional spokesperson for the mind.

Through this process, the real is made fantastic. In his portraits of Sevillan flamenco dancers, Ruven Afanador uses the symbolism and uniform of their art to articulate an energy that comes from within. Yelena Yemchuk meanwhile plants the romance of fashion squarely in the centre of the kinds of environments that 'incorporate the distilled signs of "real" life', suburban cityscapes and domestic interiors — locations 'within which narratives of the everyday could be plausibly staged'.[8] Hawkins' images feel like a gloriously plasticised fantasy, yet her source material is as 'straight-up' real as Knight's skinheads. Any artifice is a product of the individual in question. It is a celebration of the audacity of self-expression; the emotional vigour is written all over the faces of her willing collaborators, depicted with an outrageous positivity. She even indulges in it herself, making herself up as Dolly Parton in 'Dolly Parton is my Religion' to express her own playful ideals and desires.

The power of physical appearance as an assertion of the internal map of the individual is particularly prescient in a cultural moment where social identity has, for the first time, become inextricably linked with virtual manifestations of ourselves. It started with avatars to the human self in shared online worlds in which the individual could refashion their own image as they saw themselves inside their own heads — in effect, their own models to aspiration. The emergence of social networks has encouraged virtual identities and the selective editing of personal histories, refined to match the way we view ourselves in our own perfect worlds. In this construction of identity there can be found parallels with the role of fashion as an indicator of inner hopes, fears, beliefs and aspirations. This echoes Terry Jones' suggestion that 'fashion is not just about clothes; it's about how you think;' that in an 'outward expression' that marks a transient moment, 'you can be successful in your own right by expressing yourself'.[9] The question of constructed identities may raise some troubling questions, but here, at least, those questions are brought out into the open. The relationship between the real and the imagined, as a result, offers an optimistic message for fashion and its role in the vitality of self-expression.

The revolutions in the pioneering style magazines of the last twenty years have left another legacy too: the democratisation of the photographic process; the increased focus on the mutual relationships between photographer, stylist, model and audience. Collaboration repeatedly asserts itself. The lessons of stylists such as Corinne Day, who introduced personal intimacy to the fashion shoot, have been absorbed, dismantling the hierarchy of the creative process. Now, the stylist has become an integral part — Nicola Formichetti, whose diverse collaborators in this volume include Tim Richardson, Pierre Debusschere and Takahiro Ogawa, has enough credibility to take centre stage on the November 2012 cover of

POP. Alongside this is the ongoing evolution of the relationship between photographer and model to something more creatively codependent. This is another step in a gradual process. In the 1960s, David Bailey was already pushing in this more intimate direction, foreshadowing the realist photography of the nineties with his shots of models such as Jean Shrimpton, who took control of her own identity in front of his lens. Bailey's technique, to encourage the model to let loose and fire away with the camera as they did so, gave voice to the subject and was the first step in breaking down the uncomfortable tradition of the photographer-male and woman-as-object. Nineties-era realism suggested that the relationship between photographer and subject was even more up-close and intimate; sometimes uncomfortably up-close. If the camera has withdrawn from that claustrophobic proximity, the potential for the model to 'speak' before it has become dominant.

With this new freedom, it is as if fashion photography is able to enjoy itself again; to indulge in escapism with a knowing awareness of its own role in a bigger picture. Technological proliferation has created a layered lattice of multiple meanings; identity has multiplied into virtual spaces, and fashion photography is channeling the levelled playing field of this complex new world with a considered awareness of its entire history. How best to sum up this turbulent yet intoxicating moment? Nick Knight's photograph of Lady Gaga provides a neat visual answer. His subject is iconic; she represents a generation and a moment but her self-presentation has repeatedly been reborn in the fashion media, the mainstream and independent press. She traverses boundaries of style and taste that confuse her identity. Knight's answer is to echo this exhilarating impermanence in a photograph in which she appears to move sluggishly under the weight of her endlessly shifting identity. Self and image are in a continual discourse with each other; moving, mutating, ever revising a transient point. She is the embodiment of Habermacher's 'expression of momentum', the outward assertion of the individual in the face of the multiplicity of meanings and realities that define a social era in transition.

A NOTE ABOUT THE COLLECTION

In this volume, the contemporary practice of photographers who have helped to shape the current moment appear alongside emergent artists who operate at the boundaries of experimentation, sometimes in collaboration with those pioneers. It is a hierarchy-free space, reflecting the collaborative process of contemporary photography, something that is occuring between artists and generations. It weaves an international path across territories, organised not by alphabet but by thematic arrangement, drawing conceptual and visual parallels that shift loosely throughout. In doing so it attempts to generate thought-provoking associations and encourage new discussions about the role of fashion photography in the context of the twenty-first century.

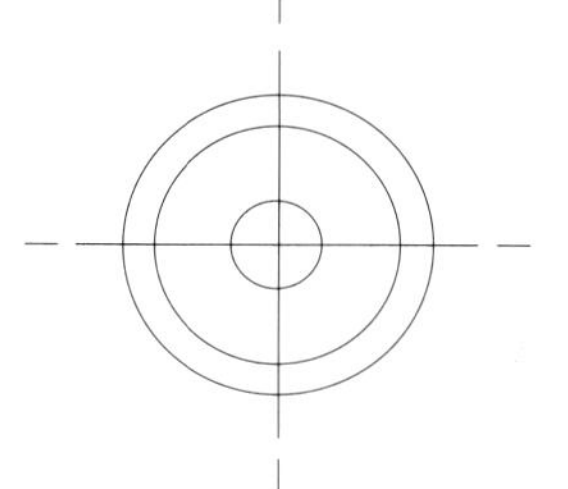

Angel from 'La Beauté en Avignon', 2000
collaboration with Alexander McQueen
photography by Nick Knight
courtesy Trunk Archive

pages 20–1:
Gisele for British *Vogue*, 2006
photography by Nick Knight
courtesy Trunk Archive

page 22:
'Body Language' for *AnOther Man*, 2010
photography by Nick Knight
courtesy Trunk Archive
styling by Alister Mackie
with Lucy McRae and Bart Hess

page 23:
Lady Gaga, 2011
photography by Nick Knight
courtesy Trunk Archive

Nick Knight puts process before product, elevating the act of creation to the status of art. It is a focus that has its genus in his first major 1978–80 series, *Skinheads*, in which he captured a point in time through the interaction of one skinhead observing another. His continuing relationship with the performance of image-making defines the work he produces, each photograph developing through a communication between subject and object to embody the movement and energy of a transient moment.

Emphasising message over medium, Knight's unique approach leads not only to photography that captures movement, but also to experimentation with the moving image itself. During *Pagan Poetry*, his film for Björk – a musician who shares his fascination with the creative potential of new media – he incites the artist to engage in a performance with the camera as it explores her face and body, generating close-up studies that slip in and out of a mutating abstraction. It is as if the film itself is seeking something, capturing it and losing it again, as it progresses. In Knight's still images there is a similar energy at work: in a portrait of model Lily Donaldson, powder bursts off her body in an explosion of colour (page 25); in 'Body Language' for *AnOther Man* magazine, paint saturates a figure posed on a stool (page 22). She is the embodiment of a portrait in progress, a painting interrupted in mid-flow.

Knight's long-term working partnership with Japanese designer Yohji Yamamato is another relationship based on a shared exploration of process. Just as Yamamato exposes the architecture of his garments, placing seams on the exterior and in doing so deconstructing his method, so Knight explores the architecture of fashion and beauty through his web-based project SHOWstudio. In this digital space he nurtures innovation and communication within the context of an online creative community. Film, text and photography are able to exist together in an environment that, unlike print, can shift and evolve from one moment to the next. More recently, SHOWstudio has set about collecting footage of photoshoots in an effort to catalogue what Knight sees as a form of theatre. For him, the shoot itself is a valid expression of the creative act as it moves towards the ultimate captured moment that appears on the screen or printed page.

Knight's deconstructive fascination with fashion is a product of an analytical mind, the scientific approach of someone who studied human biology before moving on to photography. His shoots are like calculations on a blackboard. The methodology of science – to search for something, fail and repeat, and perhaps discover something else (a beautiful mistake) – is hardwired into what he does. This is creation and response: a social synthesis of ideas that leads to images that are alive with movement, exploring the ephemeral nature of the present, the fallibility of the still image, and the persistent need to evolve. A confluence of independence and interaction leads to a visual dialogue made concrete, and one of the most dynamic bodies of work in fashion photography.

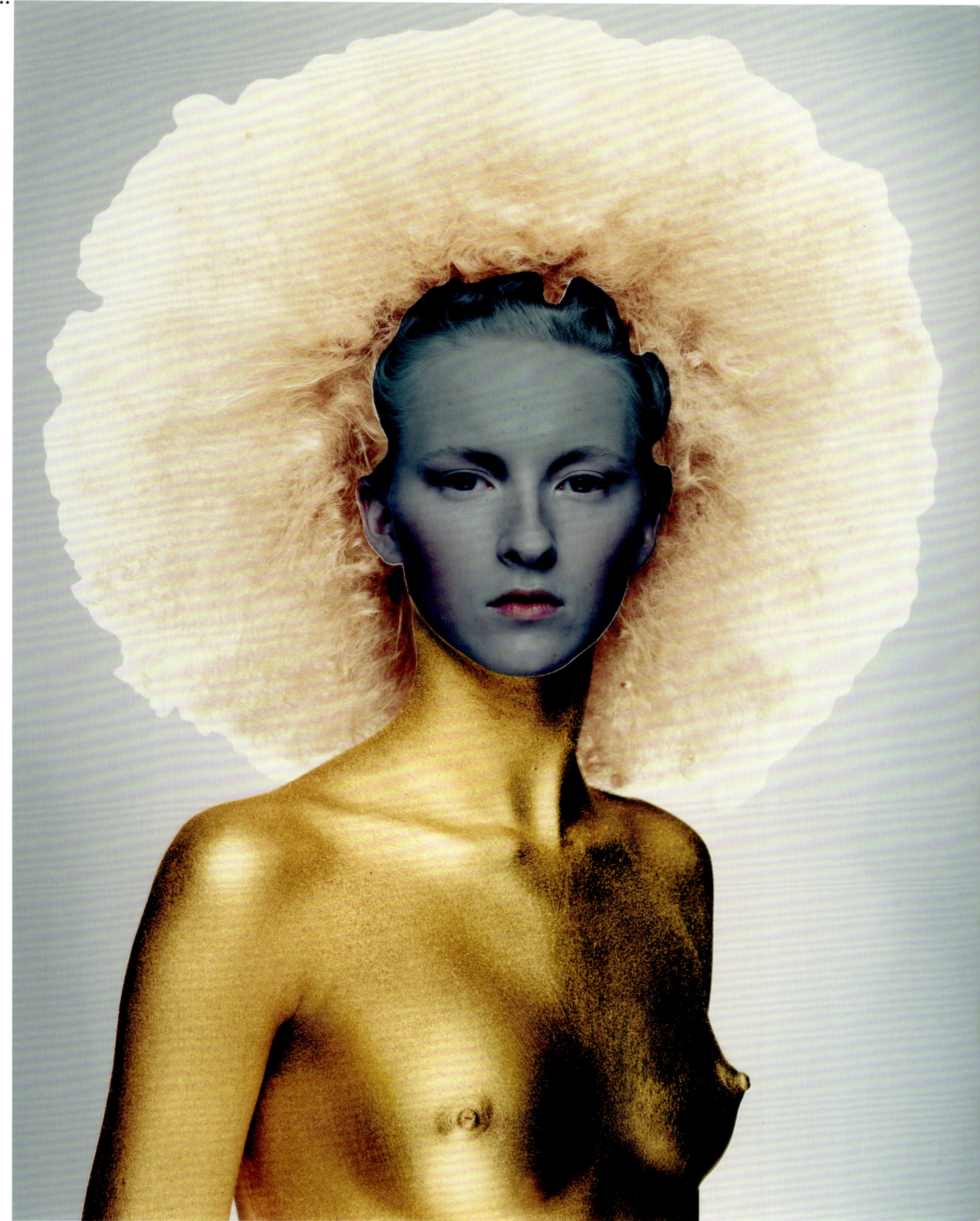

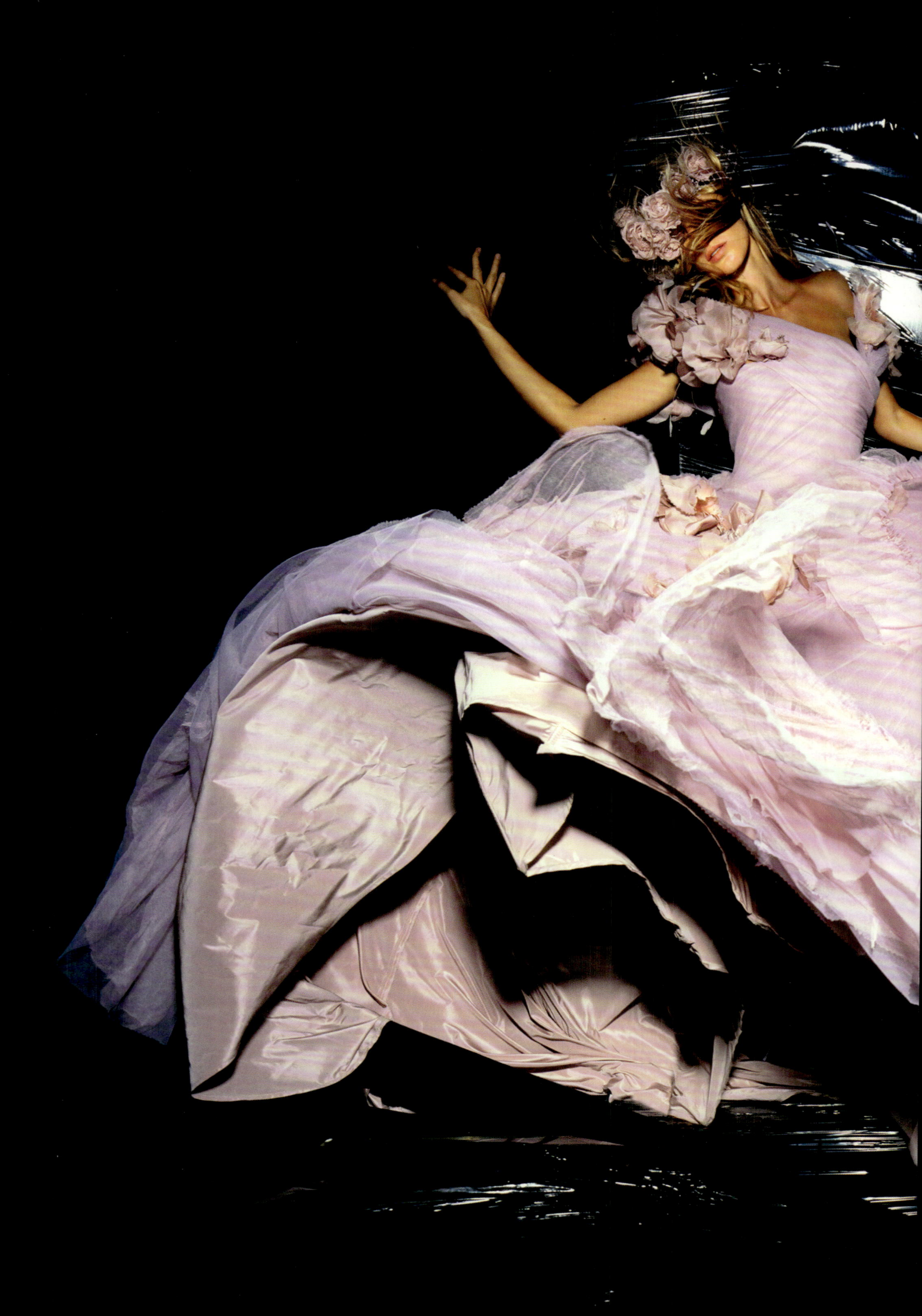

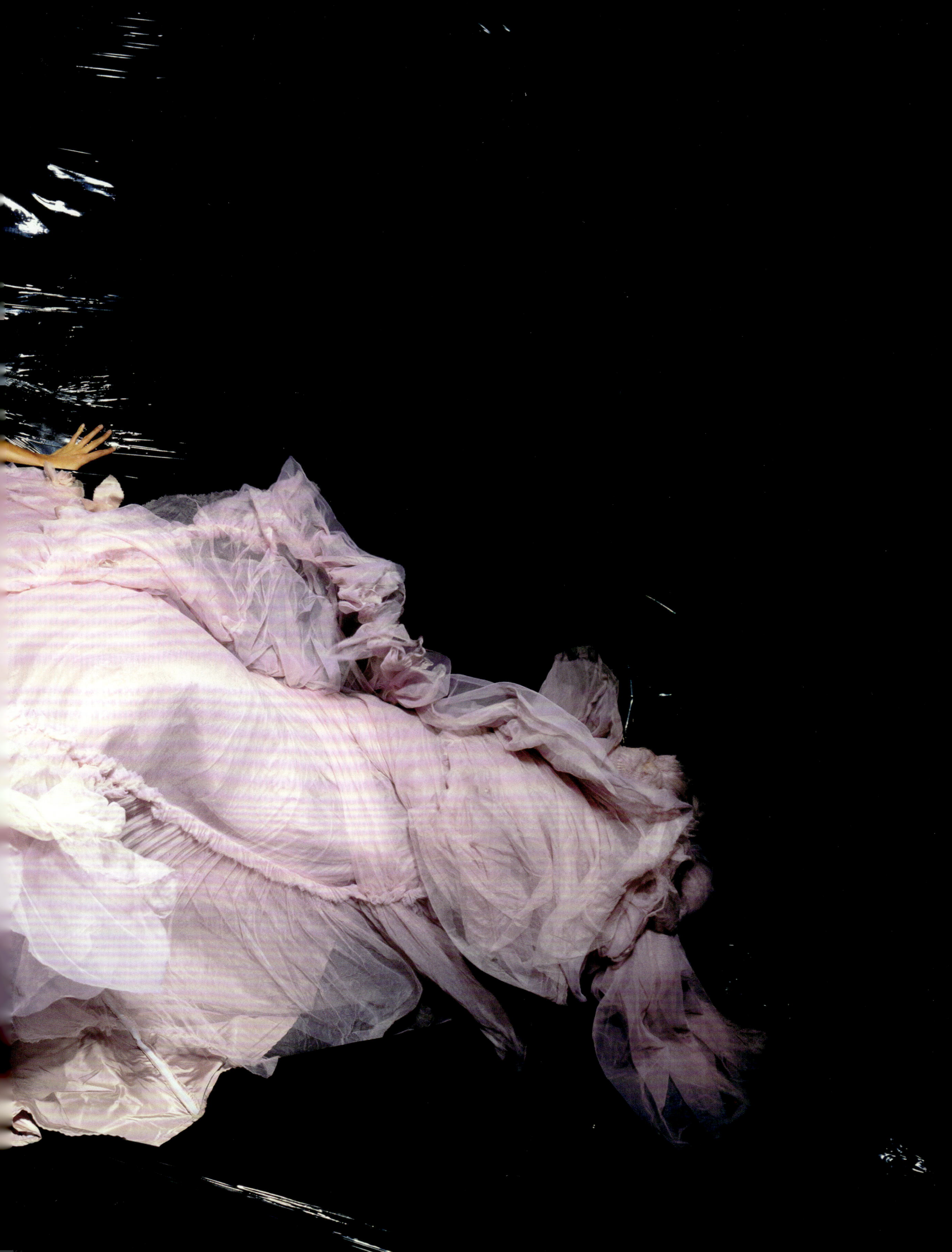

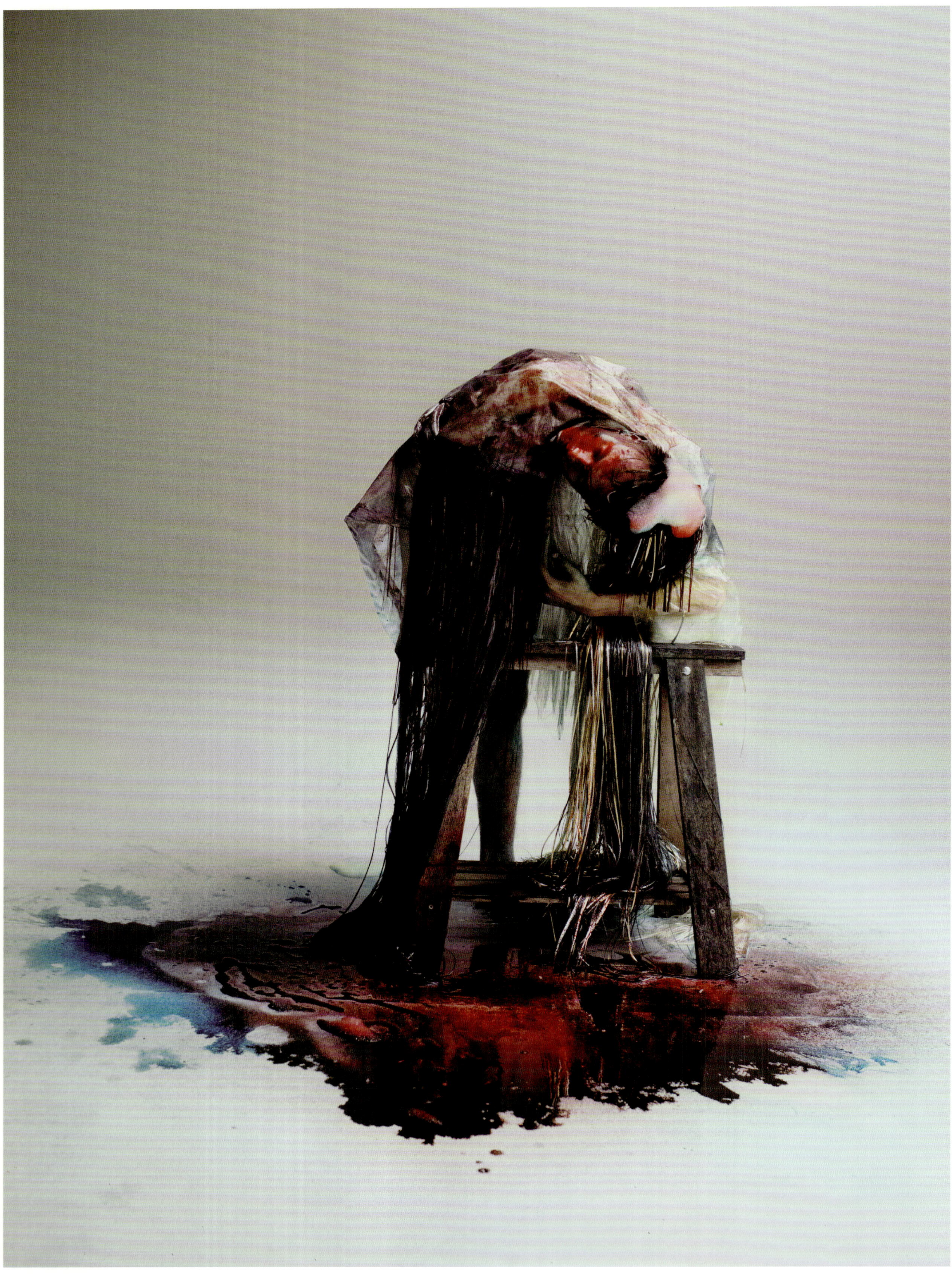

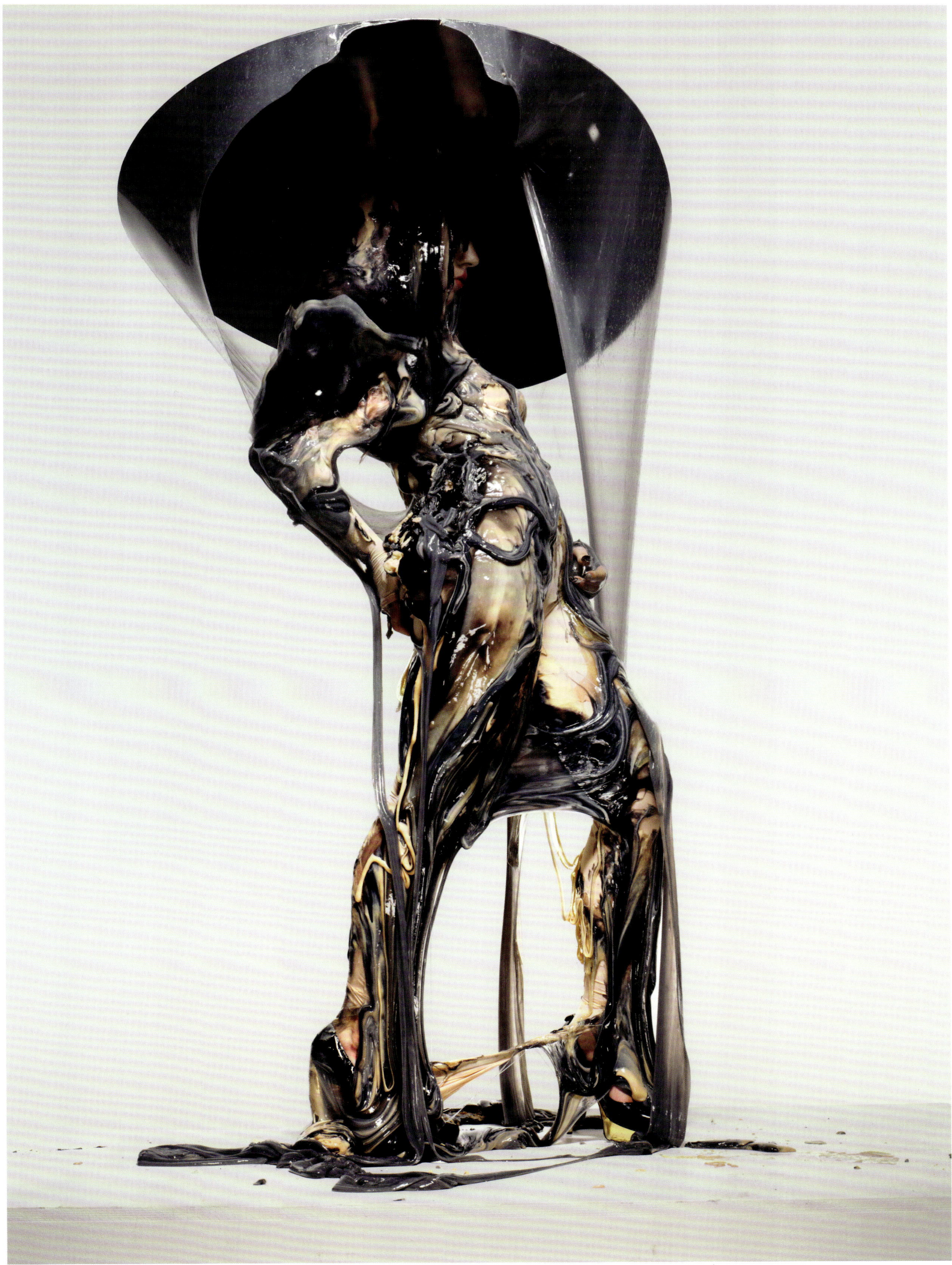

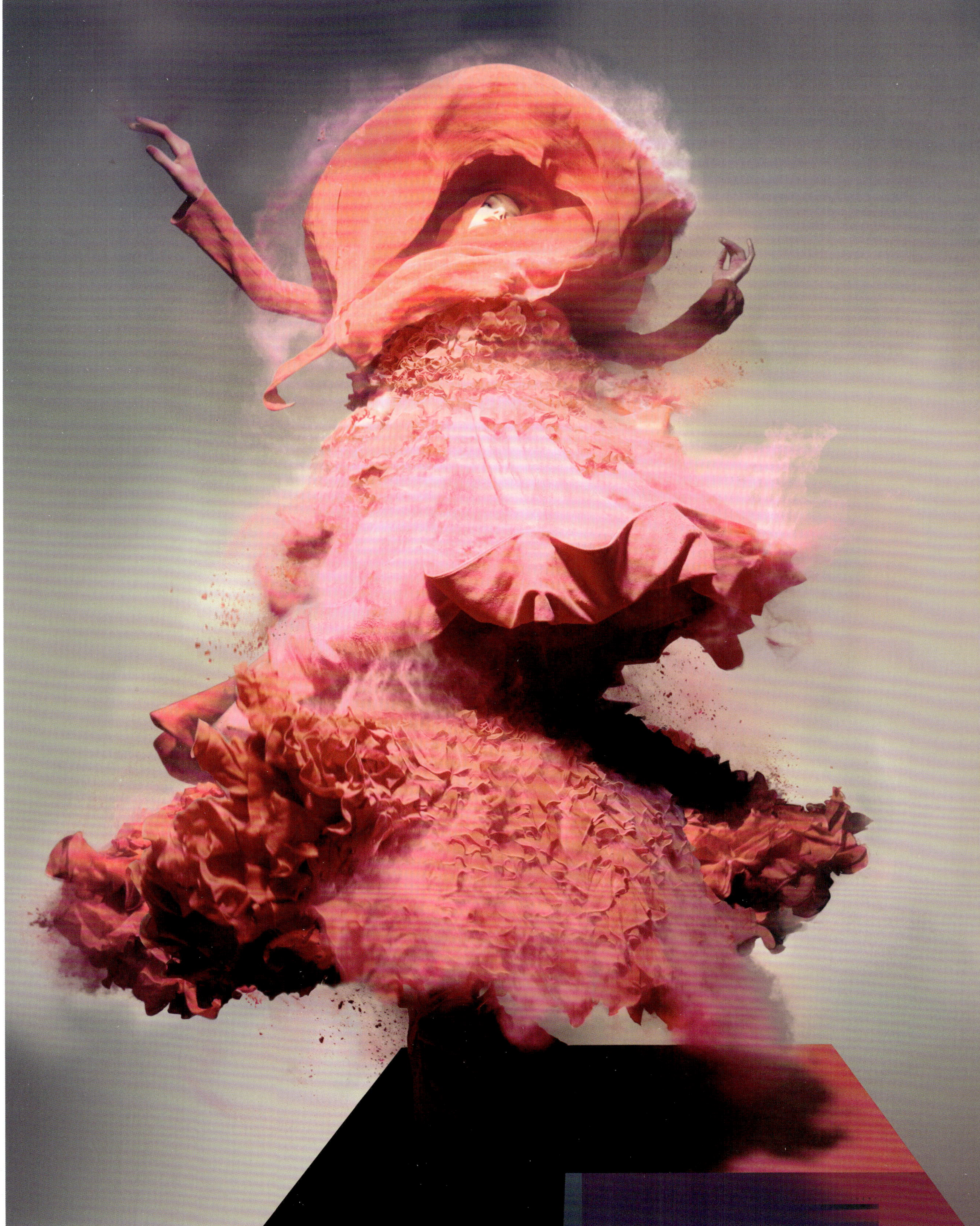

'Spotted Shadow'
from *Caroline Saulnier by Rankin*, 2010
collaboration with Caroline Saulnier
photography by Rankin

page 28:
'Enigma'
from *Rankin Spirit Of Ecstasy:
100 Years Of Inspiration*, 2012
collaboration with Rolls-Royce Motor Cars
photography by Rankin
makeup by Andrew Gallimore
styling by Scott Robert Clark

Page 29:
'Detail Chrome'
from *Rankin Spirit Of Ecstasy:
100 Years Of Inspiration*, 2012
collaboration with Rolls-Royce Motor Cars
photography by Rankin
makeup by Andrew Gallimore

pages 30–1:
'Studded'
from *Caroline Saulnier by Rankin*, 2010
collaboration with Caroline Saulnier
photography by Rankin

Rankin's simple yet monumental photographic approach was cultivated in the pages of *Dazed & Confused*, the magazine he and journalist Jefferson Hack gave birth to in the 1990s. Identifying a new era of material obsession in which the power of image works in subservience to a consumerist aesthetic, the magazine served as a platform for Rankin to develop a style that would oscillate between serious documentary photography, experimental portraiture and seductive fashion work. Despite this diverse focus, Rankin's imagery has always retained a purist aspect: attention ultimately returns to form and the body, and fashion is brought to life as freedom of expression is given over to the subject before the camera.

Rankin does not strive to make grand theoretical statements, but grand images. Pursuing this through select collaborations with stylists and makeup artists, he transforms the human form itself into an artistic canvas. His 2011 and 2012 projects with Alex Box and Caroline Saulnier rework the body through pattern and colour (pages 27, 30–3). Adornment and makeup are deployed in what is often an abrasive and visceral style, the photographer showing a fearlessness in the face of the extreme as he explores the human form and the potential we have to modify it. The intensity of this approach is consciously deployed – he locates it in a desire to shoot images that encourage responses in two areas, the cerebral and the gut.

It is this methodology that gives rise to *Myths, Monsters and Legends*, a collaboration with artist Damien Hirst that gets to the heart of his contrary preoccupations. In a series of images laced with the macabre, model Dani Smith acts out mythical stories as a play on the notion, in Rankin's own words, of 'taking something beautiful, and making it ugly'. For all its amplified horror, however, there is an optimistic undercurrent: a desire to momentarily overcome cynicism and renew a belief in the fantastic.

Even in these more escapist exercises, portraiture lies at the core of Rankin's work. His pursuit of the perfect portrait undergoes a process of constant development and refinement, and with his 2006–7 series *Eyescapes* he takes the practice to its logical extreme. The series of photographs of the human iris explores beauty in portraiture as alchemy, a distillation of the subject to its purest form. In the muscles and pigments of the eye – both the focus of his photography and the mechanism by which we absorb it – he draws out beautiful landscapes that verge on abstraction.

Such projects deal with beauty, but for the fashion industry they often go against the grain. The typical symbols of fashion – women, youth and fame – all have their place, but Rankin's practice is never limited to them. Looking to explore new terrain and depict elements that are rarely addressed, some of his more explicitly attention-seeking shots include extreme intimate closeups or elements of the human body usually shunned by an industry focused on more typical aspects of beauty. What convinces is not so much the taboo-breaking aspect of this work as the honesty of its portrayal, and it is this commitment to authenticity that makes such a vast body of work cohere.

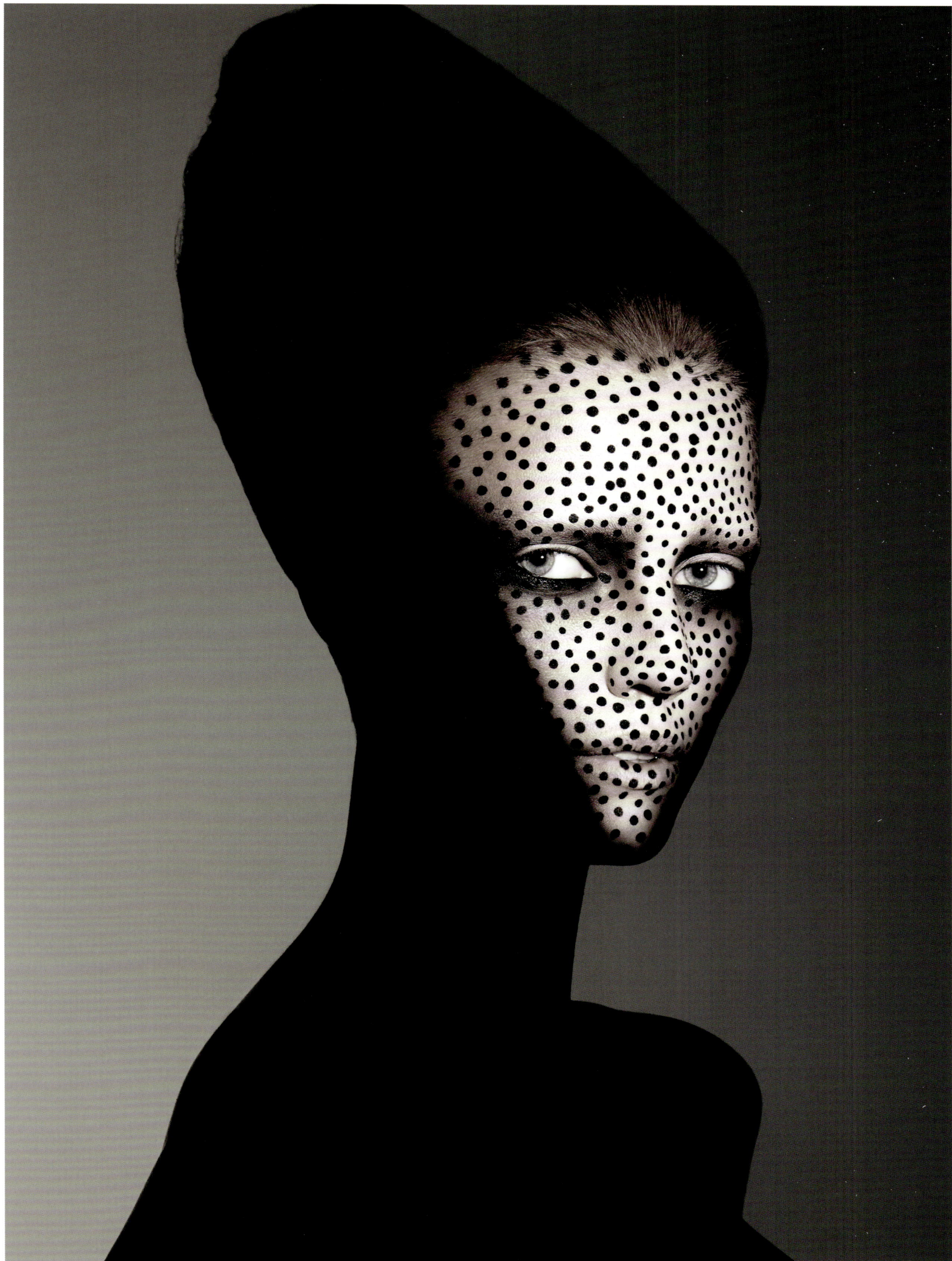

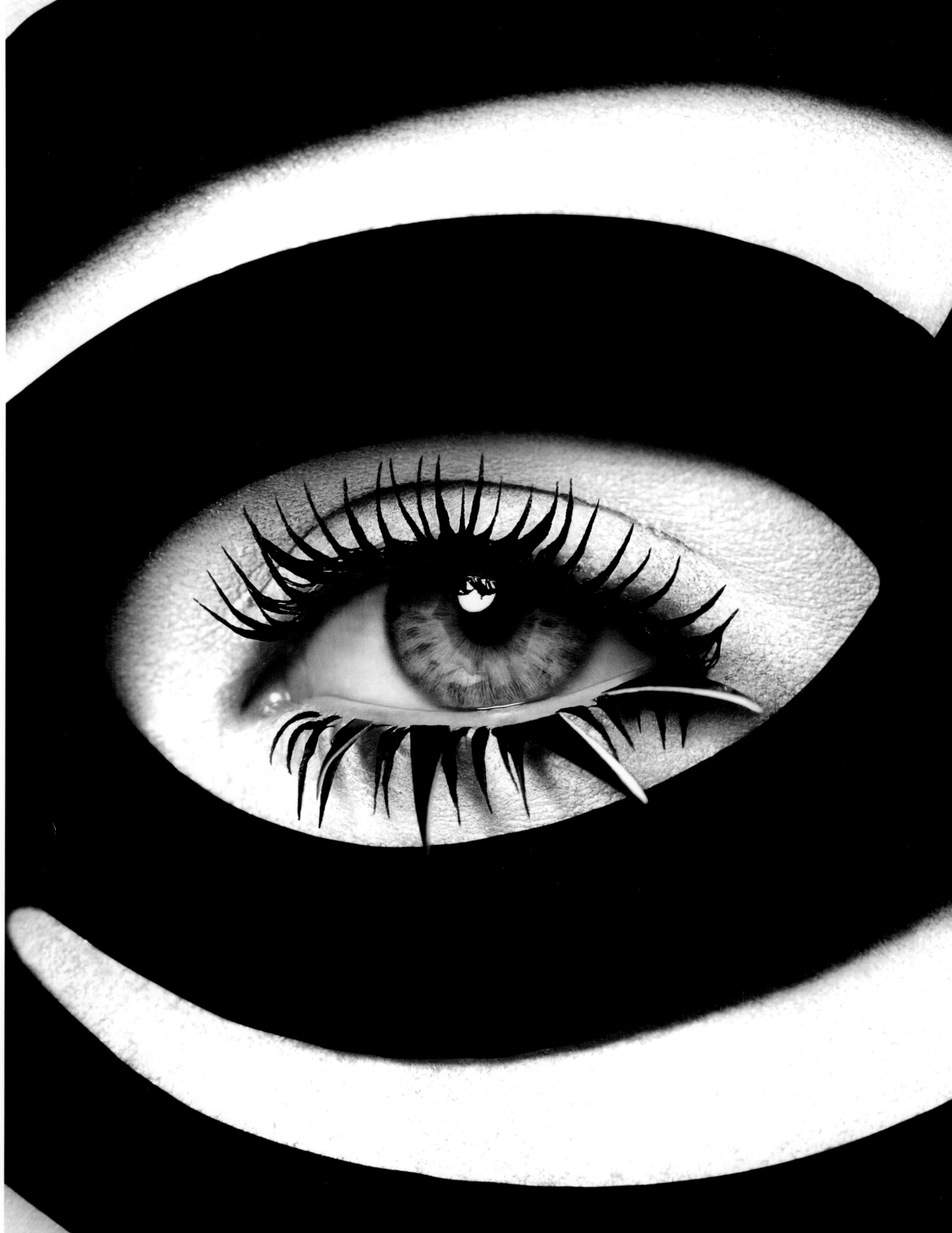

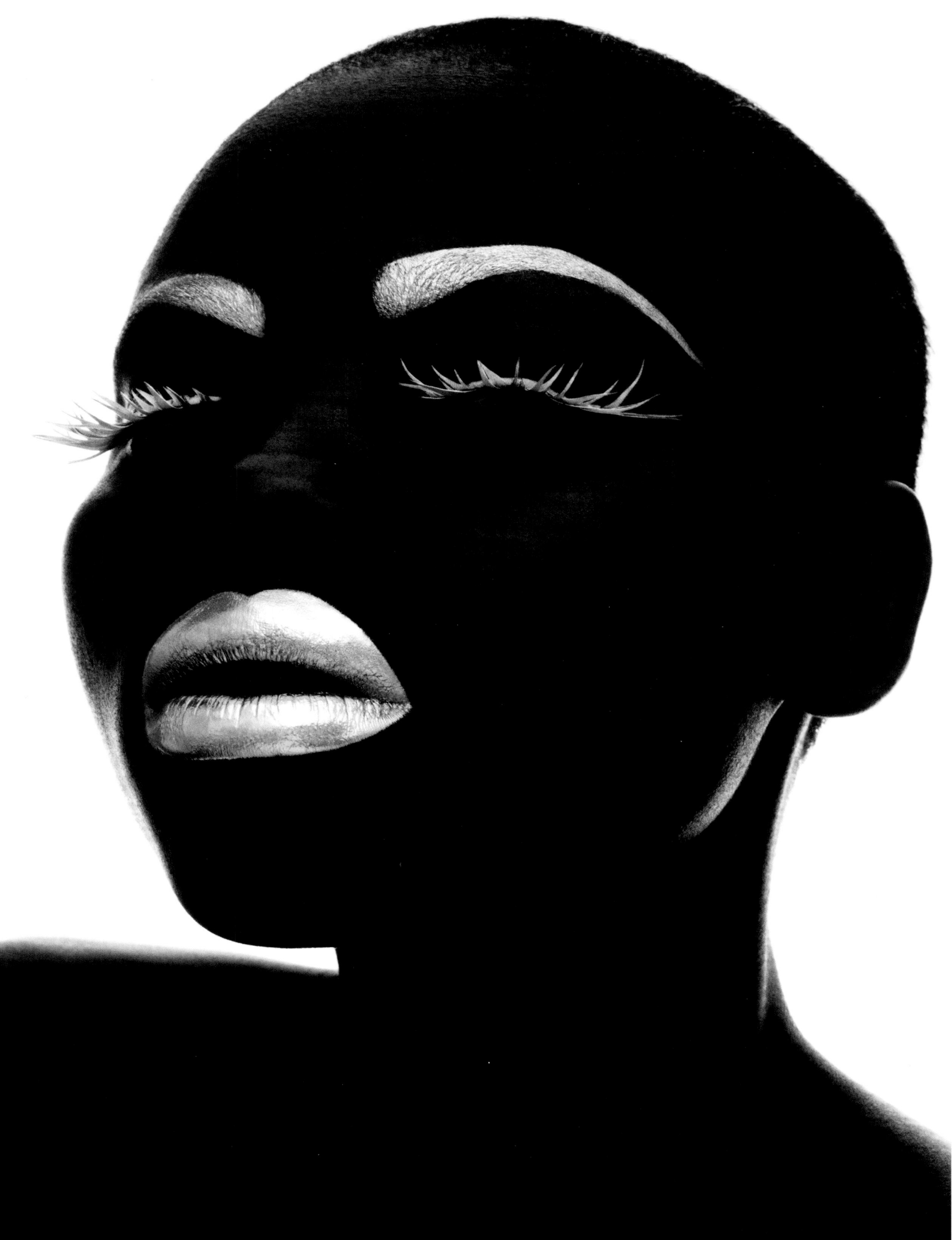

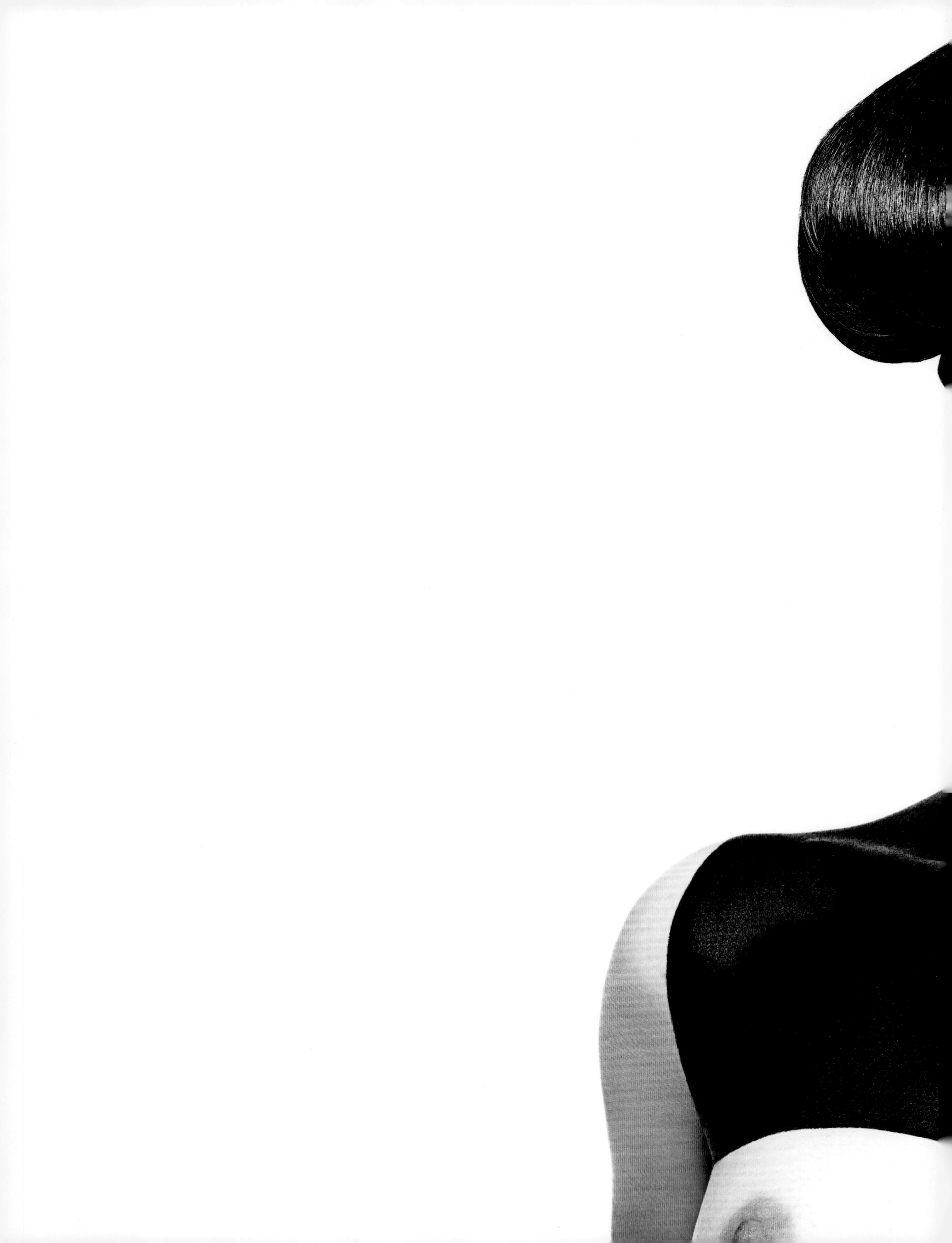

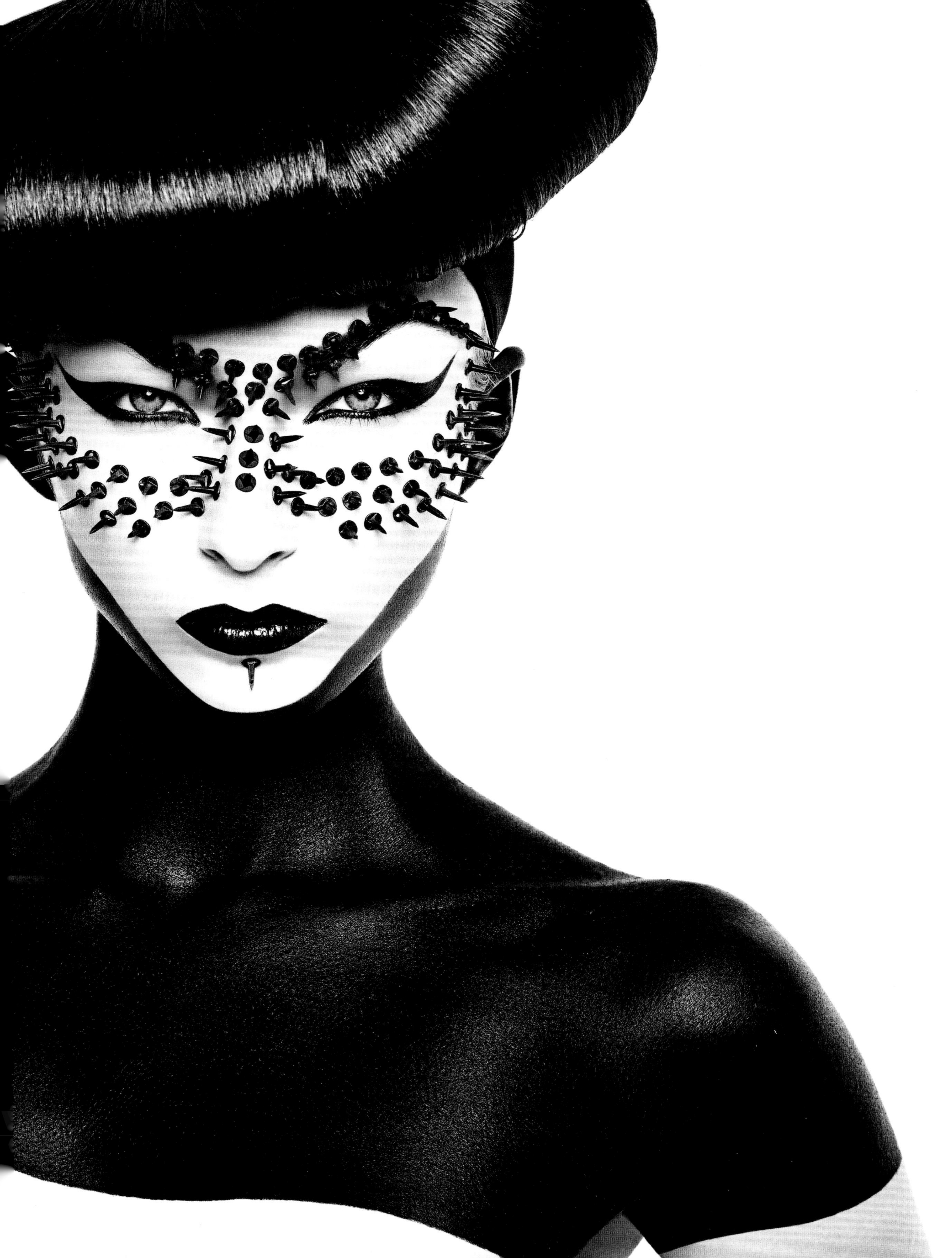

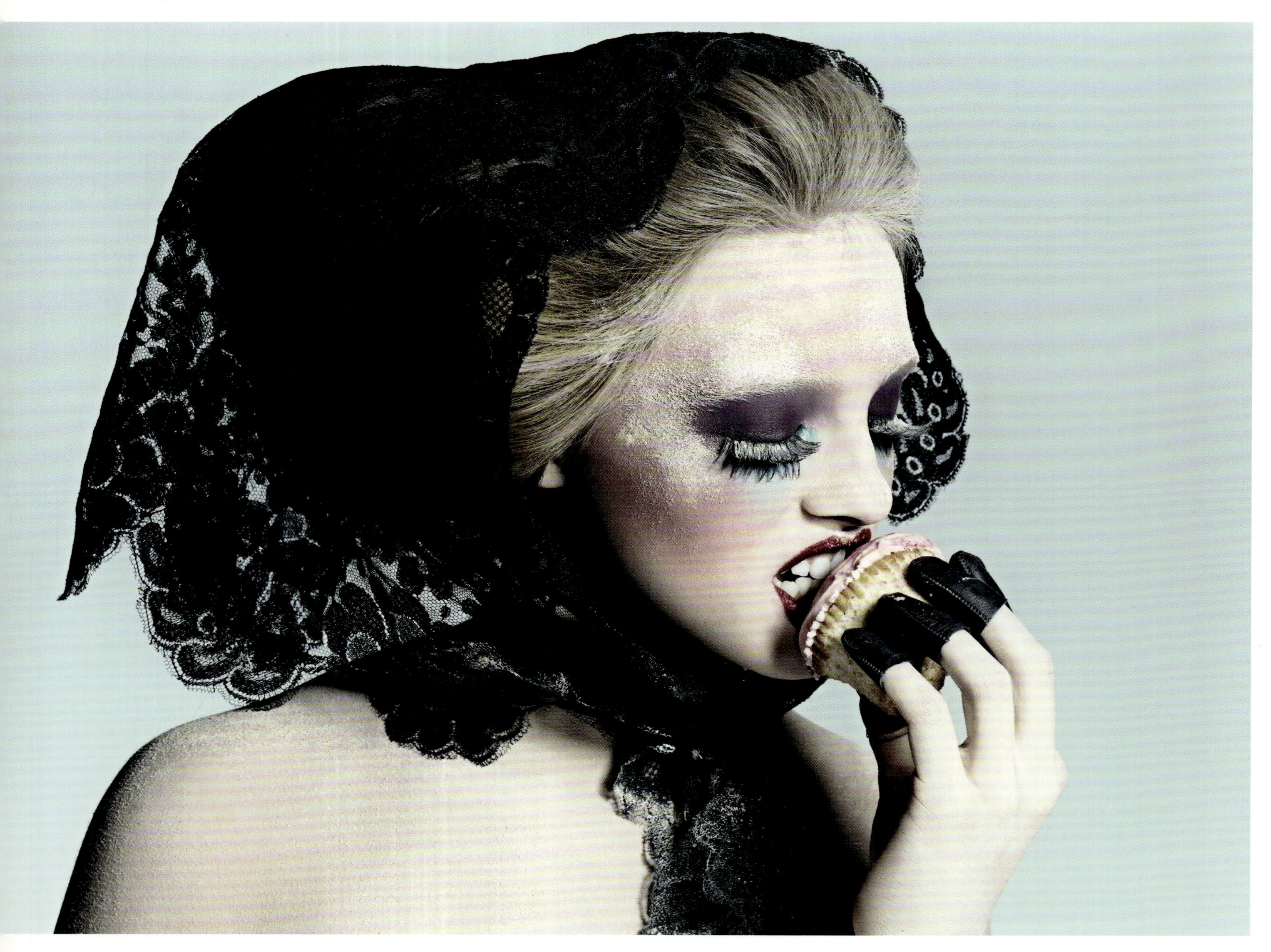

R A N K I N

'Let Them Eat Cake'
from *Caroline Saulnier by Rankin*, 2011
collaboration with Caroline Saulnier
photography by Rankin

'Lots of Lash'
from *Caroline Saulnier by Rankin*, 2011
collaboration with Caroline Saulnier
photography by Rankin
styling by Scott Robert Clark

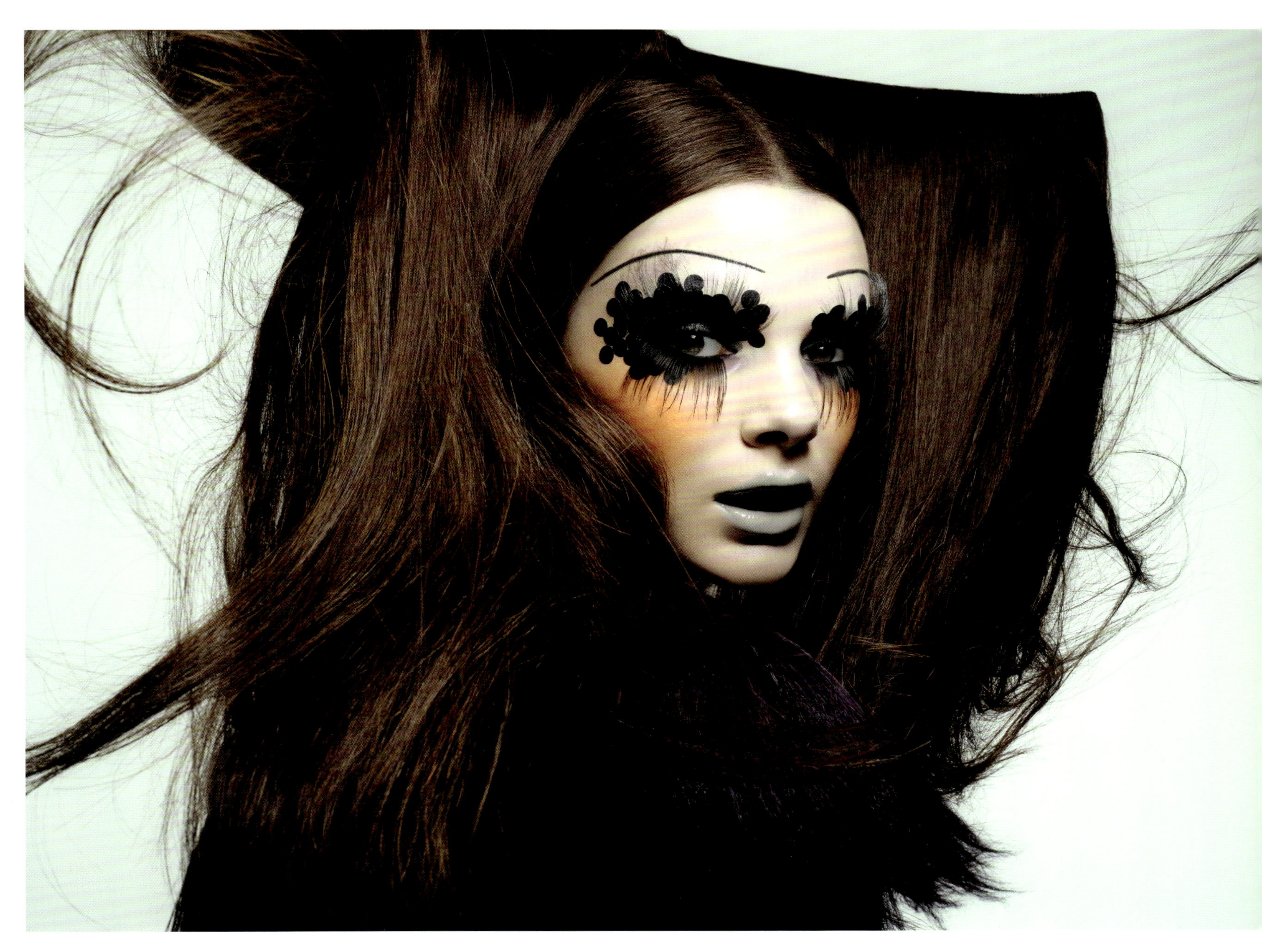

Miles Aldridge's images are highly processed and saturated with colour, but conceptually they are defined by something darker. A neo-gothicism borders on the surreal in everyday scenes that are given a disconcerting twist: a pool game; a meal in a diner; even a trip to the supermarket gives the viewer a sense that something is not quite right. The setups are drenched in unsettling artifice and otherworldly light, creating a sense of disquiet that is only occasionally offset by an intriguing sensuality.

Aldridge's heavily made-up models appear to be captured in a state of frozen motion, as if lifted from a cinematic sequence and immortalised in a single frame. His models are like plastic mannequins, their eyes glazed over as if the mind has disconnected from the body. The vacant gaze is not suggestive of an emotional absence; rather, the eyes, thick with mascara and eyeliner, are the window to thoughts that are operating elsewhere. These are the empty expressions of subjects lost in distant contemplation, like those of commuters on a train or, in Aldridge's own words, of people 'troubled by something secret'.

Aldridge's dark surrealism invites Lynchian parallels, and the two artists have voiced their mutual admiration. Aldridge photographed the filmmaker for *L'Uomo Vogue* in 2006, and references Italian actress Isabella Rossellini in the subversive classic *Blue Velvet* as an iconic inspiration. David Lynch himself has described Aldridge's work as representative of a 'colour-coordinated, graphically pure, hard-edged reality'. His sense of vivid noir, too, is reinforced by his preference for subjects such as fashion designer Rick Owens and musician Marilyn Manson, who describes the photographer as moving in 'Hitchcock and Bergman strides, [painting] stories like a colouring book made from equal parts Nabokov, Bataille, Buñuel, Fassbinder and George Hurrell'.

But while much of Aldridge's imagery draws on twentieth-century culture, his frames of reference are capable of reaching further back into the past. The haunting images of his shoot 'Imaculée' for *Numéro* in 2007 are reminiscent of the evocative statues carried through the streets during the Semana Santa, or Holy Week, in Spain's Andalucia (pages 35–7). Referencing the medieval tradition, frail models are cursed with a sickly pallor and shed thick droplets of water, much like the plasticised sweat and tears that run down the face of the Virgin Mary in Semana Santa statuary.

Perhaps the clue to the sense of tender intrigue that remains in these images, despite the fact that Aldridge seems to suck the life out of them so deliberately, is in the freeform sketches that precede their creation. In his book *Pictures for Photographs*, published by Karl Lagerfeld's publishing imprint Edition 7L, Aldridge's illustrations contrast strongly with the stylised polish of his final works; the line is light and loose as his pen sketches out ideas that are only infrequently splashed with colour, the results operating as a map to the interior life of the final piece.

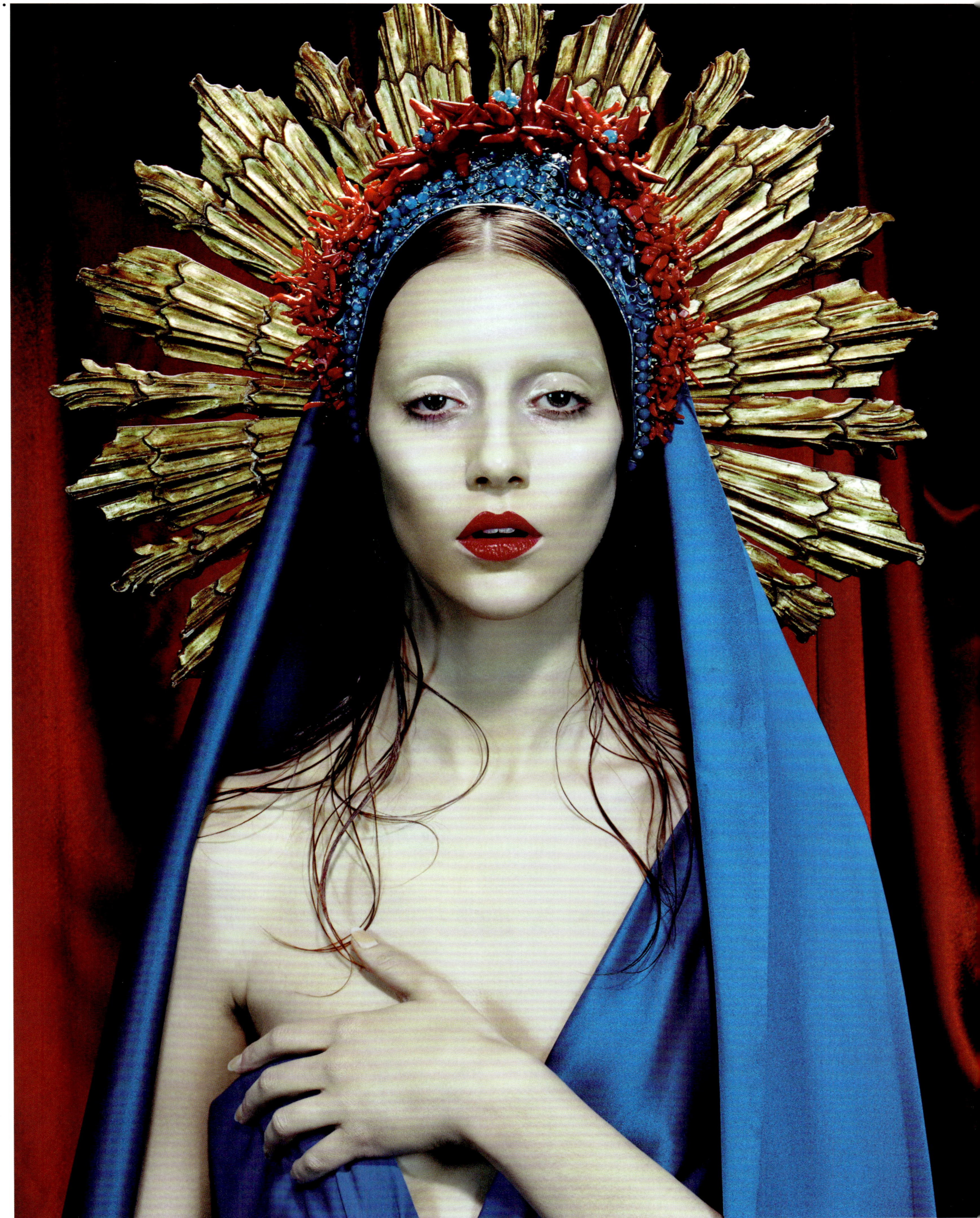

MILES ALDRIDGE

'Imaculée' for *Numéro*, 2007
photography by Miles Aldridge
courtesy Steven Kasher Gallery/Trunk Archive

pages 38–9:
'First Impression' for *Vogue* Japan, 2006
photography by Miles Aldridge
courtesy Trunk Archive

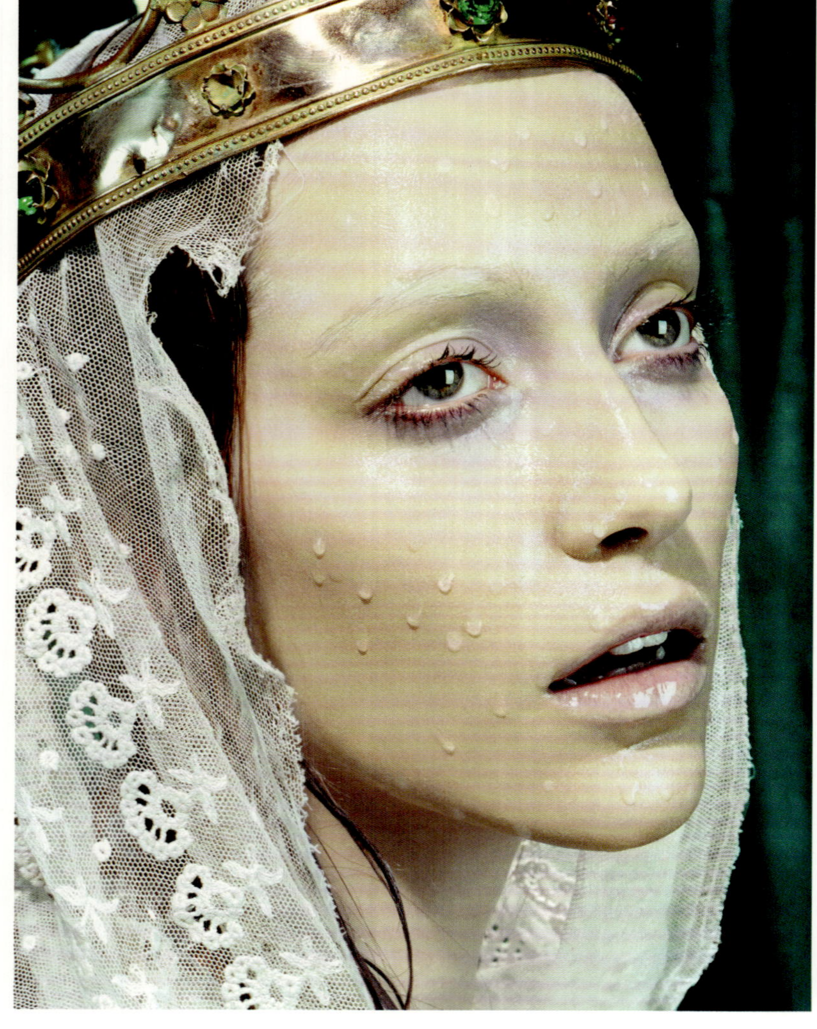
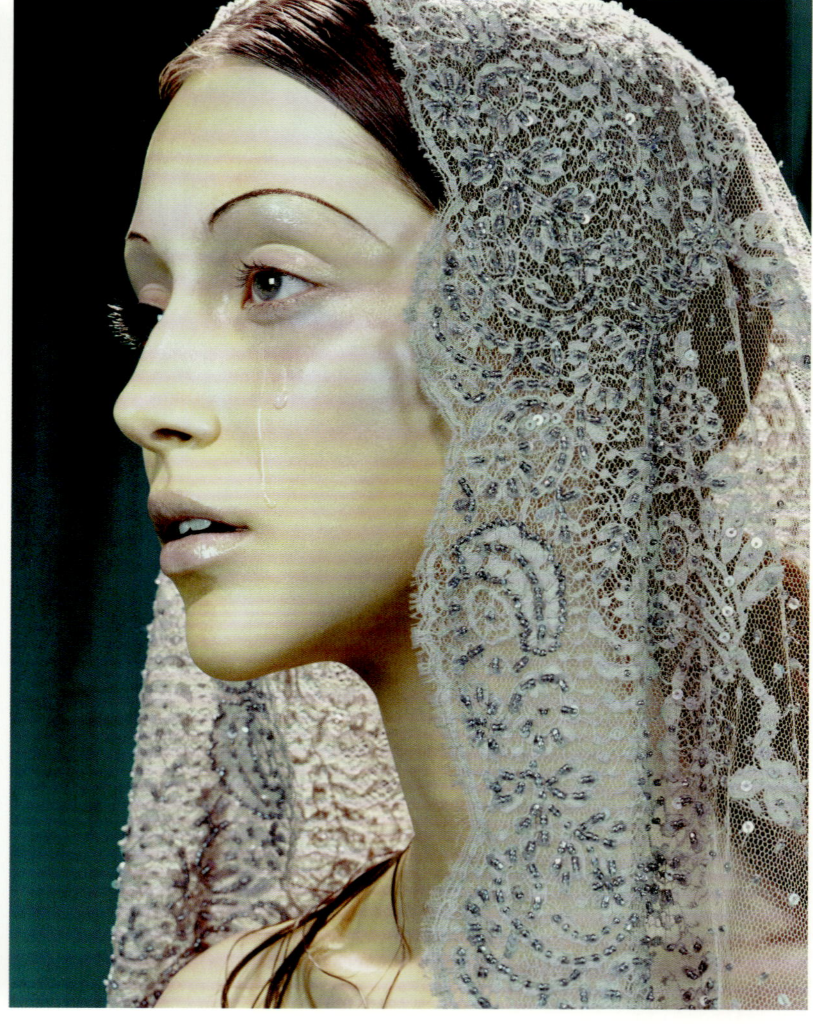

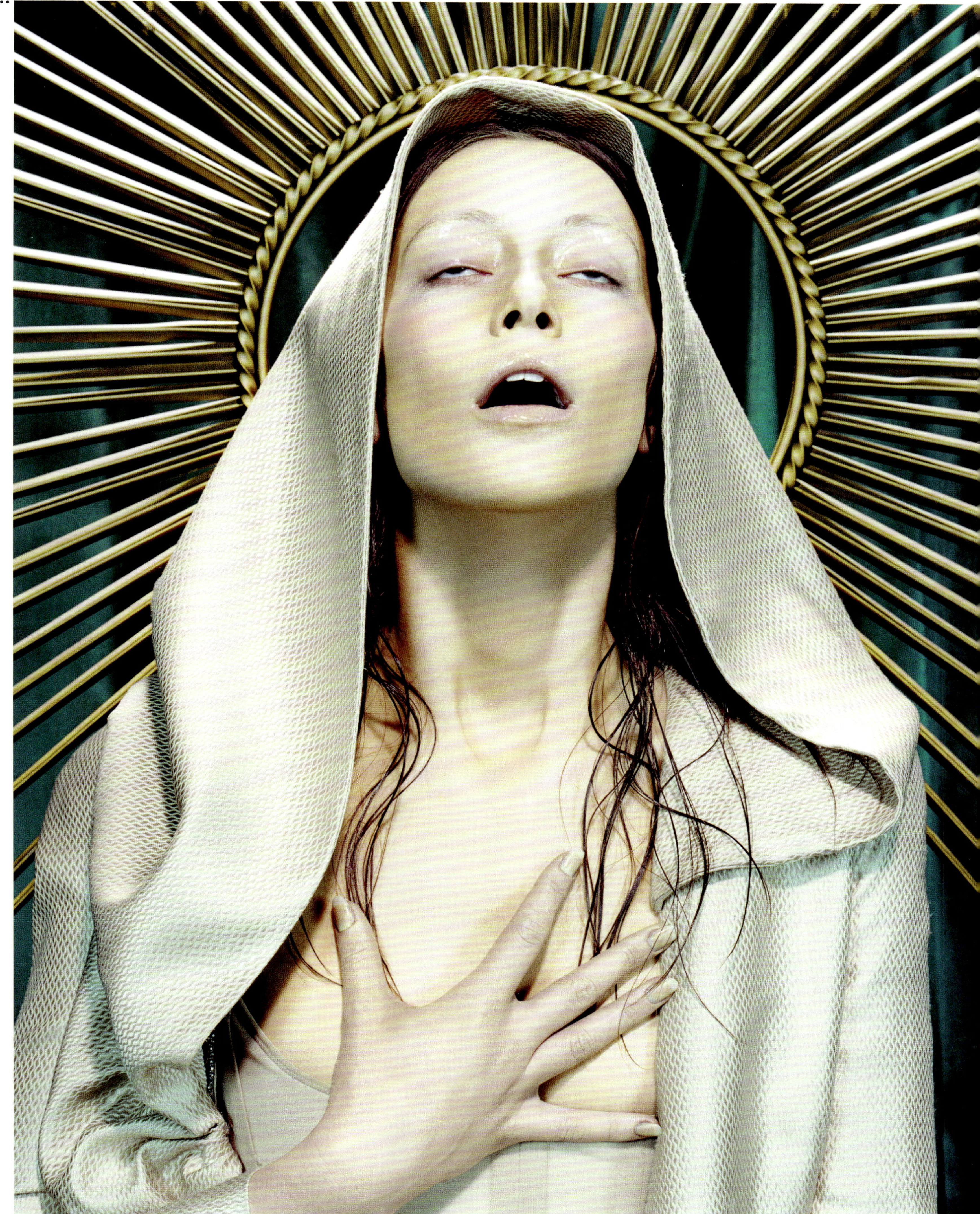

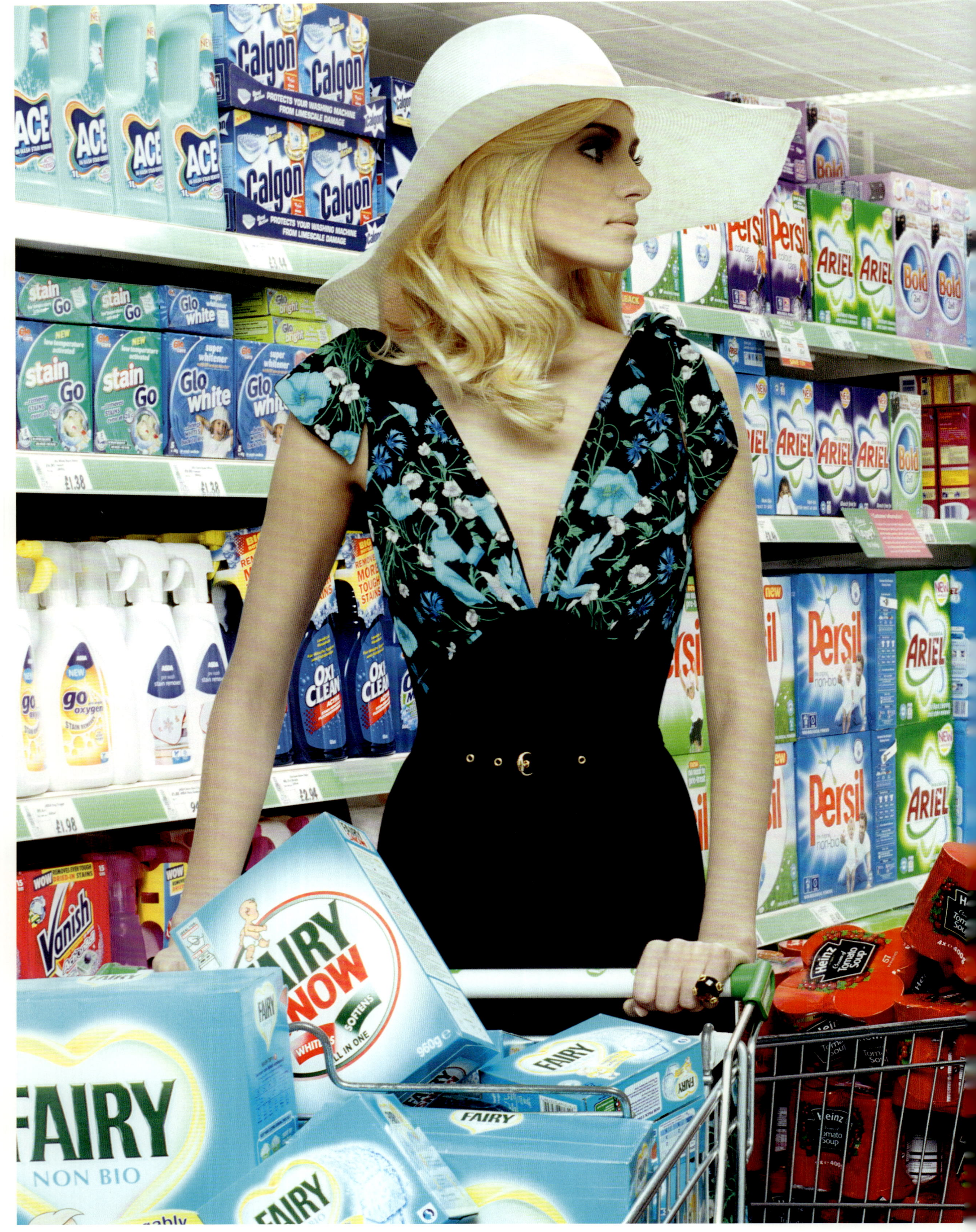

ACE
Calgon
PROTECTS YOUR WASHING MACHINE FROM LIMESCALE DAMAGE
stain Go
Glo white
Glo bright
Persil
ARIEL
Bold
go oxygen
OXI CLEAN
Vanish
WOW
FAIRY NOW
SOFTENS WHITENS ALL IN ONE
960g
FAIRY
FAIRY
FAIRY NON BIO
Persil
Heinz Tomato Soup

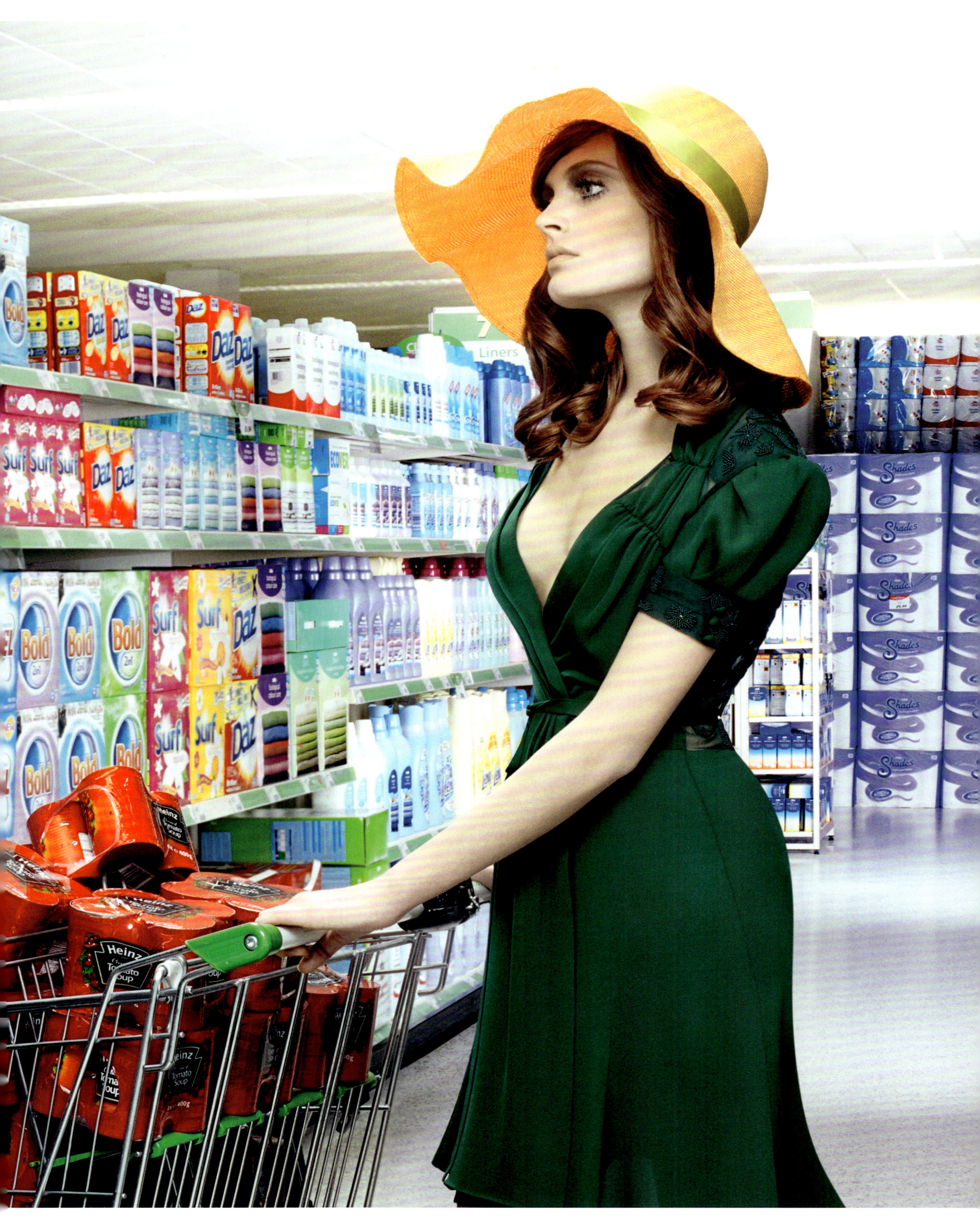

Bold
Daz
Surf
Heinz
Tomato
Soup
Shades
Liners

from *Glamorous Monique*, 2011
photography by Alice Hawkins
courtesy Patricia McMahon

The gloriously brash photography of Alice Hawkins documents a world of excess that stretches from the casino floors and motels of Vegas to the showgirls of Blackpool. Hawkins's models are invariably not from the catwalk; instead they are the people that inhabit the kitsch environments to which she is attracted. There is, however, a uniting theme that speaks to the world of fashion: each of these men and women has worked hard to achieve an image they have made quintessentially their own.

Hawkins's fascination with the often lurid exuberance of modern-day material culture carries echoes of the ironic photography of Martin Parr. However, perhaps unlike Parr, Hawkins does not stand in judgement of her subjects, preferring instead to find inspiration in the lengths to which they go to cultivate an identity. The outrageous nature of her portraits might initially provoke surprise and even amusement, but her eye is celebratory rather than critical. Whether depicting the chiselled excesses of men in her 2008 'Versace' series for *i-D* or the surgically enhanced dynamism of *Glamorous Monique* (page 41), Hawkins measures the appearance of her subjects on their own terms. They may be fantastic, unique and unconventional, but they are brought together by an unabashed attention to the details of their self-presentation.

In a reversal of conventions, Hawkins teases out the unreality in reality. Deploying a documentary aesthetic as her starting point, she achieves a celebration of style and fashion that offers more realism than a standard magazine editorial. It is precisely this

attentive, investigatory aspect that led *i-D* to take on Hawkins following her degree show at Camberwell College of Art in 2002, marking her entry into the fashion industry. Yet there is a subtle sensitivity to her images too, and her grasp of colour and light lends an evocative warmth to the worlds she explores. Neon-lit scenes are touched with wistful nostalgia; icons of pop America glimmer with unexpected promise. Playing to a jaded audience, Hawkins focuses on icons that initially seem tacky or in dubious taste, but in doing so she strips away that preconception and encourages the viewer to enjoy them again on a less cynical level.

Inherent in this is a gleeful innocence exercised towards adult themes, something that has led Hawkins to get away with more than most, pushing her to test the boundaries. An early entry into a fashion competition threatened to introduce coiffured pubic hair to the pages of UK newspaper *The Independent*, thanks to the support of Hawkins's long-term advocate and occasional collaborator Nick Knight. This faux-naïve exuberance lends a charm to her work, but alongside it there is a seriousness and a maturity, and perhaps even an optimistic message about the way we view fashion, the world and each other.

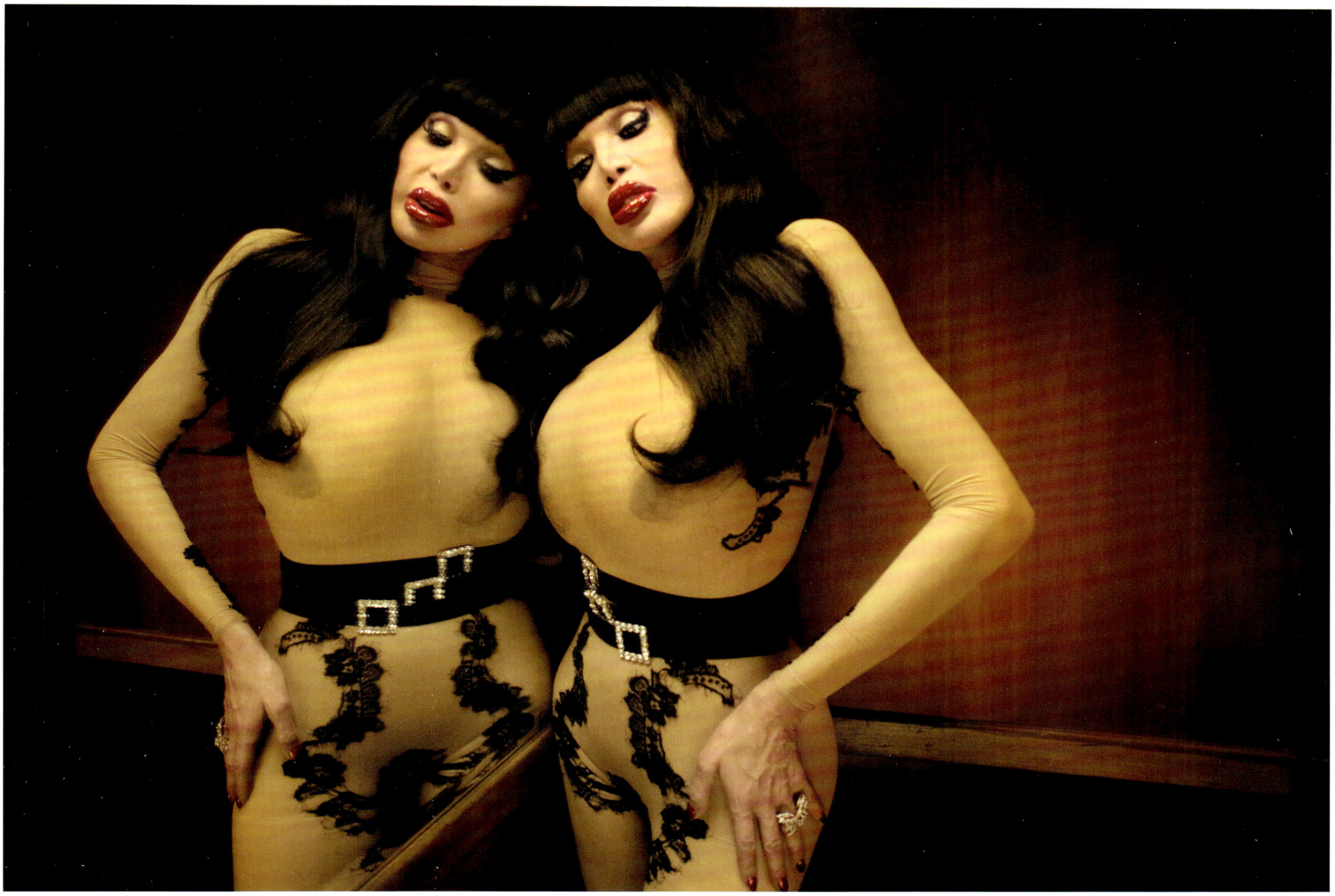

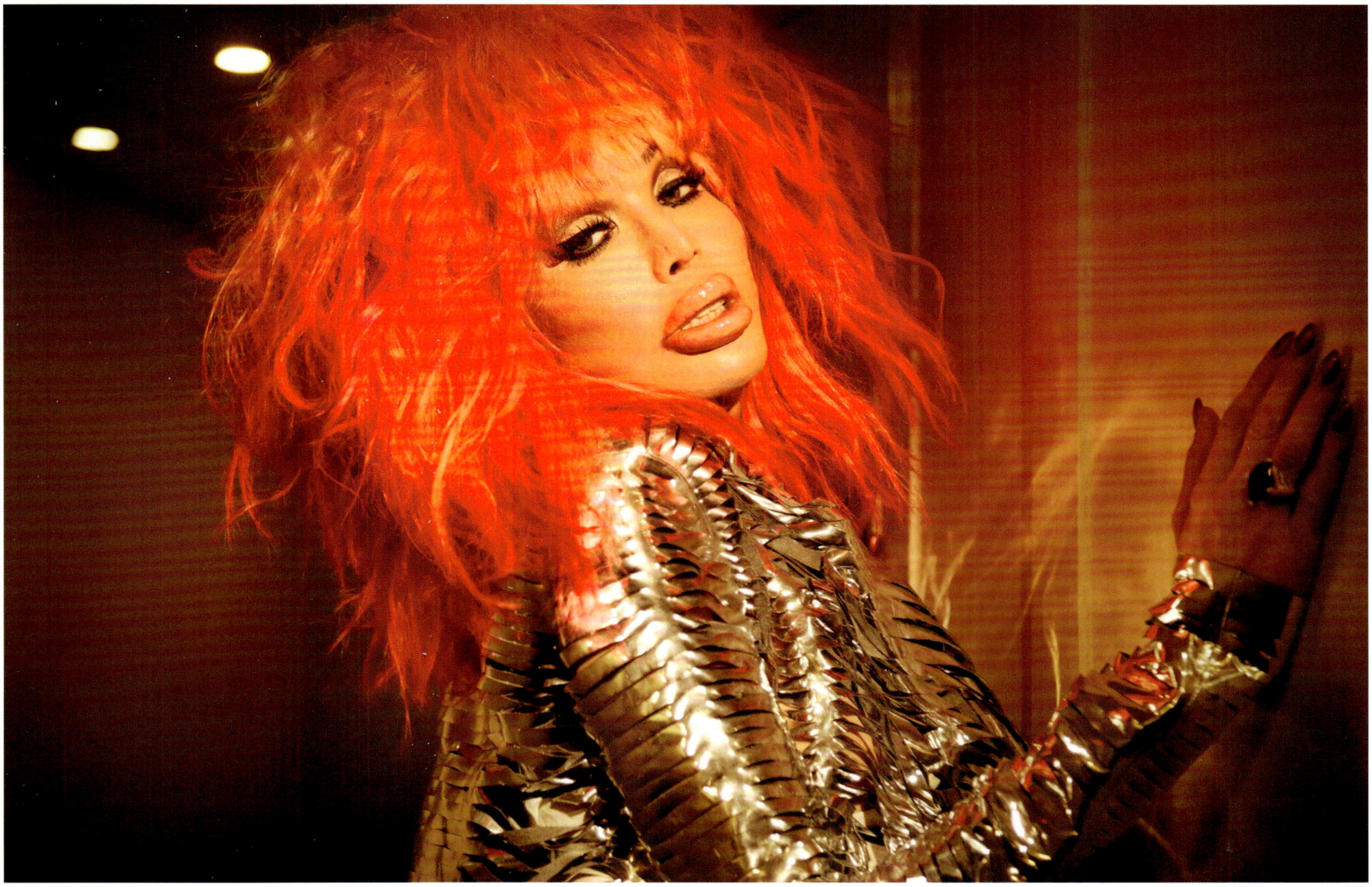

ALICE HAWKINS
from *Alice's American Safari*, 2011
Dashenka Giraldo and
Victoria the Bengal tiger
photography by Alice Hawkins
courtesy Patricia McMahon

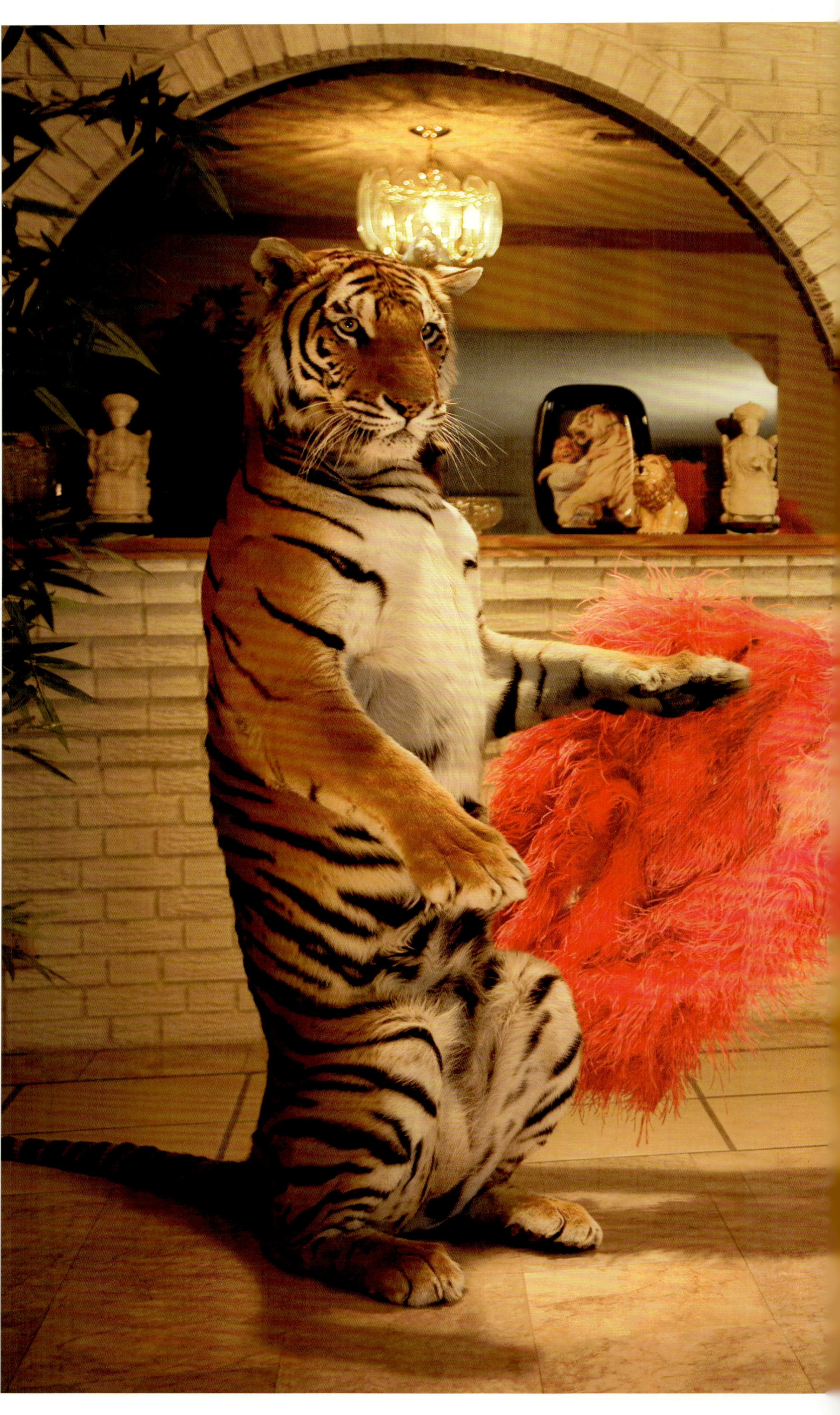

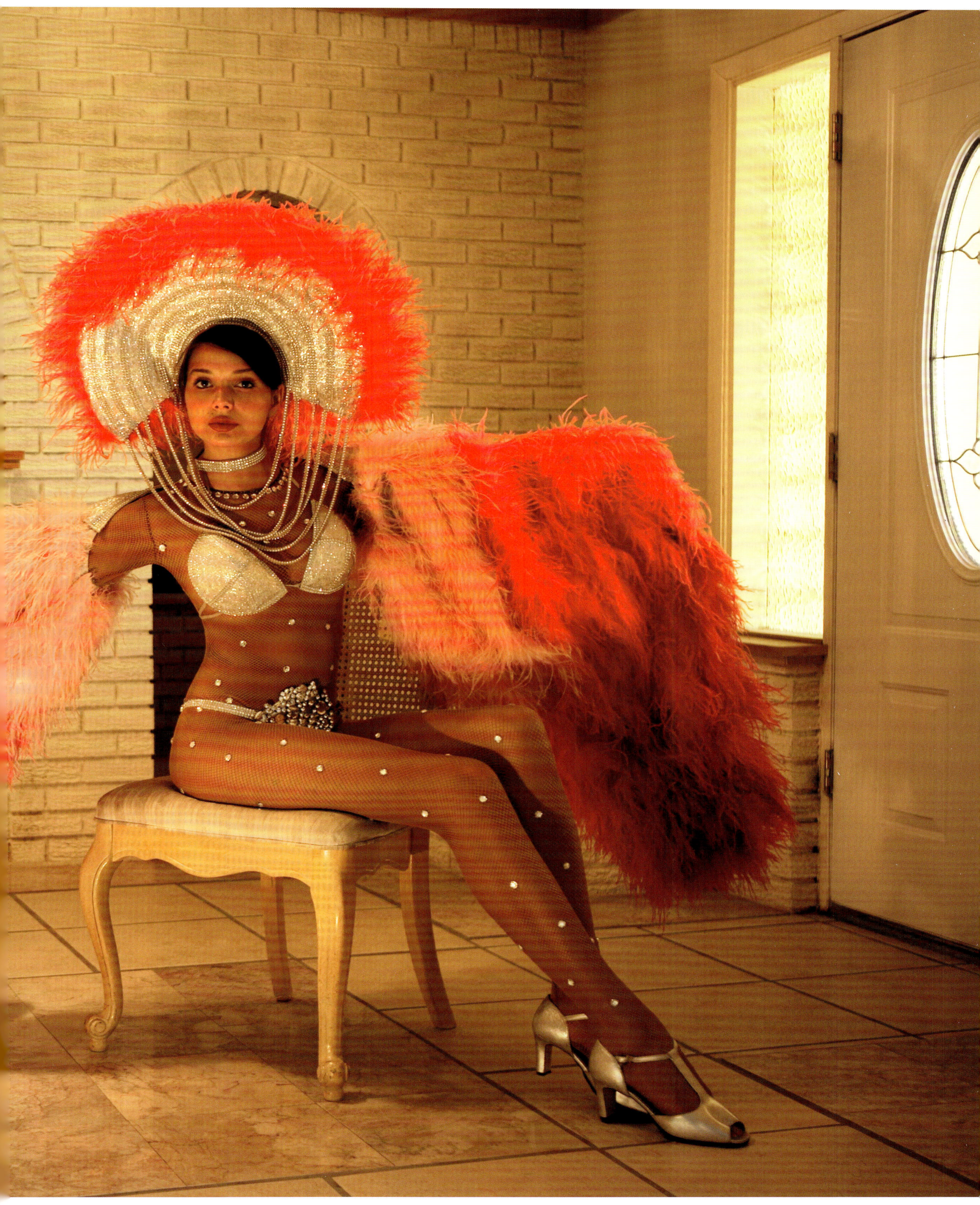

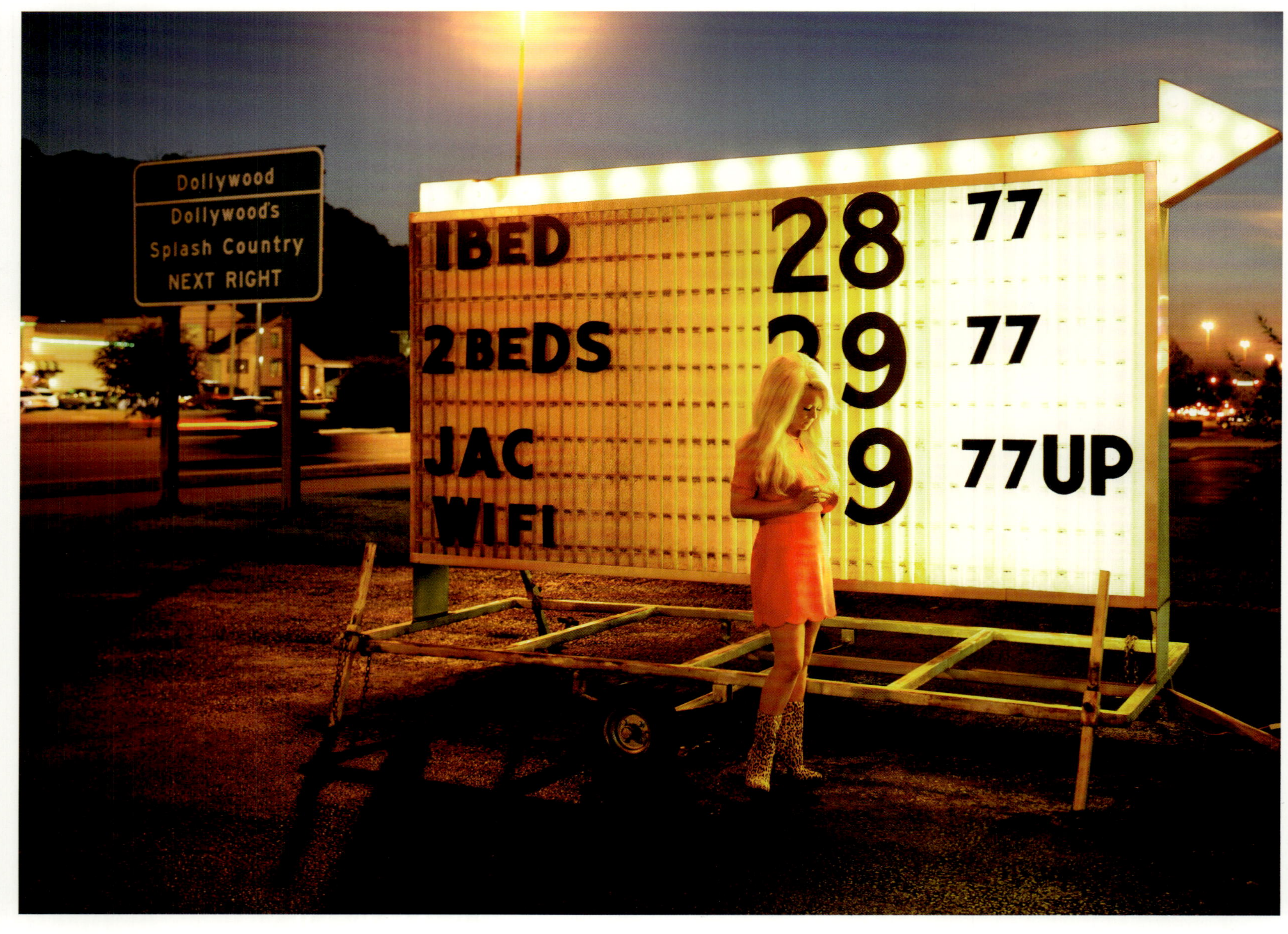
Dollywood
Dollywood's
Splash Country
NEXT RIGHT
1 BED
2 BEDS
JAC
WIFI
28
9
9
77
77
77UP

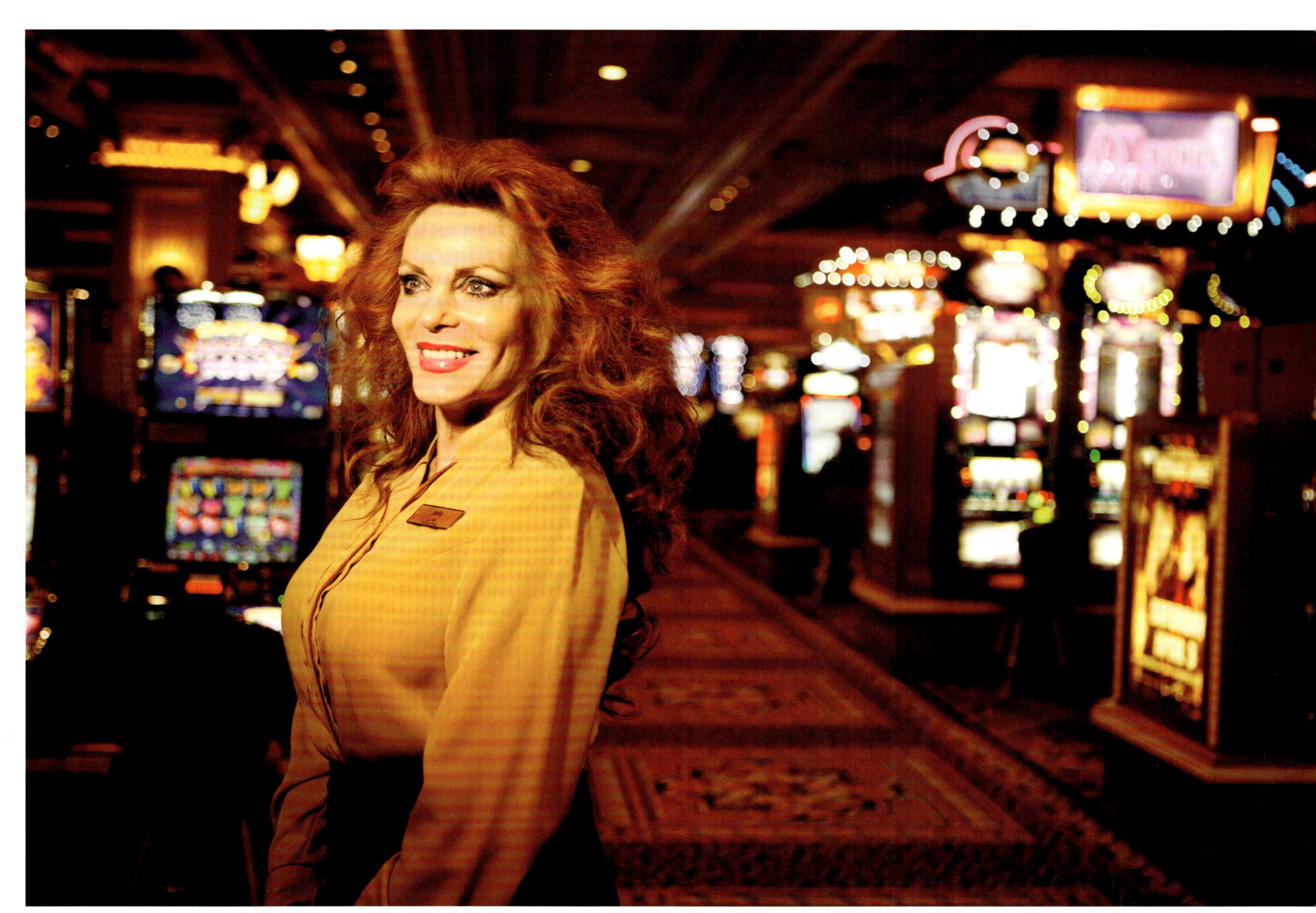

Self-portrait
from *Dolly Parton is my Religion*, 2011
photography by Alice Hawkins
courtesy Patricia McMahon

Julia, Mandalay Bay Casino
from *Las Vegas*, 2011
photography by Alice Hawkins
courtesy Patricia McMahon

Magdalena Frackowiak for *Numéro*, 2011
photography by Sean and Seng
courtesy Sean and Seng/TotalWorld

pages 48–9:
Lana Del Rey for *Interview* Russia, 2012
photography by Sean and Seng
courtesy Sean and Seng/TotalWorld

pages 50–1:
Liya Kebede for *POP*, 2011
photography by Sean and Seng
courtesy Sean and Seng/TotalWorld

Photographic duo Sean and Seng take simple, apparently straight-forward portraits and give them a sharp twist. The images feel effortless but their power is derived from a juxtaposition of ideas, as innocent depictions of beautiful people are knocked sideways by Hitchcockian elements of surprise.

Nature is a recurring motif and it emerges in uncharacteristic ways: a monkey makes an exhibition of itself on the shoulder of Frida Aasen in a cover shoot for the March 2011 edition of *Dazed & Confused*; Kendra Spears plays snake charmer in a 2011 editorial for *Numéro*; Liya Kebede faces off with a flamingo for the 2011 Fall/Winter issue of *POP* (pages 50–1). Even a recumbent elephant has made an appearance amidst Sean and Seng's eclectic menagerie. Such animal interventions are always effectively placed: on the cover of *Interview* Russia, singer Lana Del Rey wears the most simple and quietly dangerous piece of fashion attire – a bee that clings to her lip (pages 48–9). Nature seems inviting at first, but the message is mixed. There is a sting to this version of beauty, and with such instincts the photographers introduce an anarchic potential to order.

Drawing on influences that range from the dark cinema of David Cronenberg to the politicised literature of nineteenth-century French writer Émile Zola, Sean and Seng are attracted both to the timelessness of beauty and the chaos of the unexpected. Cited influences stretch through centuries and are littered with provocative artists, from the sixteenth-century German Renaissance painter Cranach to the twentieth-century photography of Francesco Scavullo. While a photograph such as Magdalena Frackowiak for *Numéro* may share the light and shadow of a Cranach *Venus* (page 47), it is perhaps the artist's predilection for more revolutionary ideas that finds its parallel in the passions of Zola or the boundary-pushing aesthetics of Scavullo. Sean and Seng's output may not carry such explicit agendas, but look closer and the motivations behind these esoteric tastes shine through. Matching these sources of inspiration is a tendency towards unusual or marginal subjects: prostitutes, street children, transvestites and the elderly, all of whom are welcomed into their pleasingly skewed visual vocabulary.

Working together as a team since meeting at the London College of Fashion and winning their first commission for Vivienne Westwood while they were still students, Sean and Seng have adopted a youthful exuberance towards their work that continues to make its presence felt. While they choose not to pursue an explicit political message themselves, the subversive motivations of their sources of inspiration infects the tone of their work; for them, eccentric beauty marries the wild and the domestic with dramatic consequences.

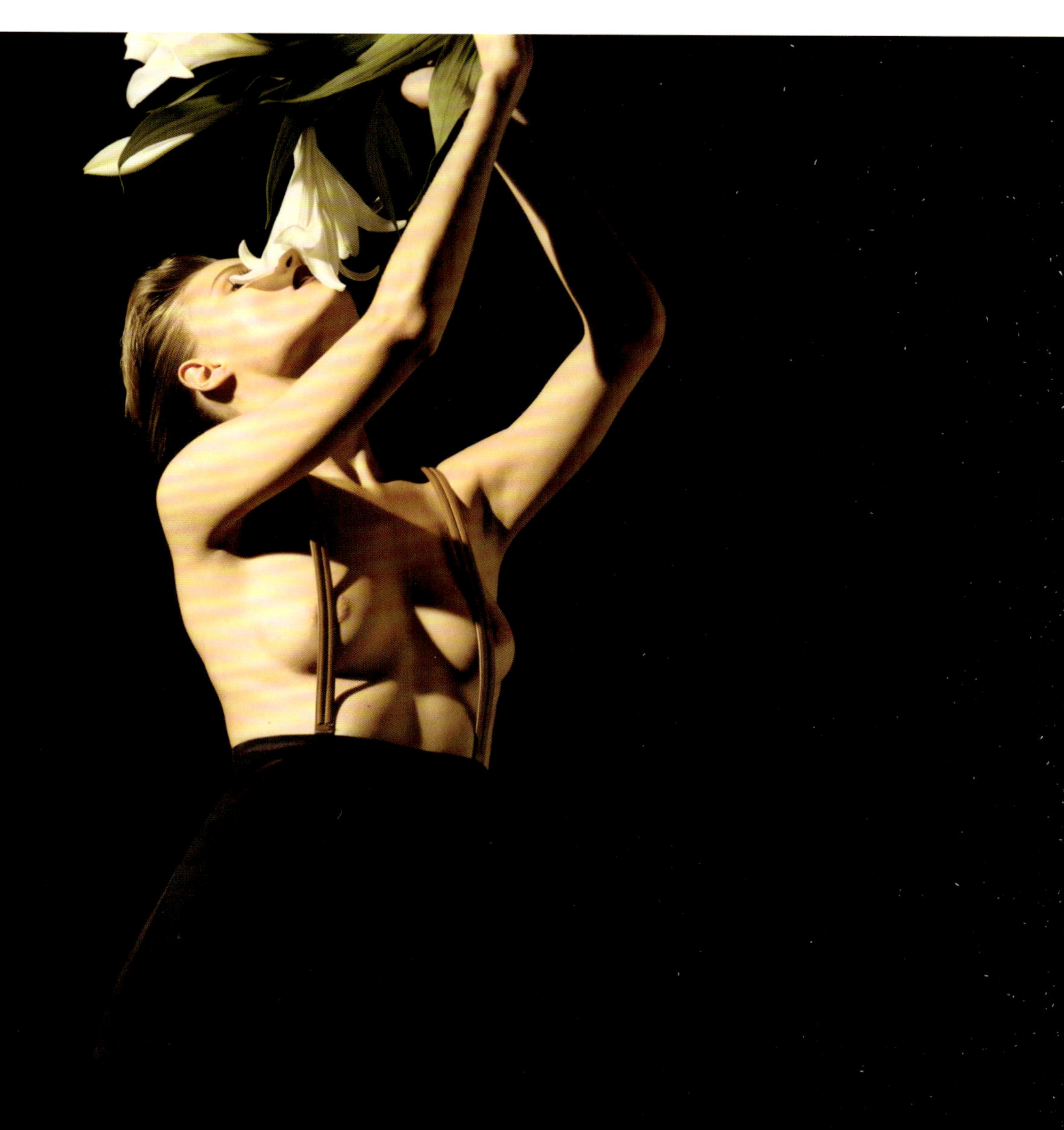

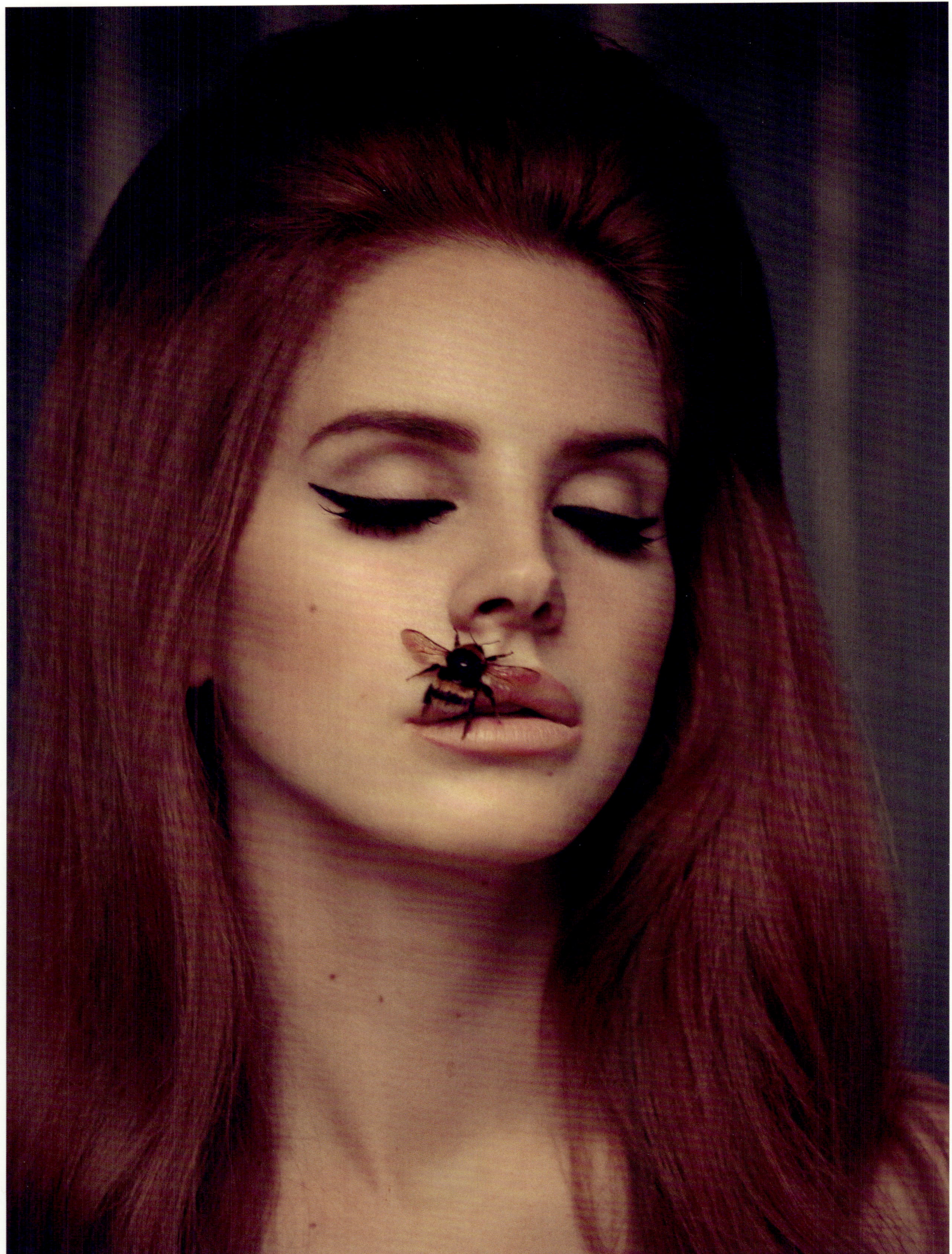

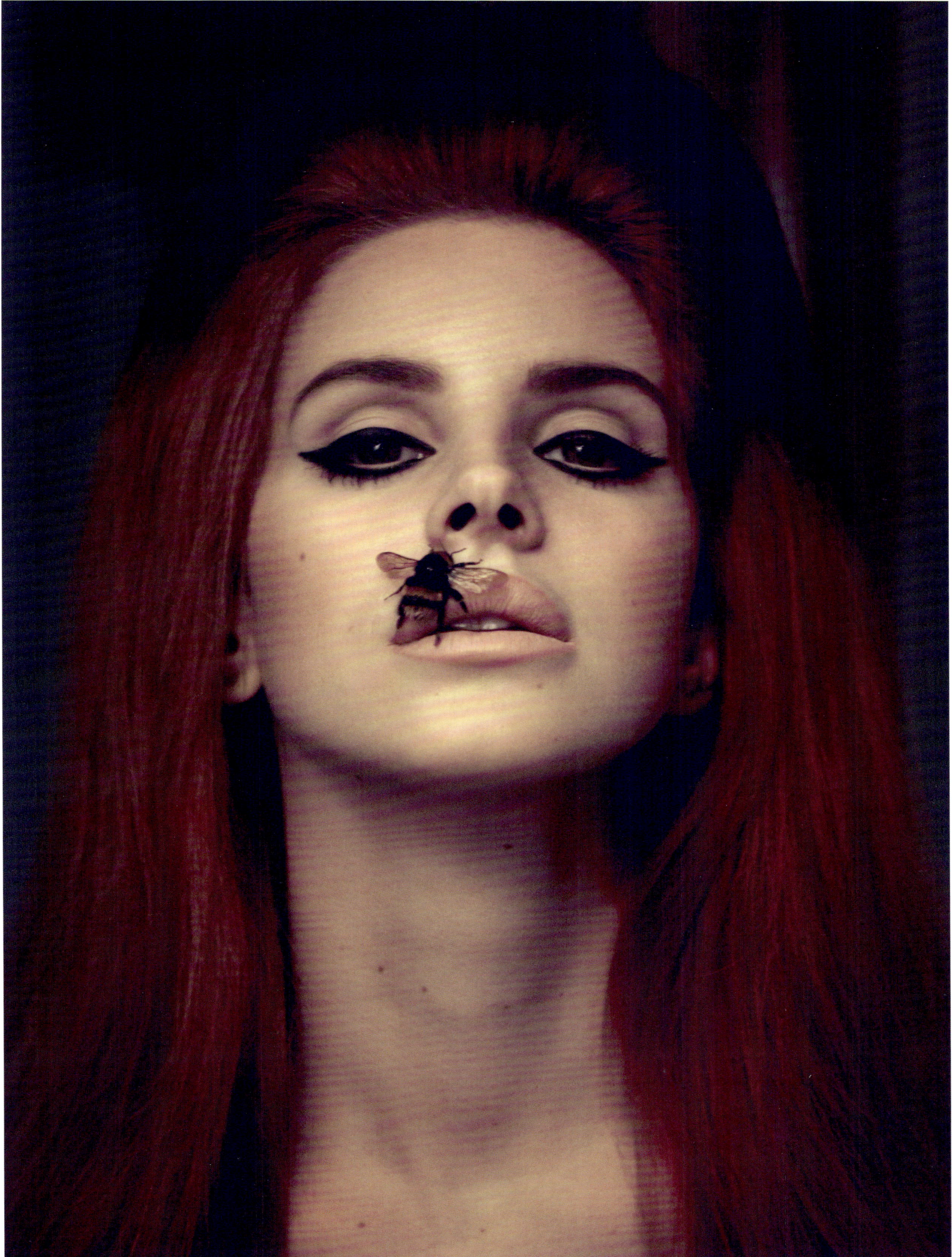

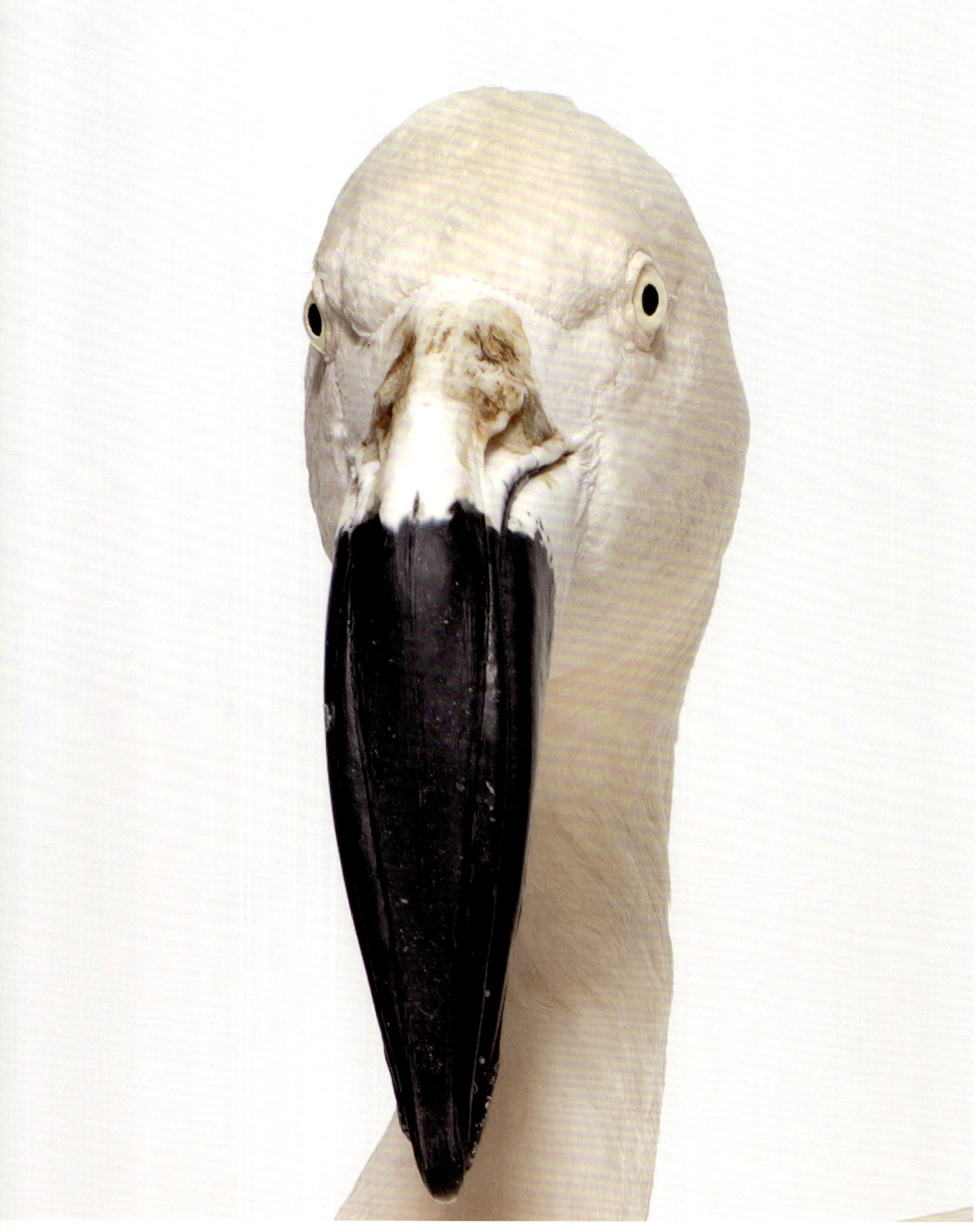

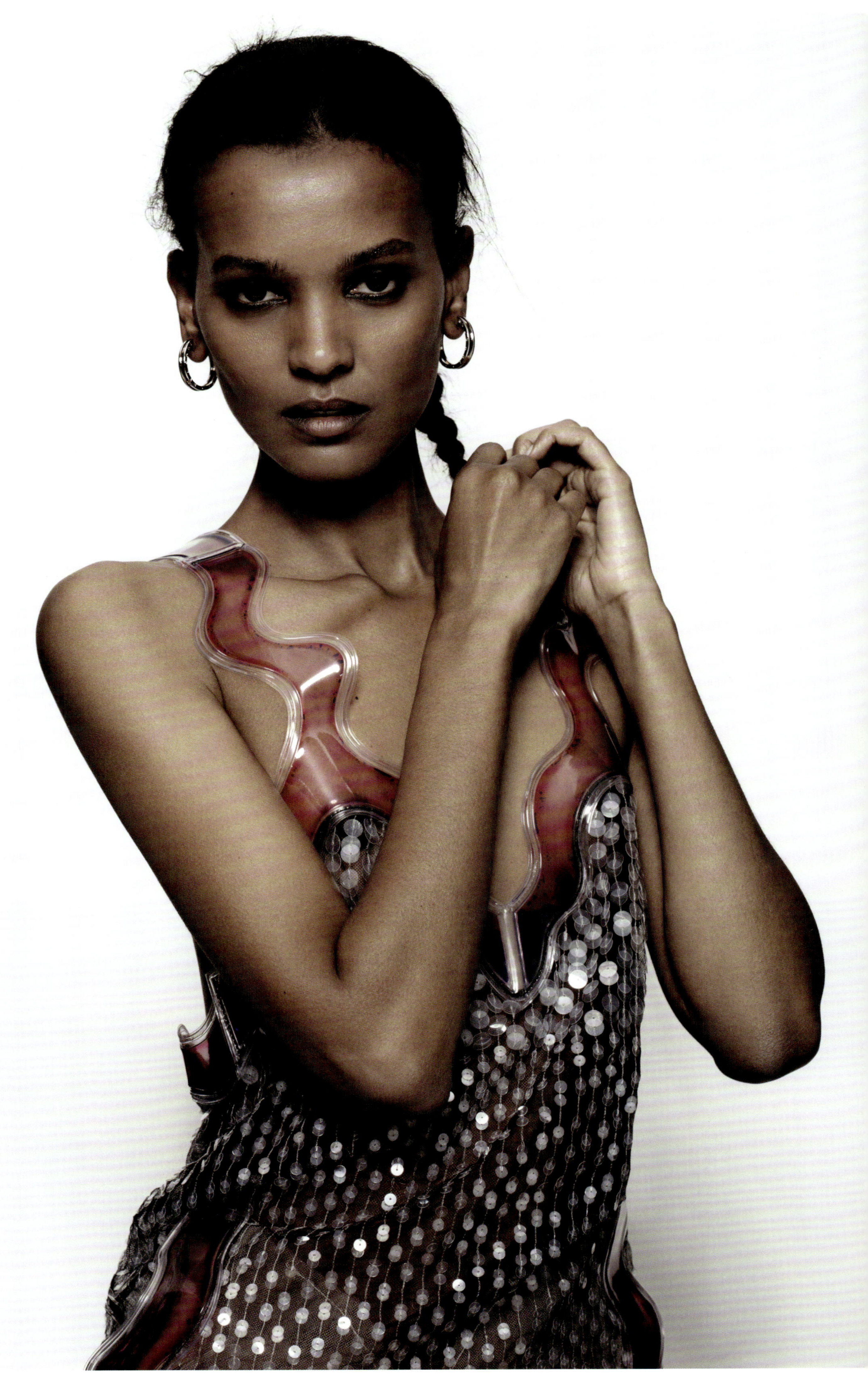

SEAN AND SENG

Frida Aasen for *Dazed & Confused*, 2012
photography by Sean and Seng
courtesy Sean and Seng/TotalWorld

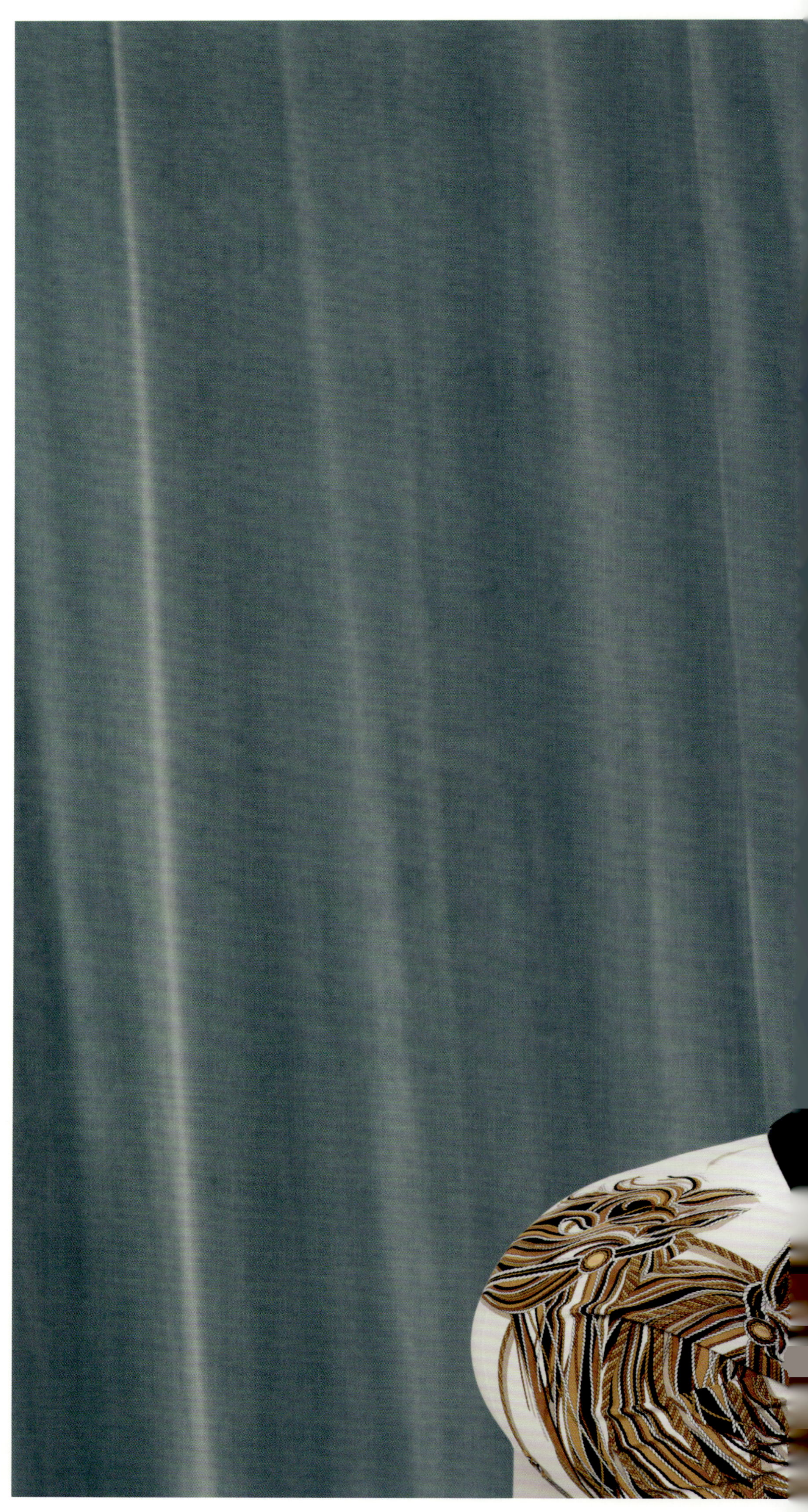

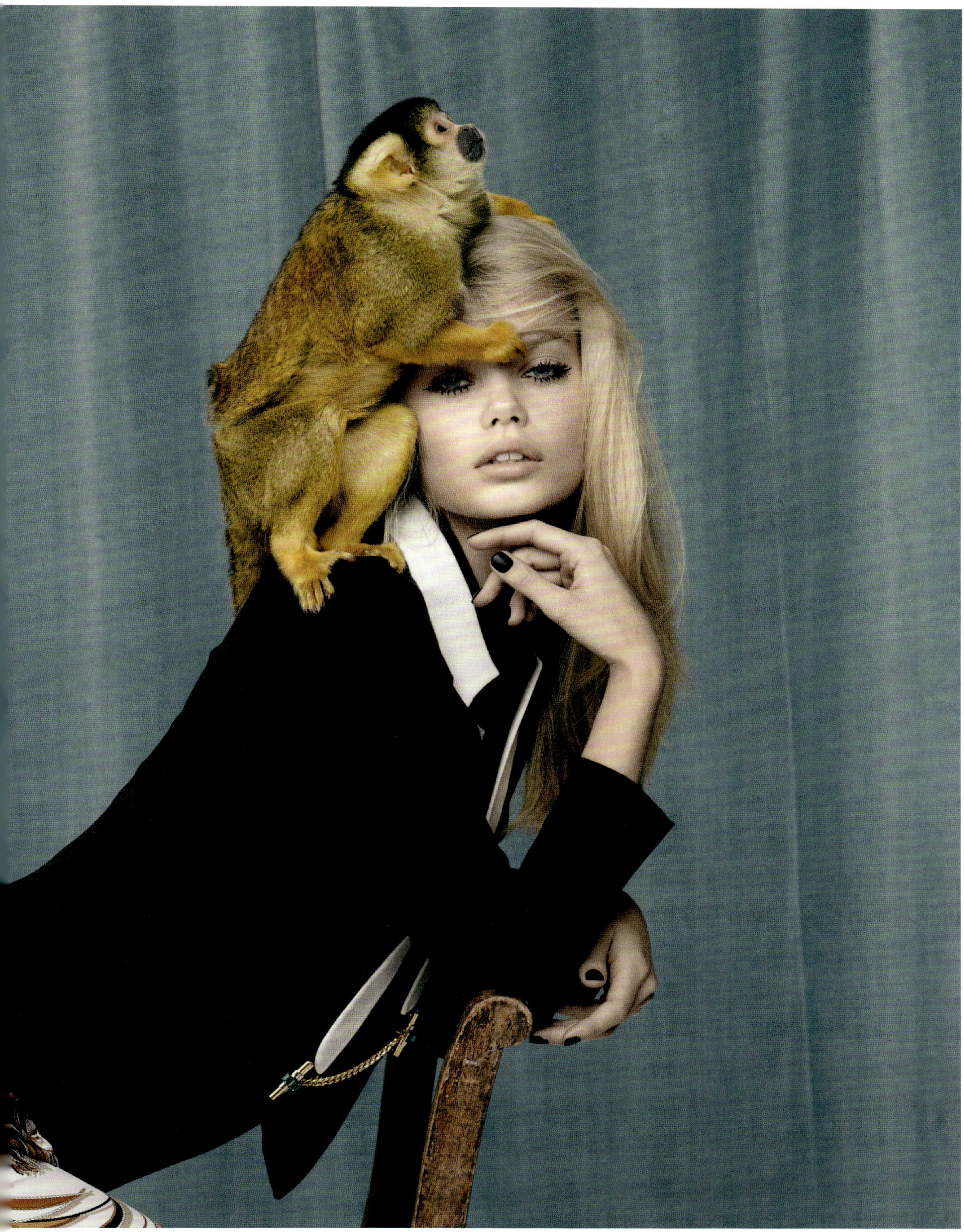

Vanessa Lorenzo and Joan Pedrola
Courances, France, 2010
photography by Ruven Afanador
courtesy Ruven Afanador

Olga Serova, St Hilarion, France, 2008
photography by Ruven Afanador
courtesy Ruven Afanador

pages 56–7:
Jenny Sweeney, Paris, France, 2007
photography by Ruven Afanador
courtesy Ruven Afanador

pages 58–9:
Bimba Bosé for *Yo Dona España*, 2010
photography by Ruven Afanador
courtesy Ruven Afanador

page 60:
Esperanza Fernández Vargas, 2007
from *Mil Besos*
photography by Ruven Afanador
courtesy Ruven Afanador

page 61:
Samantha Santiago Alcón, 2007
from *Mil Besos*
photography by Ruven Afanador
courtesy Ruven Afanador

Pairing elements of classical formalism with an irreverent eye, Ruven Afanador sets exotic portraits amidst traditional architecture and landscapes of natural beauty. Born in the sixteenth-century city of Bucaramanga in Colombia and growing up surrounded by the mountains of the Andes, high above the Río de Oro, Afanador's work carries the mark of a childhood immersed in the rich customs, ritual and pageantry of his home country. The elaborate costume and mysterious masks of Colombian festivals are echoed in expressive photographs that are relocated to French châteaux and Italian side streets; extraordinary scenes emanating from imagined places and times are treated as commonplace reality, blurring the lines between the ordinary and the fantastic to create a suspension of disbelief in the face of the unfamiliar.

Often favouring long torsos and chiseled, sinewy bodies, Afanador's taste is more in line with the conventions of Italian Renaissance sculpture than with the men and women of contemporary fashion. Nowhere does he express the glory of the body more powerfully than in the 2009 book *Mil Besos*, a series of portraits of the arresting women at the heart of Spanish flamenco (pages 60–1). Caught in aggressive, baiting poses, the women perform for Afanador's penetrating lens with the fierce energy they usually reserve for the tablaos of Seville. *Mil Besos* is a natural progression from Afanador's earlier major collections of portraits, *Torero* and *Sombra*, in which he subverts the conventions of gender representation. While *Torero* rewrites masculine stereotypes by uniting Spanish matadors with the conventions of couture photog-

raphy, *Sombra* navigates an alternative male beauty through the poses of classical masculine ballet.

Afanador's journey from Colombia to America began with a move to the Midwest in his teens, where he studied art and photography, picking up skills that he would later develop in Europe. Spending the early months of his career in Italy, a lack of studio space pushed his work into the back alleys of Milan. His experience working outdoors gave rise to a preference for alfresco shooting that would dominate his future work. Finally settling in New York, the wide-ranging elements of this journey have come together to define his contemporary photography.

Afanador's images exhibit a reverence towards the grand and spectacular, yet they are underpinned by a mischievous attitude towards the subjects themselves. His oblique take on reality often suggests the elaborate intricacies of great storytelling. Shoots such as 'Retratos de una obsesión' for *Yo Dona España* carry undertones of illicit parties or the gatherings of secret societies in the grounds and corridors of exquisite mansions (pages 58–9). In utilising multiple levels of symbolic resonance through a prism of magic realism, such imagery evokes the writing of fellow Colombian Gabriel García Márquez, whose authentic engagement with fantastic interventions into the everyday parallels Afanador's visualisations of the drama of human performance set within extraordinary narratives.

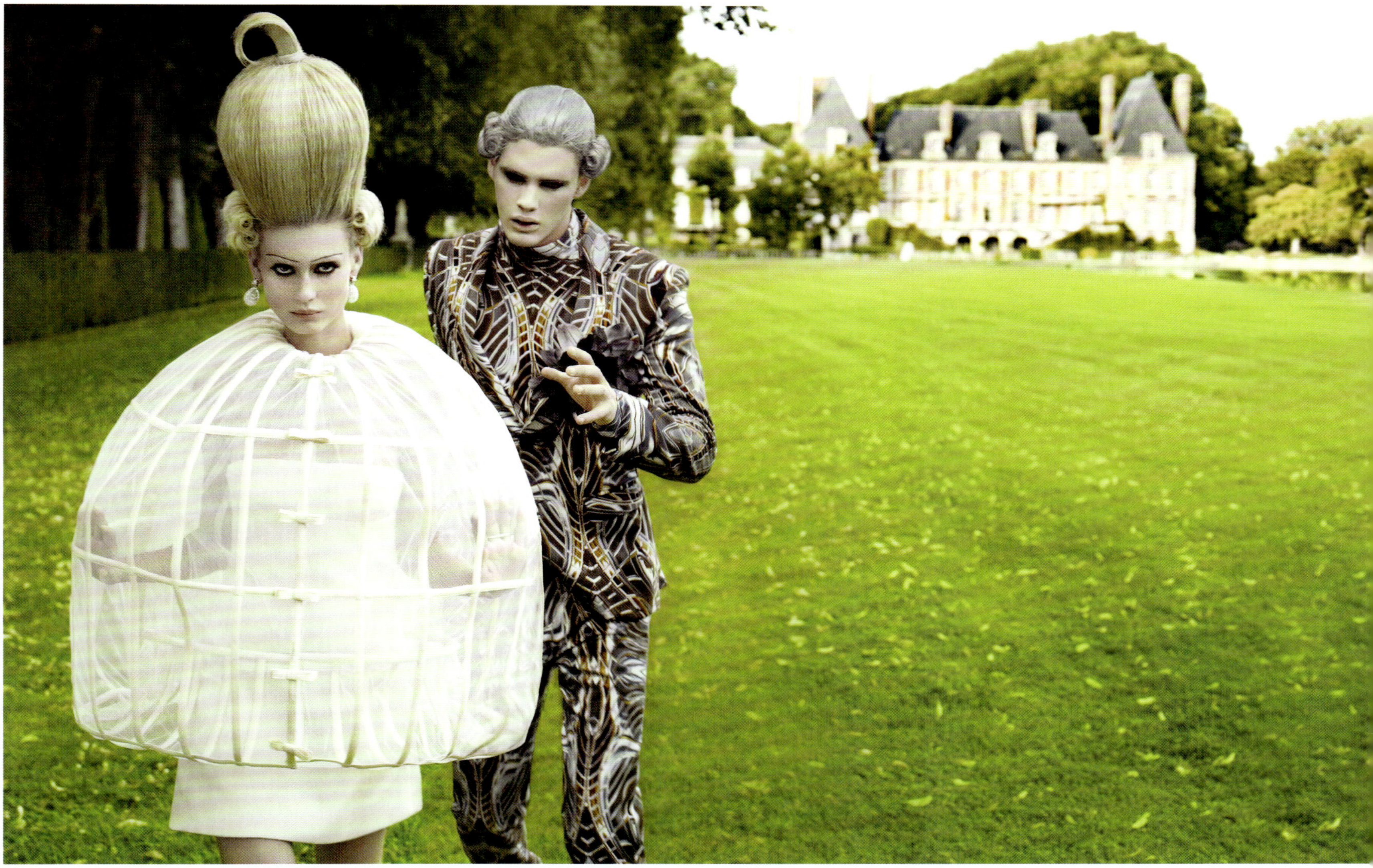

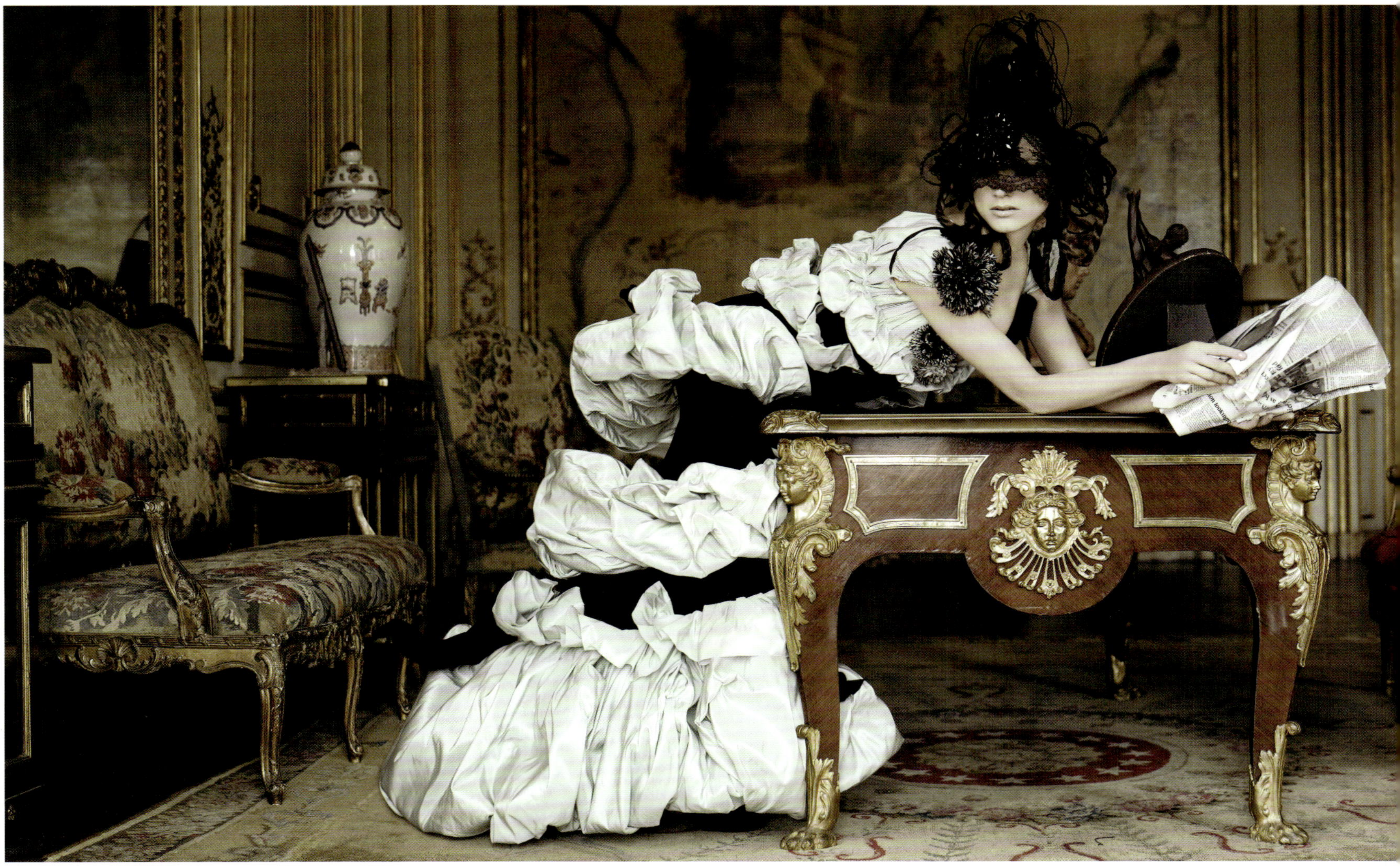

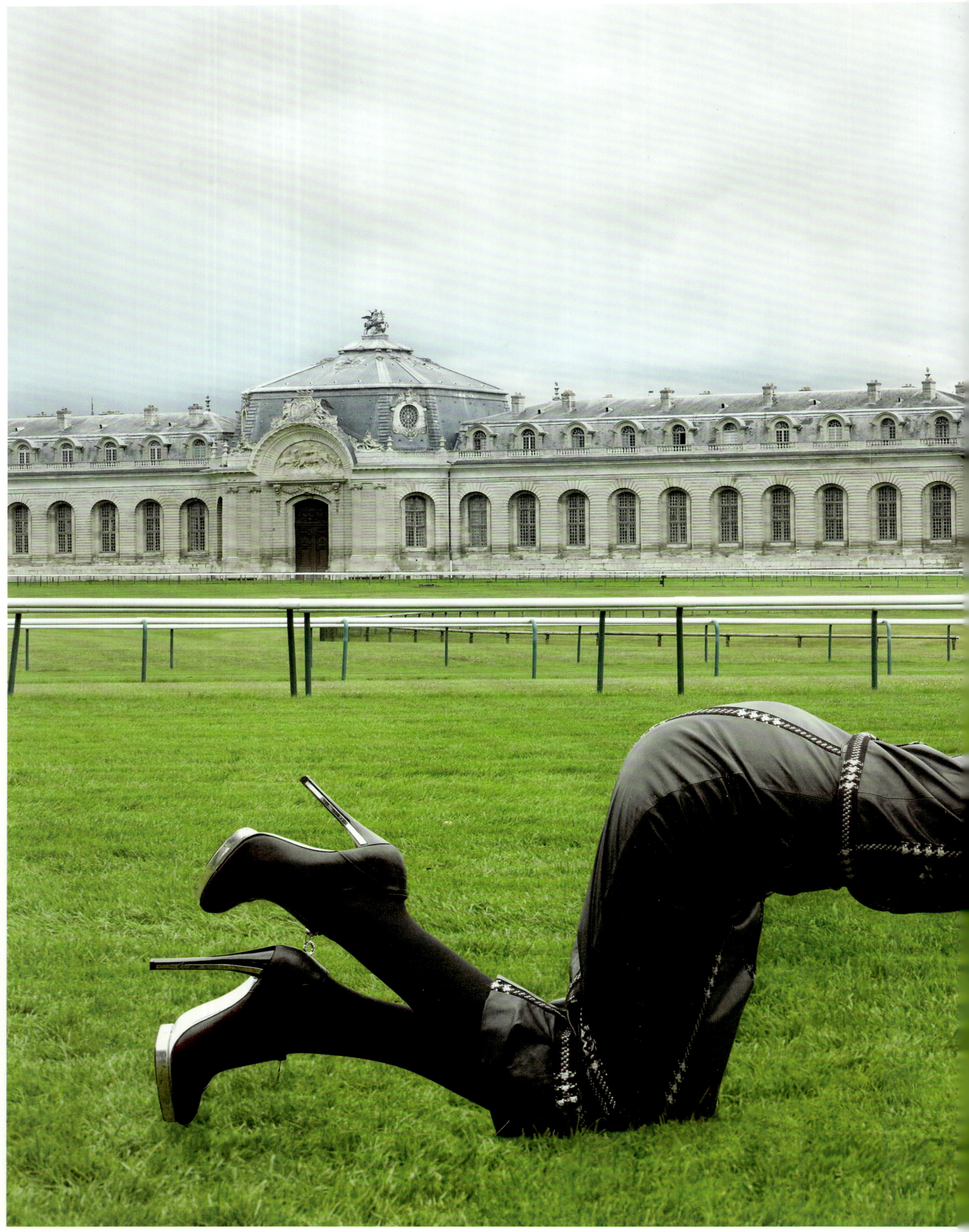

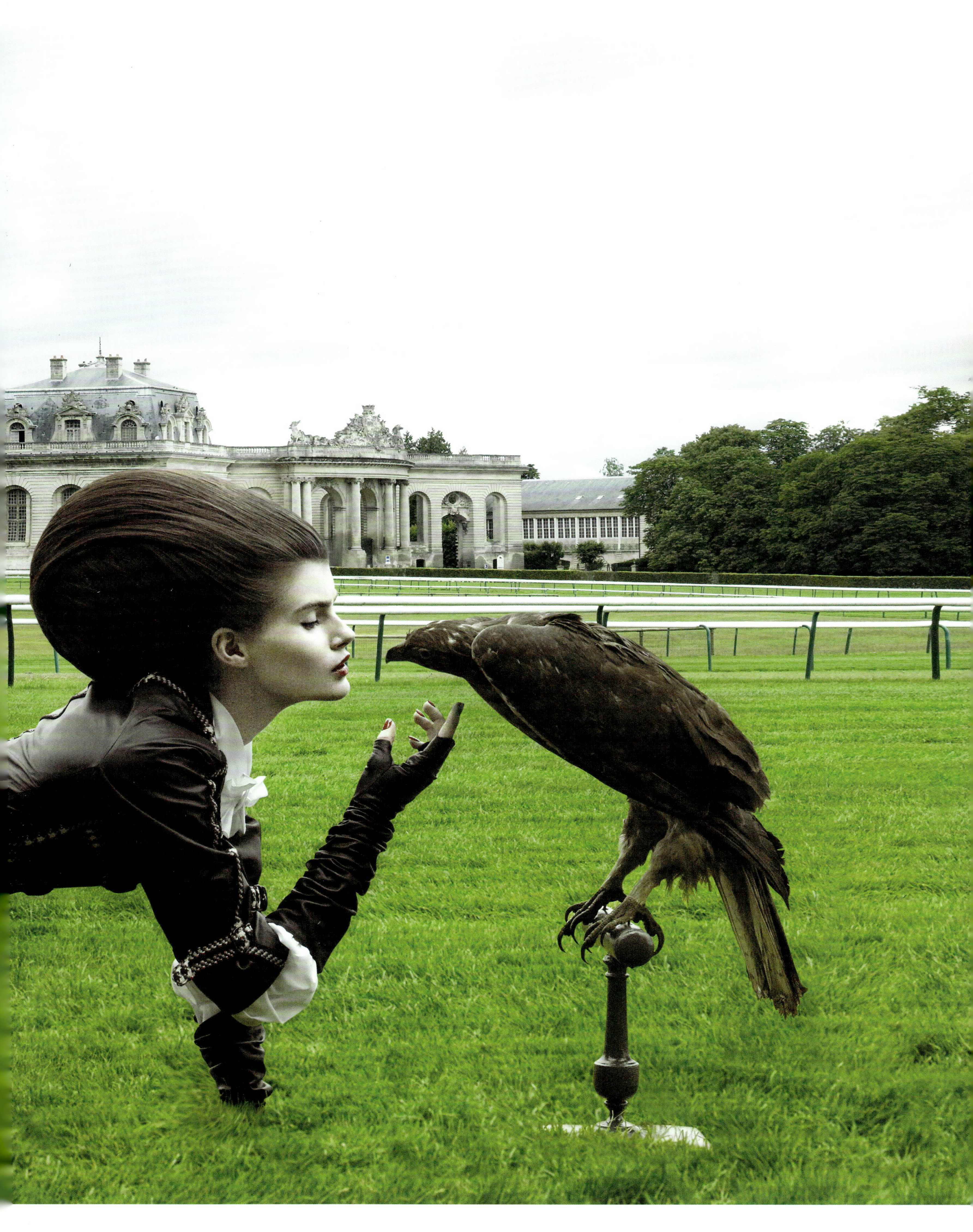

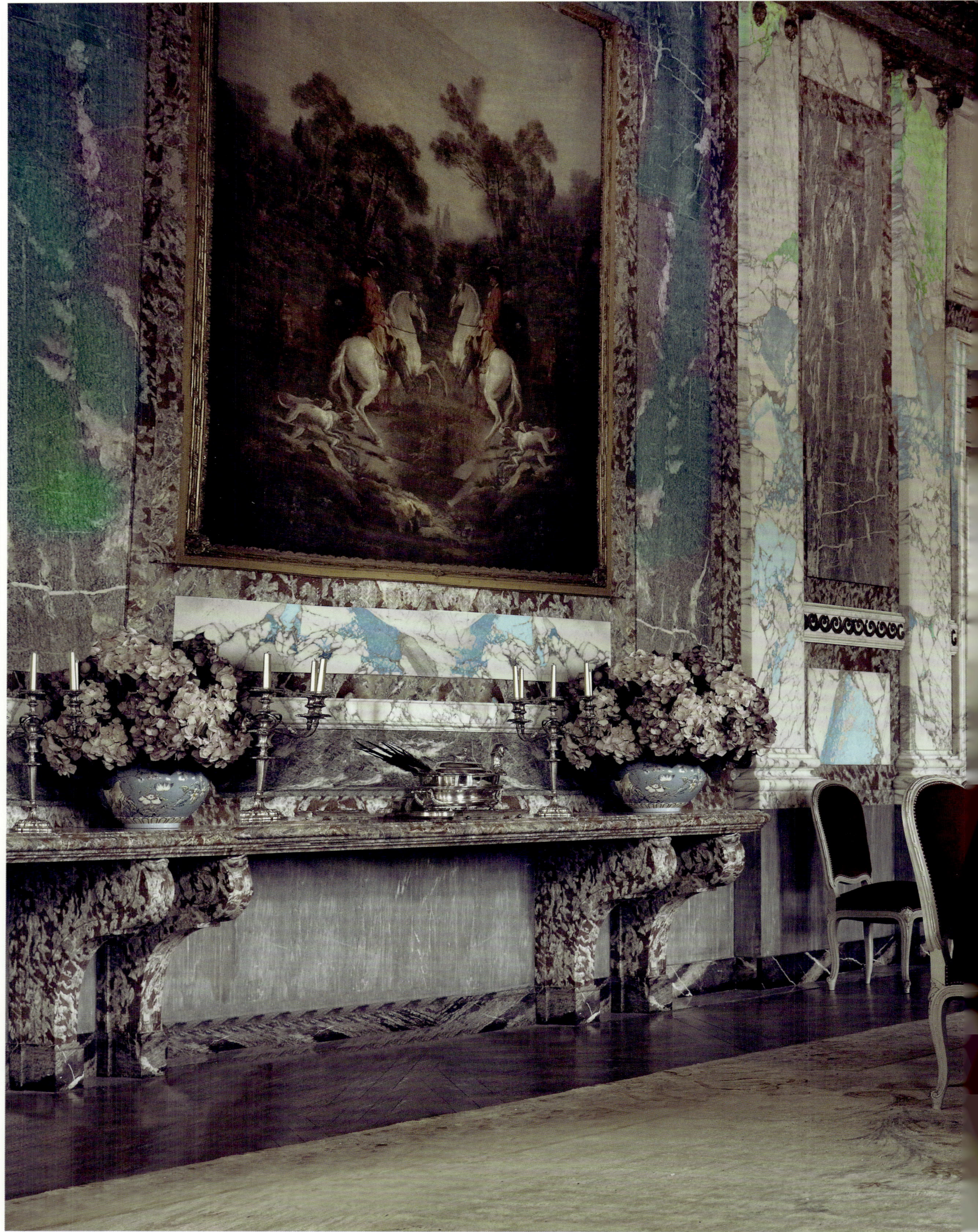

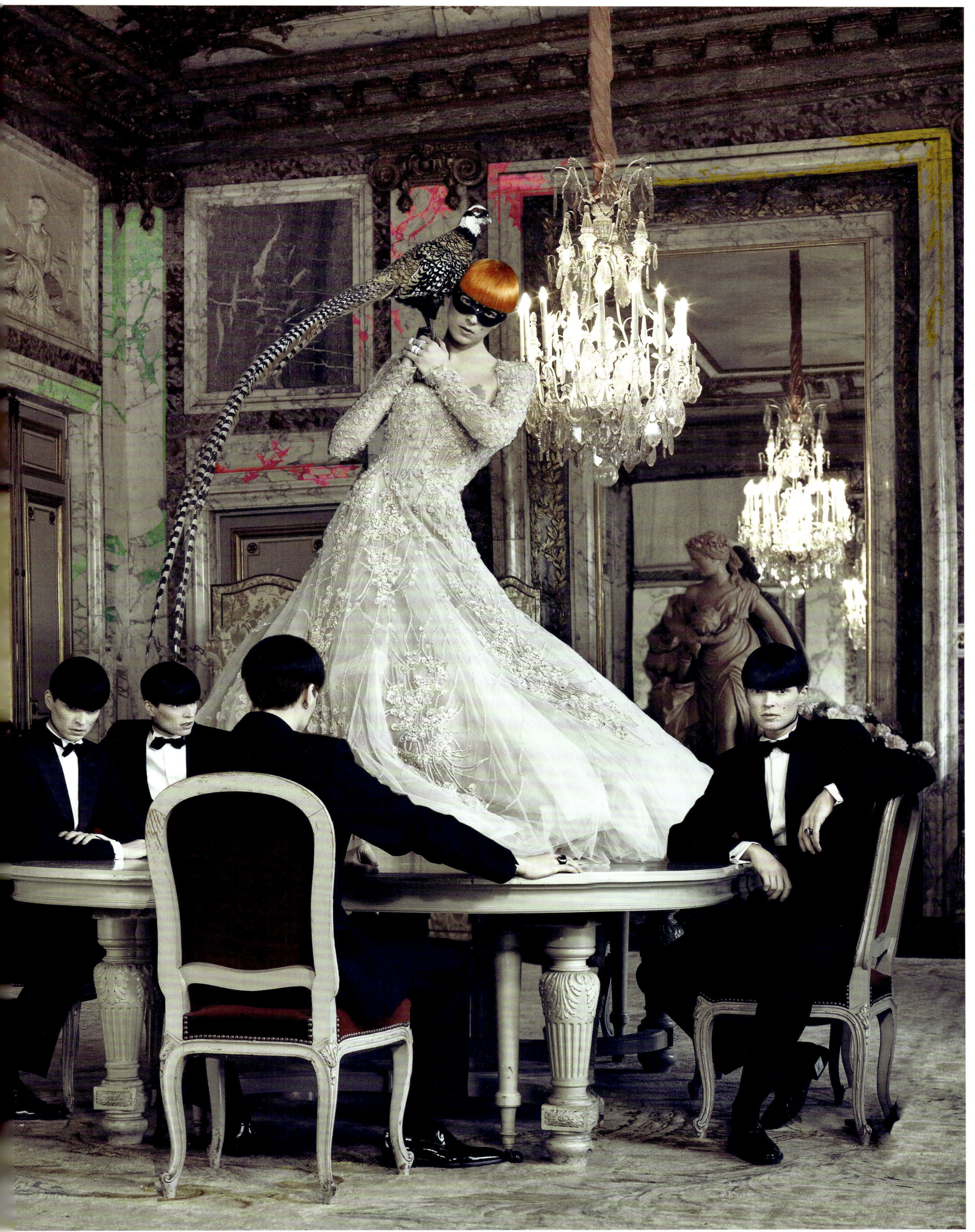

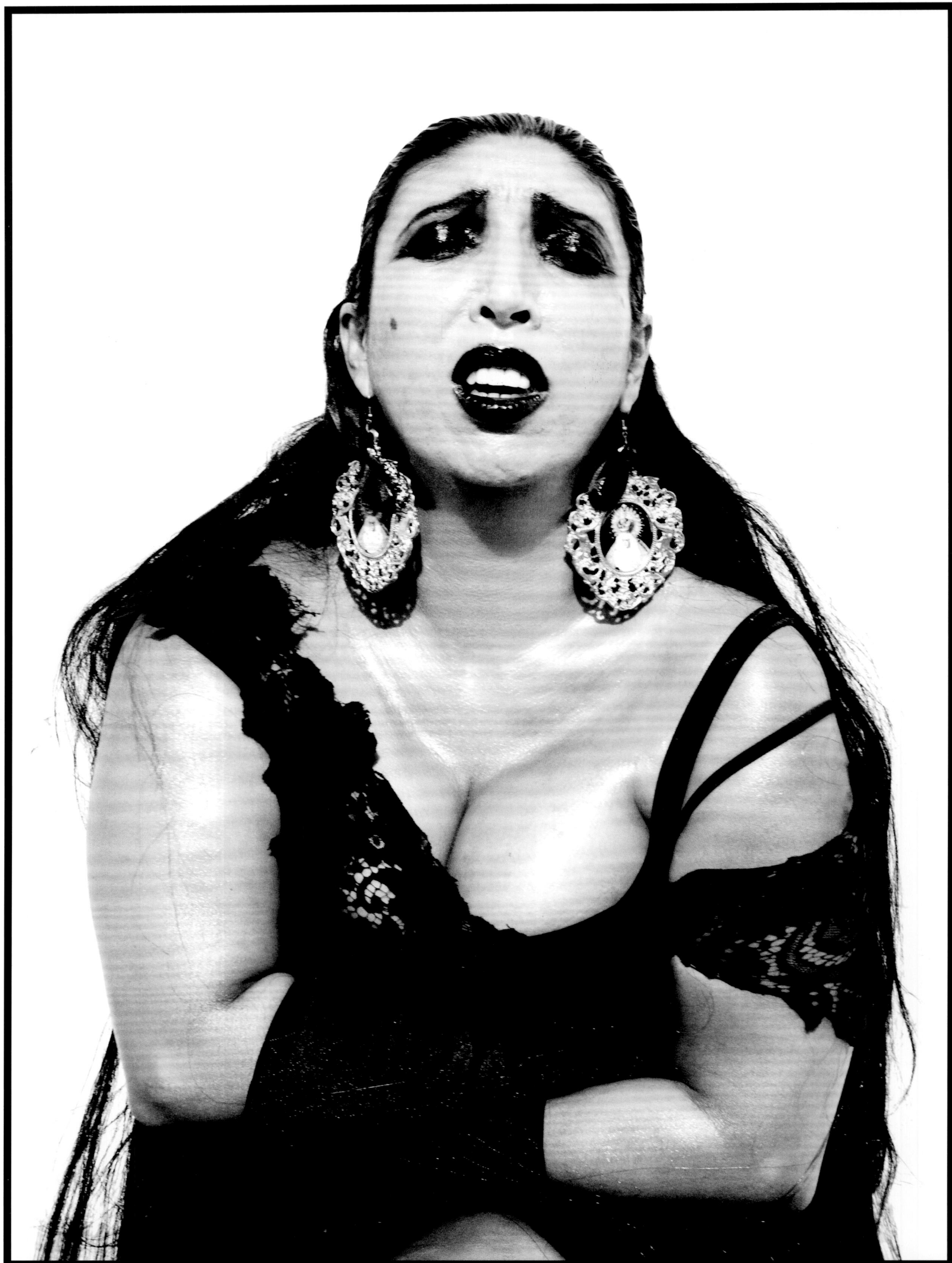

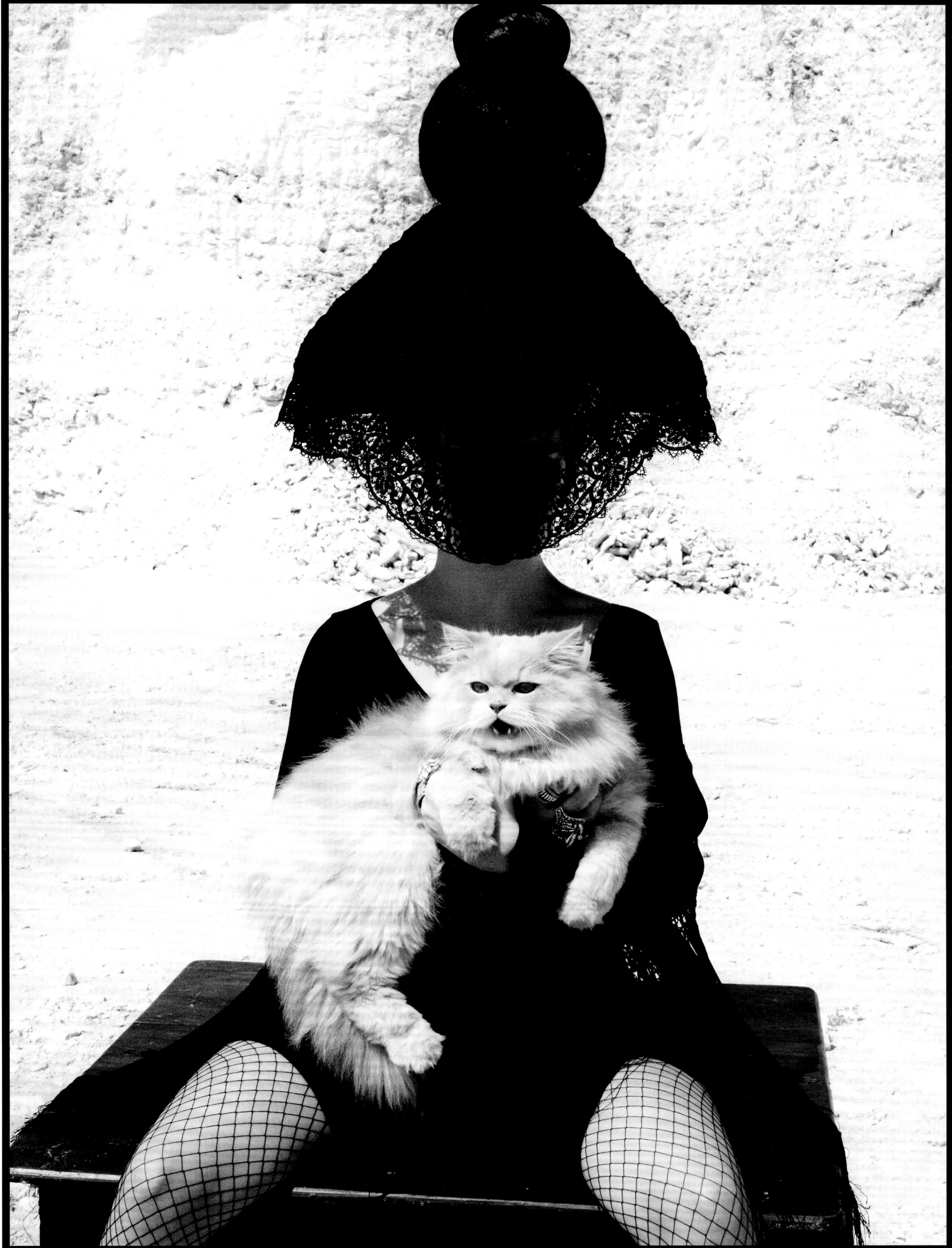

Christina Ricci in 'Religion'
by Riccardo Tisci for *Visionaire*, 2011
photography by Daniele + Iango
courtesy Streeters

Operating out of New York since 2001, the creative partnership of Italian Daniele Duella and Swiss Iango Henzi takes fashion beyond function in a self-confessed pursuit of an 'aesthetic absolute' in image making. Uniting classicism with the contemporary, they seek out avant-garde subject matter to confront the conventions of fashion and rewrite the rules for iconic photography. The images that result walk a line between beauty and provocation.

Form and function fuse dramatically with Daniele and Iango's taste for the provocative in an interpretation of a piece by contemporary designer Ron Arad for his 2008 exhibition at Arums Galerie in Paris (pages 66–7). As part of a re-edit of Arad's Spring 1991 collection, curated by Patricia Moroso, *Orgasmus* features a volatile interaction between oversize model Velvet d'Amour and a Ron Arad sculpture. The image is frenzied as movement is expressed through focused blur, the correlation of the curvature of Arad's sculpture and the photographer's model making for an explosive redefinition of beauty.

Such subtle subversion is deployed to more direct effect in a 2012 shoot for The Royalty Issue of *i-D*, in which the explicitly male archetype of the Japanese Sumo wrestler is replaced by a dominant female (pages 64–5). The substitution is matter-of-fact and effective; only a second glance opens up the question of gender. Elsewhere, in the explicit *Give a Penny for a Shot,* a similar subversive sensibility threatens to spill over into vulgarity. But the socio-political satire wrapped up in the image, alongside its desat-urated, pre-Raphaelite colouration, overwhelms its graphic nature to create something else. Daniele and Iango's rich use of chiaroscuro diverts attention from an image that shocks and encourages a reappraisal of what is being viewed. The deep, classically inspired dimensionality of this style elevates the photographs in terms of power in much the same way that the pair's preference for scale – most images are developed at 2.8 x 1.8m – operates as a visual indicator of the scope of their artistic ambition.

Favouring photography over formal study from the age of thirteen, Duella has found the perfect partner in Henzi, whose career as a dancer working with choreographers such as the legendary Serge Golovine has served to bring an understanding of movement and the body to his technique. The outcome is a unique relationship between technical precision and the vitality of movement and form. Taking their lead from the past and shooting with film rather than digital, Daniele and Iango adopt a cool attitude towards postproduction and prefer to rely on the immediacy of their equipment, an approach that echoes their historical awareness of image making. Thematically, however, they look forward rather than back. An engagement with contemporary ideas comes through in a 2008 haute couture shoot for *The Economist*, in which the work of artist Leigh Bowery is channeled to unite their conceptual view of fashion with the performance that works as an essential part of it. It is this synthesis of classical aesthetics and contemporary intuition that allows Daniele and Iango's work to achieve both timelessness and emotional immediacy.

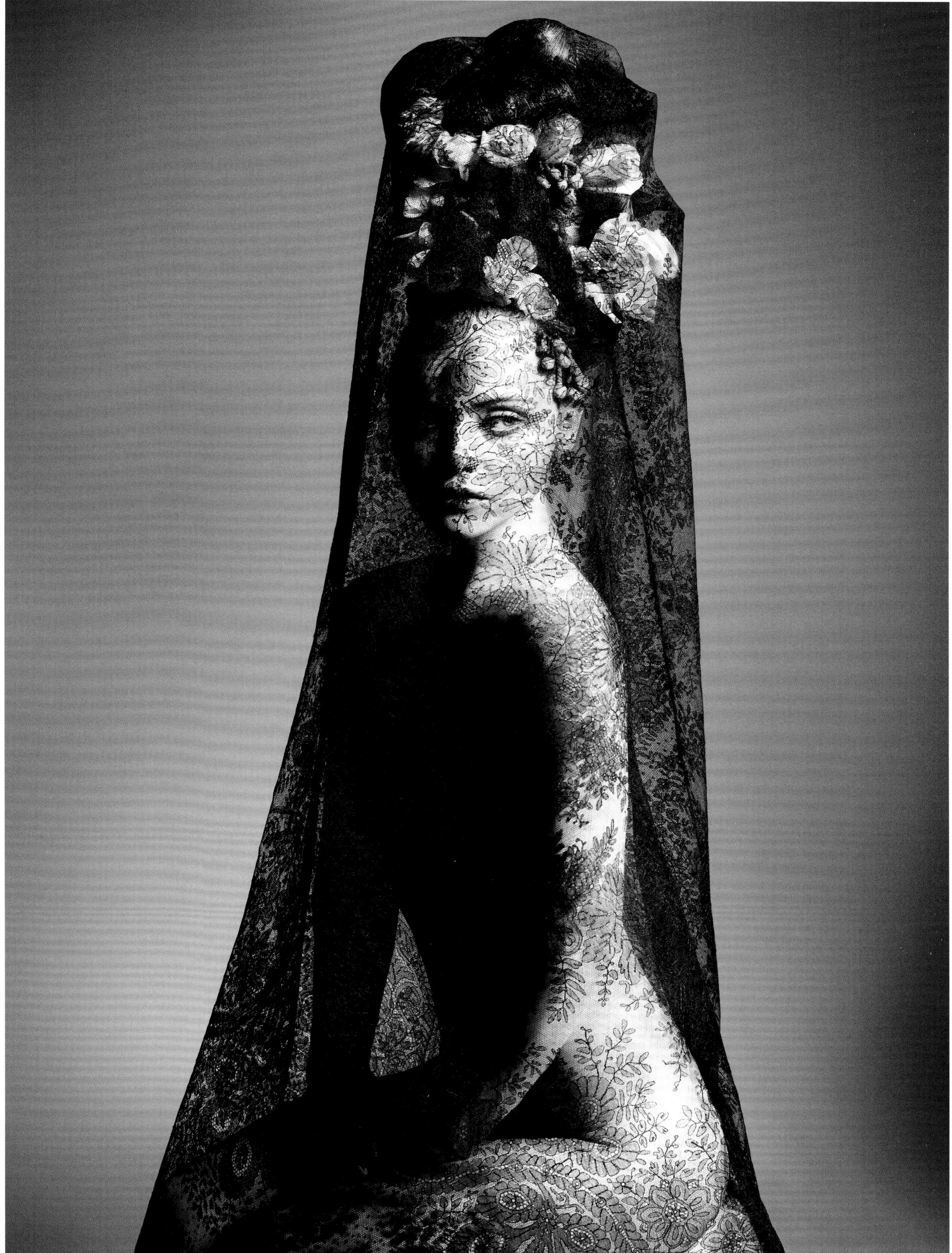

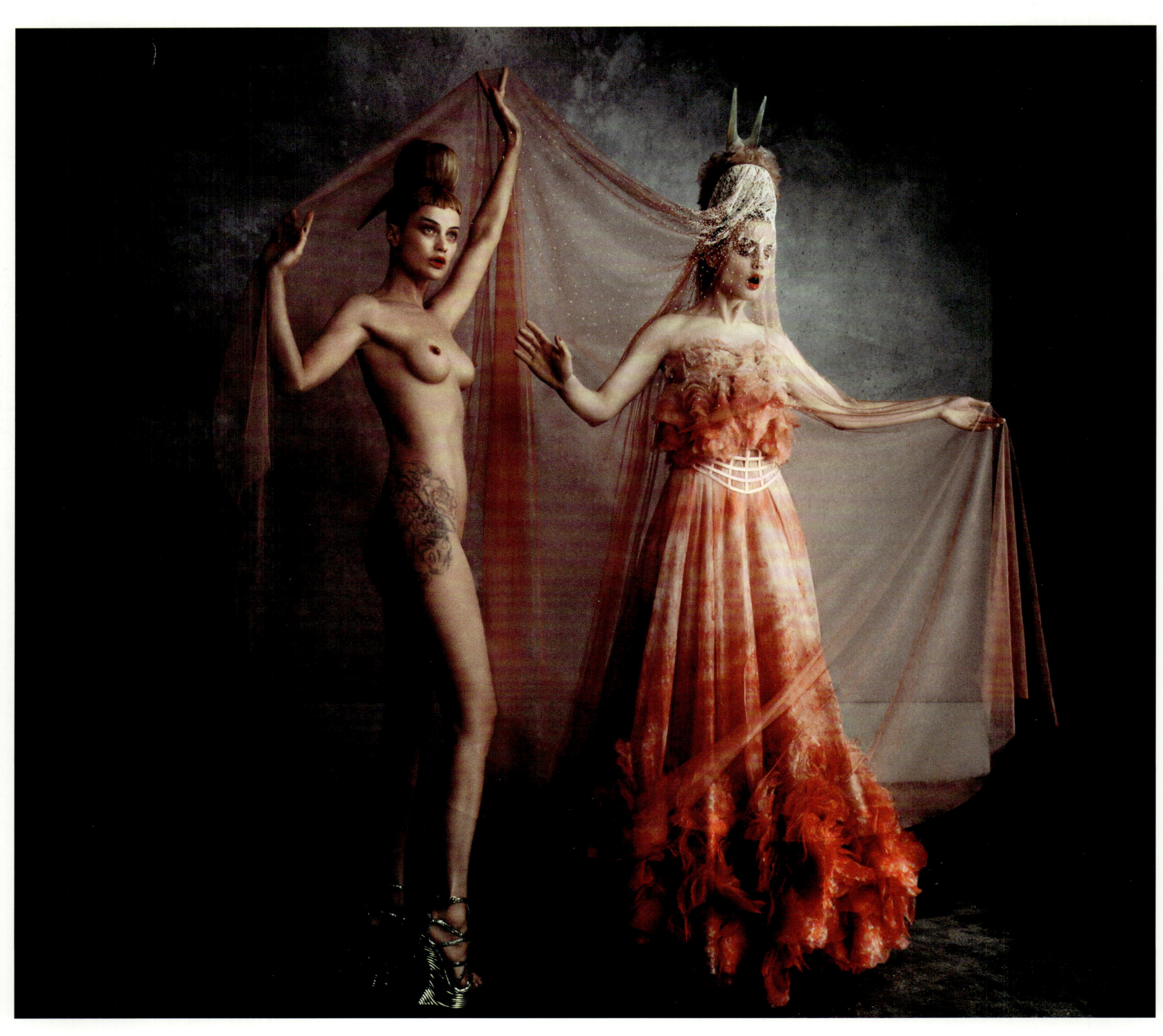

DANIELE + IANGO

Carolyn Murphy and Guinevere Van Seenus for *i-D*
The Royalty Issue, 2012
photography by Daniele + Iango
courtesy Streeters
casting by ML McCarthy
Urban Productions / Casting

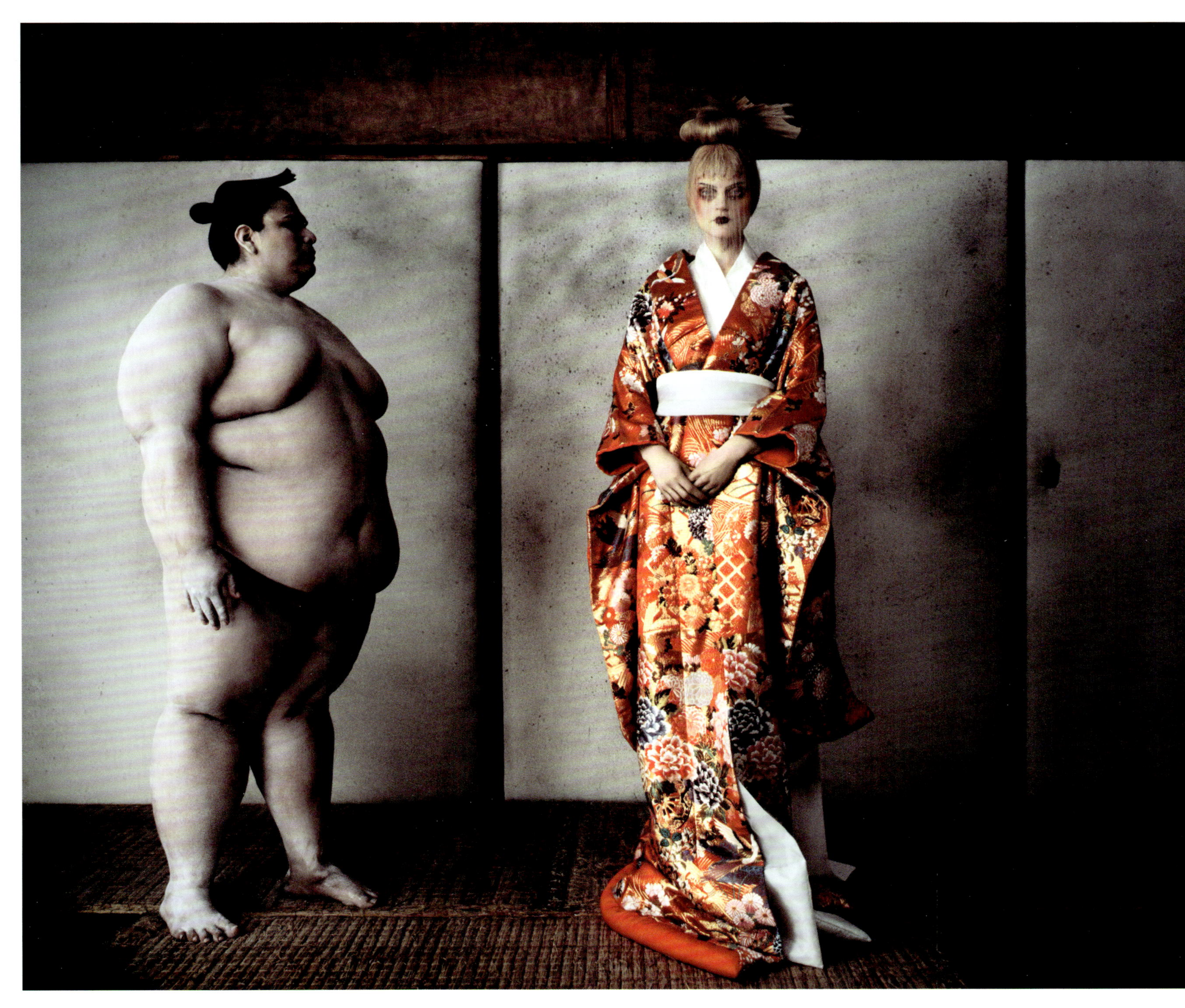

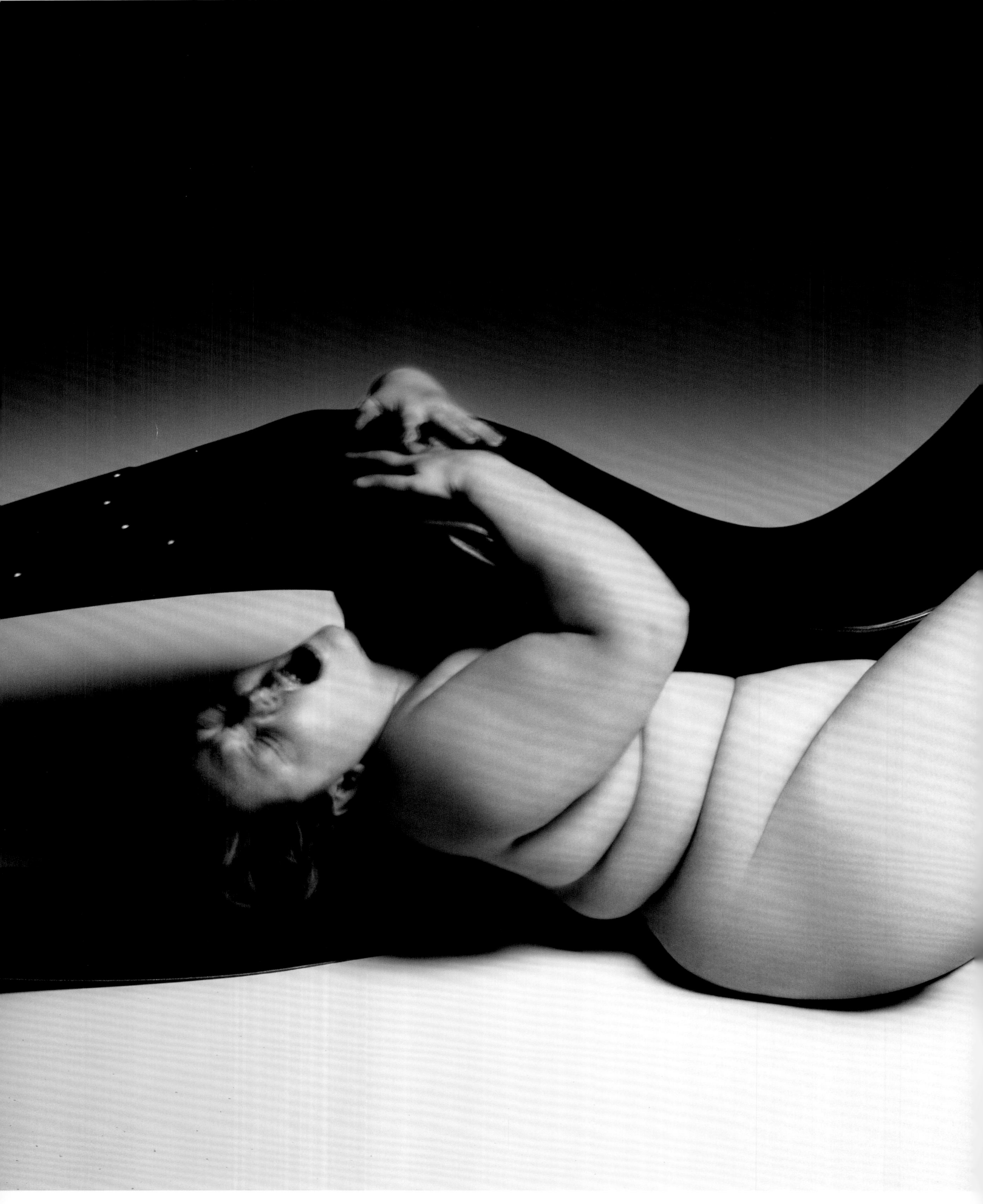

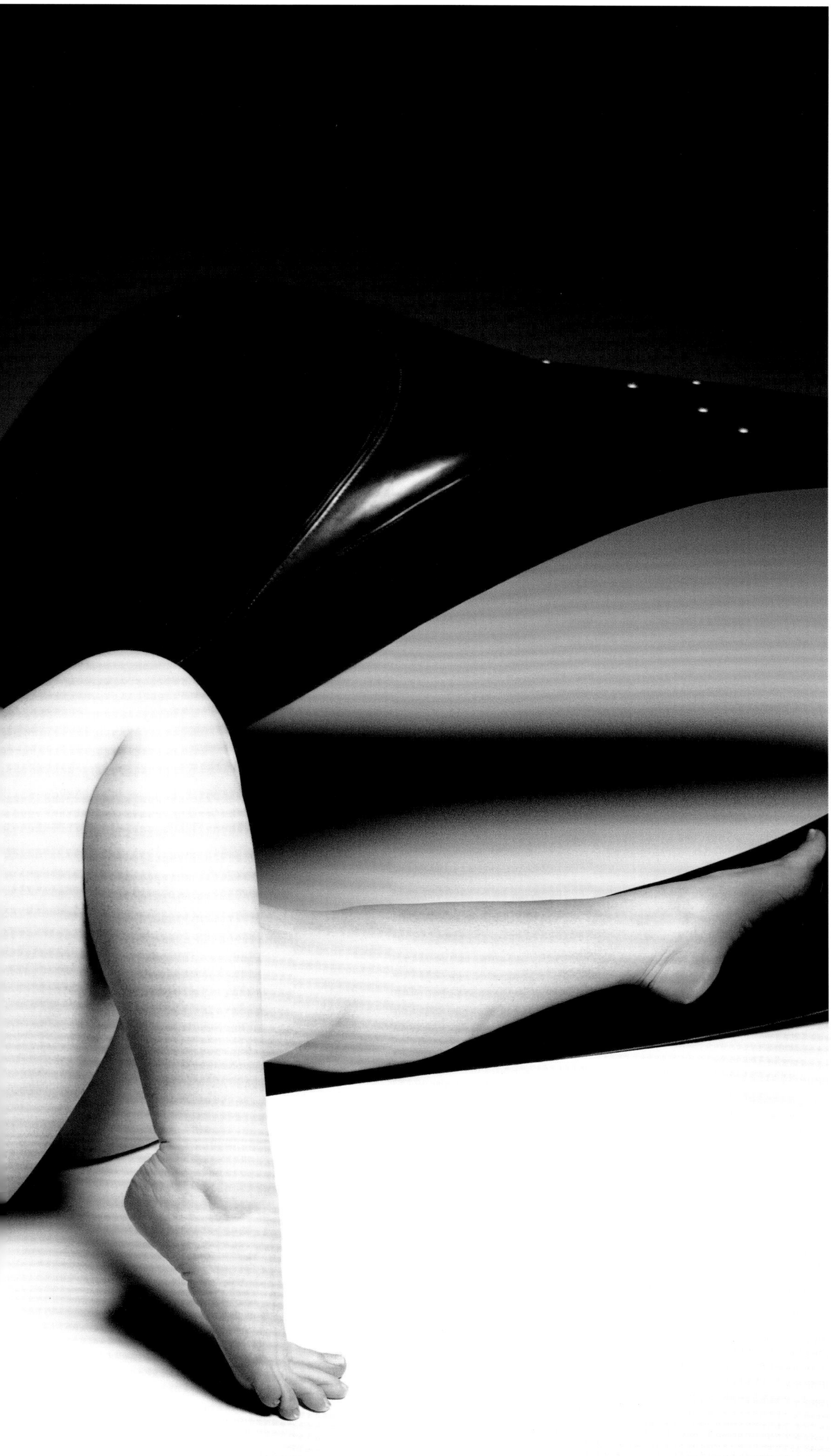

DANIELE + IANGO

Velvet d'Amour
for Ron Arad Spring Collection 2009
photography by Daniele + Iango
courtesy Streeters

page 68:
Katia, *Modern Warrior*, 2012
photography by Daniele + Iango
courtesy Streeters

page 69:
Isabeli Fontana for *i-D*
The Role Model issue, 2012
photography by Daniele + Iango
courtesy Streeters

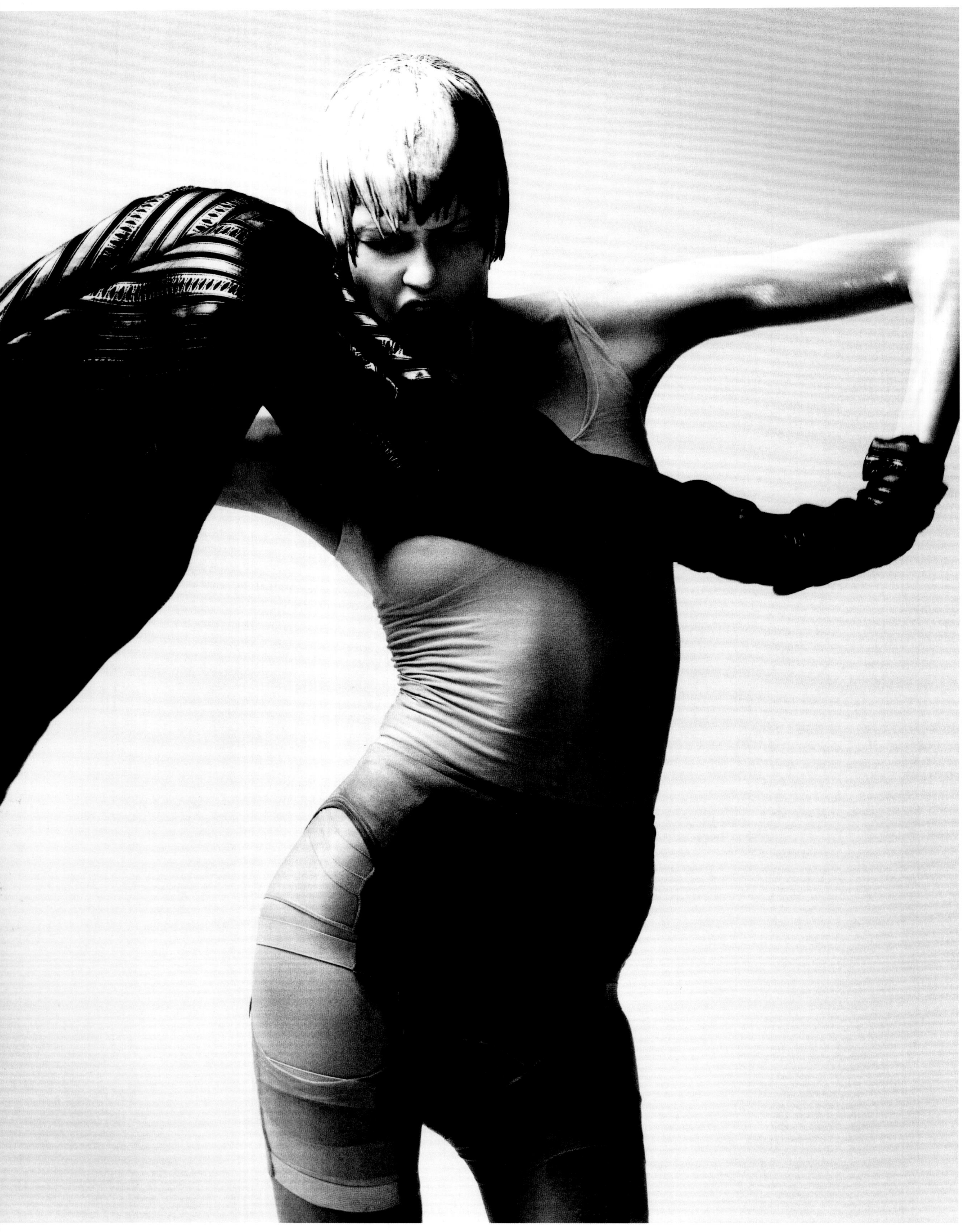

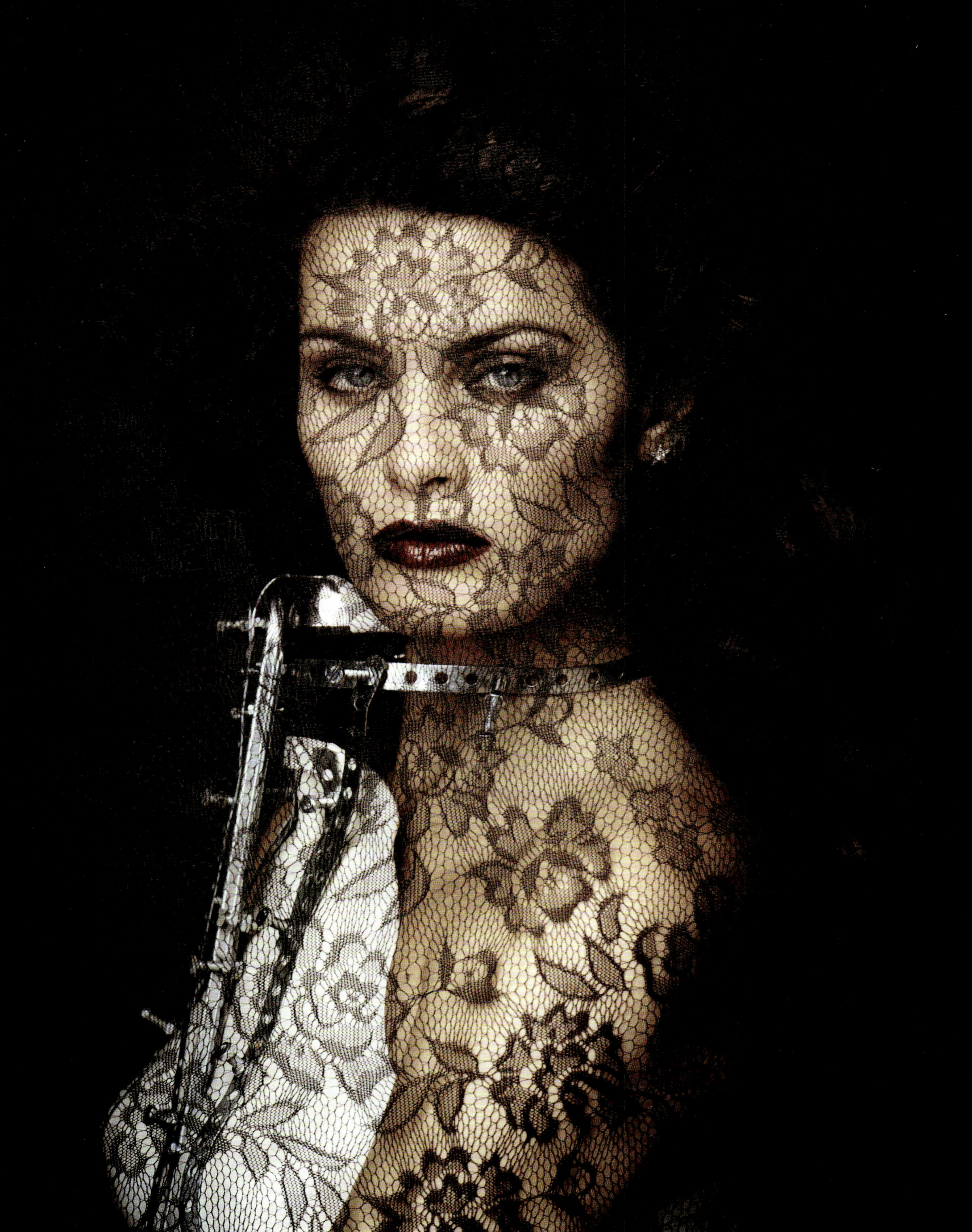

DANIEL SANNWALD

pages 71–73:
for *Harper's Bazaar* China, 2010
photography by Daniel Sannwald
courtesy Daniel Sannwald Studio
styling by Stevie Westgarth

pages 74–5:
from 'Looking for a Certain Ratio'
for *Vogue Homme +*, 2011
photography by Daniel Sannwald
courtesy Daniel Sannwald Studio

The experimental London-based, German-born Daniel Sannwald eschews a single visual signature in his fashion photography, relentlessly exploring new territories with each shoot. Taking the experimental path to a logical extreme, he pushes at technical and theoretical boundaries to create images that are layered with oblique yet compelling meaning. His style projects an atmosphere of contemporary mythicism, navigating a sea of dream-like references from the dystopian futurism of Fritz Lang to the tragic beauty of Shakespeare's Ophelia. His art emerges through a process of endless reinvention, yet his photographs are united by the symbolic parallels that run through them.

Preferring to describe himself as an 'image maker', Sannwald's technique goes beyond pure photography. Following the precedent set in his first professional editorial for *Suite*, in which he combined a Polaroid camera, an old Canon and a copy machine to capture different elements of his subject, a multi-disciplinary approach has continued to define his practice. In later works even more direct interventions are made, from chemical burns to heavy digital compression. In an August 2010 shoot for *Harper's Bazaar* China, the surface of portraits appear to have been dissected with a knife in order to reveal further layers beneath (pages 72–3); these uncanny images are symbolic of Sannwald's multi-tiered methodology.

In his 2011 shoot for *Vogue Homme +*, 'Looking for a Certain Ratio', Sannwald's juxtapositions create formal associations in a more literal search for parallels in his environment, a feature that owes a lot to a past directly referenced in his work. Believing at a young age that his late father lived on in an imagined place he was yet to discover, Sannwald set out to find it within the many films and books he absorbed. This starting point is acknowledged most explicitly in his photographic collection *Pluto and Charon*. The relationship of the satellite Charon to its parent planet, Pluto, each tidally locked and remaining face-to-face within a chaotic universe, is one of mutual dependence. It is an allusion to Sannwald's creative discourse with his father, to whom the collection is dedicated. The visual expression of this relationship not only acknowledges the transfer of ideas from parent to sibling, but is also suggestive of the alliance of photographer and subject in what is always a collaborative process.

With echoes of the deliberately contradictory oeuvre of contemporary artist Gerhard Richter, Sannwald's style is paradoxically defined by its lack of definition. His practice moves through photography, paint, collage and even performance in an endless mutation. The images that come out of this threaten to marginalise themselves at first with their elusive frames of reference, yet ultimately they succeed through the force of their conviction and delivery.

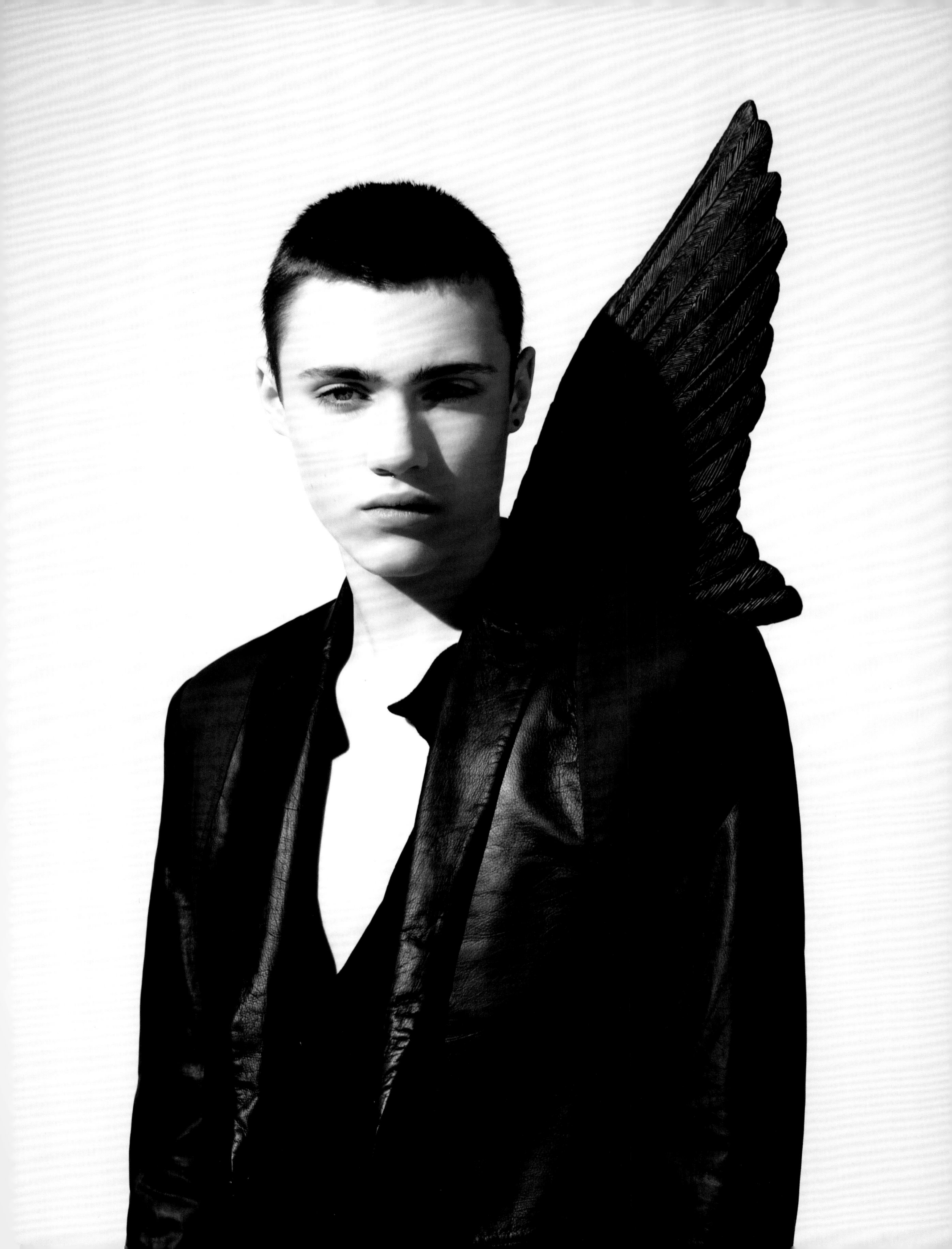

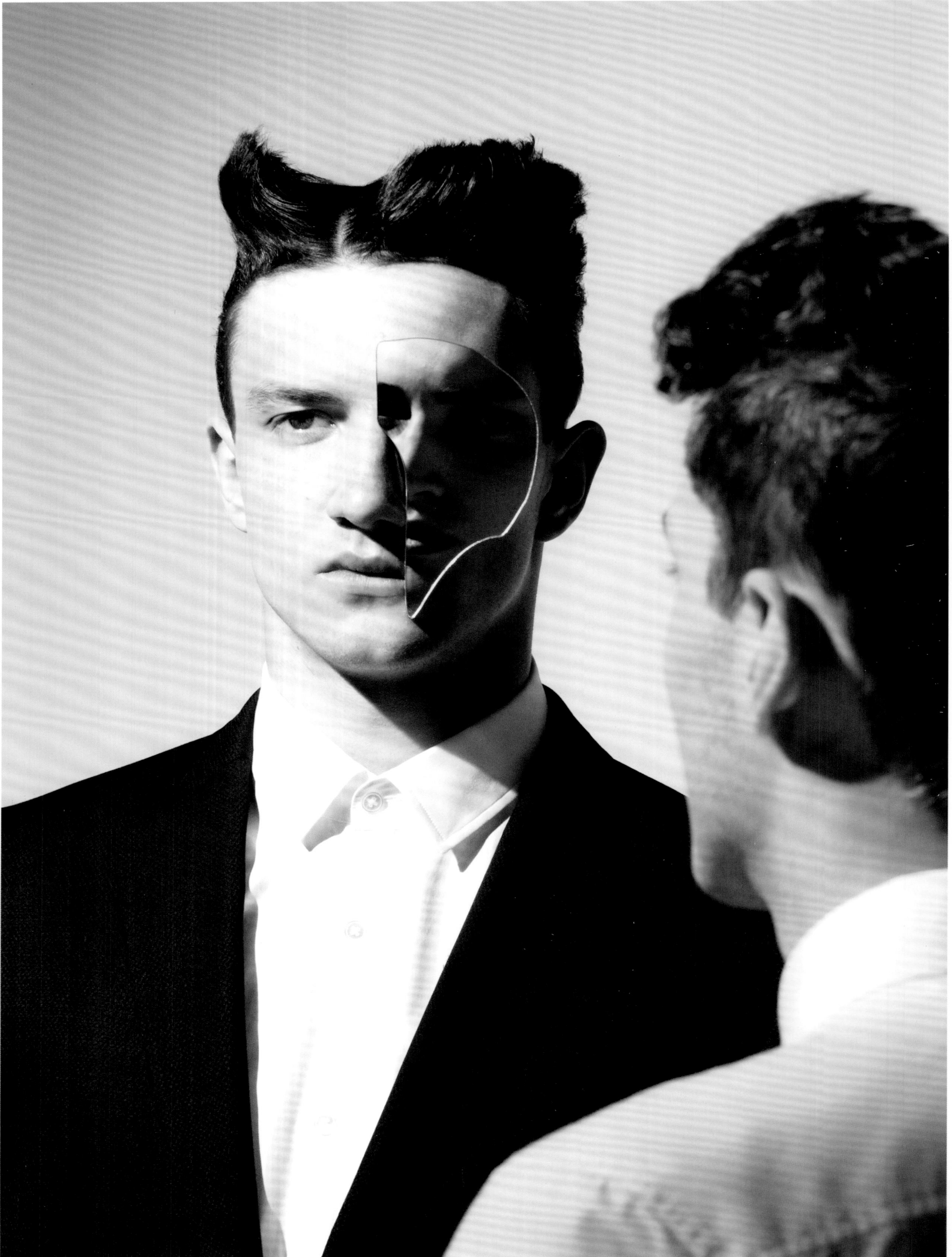

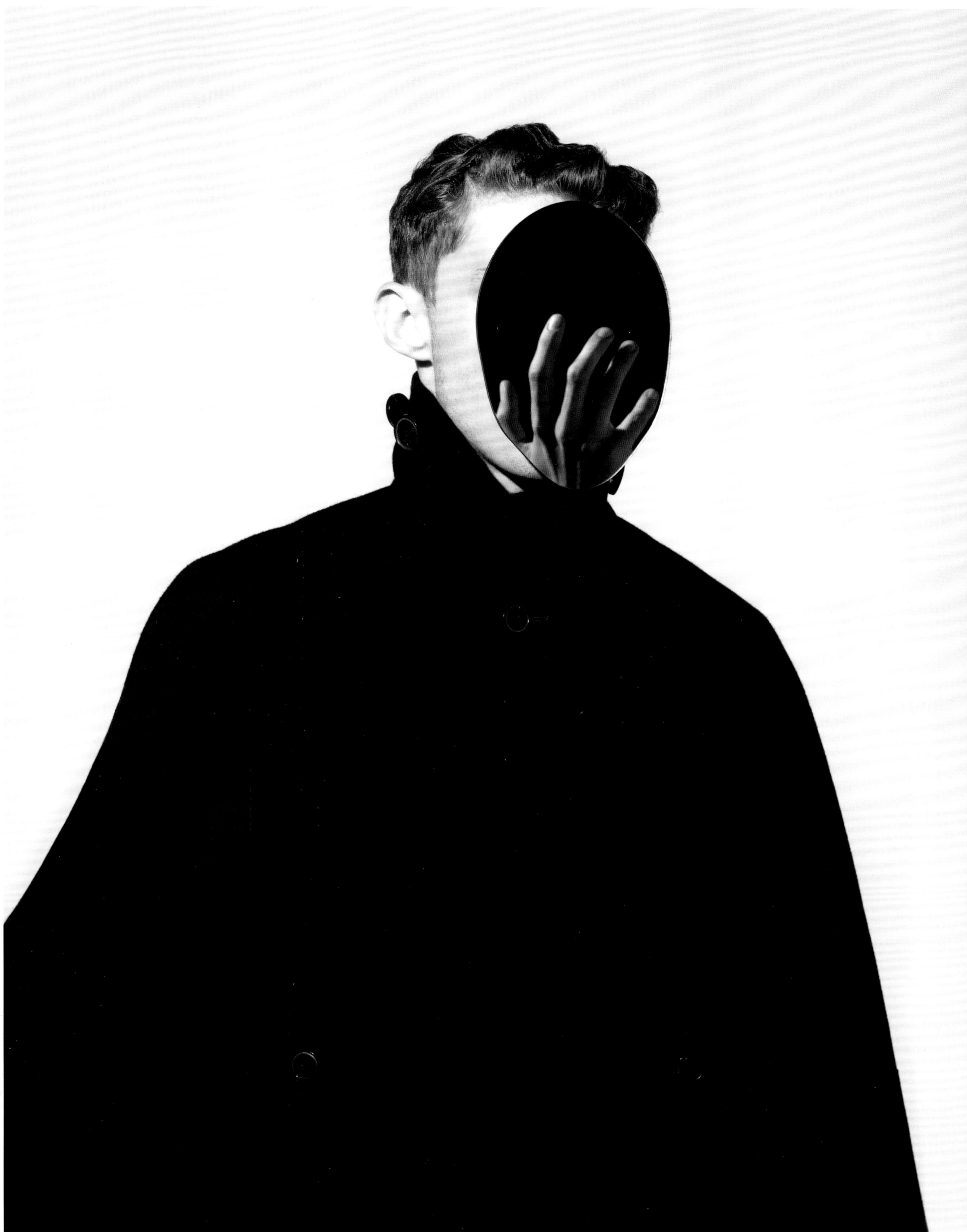

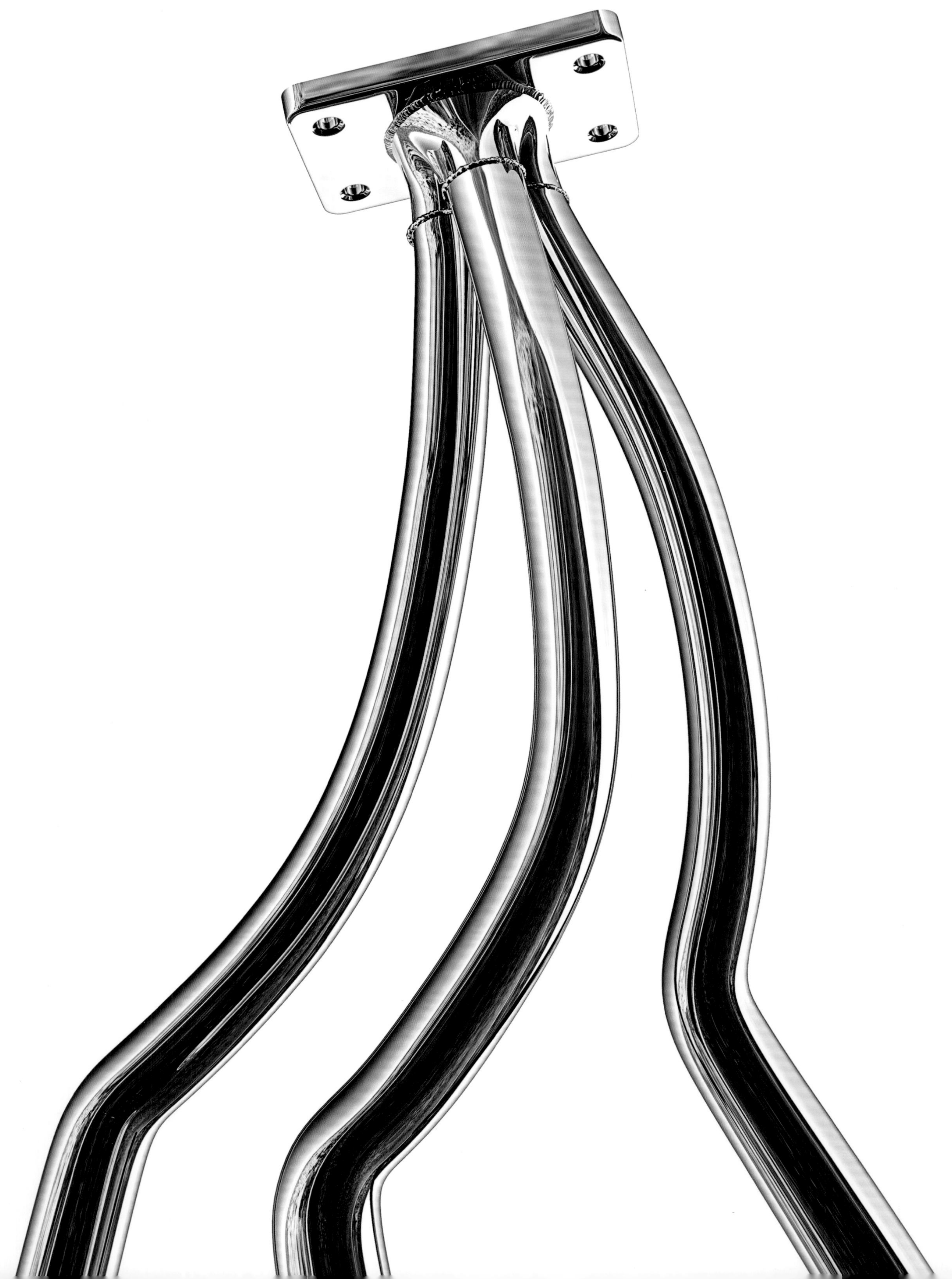

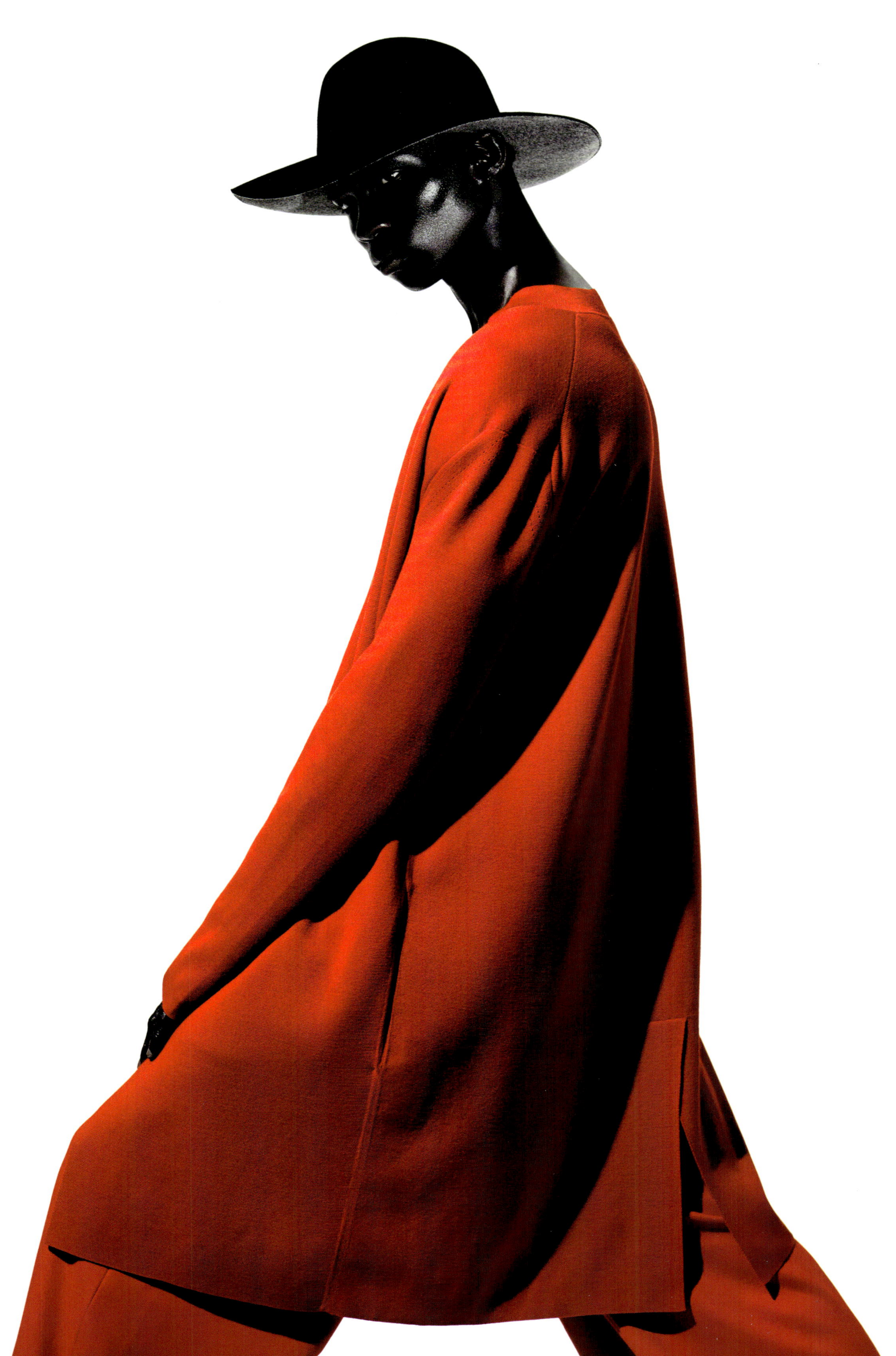

Jeisa Chiminazzo for *Hercules*, 2010
photography by Paola Kudacki
courtesy Trunk Archive

page 78:
Iris Strubegger for *Hercules*, 2010
photography by Paola Kudacki
courtesy Trunk Archive

page 79:
Tao Okamoto as Tina Chow for *Vogue* Paris, 2009
photography by Paola Kudacki
courtesy Trunk Archive

The photographic style of Argentinian-born Paola Kudacki is achieved through the elevation of simplicity in the pursuit of beauty. Expressing fashion through the seductive intimacy of a soft-focus lens, she reduces her images to sparse arrangements of essential elements. The natural tones of the flesh dominate, occasionally segueing into black-and-white or the delicate romance of a Polaroid haze. Within this pared-down approach, detail becomes transcendent and, through the suggestive traces of ideas that Kudacki works into her images, she introduces humanity to her idealised aesthetic.

Subtle symbolism invades Kudacki's minimalist canvas. In a 2010 editorial for fashion magazine *Hercules*, she shoots model Iris Strubegger against a background of reflective glass covered with paper (page 78). The sheet is torn away to reveal the reflection, but the tear cuts into the reflected image. The military detail works as a signifier of an unknown past; it is in Kudacki's words a metaphor for lost romance, the tear suggestive of broken memories. It is also, in its careful use of geometric form, a step towards abstraction. Shooting Jeisa Chiminazzo in another editorial for *Hercules* in 2010, Kudacki gives voice to her concept of femininity through the juxtaposition of a flower against the inquisitive toughness of her model (page 77). This sense of feminine identity as something graceful yet assertive is a theme to which she repeatedly returns.

Kudacki's homage to the model Tina Chow for the September 2009 edition of *Vogue* Paris is one of the most effective embodiments of this approach, successfully pitting the delicacy of feminine beauty against the more powerful reality of female identity itself. For the shoot Kudacki borrowed pieces of Chow's distinctive jewellery to dress model Tao Okamoto in the style of the famous fashion icon, who in her brief lifetime was photographed by Cecil Beaton and immortalised by Andy Warhol. In the editorial Tao puts on a rebellious front, encouraged by Kudacki's request for a disposition that would 'shatter the beauty of the picture' (page 79). Tao's hand smudges her lipstick across her face as she is caught in the eye of the lens, creating the illusion of a celebrity made for the camera yet photographed against her will. Here, she articulates the independent spirit of a person at once dictated and frustrated by her situation. Re-imagining herself as a late-night paparazzi, Kudacki tells the story of Tina Chow through the slightest of details, and the attitude of the image is reflective of the determined independence of the women she depicts.

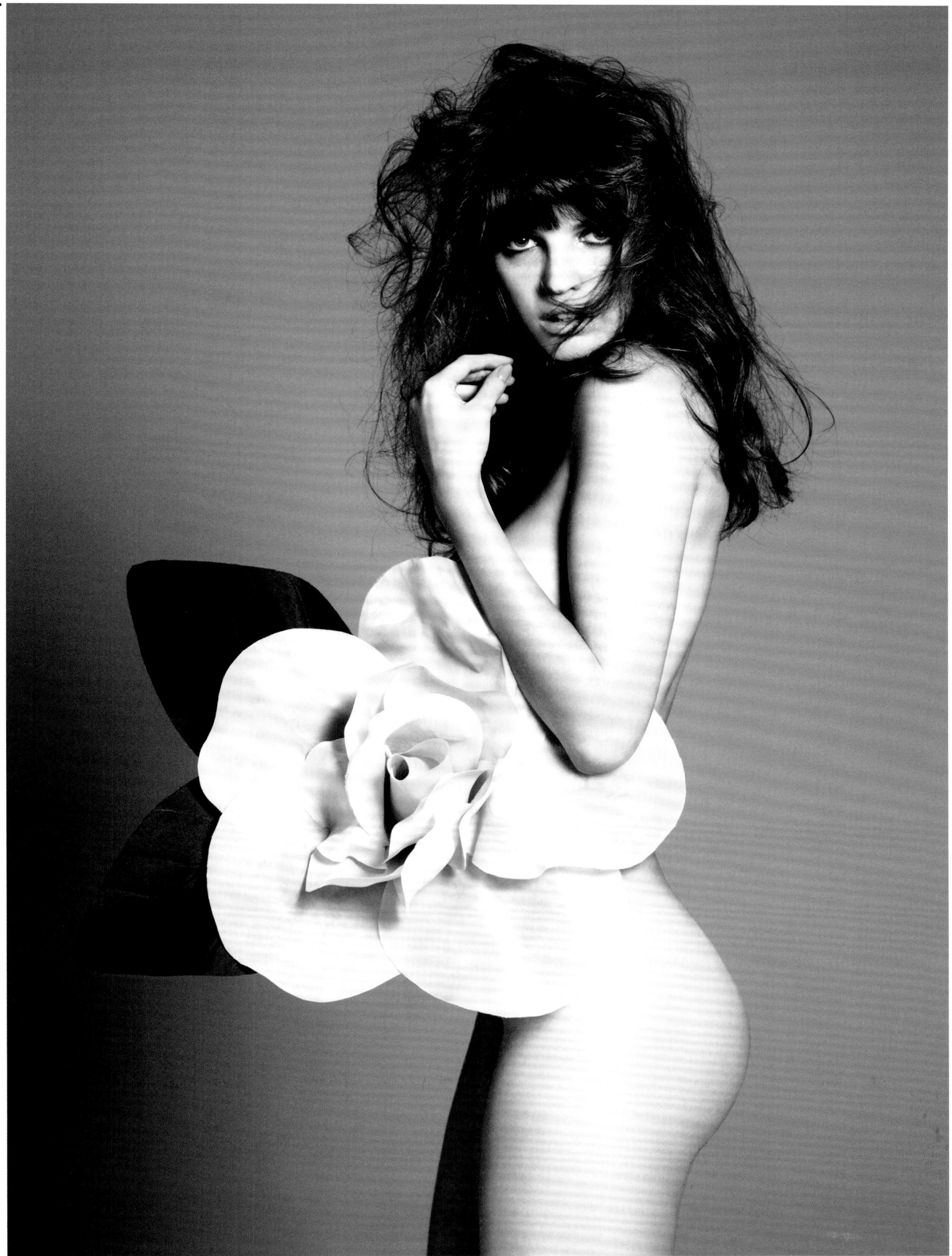

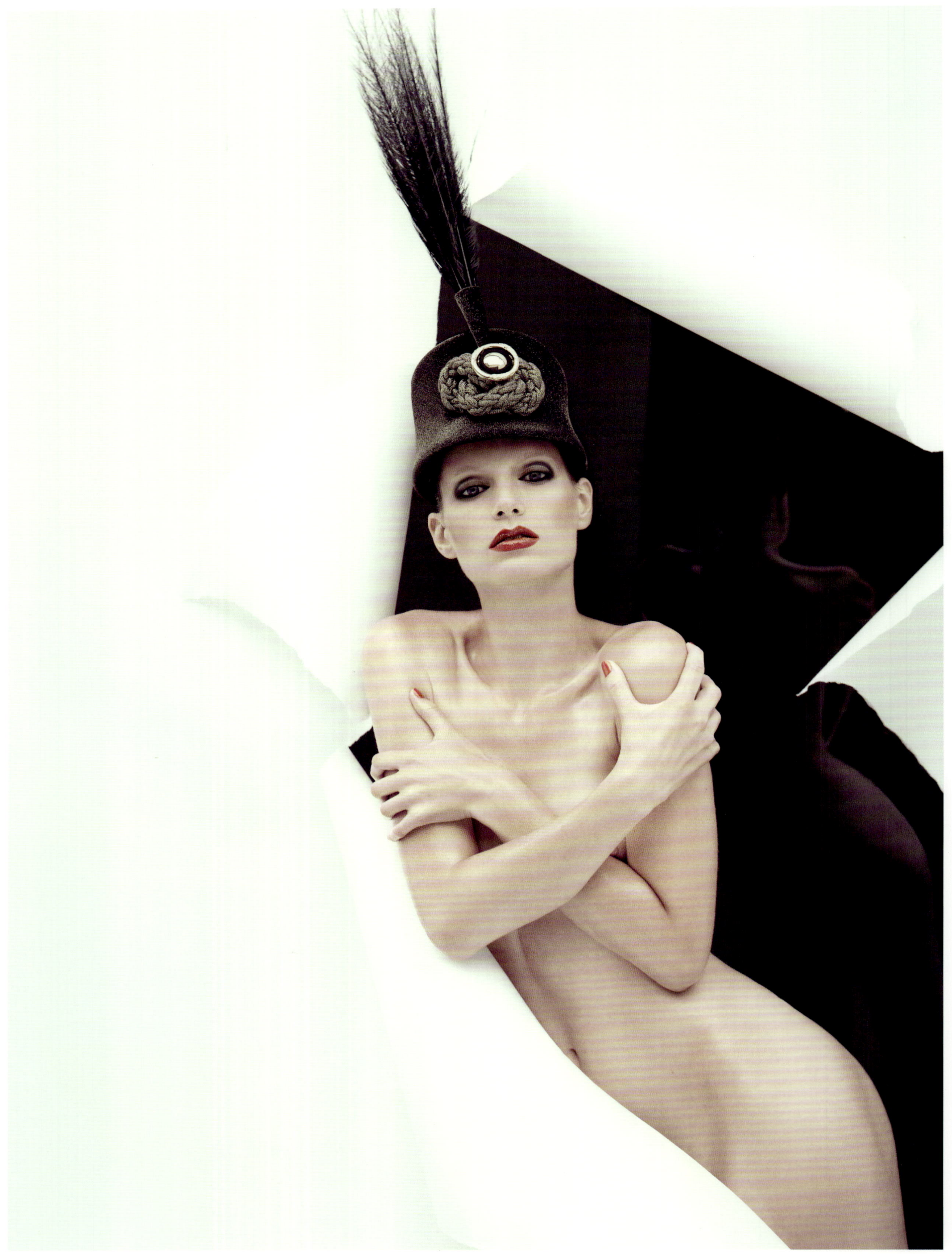

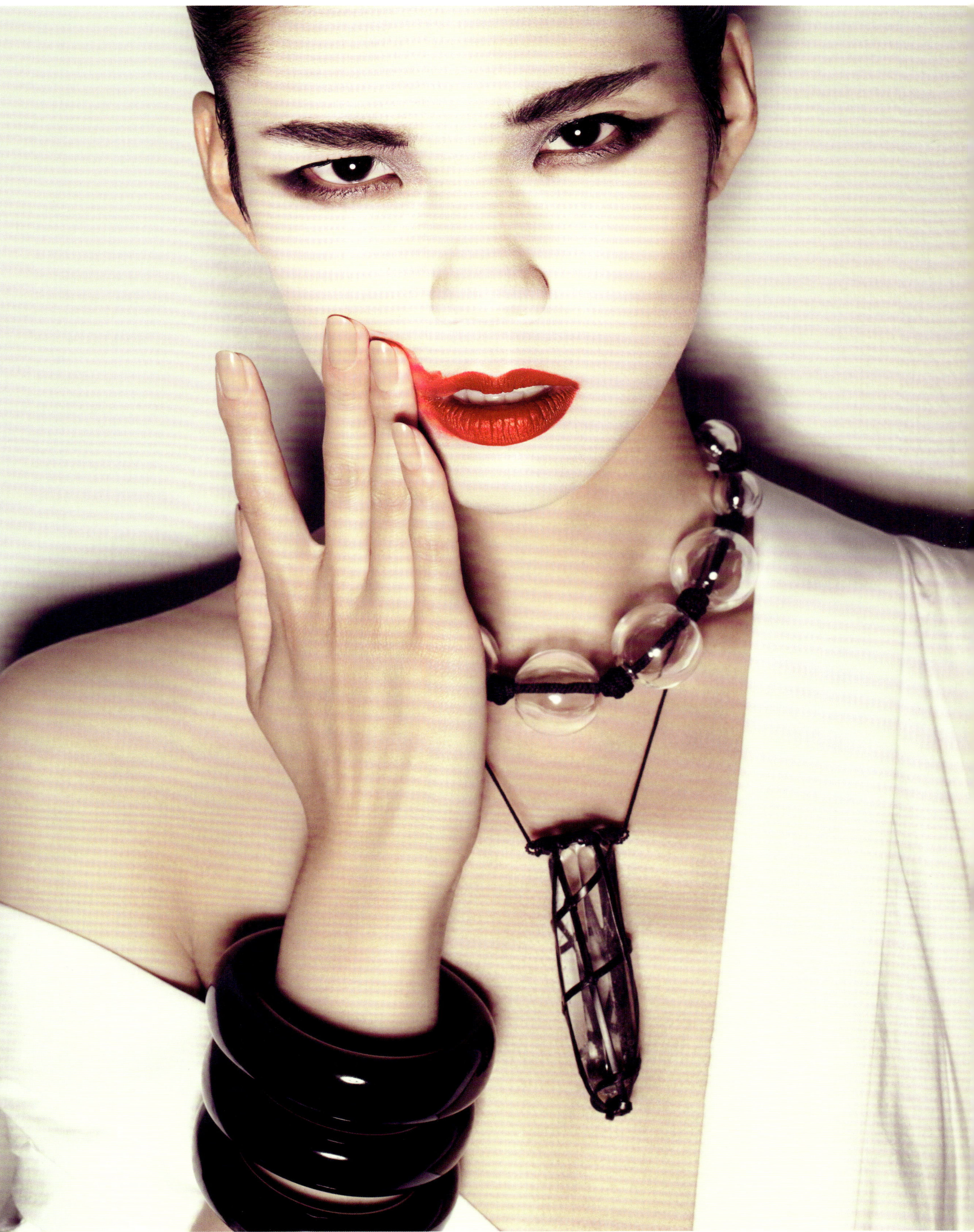

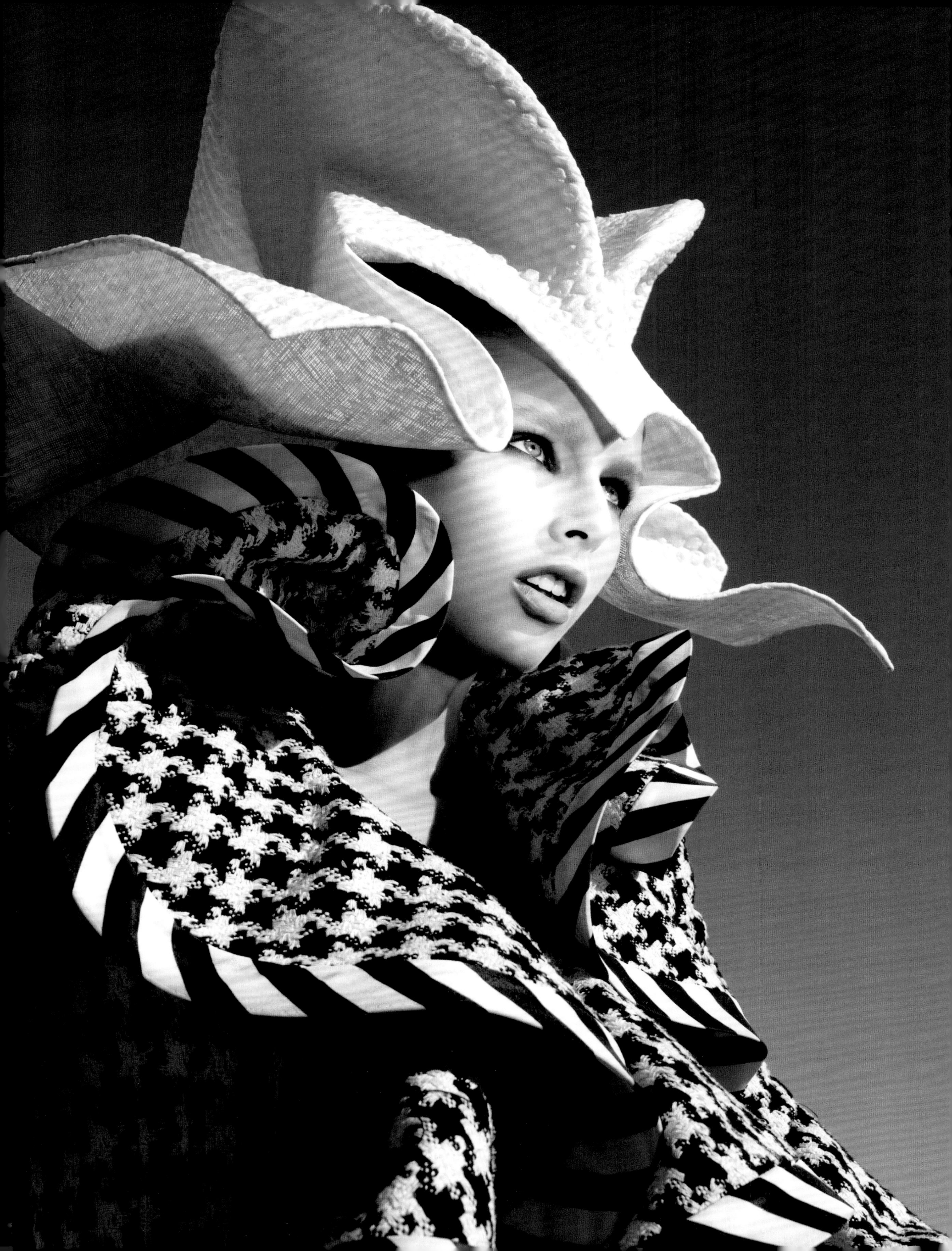

for *WestEast*
photography by Kourtney Roy
courtesy Kourtney Roy

for *Sex Mode & Digestion*
photography by Kourtney Roy
courtesy Kourtney Roy

pages 84–5:
Self-portrait
from 'The Abandoned Bride' for *Soup*
photography by Kourtney Roy
courtesy Kourtney Roy

Kourtney Roy's images exist somewhere between the strange and the familiar, playing on notions of the self and psychoanalysis to deconstruct issues of identity through black humour. Roy's method is subversive: producing images in an industry focused on facial beauty, she dares to dump her models face-first in paddling pools or beneath garage doors, creating startling episodes within the apparent safety of suburban settings. Casting herself as the protagonist in many of her photographs and often appearing as a questioning participant in stereotypical roles, Roy's taste for the bizarre is also a direct challenge to the male representations of female bodies that dominate contemporary fashion photography.

A graduate of the Emily Carr Fine Arts Institute in Vancouver, Roy cites as her inspiration artists such as Francis Bacon and Jeff Wall — artists who twist the familiar into something extreme and out of the ordinary — rather than looking to the tradition of fashion photography itself. Neither as gratuitous as Bacon nor as sombre as Wall, Roy's image-making has at its heart an exploration of the mechanics of psychoanalysis as expressed by Sigmund Freud and Carl Jung. Harnessing Freud's 'worrying strangeness', or *'unheimlich'* — the uncanny — alongside Jung's exploration of the symbolic resonance of the animal in the human psyche, Roy creates scenes that stray so close to a commonplace reality that the uncanny elements they depict feel all the more starkly rendered.

Situating herself in front of the camera, Roy's 'self-objectification' places her in different narratives that break down the space between subject and photographer, taking out the exploitation of the 'other' in the objectifying process — a neat riposte to the tradition of the male photographic gaze. In these self-portraits Roy is reborn as a projection of her own myths and concepts of femininity, her identity a collection of fragments of past and future desires. The photographs are forward-looking, nostalgic and fantasized all at the same time, multiple realities operating within single frames.

In these images, uniform and costume are used to set existentialist longing within mundane contexts: a bride stands, as if misplaced, in a sparse pastoral setting; a woman with a cape sits in an empty playground; a cheerleader poses blankly before a printed Americana backdrop (pages 84–7). In an unpublished shoot from 2012, this idea is taken further. A series of women reminiscent of housewives from vintage American advertisements pose in front of idyllic beach scenes with palms, but the beach scenes are not real. They are papered onto the walls behind them and peel at the edges. This face-off between the real and the subconscious goes to the heart of Roy's conceptualism, leading to photographs that reach out to unveil the sublime in the everyday.

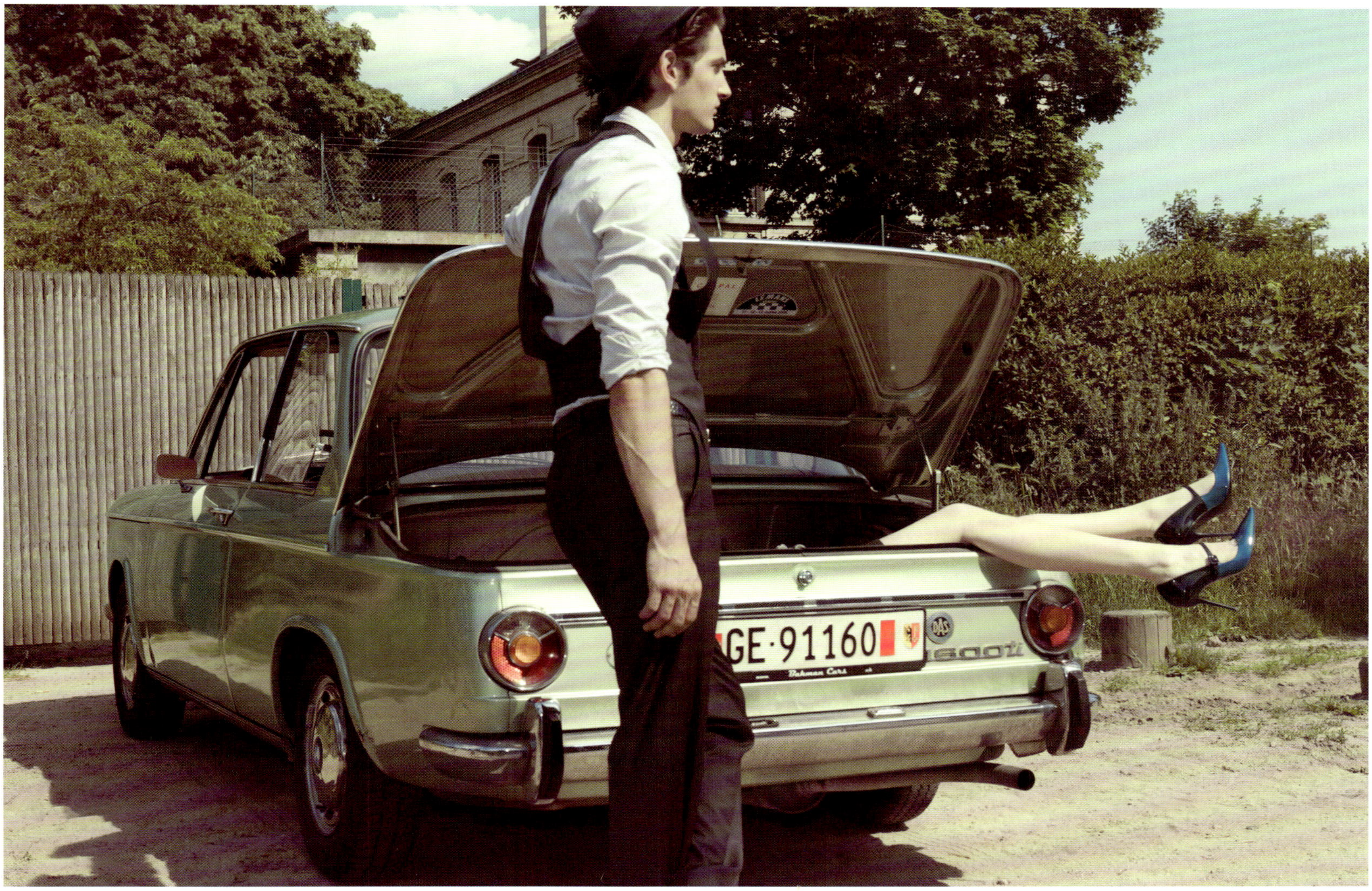

GE·91160

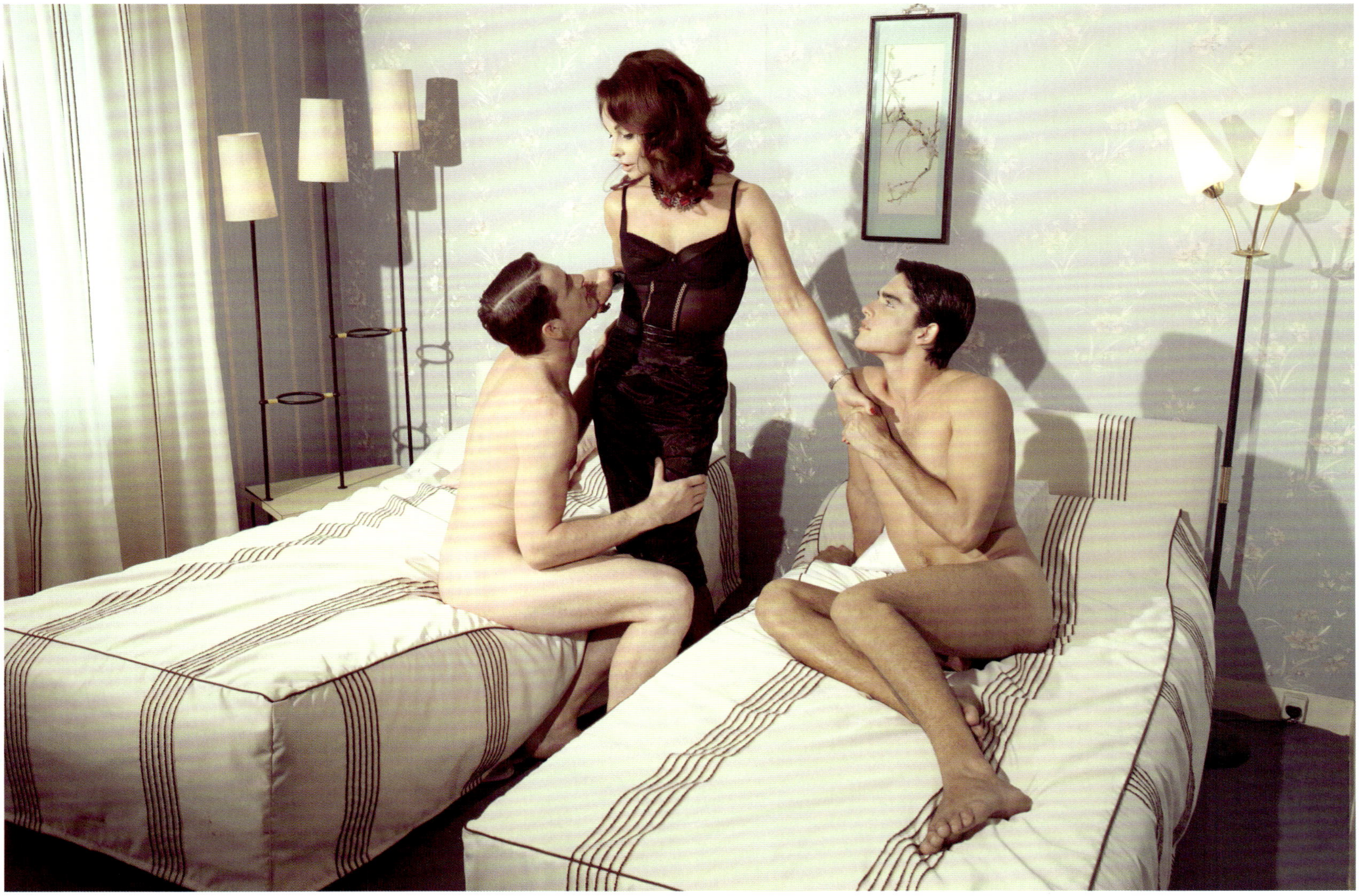

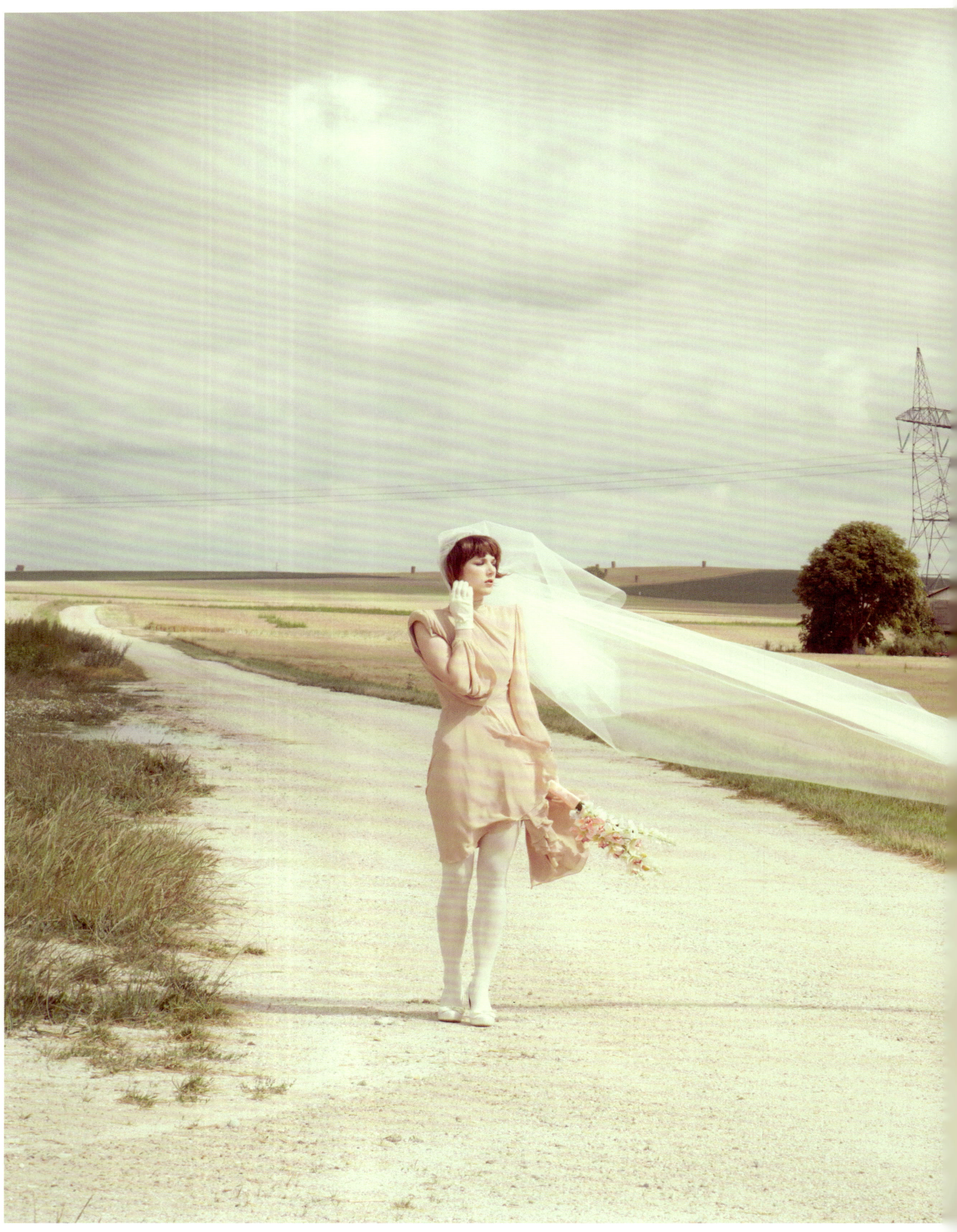

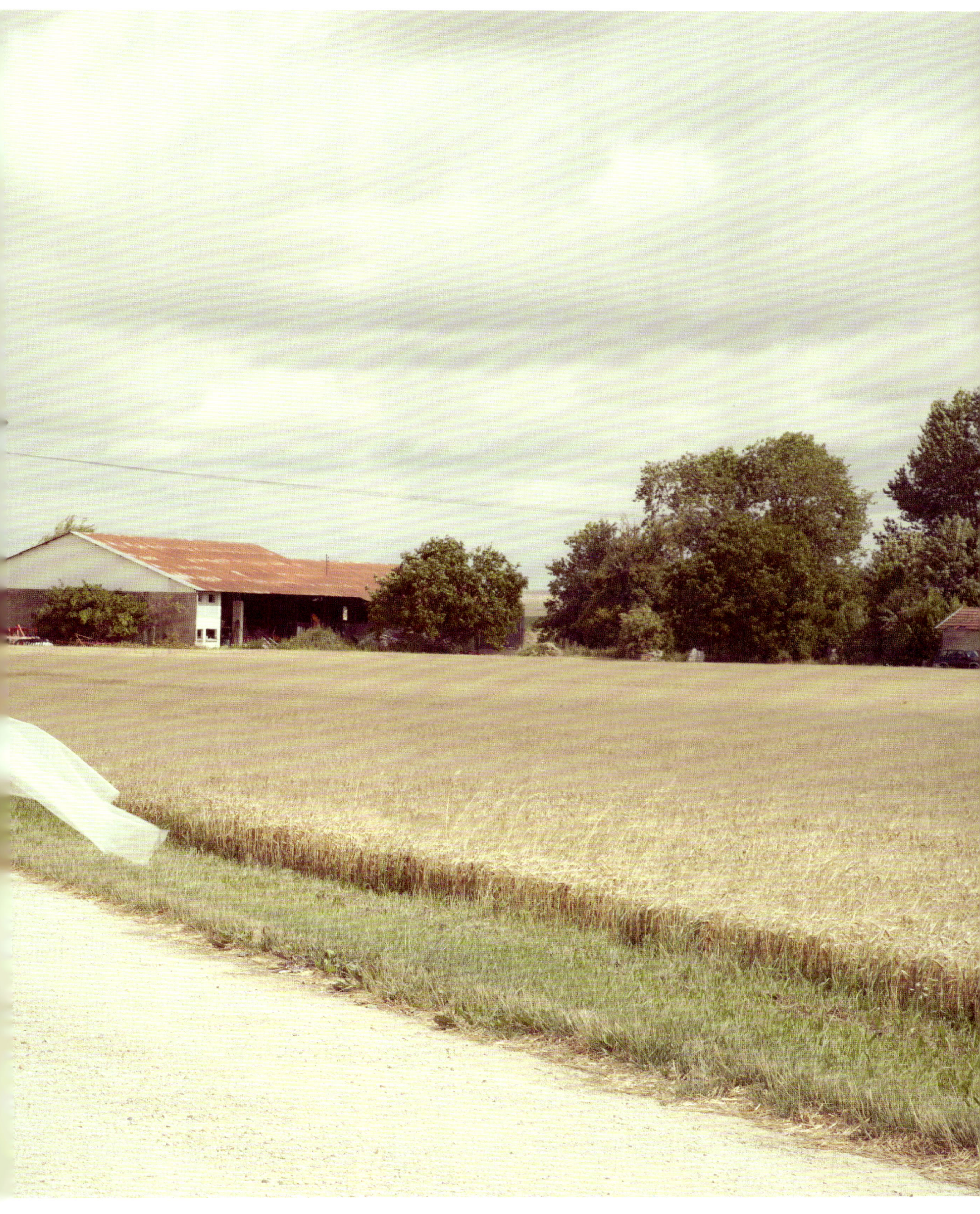

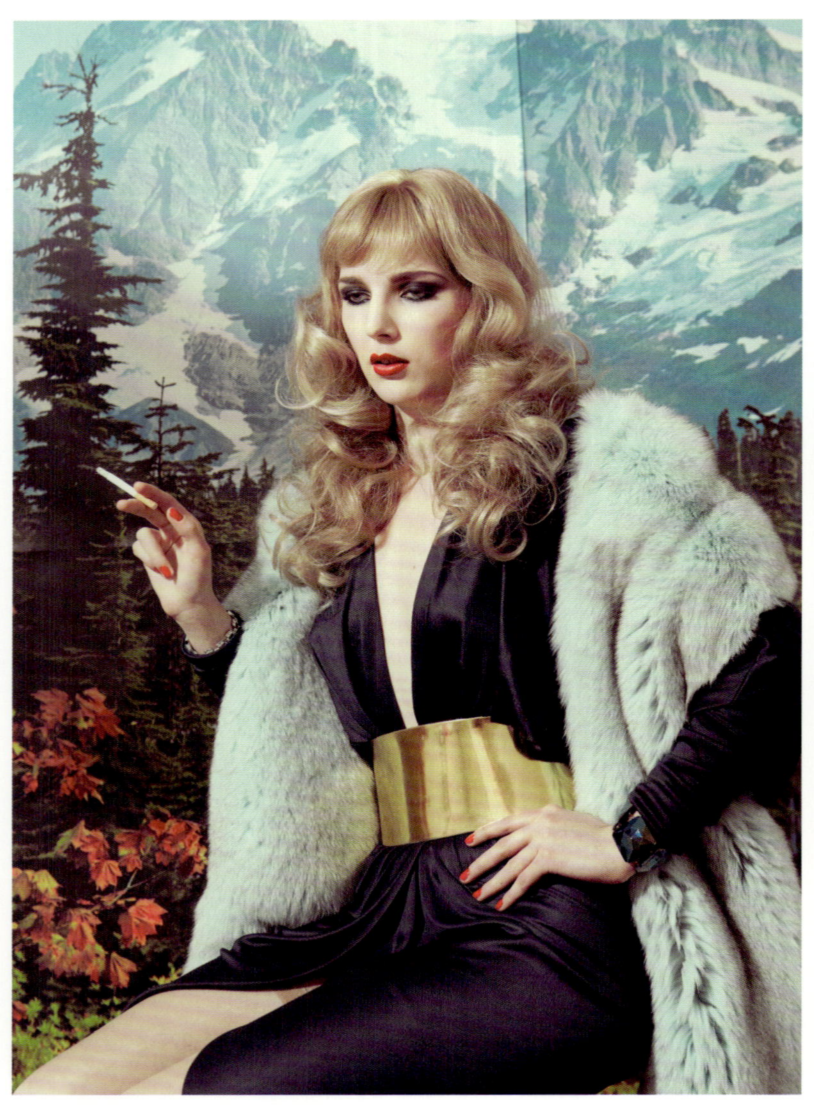 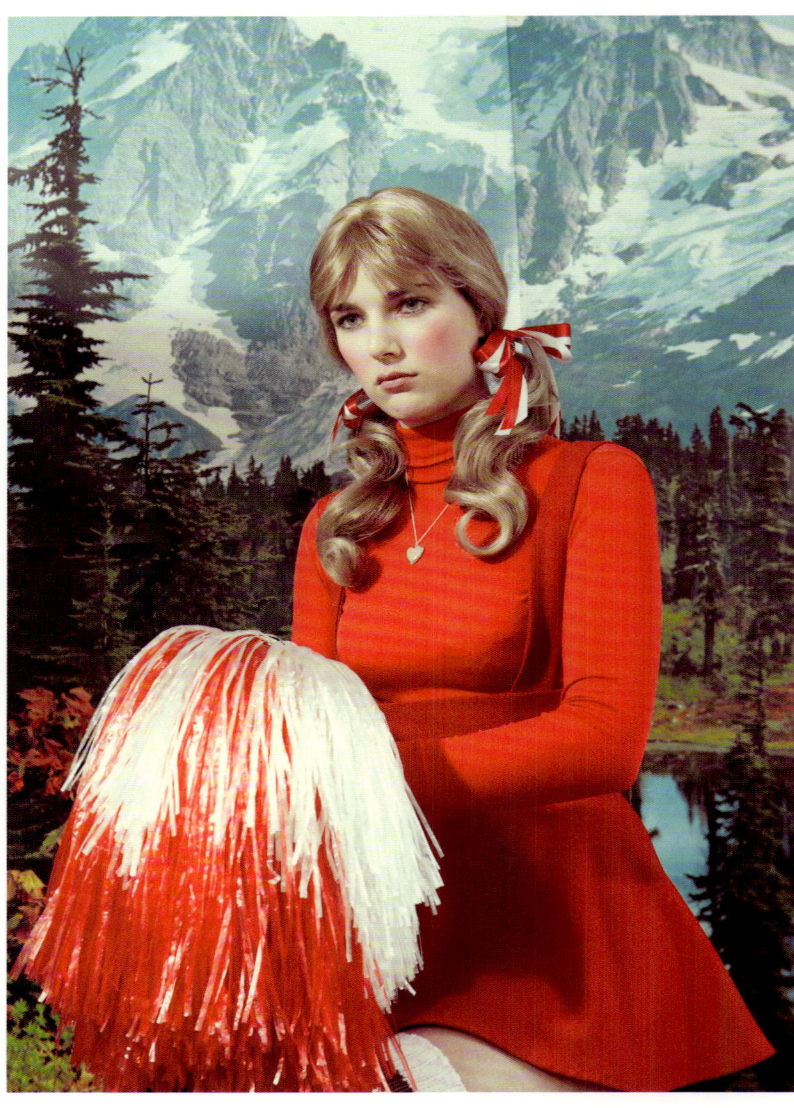

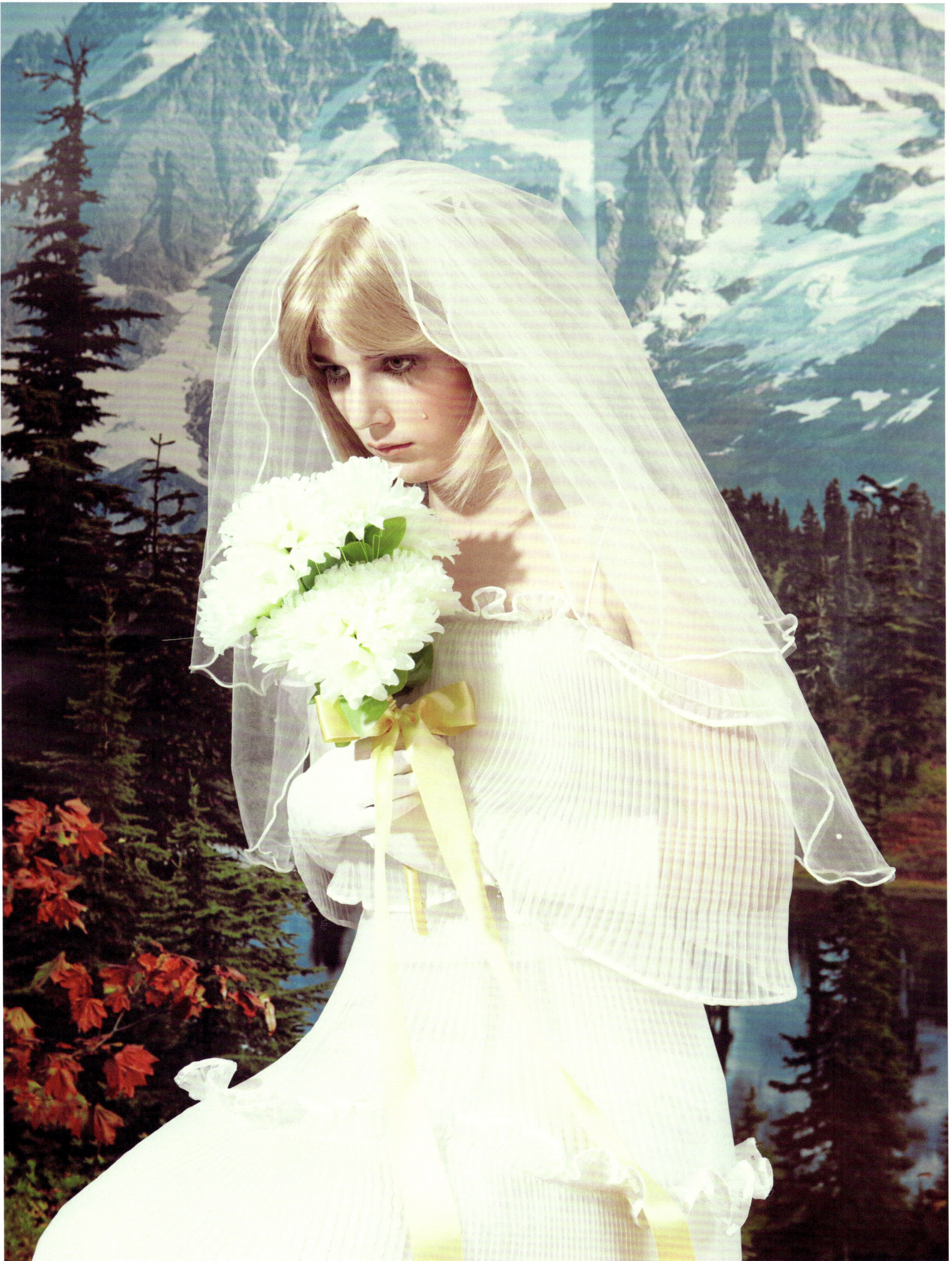

pages: 89–91:
from *La Niña Santa* at La Toute Petite Agence, 2011
photography and styling by Sanchez and Mongiello
courtesy Sanchez and Mongiello

The Argentinian-born, Paris-based duo Sofia Sanchez and Mauro Mongiello have a visual language that is deceptively simple. Bold colours are set against minimal backdrops to create the kind of eye-catching images that feel commercially vibrant and instantly seductive. Yet beyond this lies something less definable, a point of reference that takes its inspiration from a more mysterious place and promises a hidden depth. Discovering, some twenty years ago, a shared fascination with magic realism that could be traced back to their Argentinian roots, Sanchez and Mongiello have steadily built up a portfolio that has infused elements of this tradition with their distinct take on fashion.

It is when Sanchez and Mongiello allow themselves free rein to fully pursue their own conceptual interests that the glorious warmth exhibited in their work becomes offset by something more curious. Photographing Dree Hemingway, Anja Rubik and Hanne Gaby Odiele for their debut solo exhibition *La Niña Santa* at the Parisian gallery La Toute Petite Agence, Sanchez and Mongiello have produced a series of portraits that suggest the fragility of youth on the verge of imminent corruption (pages 89–93). Features are disguised by ill-applied makeup or obscured altogether by fabrics, accessories and handmade masks to unsettling effect. Citing the dream-like literature of fellow Argentinian Jorge Luis Borges, the pair draw on a cultural history of paganism, Catholicism and lost innocence to create portraits that suggest there is something beyond what meets the eye. If Borges's language is of

dreams and illusions, Sanchez and Mongiello's is of a corrupted, sensualised mysticism. Punctuating the exhibition are a series of still lifes — crosses adorned with flowers, knives, candles and pieces of fruit — apparent visual non-sequiturs that serve to suggestively illuminate obscure themes.

The work of the photographers is very much a marriage of two creative minds. To unite their styles the pair have developed a unique photographic process that involves simultaneous shooting. Photographing side-by-side, but independently, they pause inter-mittently to share their progress. This allows both for individuality and a synthesis of ideas in the final image, which they also select, edit and retouch together. It is a collaborative process that has proved so consistently effective that they have remained the pho-tographers of choice for style magazine *Numéro* for several years.

Sanchez and Mongiello's world is bright and bold, and though their more personal work carries a haunting edge, any darkness is handled with a lightness of touch. This is a quality that develops out of their private attitudes. When the pair found a statue in the street outside Sanchez's Buenos Aires house, of a black figure representing death, they chose not to see it as a morbid omen but a creative talisman. It is this warm enthusiasm for the unusual and esoteric that makes for such a pleasingly double-edged collection of work.

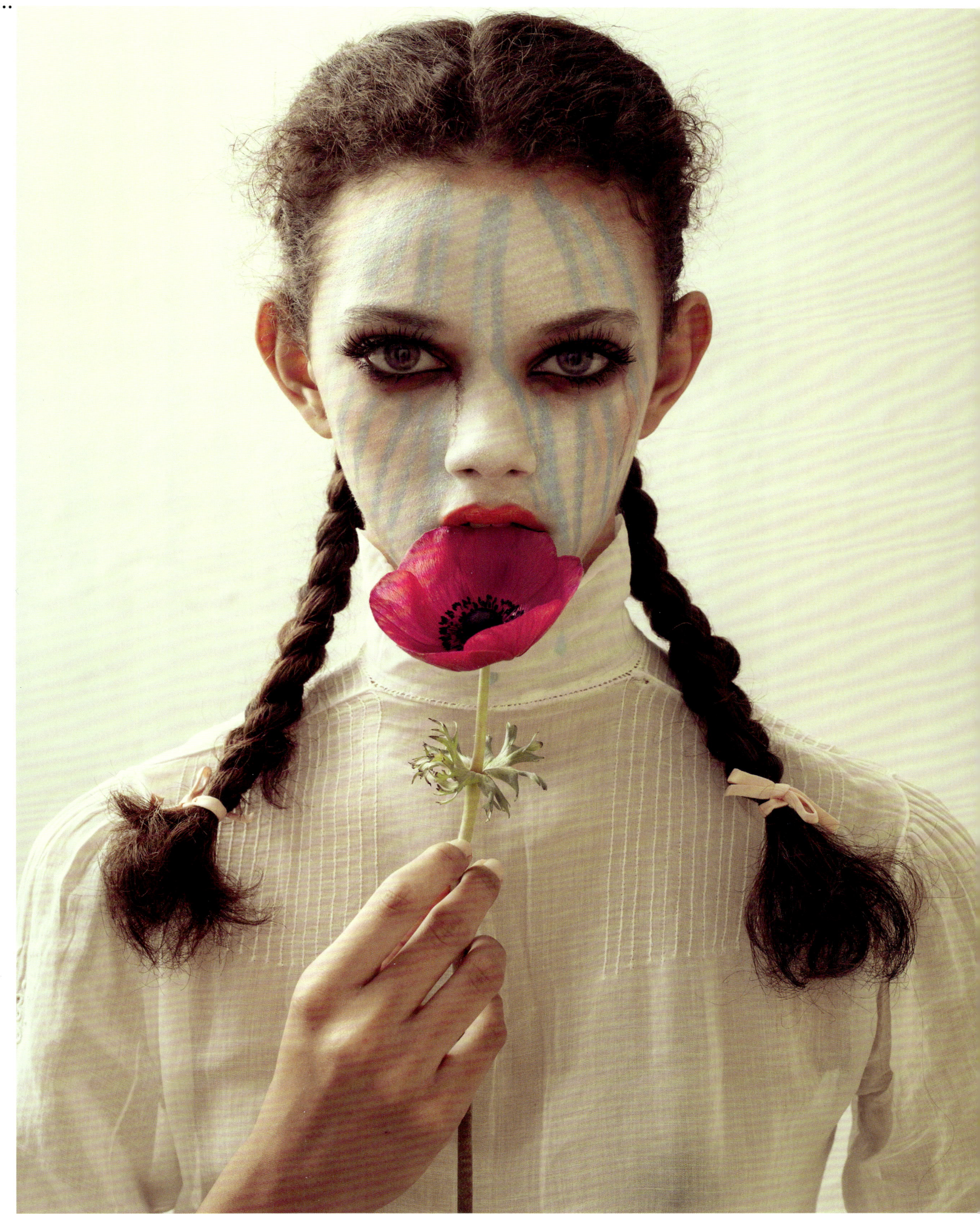

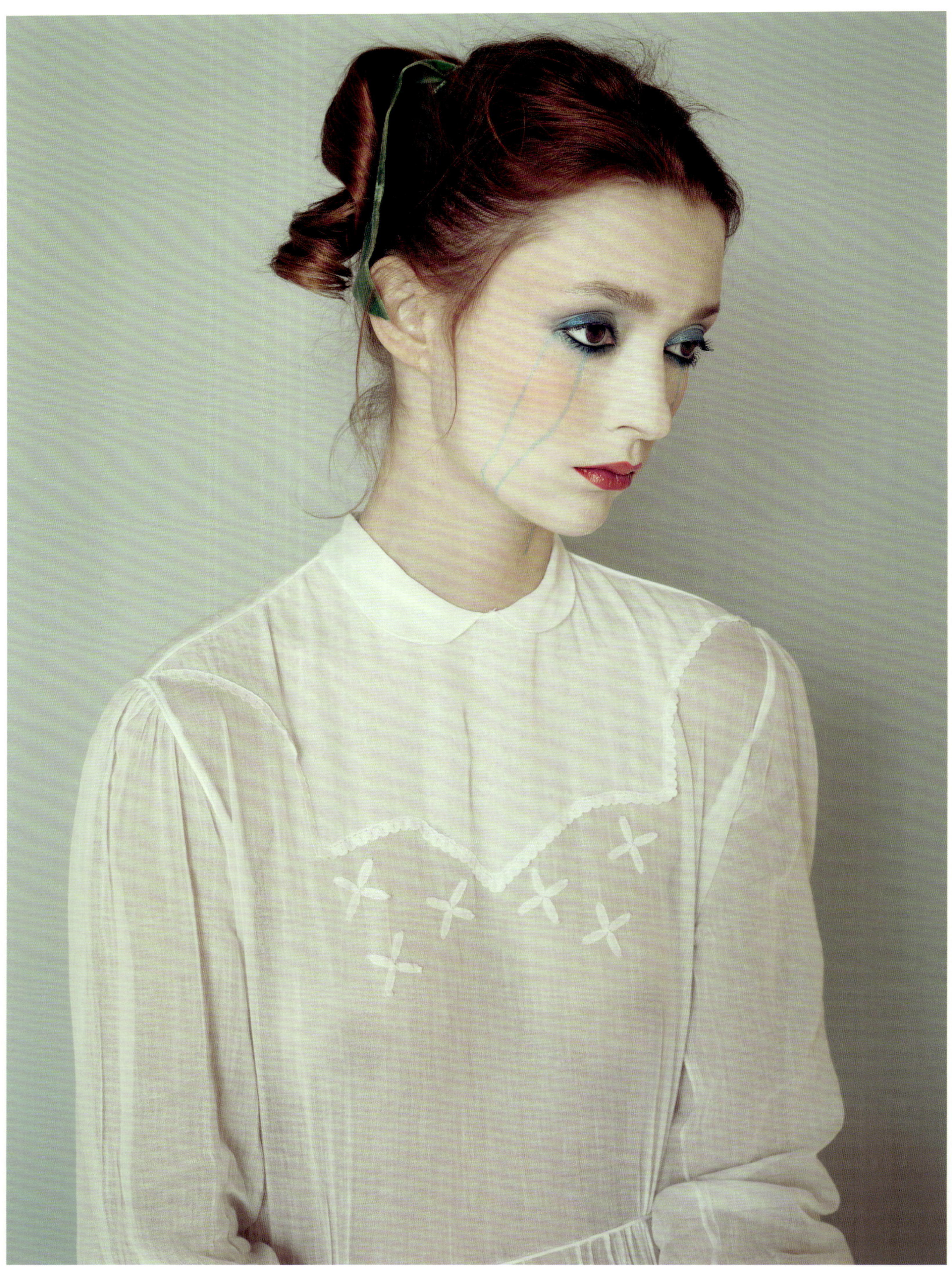

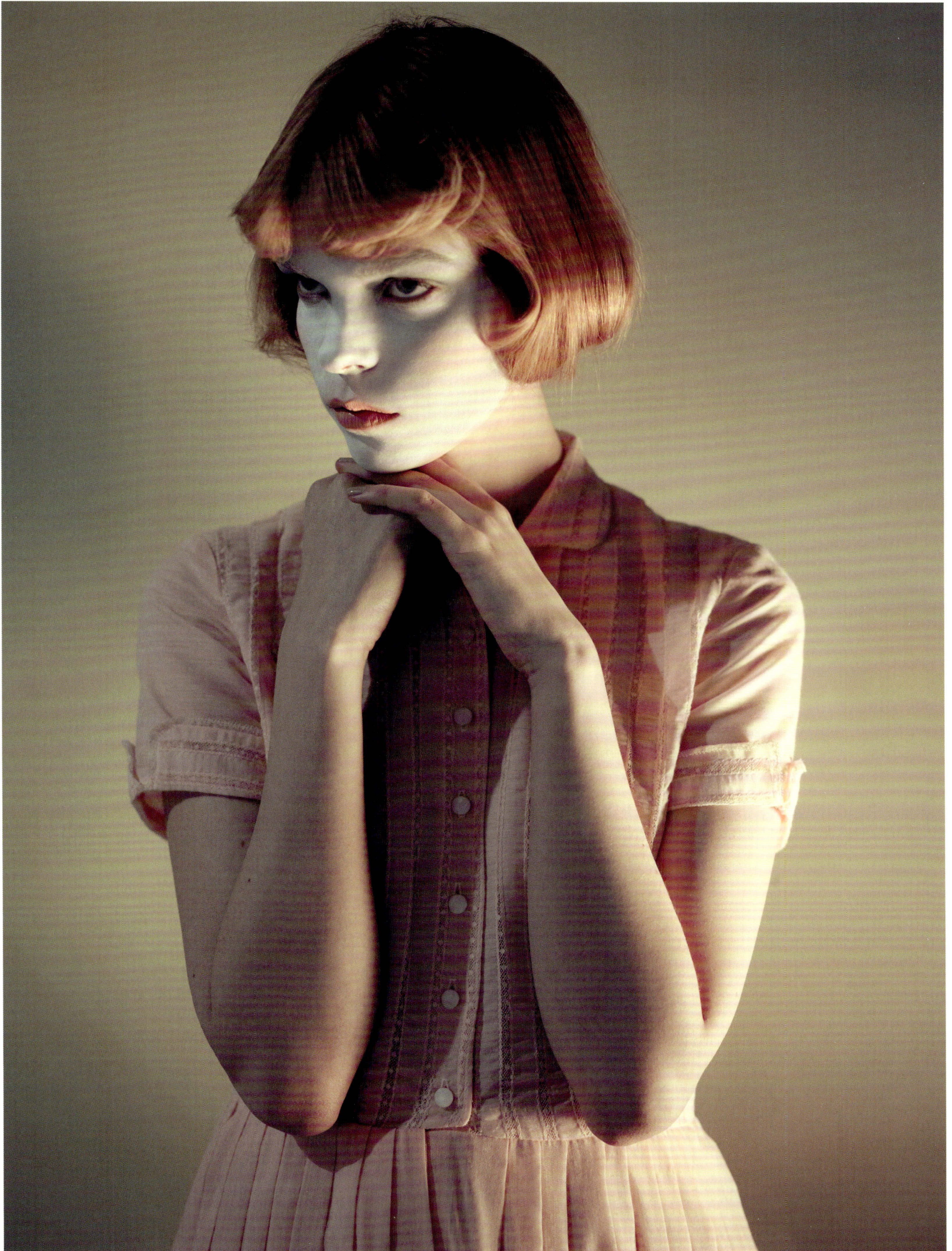

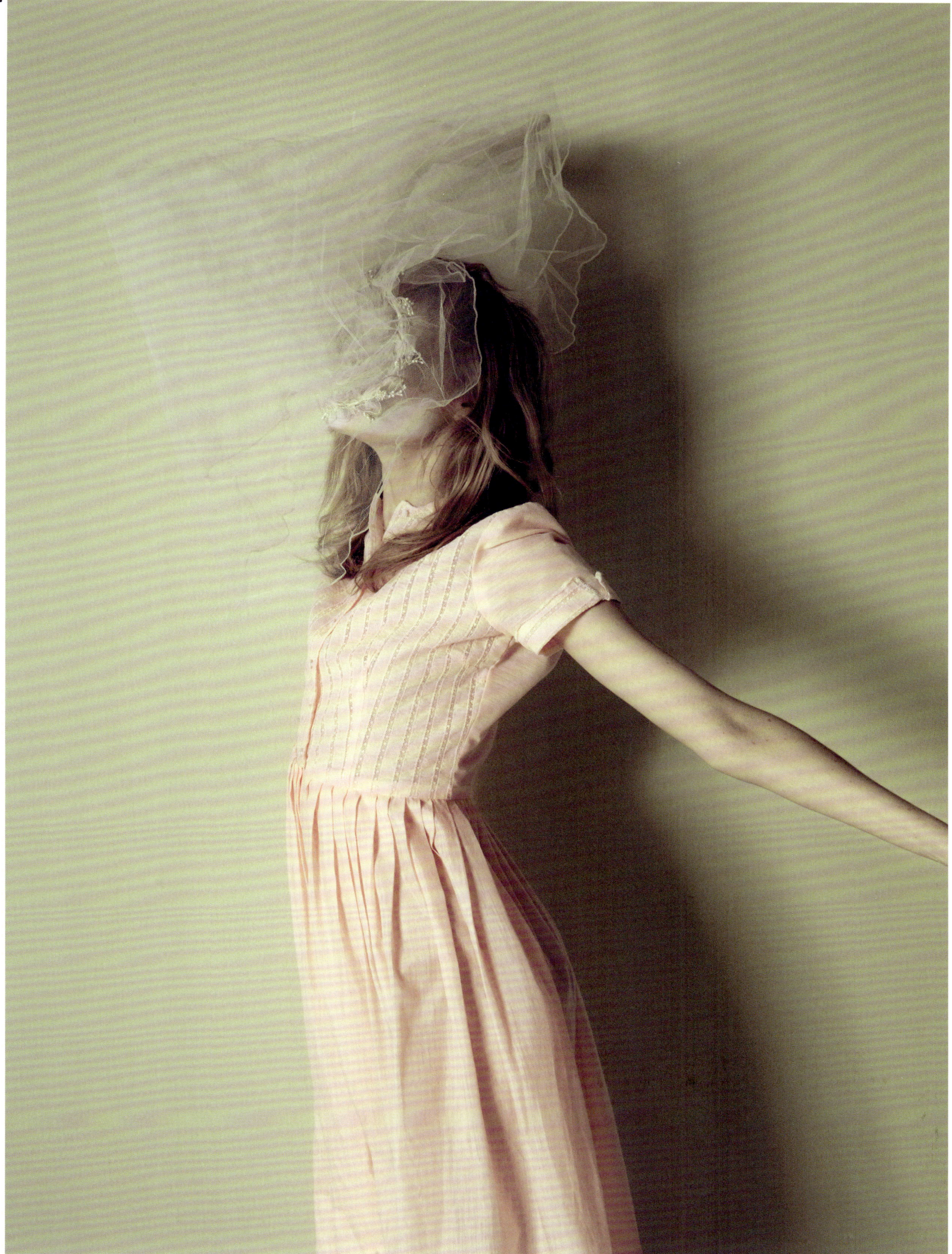

from *Icons* by Markus + Indrani, 2012
photography by Markus + Indrani
courtesy Markus + Indrani and
Angela de Bona Photo Agency

pages 96–9:
from *The Legend of Lady White Snake*
photography by Markus + Indrani
courtesy Markus + Indrani and
Angela de Bona Photo Agency

The unlikely coming together of Markus Klinko, a former international harpist, and Indrani Pal-Chaudhuri, a former model and Princeton Anthropology graduate, has given birth to an equally extraordinary photographic outfit committed to the ostentatious and the fantastic. Rather than deconstructing society's obsession with fashion and fame, the duo hold a mirror up to it, reflecting the creative exhibitionism of the icons of celebrity in all their outrageous glory.

Markus and Indrani have a non-judgemental eye when it comes to the gratuitous excesses of the cult of celebrity. Their work brings these fantasies of ambition to life in portraits that are fiercely colourful and polished to post-production perfection. At the same time there is a clear attraction to subjects that share the pair's commitment to pushing the boundaries of the imagination, something that goes back to their first commission. The late Isabella Blow — one of fashion's most strident experimentalists — took them on for their first shoot for the cover of the *Sunday Times Magazine*, and work for other similarly minded artists followed. Early portraits included the musician David Bowie and the model and campaigner Iman, forming the foundations of their subsequent dynamic style of portraiture.

If the grand 2009 *Icons* installation at the Pacific Design Center in Los Angeles sums up their obsessive search for the iconic portrait, it is their taste for escapist fantasy that has taken them down more experimental paths. A simultaneous film and photographic collaboration with Daphne Guinness led to the 2011 project *The Legend of Lady White Snake*, featured as part of the Daphne Guinness exhibition at the Fashion Institute of Technology in New York (pages 97–9). Using the fashion of the late Alexander McQueen, to whom the work is a tribute, the team re-imagined a Chinese legend as a transcendental dream. In this project, film and photography are not far apart. As the camera moves through artistically composed architectures, the film oscillates between still shots and rapid, repeating moments. It is a vision of the art of photography shifting in and out of movement. McQueen's clothes take on a life of their own: in a repeated sequence Daphne wears a dress that moves in the wind like an ethereal liquid, imitating the water that surrounds her. While the origins of the story — a macabre oral tale that, over the centuries, has evolved into a romance — works as the perfect tool to showcase the designer's dark duality, it is the photographers' visualisation that captures the warmth of its romantic beauty.

Despite the persistent air of escapism that hangs around their work, Markus and Indrani retain a commitment to the real. In 2010, four months of photography were dedicated to a project for the charity organization Keep a Child Alive, in which the pair laid a series of famous figures in coffins and photographed them in situ as a reminder of a mortal reality. It is this underlying humanity that allows Markus and Indrani to flirt so outrageously with the joy of iconic image-making and get away with it. In choosing such a celebratory approach to the idealised world of fame, they get to the heart of what feels so exciting about it while retaining their genuine commitment to the sincerity of human self-expression.

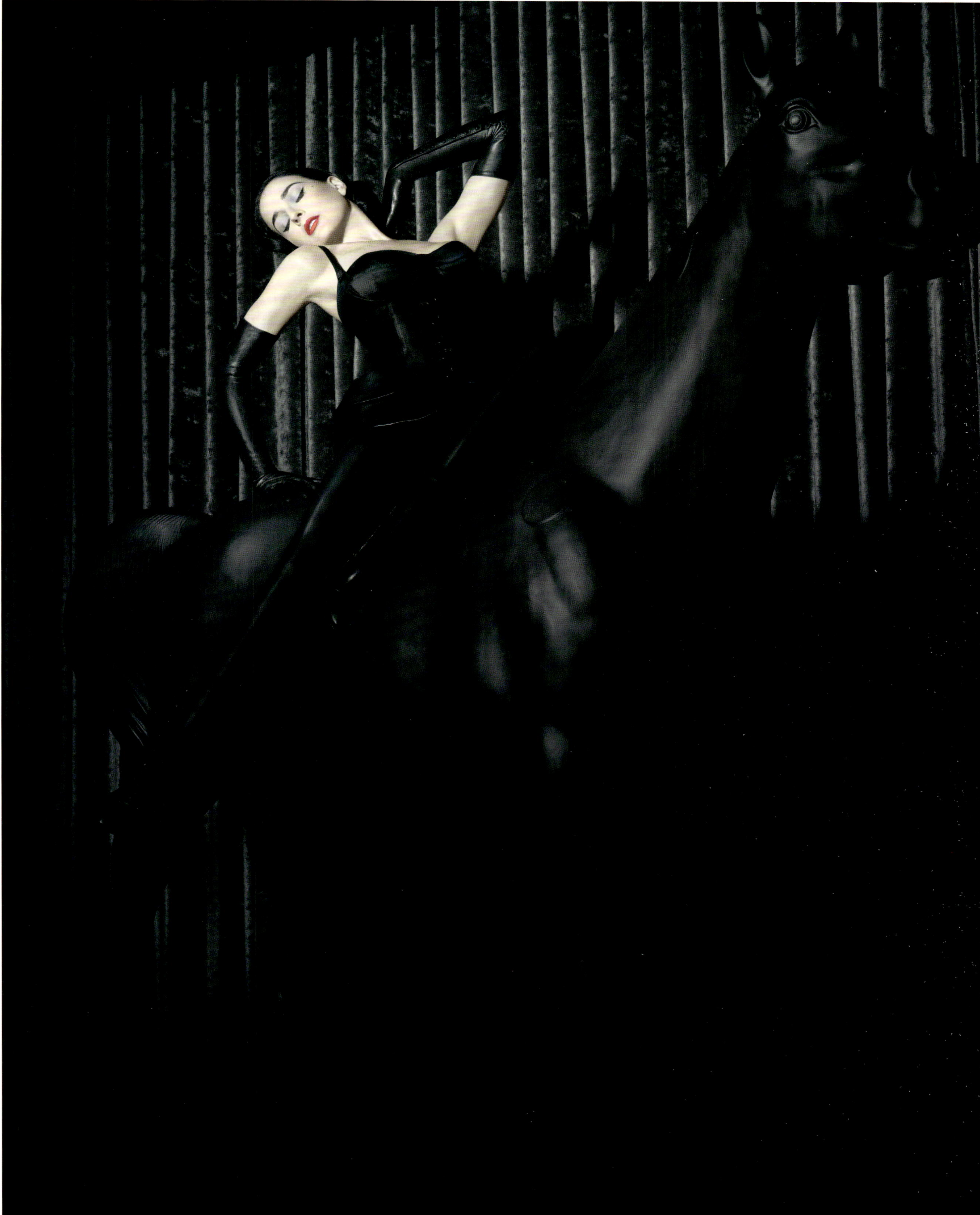

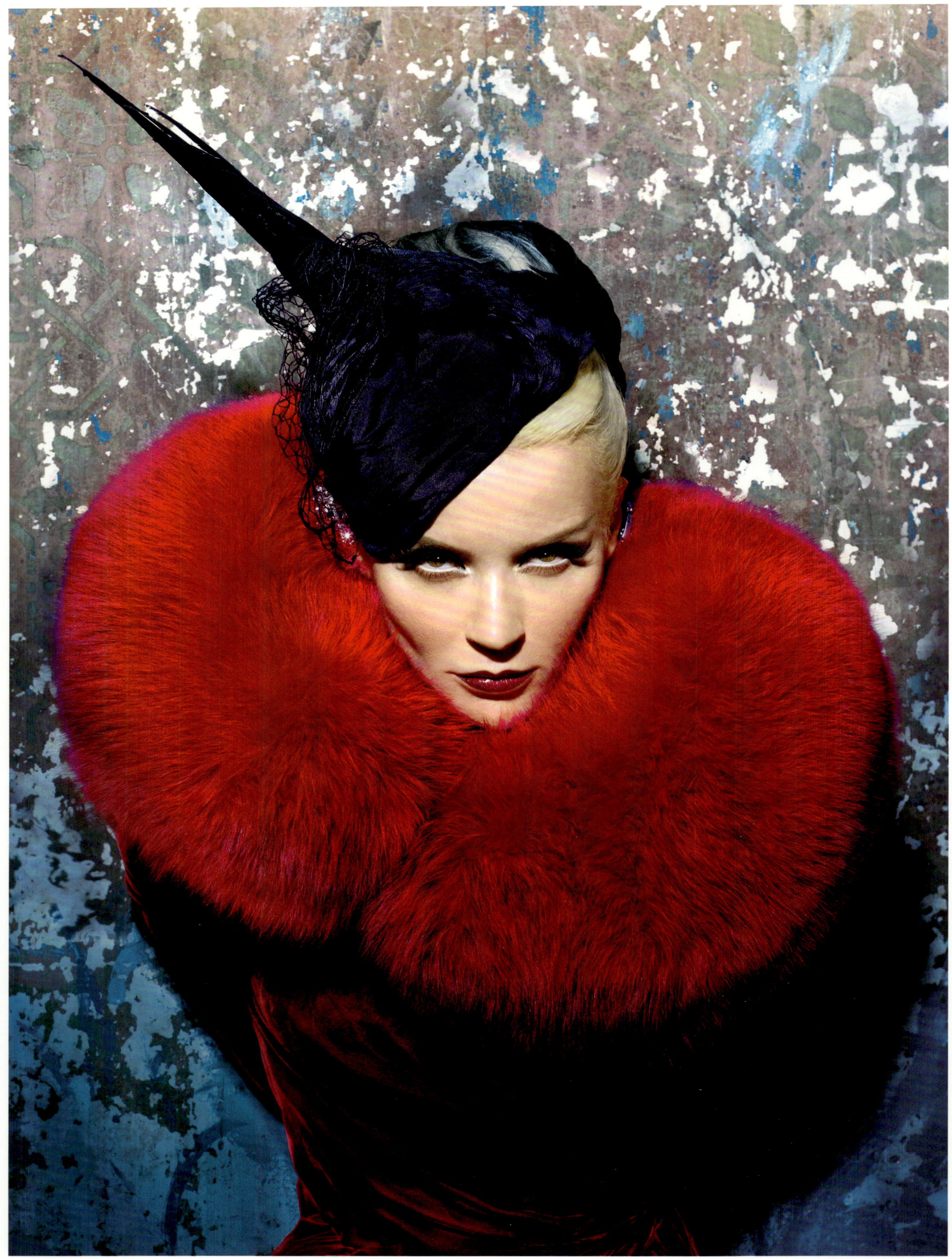

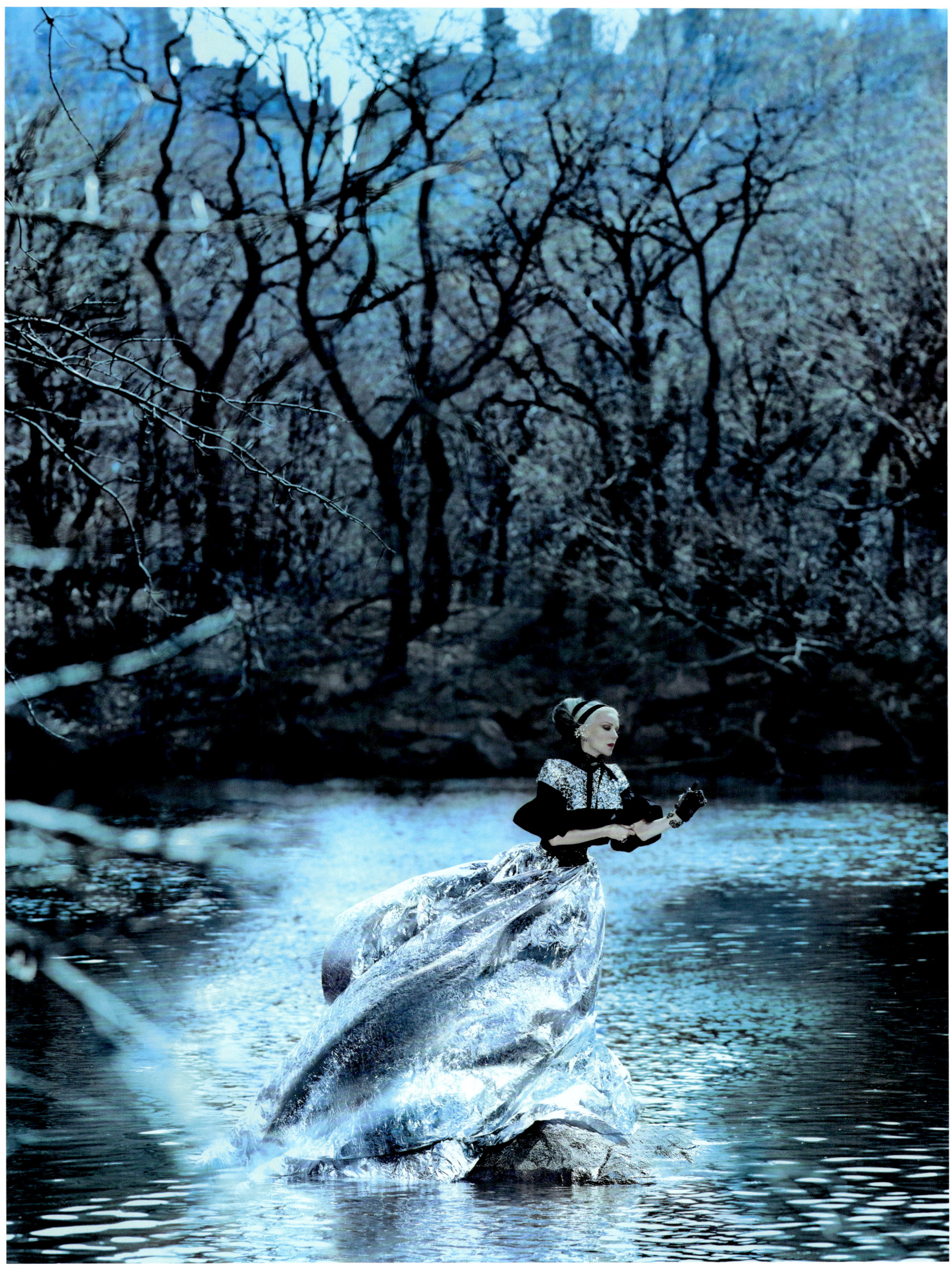

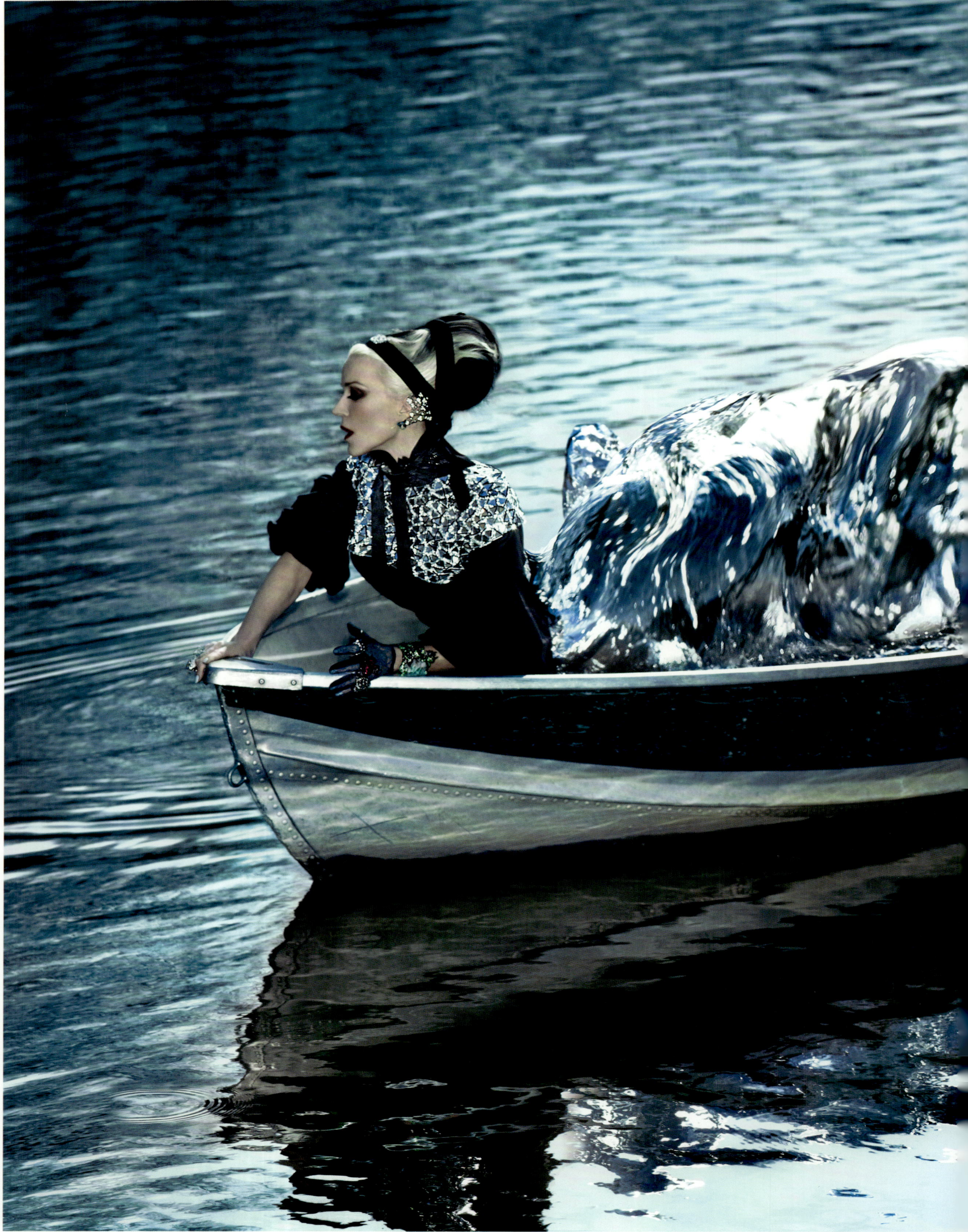

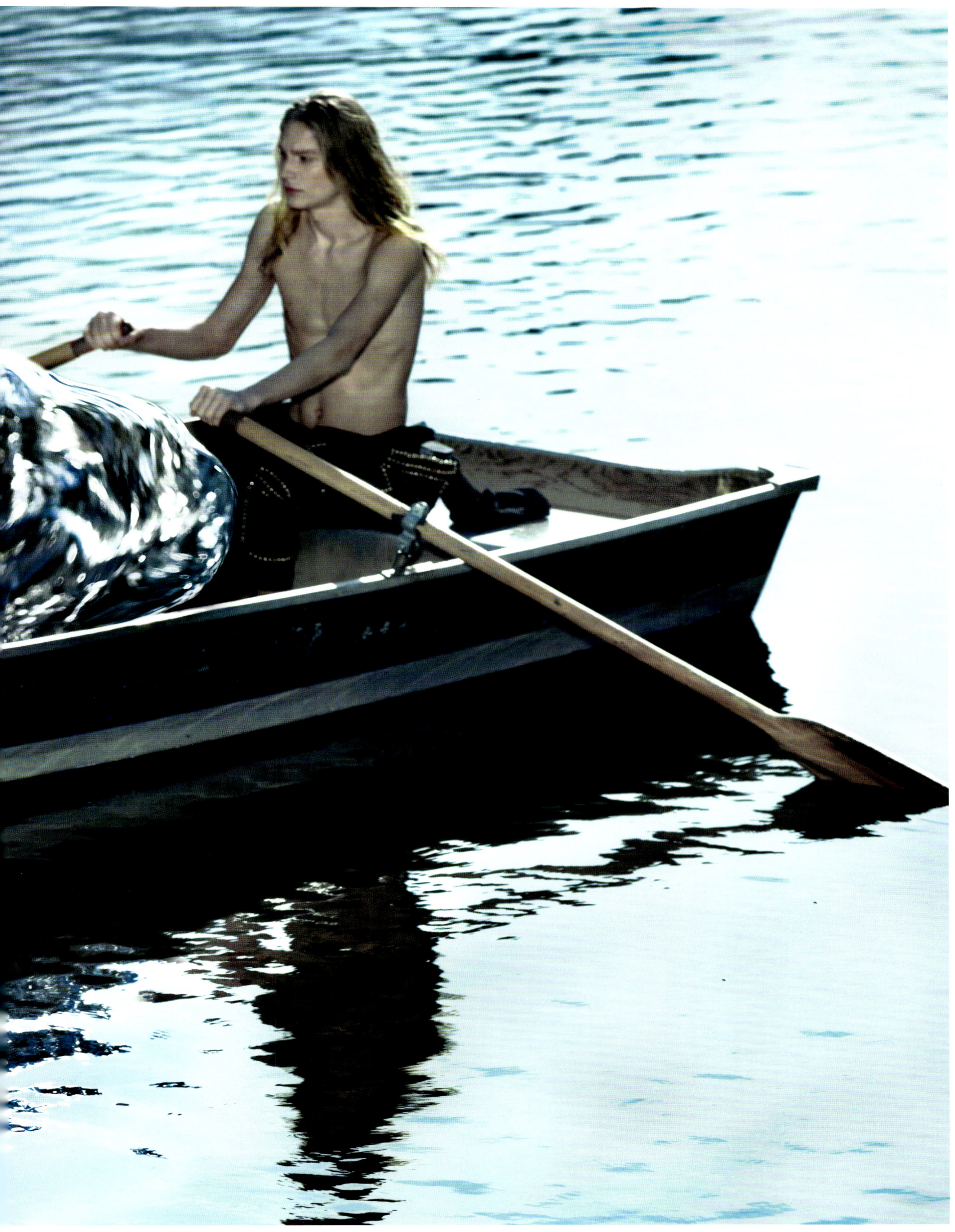

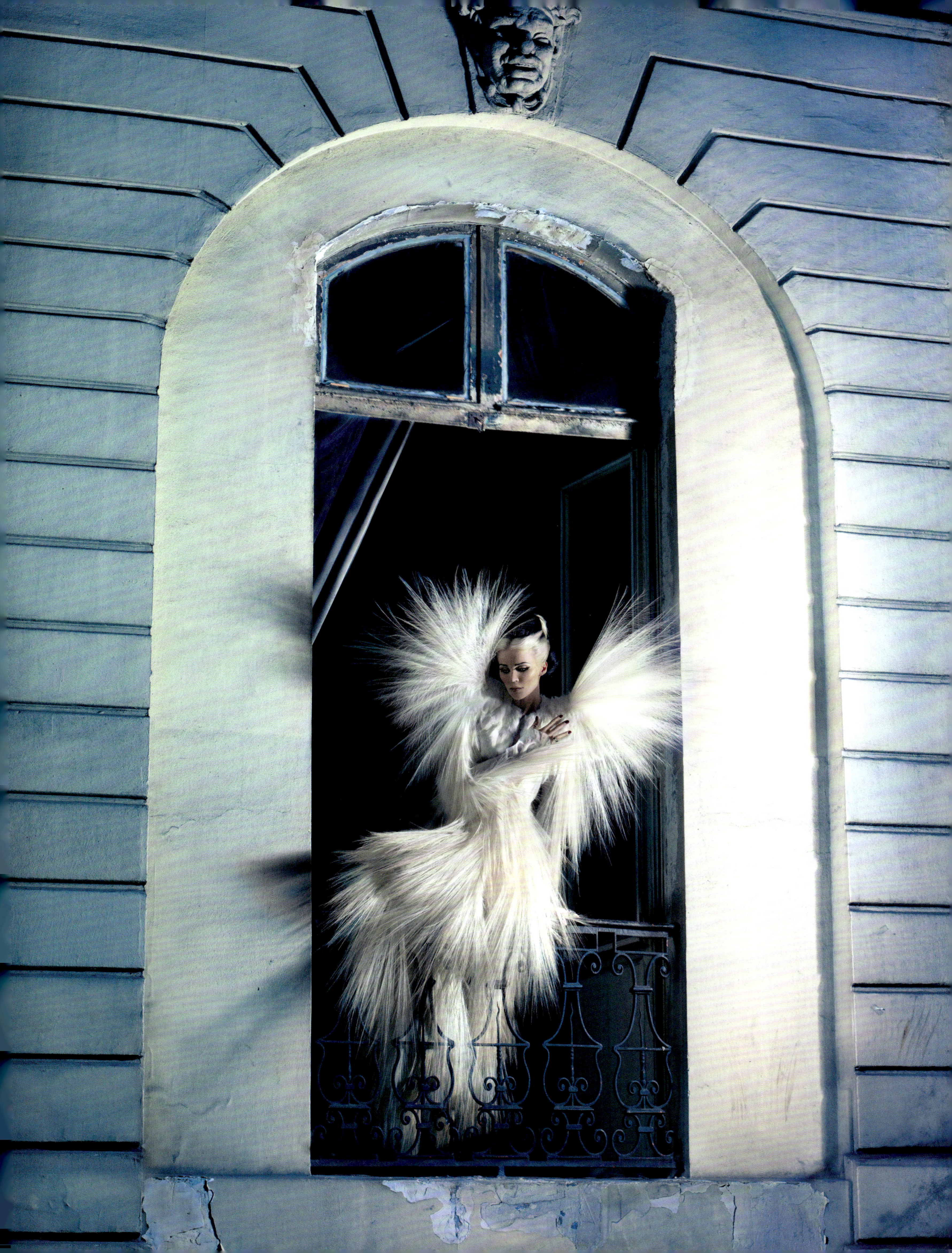

'She Loves the Wet and Wild'
for *Vogue* Japan, 2008
photography by Yelena Yemchuk
courtesy Trunk Archive

The enchanted realism of Ukrainian-born Yelena Yemchuk draws upon the post-Soviet environments and folk traditions of her Eastern-European birthplace to re-imagine an art that belongs to a different place altogether – that of the New York fashion scene. The images that result are immersed in contrasts.

Yemchuk's photography has a quiet objectivity. Her lens chances upon previously unseen episodes in unassuming environments, whether it is a public swimming pool, a crumbling sauna from a previous era or the clinical ambivalence of a hotel foyer. This documentary effect is reinforced by her personal photography, through which she has explored the geography and cultural heritage of her youth. In *Gidropark*, a series created over several years, Yemchuk's 35mm camera has repeatedly returned to scrutinise the human landscape of an island on the Dnieper River that runs through Kiev in the Ukraine. Revisiting this, an area she knew well as a child, Yemchuk celebrates the day-to-day interactions that occur on what she has described as a 'Soviet Coney Island'. Even in these most modest of conditions, people are captured at leisure, and it is here that performance takes over. Gradually, the immediate disparity of New York and Kiev gives way to the similarities of human self-expression across cultures and continents.

Yemchuk's esoteric inspirations twist her documentary style, pushing it into the terrain of the real made unreal. Her fascination with folk storytelling and the bizarre shapes the approach she takes toward her subject matter. In urban settings Yemchuk situates these unlikely moments of beauty in a colder and more mundane reality (pages 106–7). The women that populate her inner-city world have stepped out of a fairytale and into the ordinary, somehow remaining unaffected by the starker realities of their new environments. The effect is a conjured place in which both bliss and melancholy never seem far off (pages 104–5).

When her attention moves away from the cool concrete of urban centres, grittiness makes way for eery lakes and mysterious woodlands. Such folk-inspired landscapes are an unsurprising aspect of a photographer whose simultaneous artistic practice carries echoes of the imagery of Russian Surrealist novelist Mikhail Bulgakov and the enigma of traditional Eastern-European storytelling. Exhibited under the title *Notes on Fantômas* at the Dactyl Foundation in 2008, Yemchuk's lightly executed illustrations depict a trade-off between the romance and magic of fables and a darker, more threatening aspect. Applying childhood folklore and the sense of failed urban aspiration in a post-Soviet Kiev to the world of fashion might threaten uncomfortable juxtapositions, but Yemchuk allows them to coexist, sublimely at odds, in scenes that locate the strange and disquieting in the familiar. In the chasm between the raw energy of Eastern Europe and the society excesses of New York fashion, she carves out the parallels that give rise to the troubled yet engaging romanticism of her work.

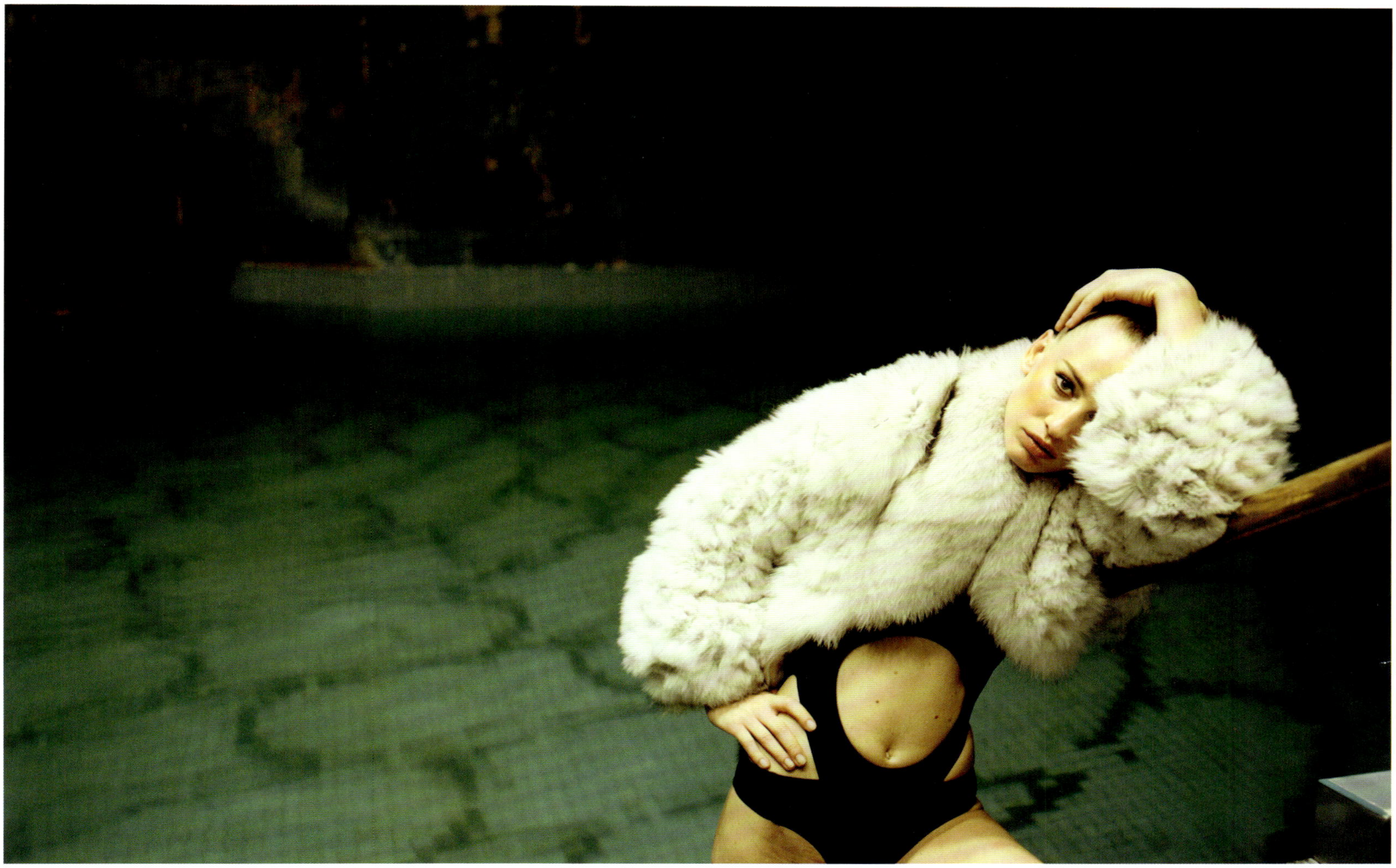

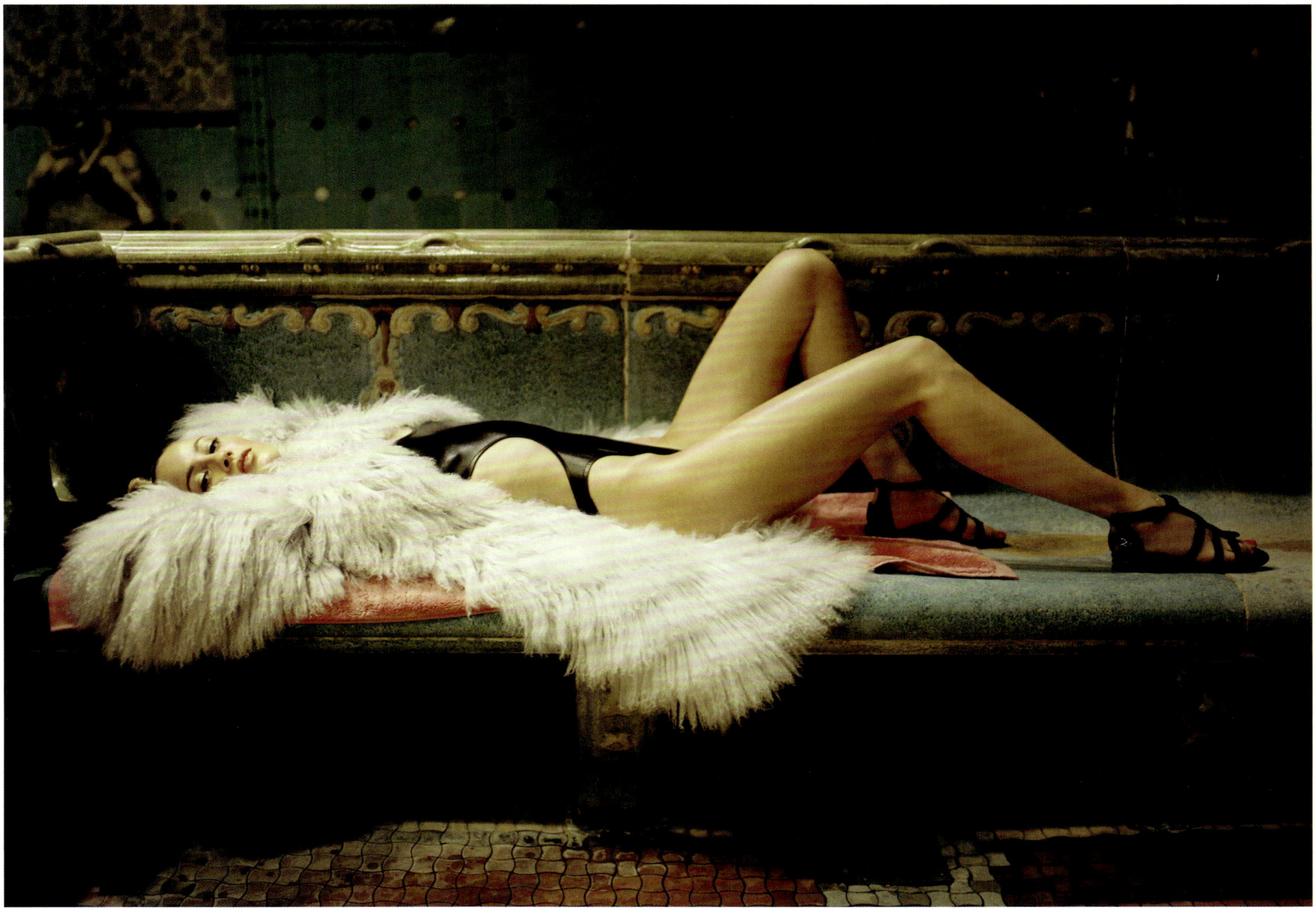

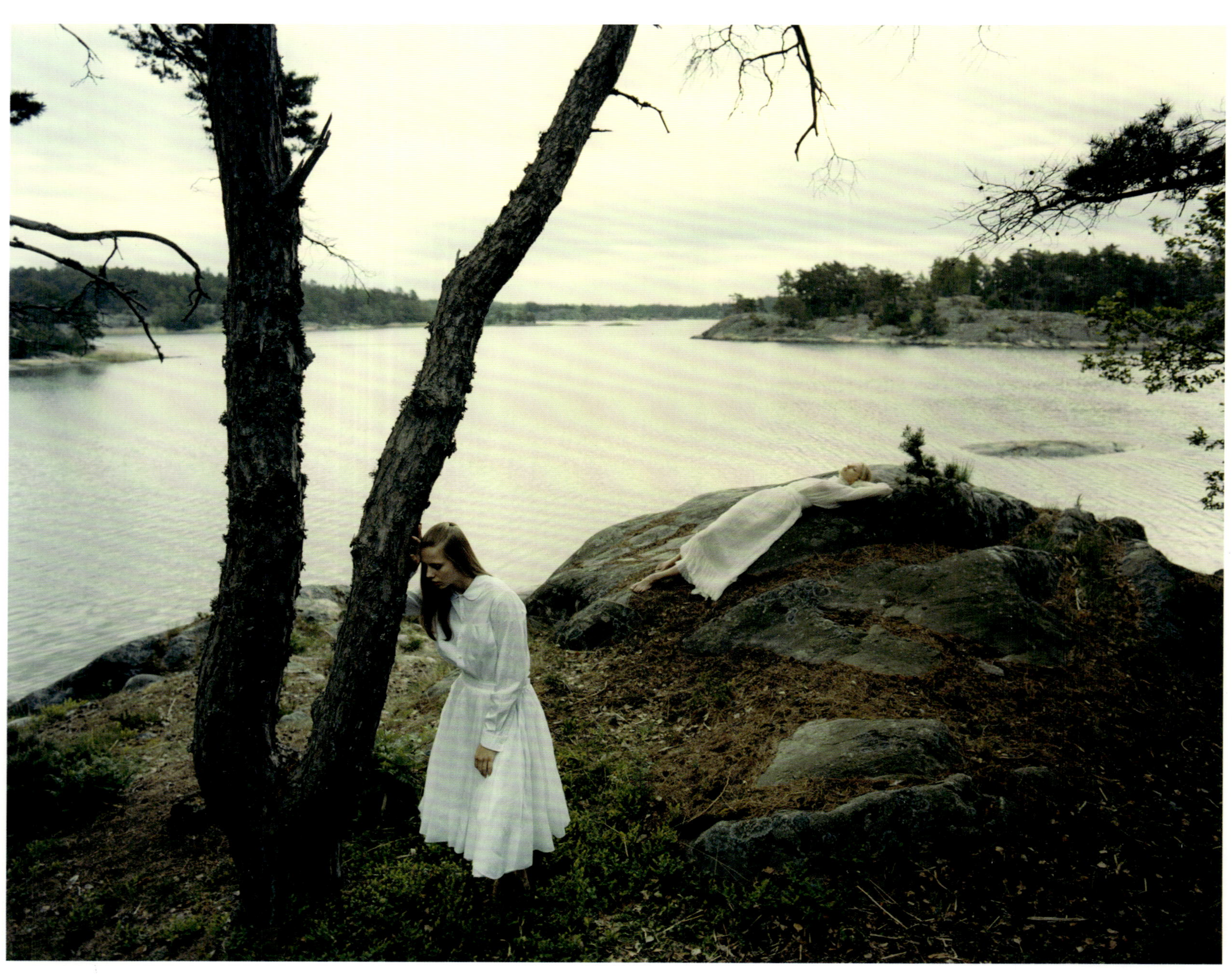

YELENA YEMCHUK
from 'The Nordic Light' for *Vogue* Japan, 2006
photography by Yelena Yemchuk
courtesy Trunk Archive

pages 106–7:
from 'Signora in Nero' for *Vogue* Japan, 2005
photography by Yelena Yemchuk
courtesy Trunk Archive

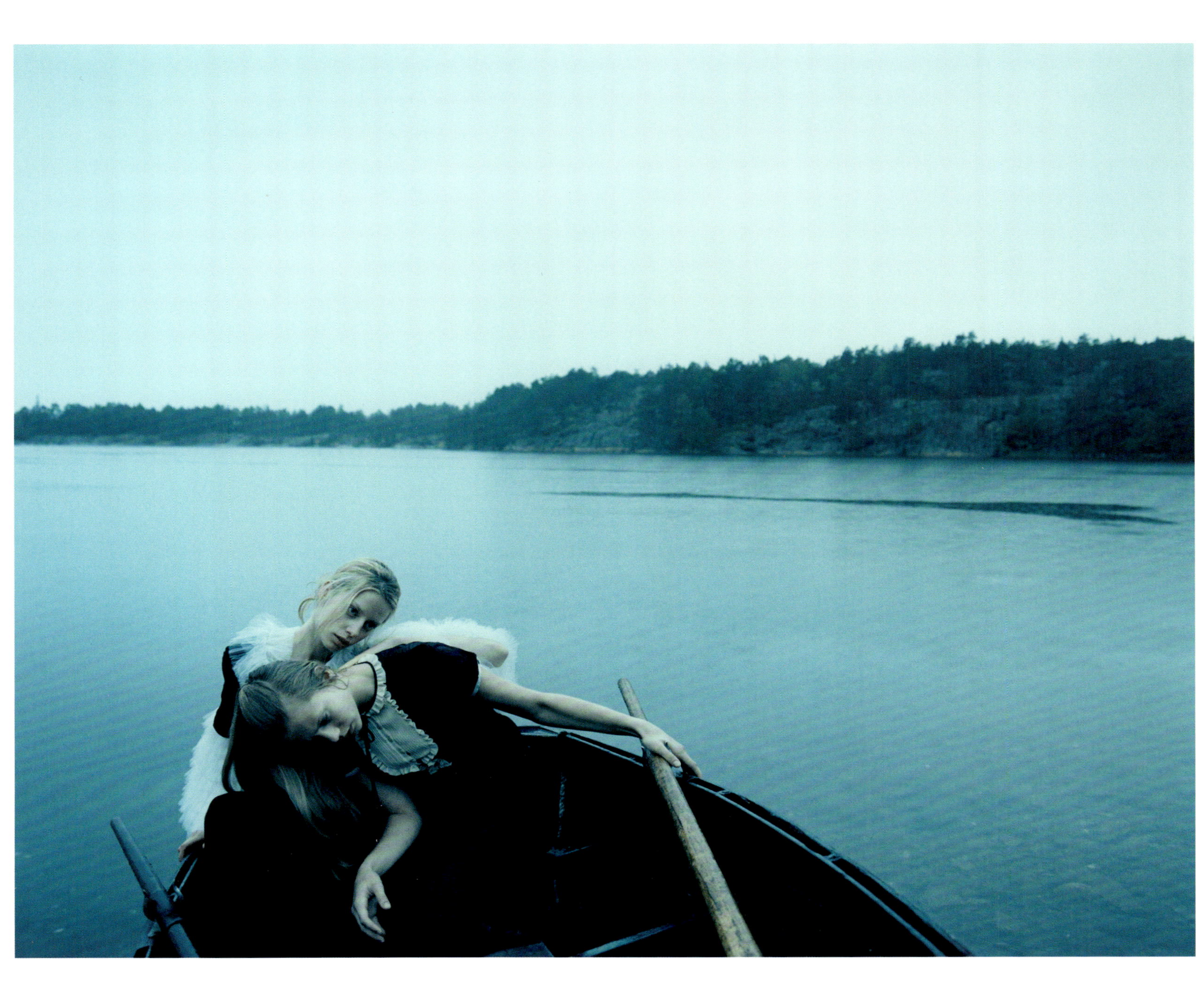

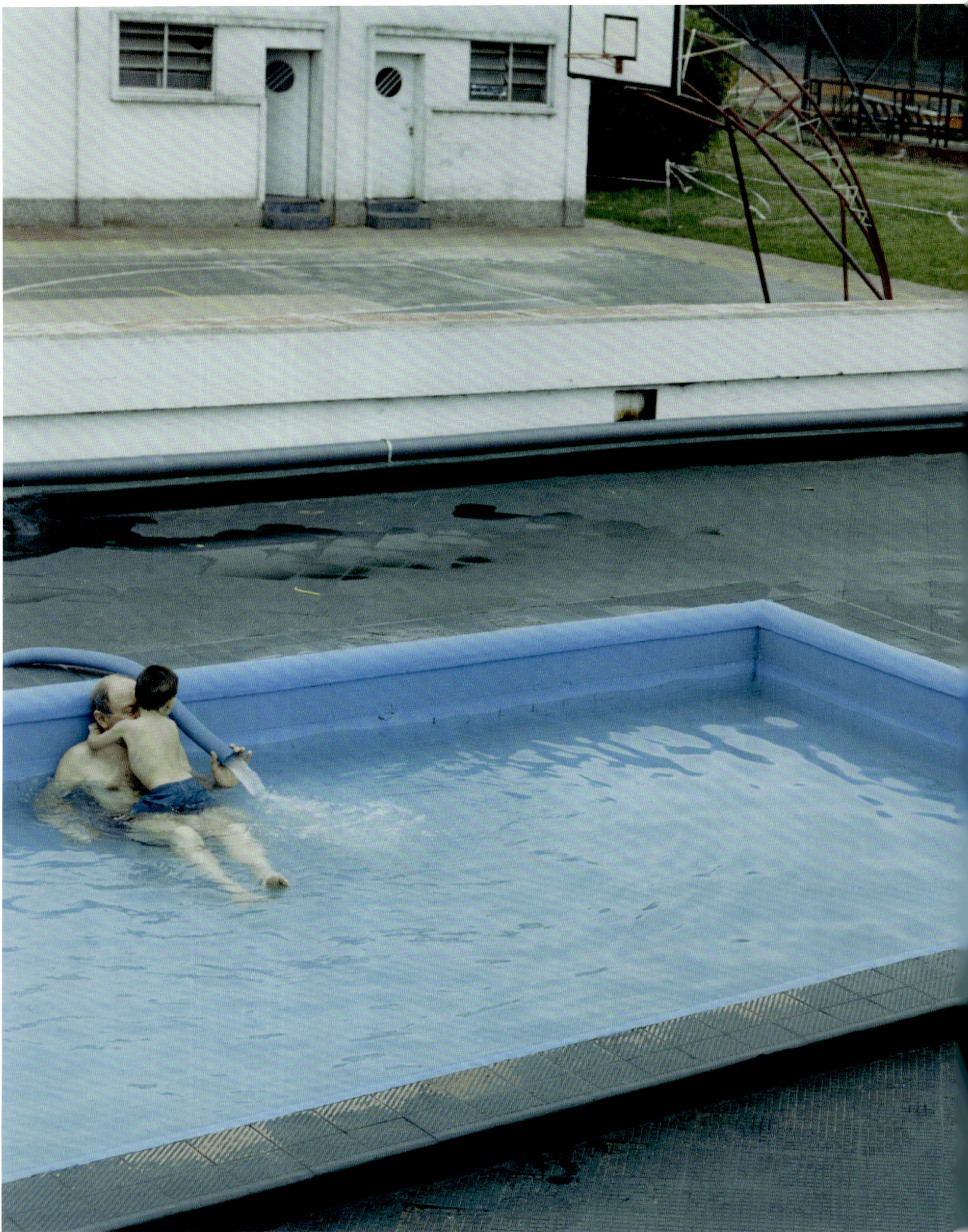

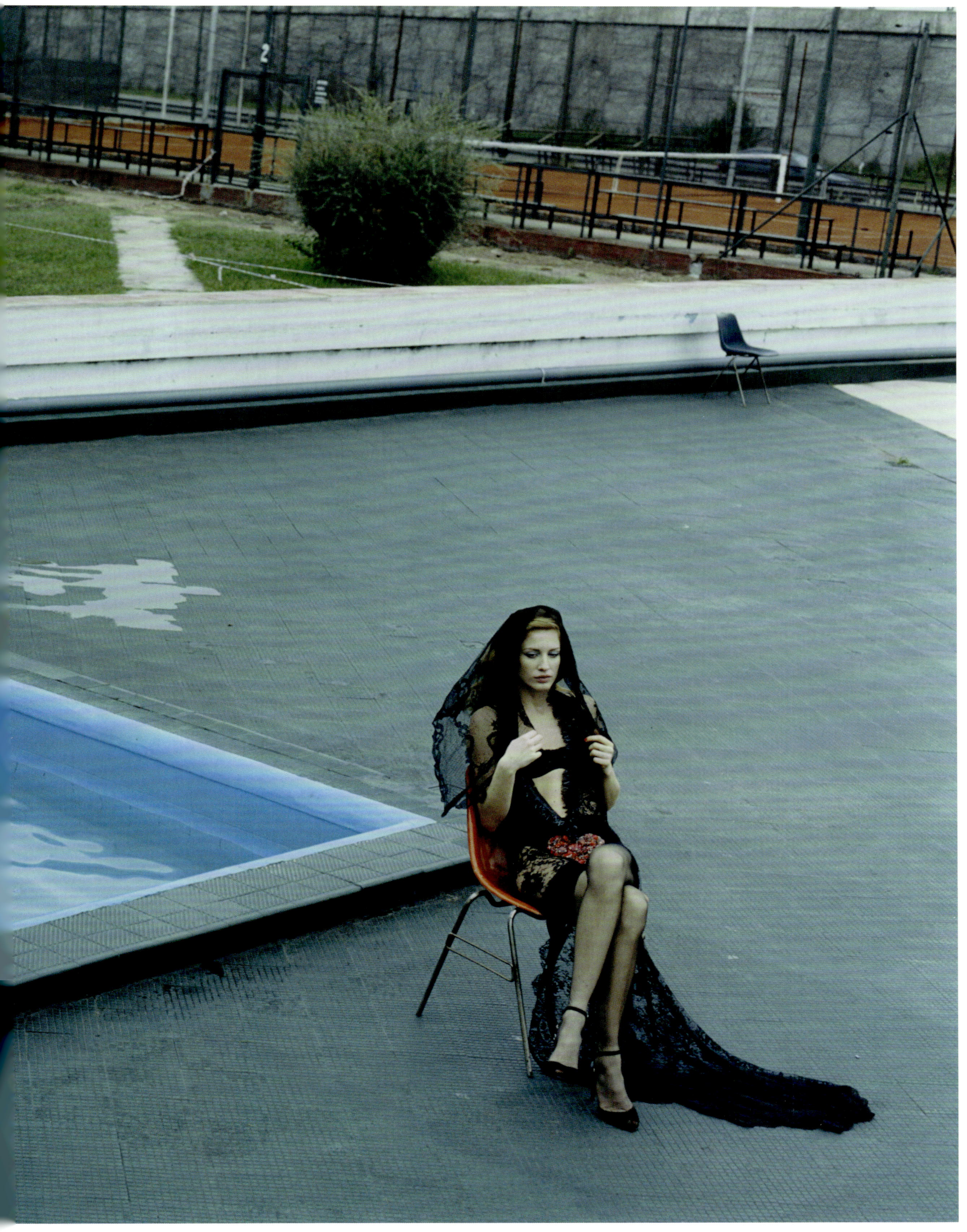

'Hay que adaptarse a los tiempos'
('You Have to Adapt to the Times'), 2010
personal project from *Serie 365*
photography by Eugenio Recuenco
courtesy Eugenio Recuenco Studio
and Gianfranco Meza

The imagery of Spanish photographer Eugenio Recuenco comes from a place where history and the imagination meet. Recuenco takes his lead from the past, plundering the history of art and literature for inspiration then twisting what he finds towards the sensual, grotesque and comedic. His use of light and colour is unique. His subjects dwell within the muted palettes of old paintings, occasionally offset by the vivid glow of their costume. The dramatic use of shadow and light often suggests the melodrama of theatre, creating narrative mystery amidst historical fantasies. Within these moody arrangements the images often look like they may have been gathering the dust of centuries, yet the allusions they incorporate thrust them straight into the contemporary. The effect is that they seem almost timeless, sitting with joyful awkwardness in any context.

In 'Les Costumes' for *V* and *Madame Figaro*, a domestic scene recalls the sublime beauty of Jan Vermeer. Look again, however, and something unexpected reveals itself: an illicit act that appears outrageously out of place (page 109). The element of surprise in these time-travelling juxtapositions epitomises Recuenco's narrative playfulness, a characteristic that runs throughout his work. Fashion, here, is not about refining appearance to fit in with the whims of the present. Such constant re-imagining of the self through the lens of fashion is challenged in images which depict style and dress as a more personal form of self-expression to be located and nurtured anywhere and within any moment.

Recuenco is responsive to his equipment. He believes in the relationship between photographer and camera and is not afraid to resist the draw of the new. In a high-profile shoot for Chanel, the rustic analogue of an old Hasselblad takes precedence over the 22-megapixel digital alternative proposed by his client. In conversation, singling out the Pentax as the only model to offer an intimate relationship with its user, Recuenco describes how the camera itself breathes life into the photographic process. Here again, Recuenco's method relies on human warmth, even towards the mechanics of the medium itself.

When asked to shoot a self-portrait for iconic coffee brand Lavazza, Recuenco chose an icon from Spanish – and world – literature, styling himself as Miguel de Cervantes' hapless wanderer Don Quixote. Sitting triumphantly astride a horse in full armour, Recuenco seems grand and idealistic. But this is Quixote – though he may appear gallant and bold in the pursuit of his craft, ultimately the implication is that he is on a fool's mission. It is an interesting conflation, yet Recuenco has the edge over Cervantes' warrior: he enters into his madness all too knowingly. His is a very serious quest underpinned by a playful grasp of the absurd.

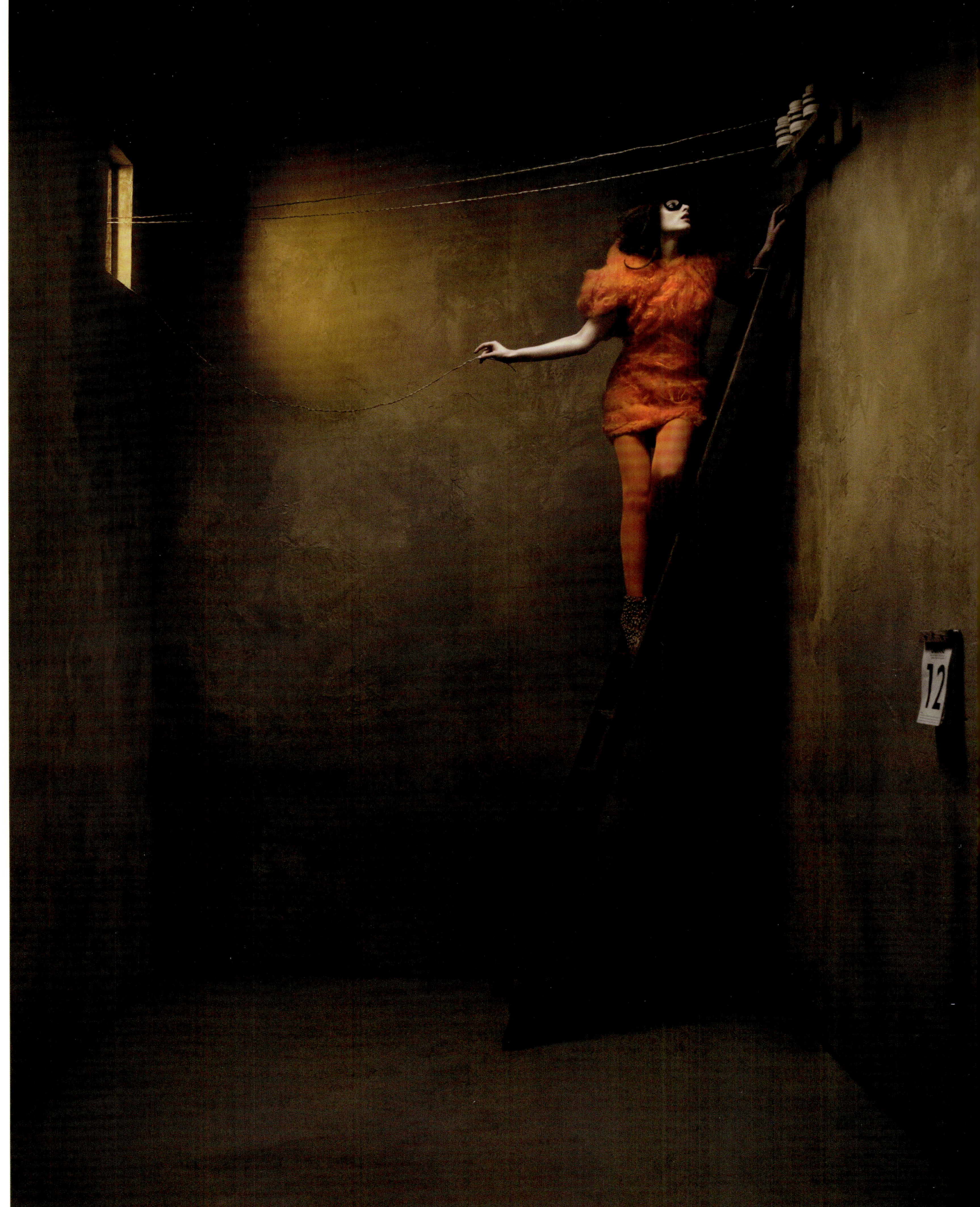

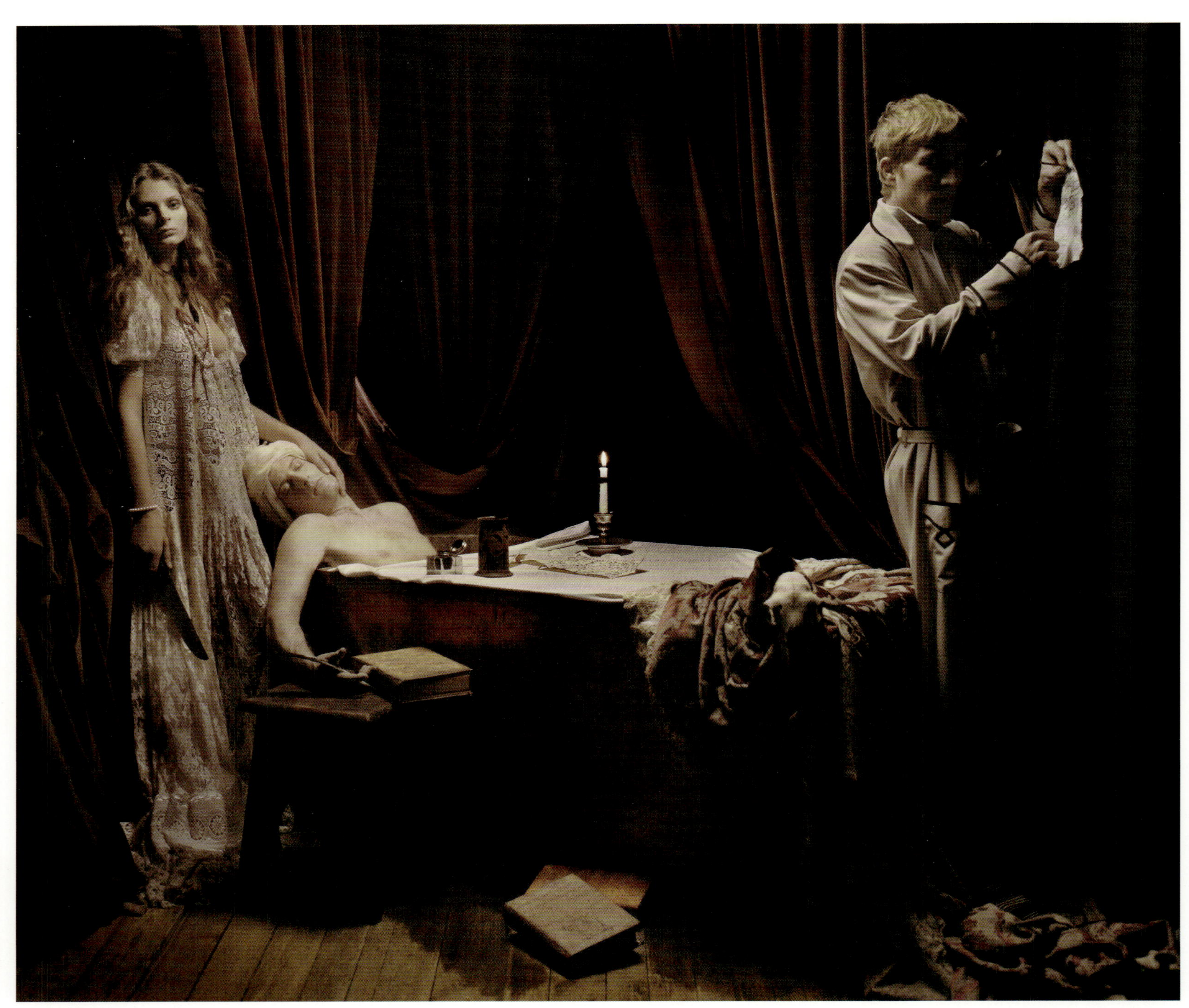

EUGENIO RECUENCO

'La mort de Marat' for *Madame Figaro*, 2009
photography by Eugenio Recuenco
courtesy Eugenio Recuenco

'Les Costumes' for *V / Madame Figaro*, 2009
photography by Eugenio Recuenco
courtesy Eugenio Recuenco

pages 112–13:
'Esencia de Seducción' for *Yo Dona España*, 2009
photography by Eugenio Recuenco
courtesy Eugenio Recuenco

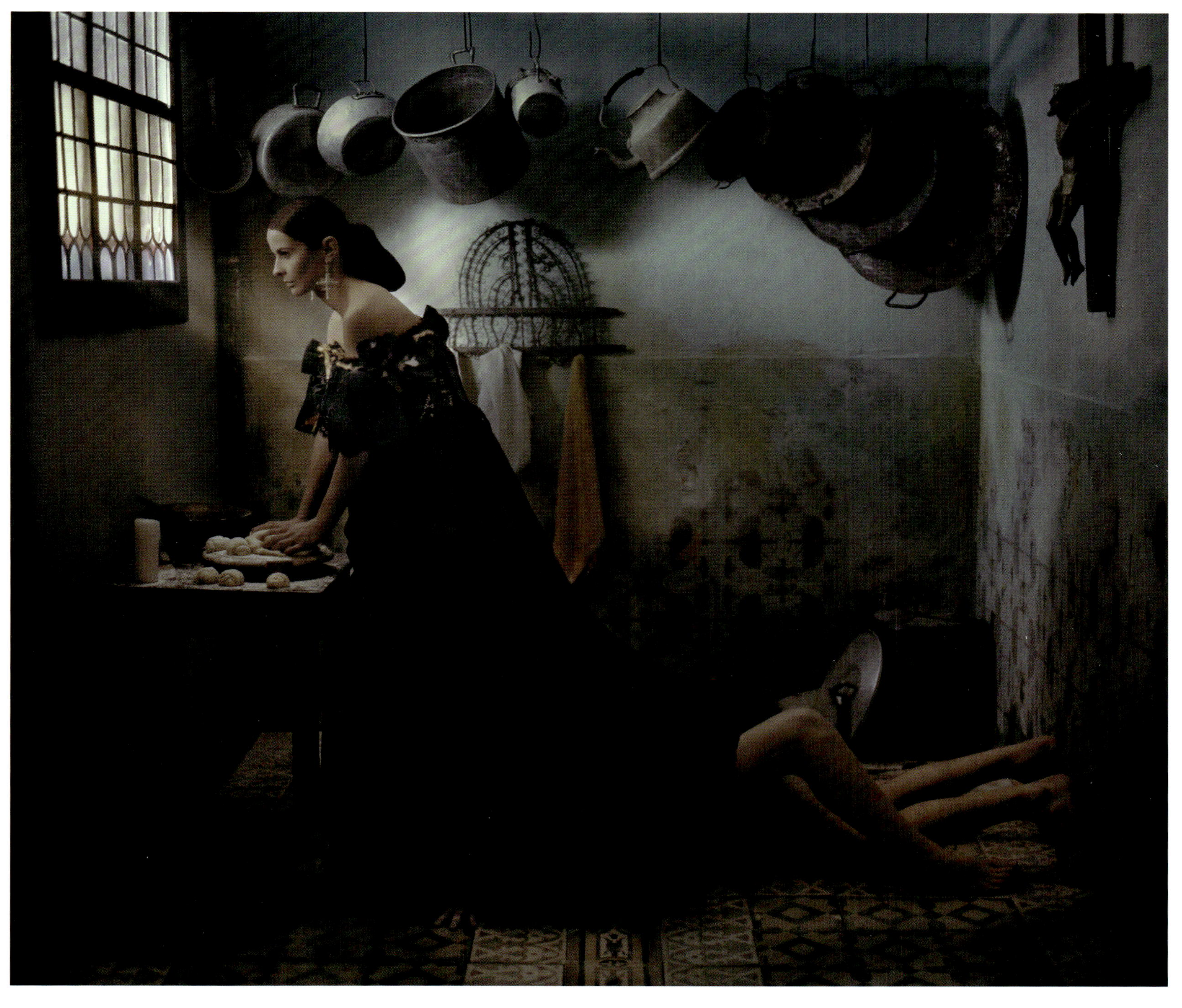

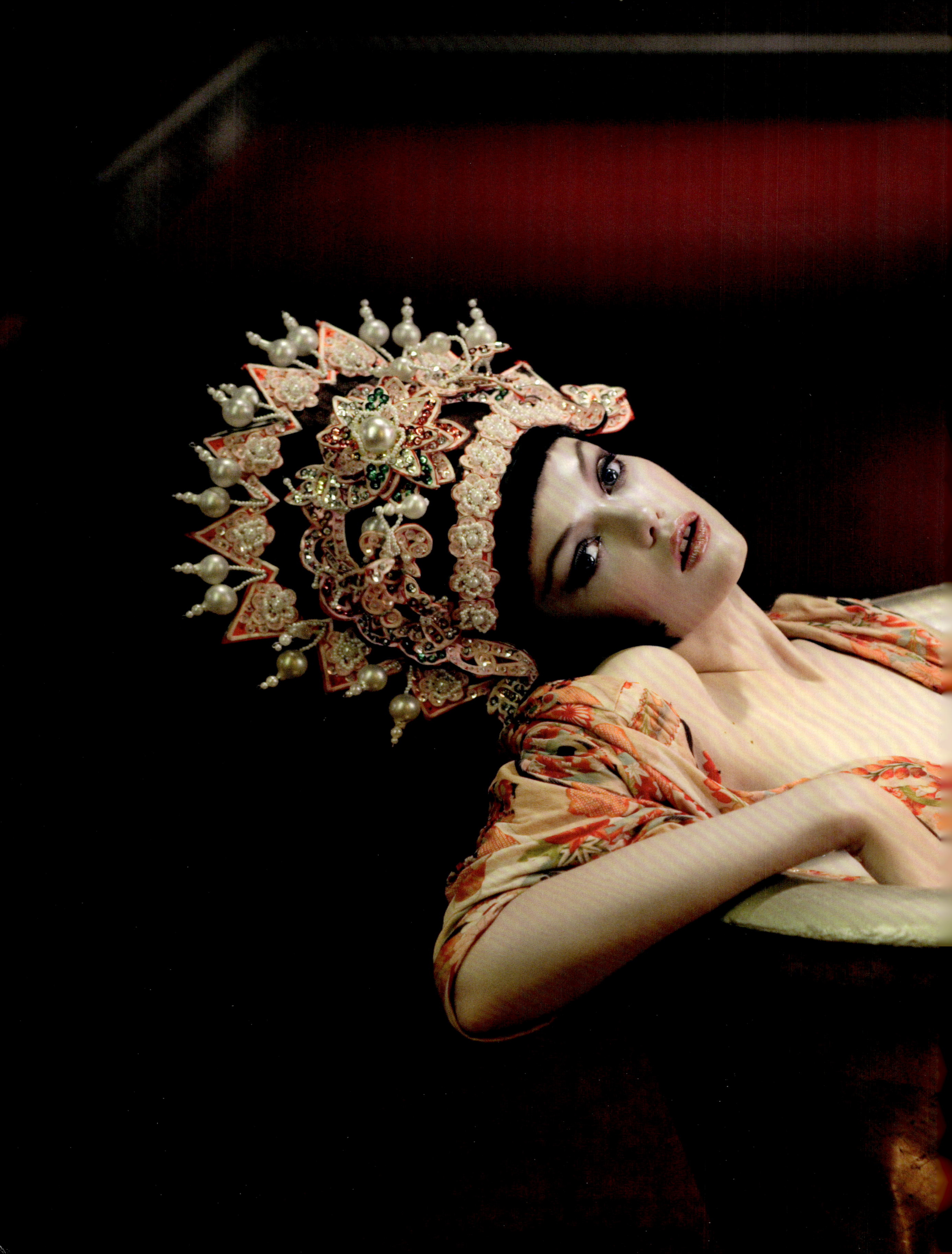

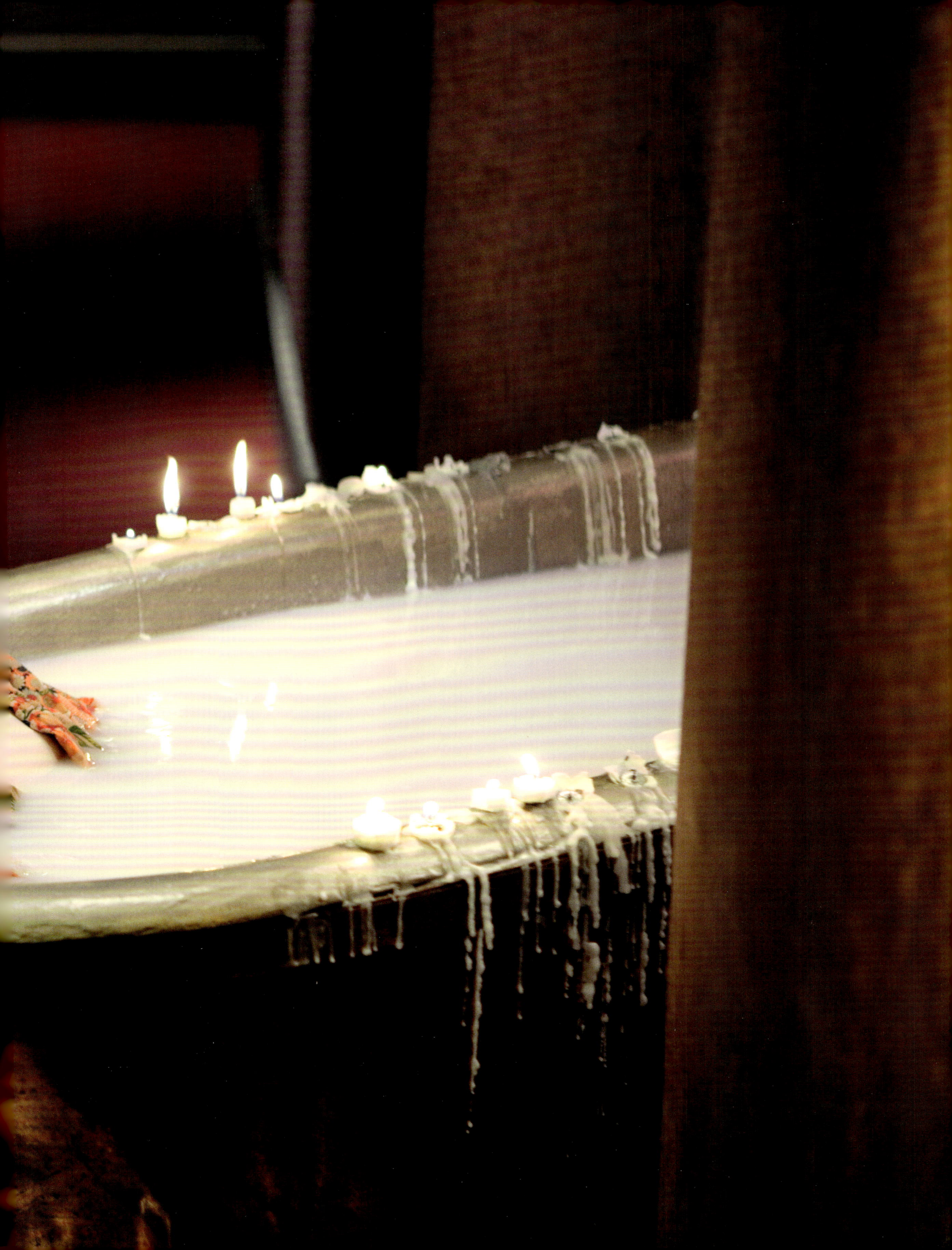

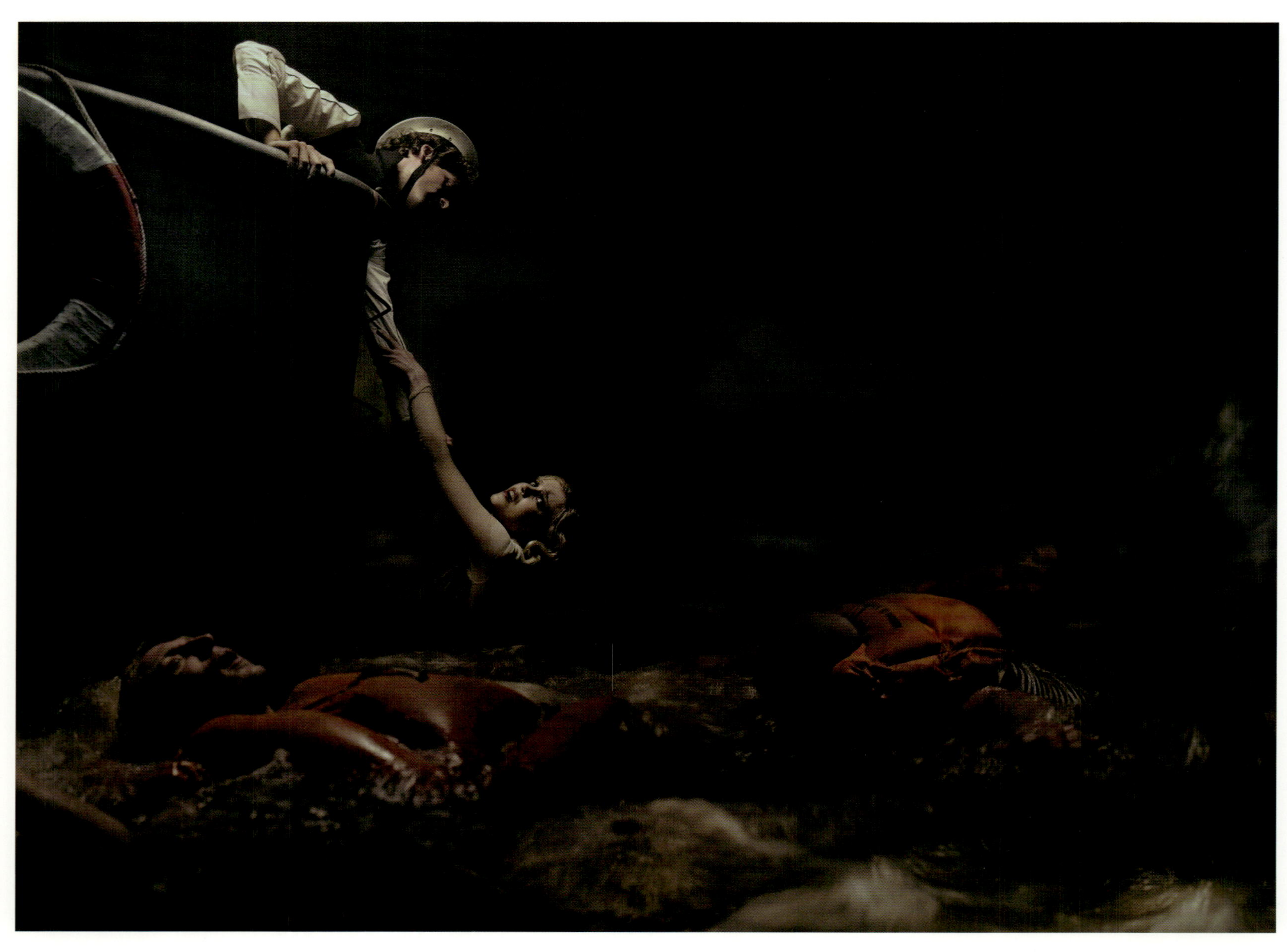

ELGENIO RECUENCO

'Crew member Number 0308: Unidentified Passengers'
from *Tempestad* for *Yo Dona España*, 2007
photography by Eugenio Recuenco
courtesy Eugenio Recuenco

'All in One' for *Blue Bretzel*, 2010
photography by Eugenio Recuenco
courtesy Eugenio Recuenco

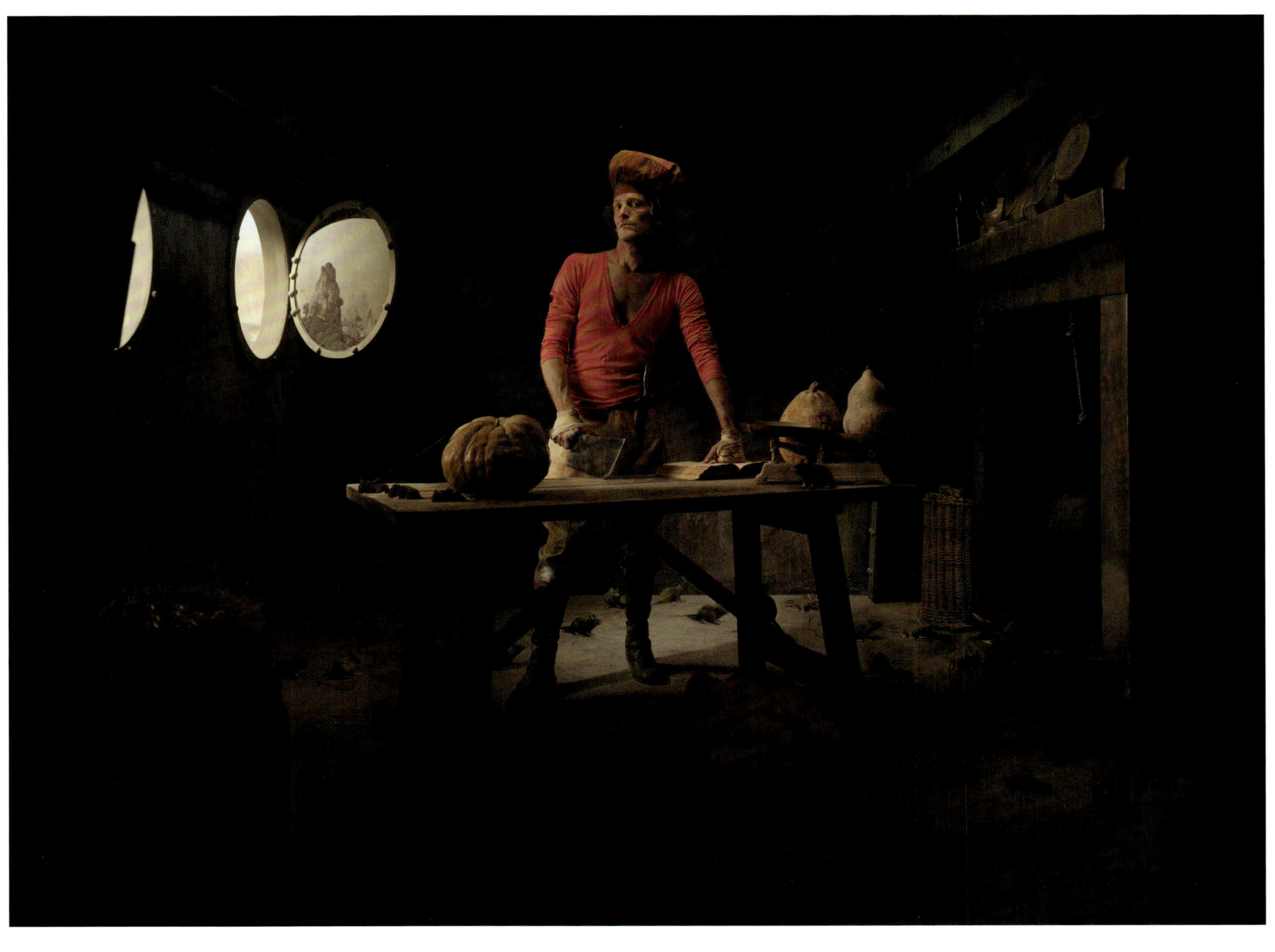

'Obscurité' for *Schön*, 2010
photography by LaRoache Brothers
courtesy Factory 311

page 118:
'Mechanical', 2008
photography by LaRoache Brothers
courtesy Factory 311

page 119:
Lily Cole for *Wig*, 2007
photography by LaRoache Brothers
courtesy Factory 311

When creative duo Wolfgang Mustain and Laurence Edney work together as the LaRoache Brothers, things take on an atmosphere of gloomy theatricality. Intoxicated by the symbolism and imagery of Victorian gothicism, the pair feast on a diet of moody noir that creeps out of their operational base in East London to infect the world of fashion. Dangerous portraits laden with menace are lifted from the darkness using the techniques of liquid light, a process that allows their photographs to be developed on found textures such as rusted sheet metal and concrete.

Mustain and Edney are relentlessly attracted to pseudo-horror. Miscellaneous pieces of equipment provide industrial backbones to a series of portraits in 2007 that reconstruct models as mechanised beings from an urban nightmare. For a 2008 editorial in *Wig*, model Lily Cole is pictured in the style of a sinister faded family portrait from a copper-coloured past (page 119). The process that gives substance and physicality to these monochromatic photographs involves the painting of light-sensitive photographic emulsion onto unusual materials to create a disturbance in the image surface. As the picture develops it creates an ethereal glow that offsets the darkness of the photograph.

Mustain and Edney, two former photographer's models, first met in Japan on the modelling circuit in the 1990s. Resurfacing as a photographic team themselves many years into their careers, this history has shaped their own approach. Allowing them first-hand experience with legendary photographers of the twentieth century,

such as the late Irving Penn, this long gestation period has shaped their understanding of the people they portray. The fictional exuberance of their style is hardly disguised and yet the techniques, which hark back to the early days of photography, lend a false authenticity to the images.

In the black-and-white 2011 editorial 'Holy Rollers', there is a touch of the supernatural as we are witness to a man apparently submitting to a spiritual levitation (pages 120–21). Here the photographers flirt with a realist style, compelling the viewer to indulge a faith in the impossible. Ultimately Mustain and Edney are in thrall to techniques that echo the black magic of their subject matter. Such technical innovation ties the pair both to the past and the future, their approach simultaneously forward- and backward-looking, as if their imagery is lifted from a parallel past richer, darker, yet more magnificent than the one with which we are familiar. In these portraits there is always something lurking in the shadows that creeps under the skin and embeds itself in the mind. Following their process beyond the photograph itself to explore old-world techniques of printing and post-production, Mustain and Edney have realised that images are more than just surface — but that surface can be exploited too.

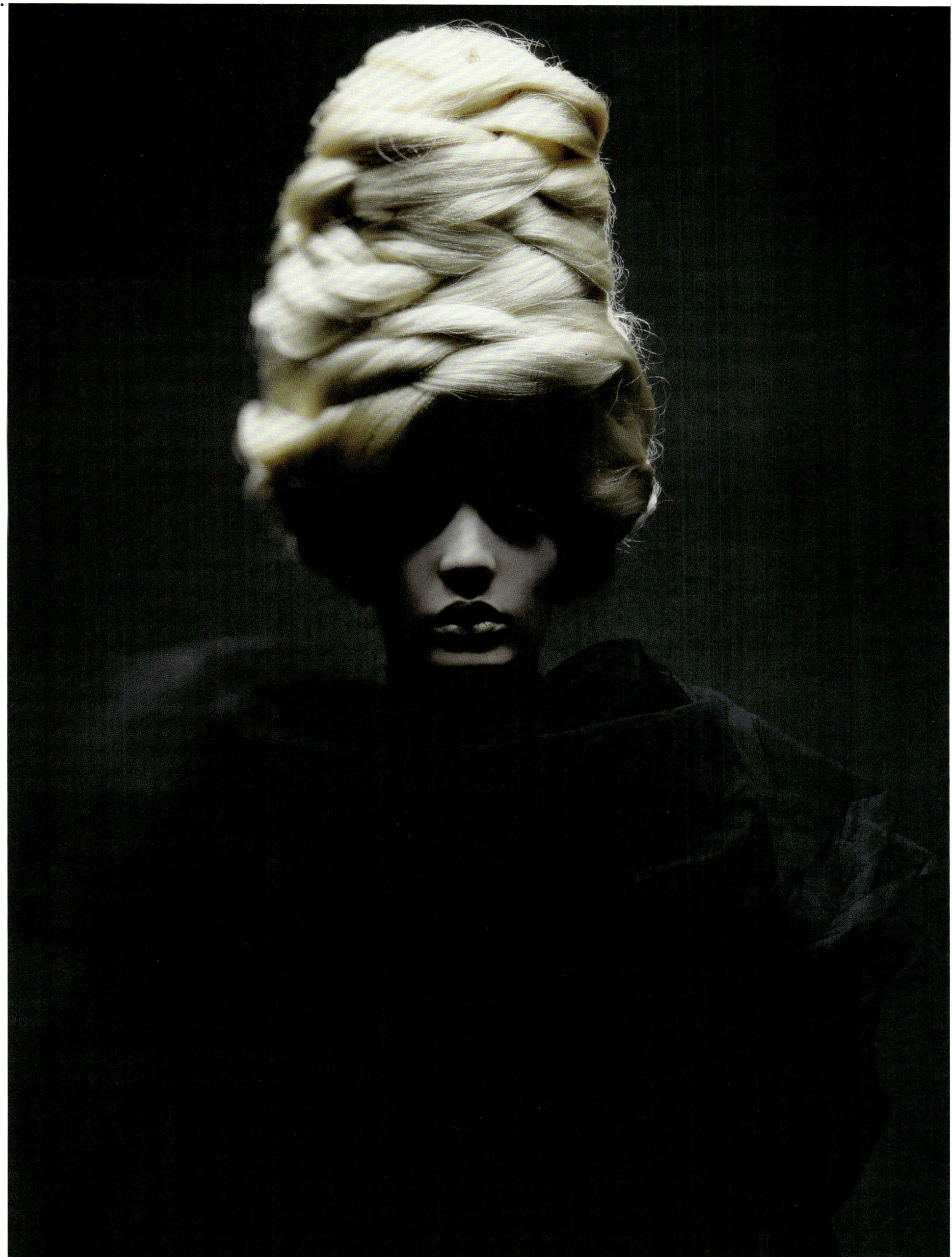

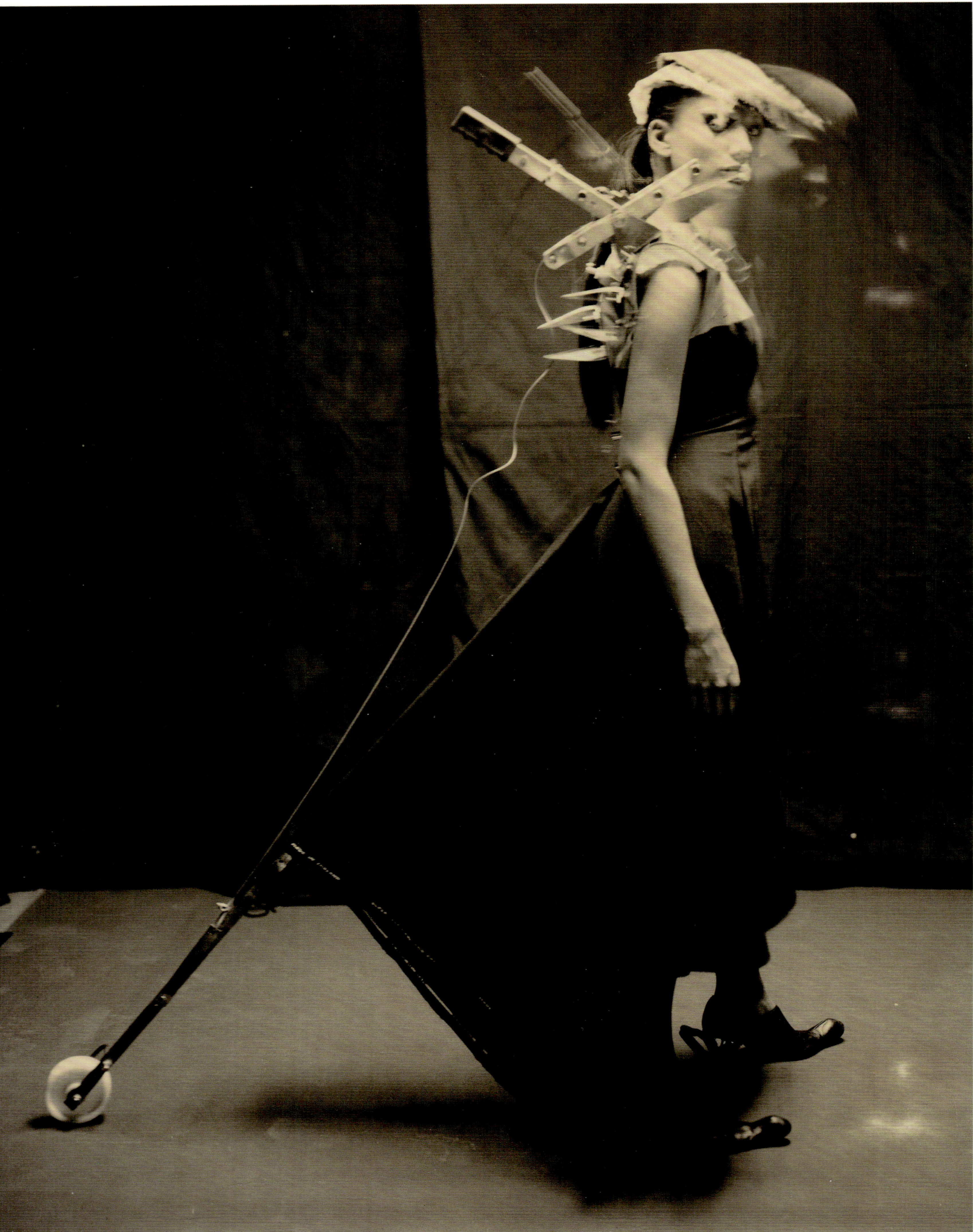

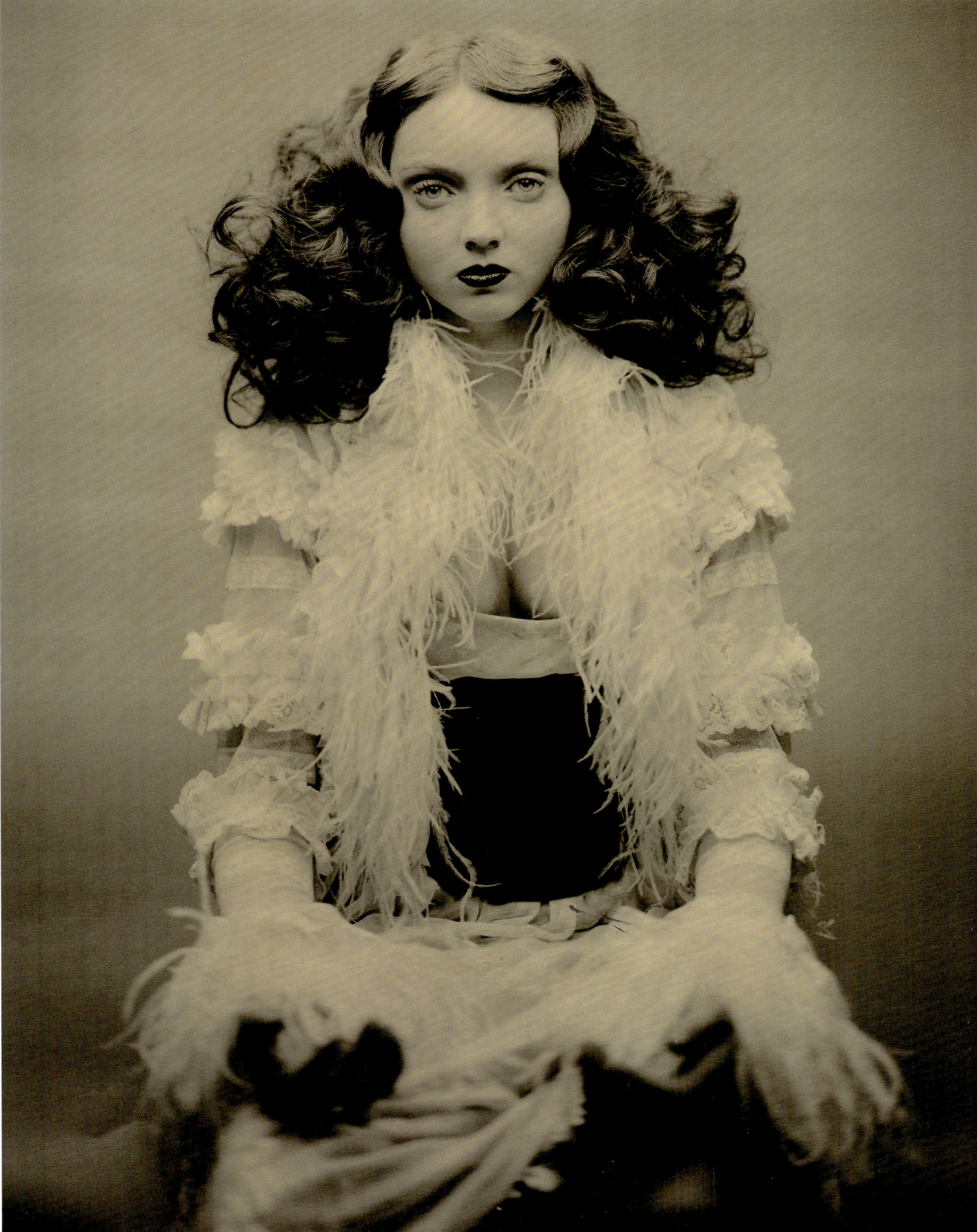

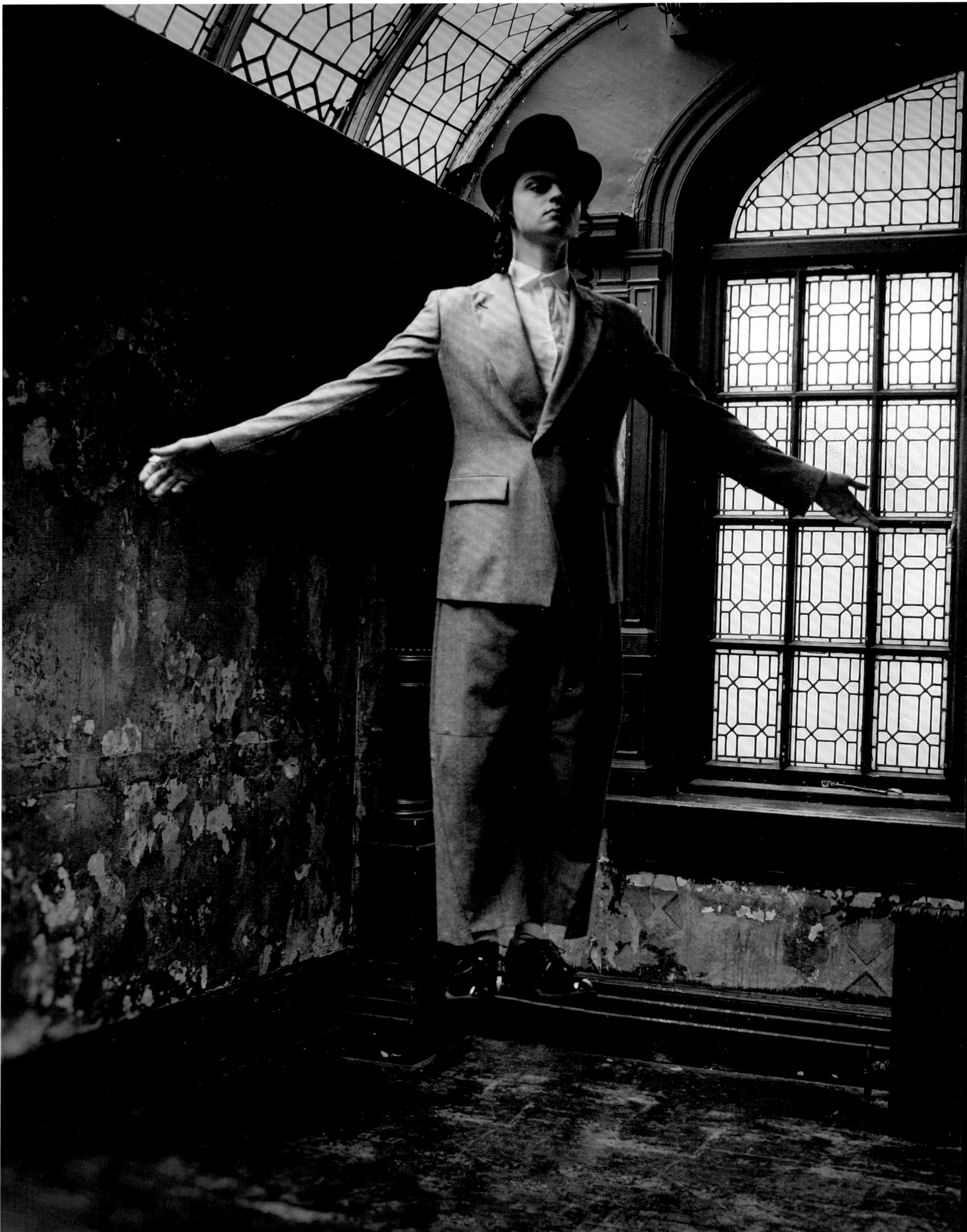

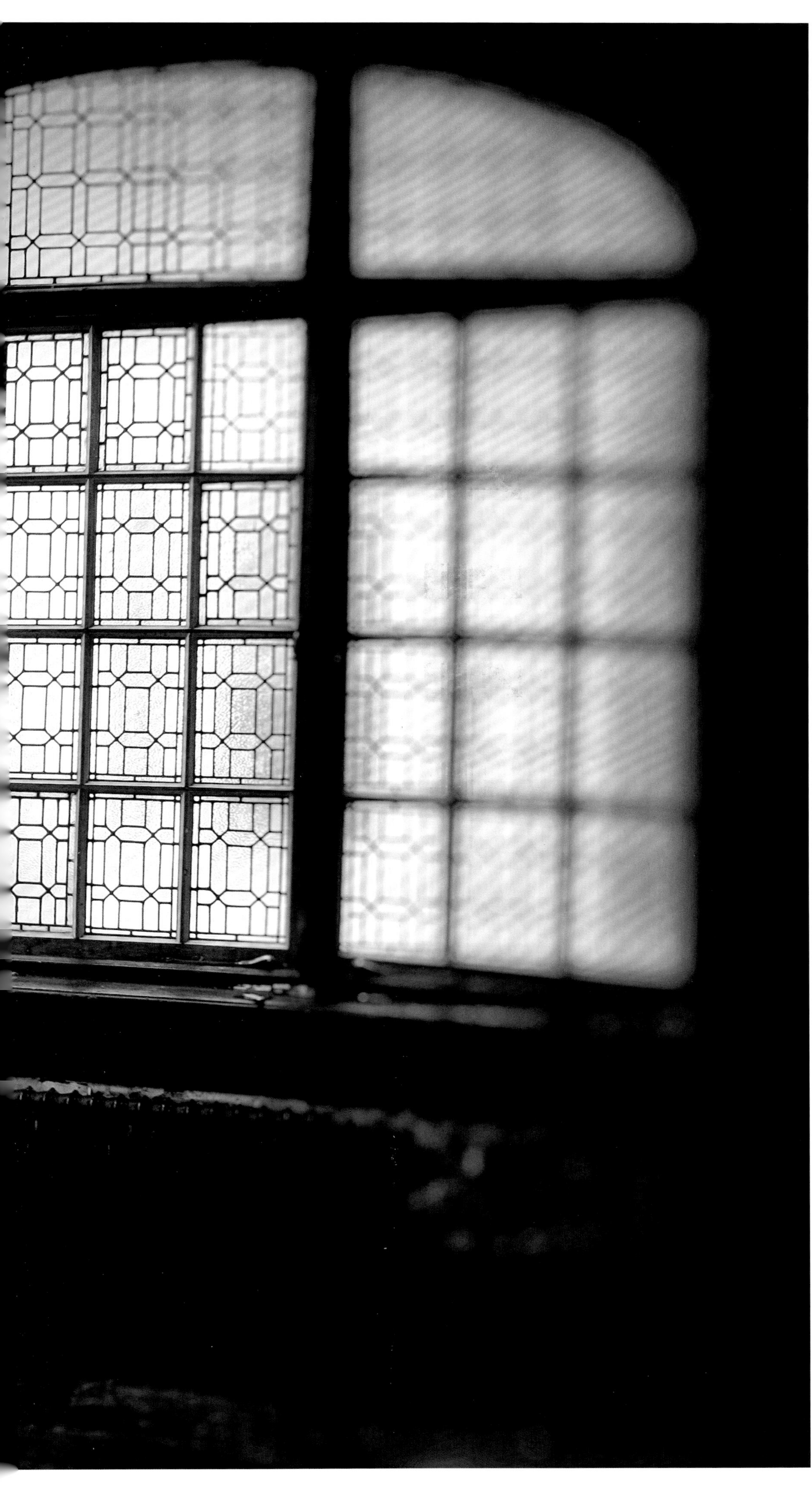

LAROACHE BROTHERS

'Holy Rollers' for *121 Magazine*, 2011
photography by LaRoache Brothers
courtesy Factory 311

Julia Hafström for *Bad Day*, 2011
photography by Chadwick Tyler
courtesy Chadwick Tyler

The women caught in the barrel of Chadwick Tyler's camera are trapped in a monochrome melodrama. Edging between euphoria and hysteria, they surge like spectres in and out of scenes that are otherwise enveloped in an inky blackness. It is an environment dominated by extreme emotions; gaunt faces portray terror as others appear transcendent. At times, Tyler's models have more in common with the disturbing apparitions of an Ada Emma Deane photograph than the world of fashion and glamour to which they are directed.

Tyler approaches photography in the manner of a painter locked away in a studio. Images such as that of Kelsey Van Mook for Christian Lacroix seep with the Romanticism of eighteenth-century portraiture (pages 126–27). Eschewing contemporary polish, he favours natural light – even in interior conditions – and lets his camera take its time to capture the scene. Slow shutter speeds and small-format film lend a blurred vagueness to melancholic arrangements. Movement becomes an element of its own in images that depict the body as something other than bodily. In an editorial for *Black*, model Gertrud Hegelund is captured at what appears to be the moment of rapture; in a series of photographs of Constance Jablonski for the fashion photography showcase *Grey II*, fabric takes on the characteristics of an object caught in poltergeist activity (page 124). But these images are visualisations of subconscious desires rather than anything explicitly mystical. Suppressing conscious thought in favour of shooting by instinct, Tyler keeps his focus on the subliminal and speaks to an introspective space where emotion takes over. In his 2008 solo show

Tiberius, this approach reaches a crescendo as over fifty models surrender to the photographer's lexicon of ecstasy and horror. While Tyler appears to wrestle with a world beyond the physical, his style plays with the illusion of the photograph as an archive of a more concrete reality. Images such as those of Julia Hafström for magazine *Bad Day* work as false documents, capturing individuals in contexts that, in the unstaged nature of their composition, seem to convey a genuine moment (page 123). This focus both elevates his art and plays games with its sincerity.

Coming from a farming background in Florida, the history of the twentieth-century Dust Bowl era and the imagery of the Great Depression is echoed in the grainy finish of Tyler's photographs, which carry the mood of the environment in which he first began to experiment with the medium. It is an atmosphere of extremes, and it suits fashion only when fashion can accommodate it. In the oeuvre of a photographer for whom emotion takes over from reason, the beauty of the subject takes precedence over the beauty of fashion, and in this supporting role its function is expressed all the more clearly.

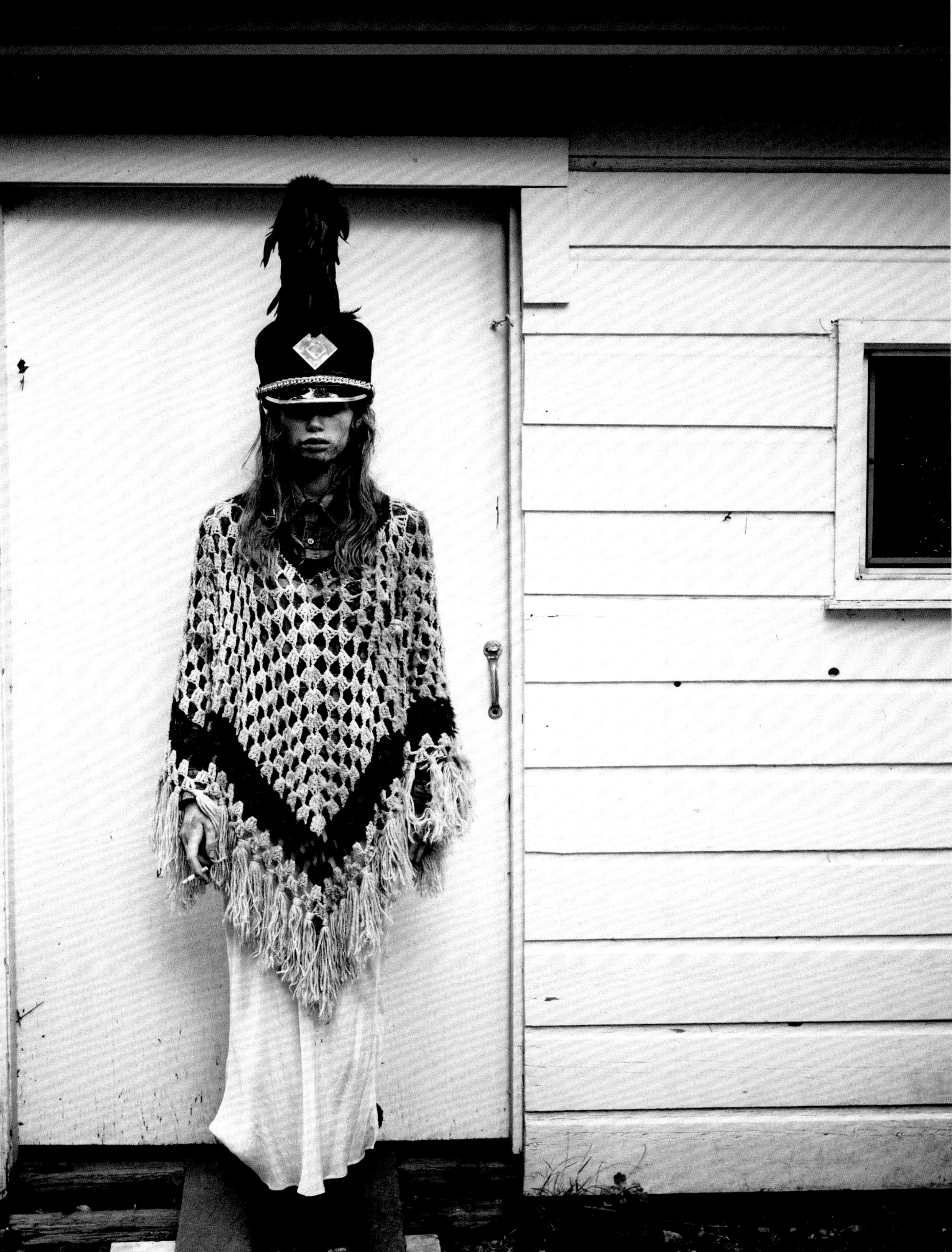

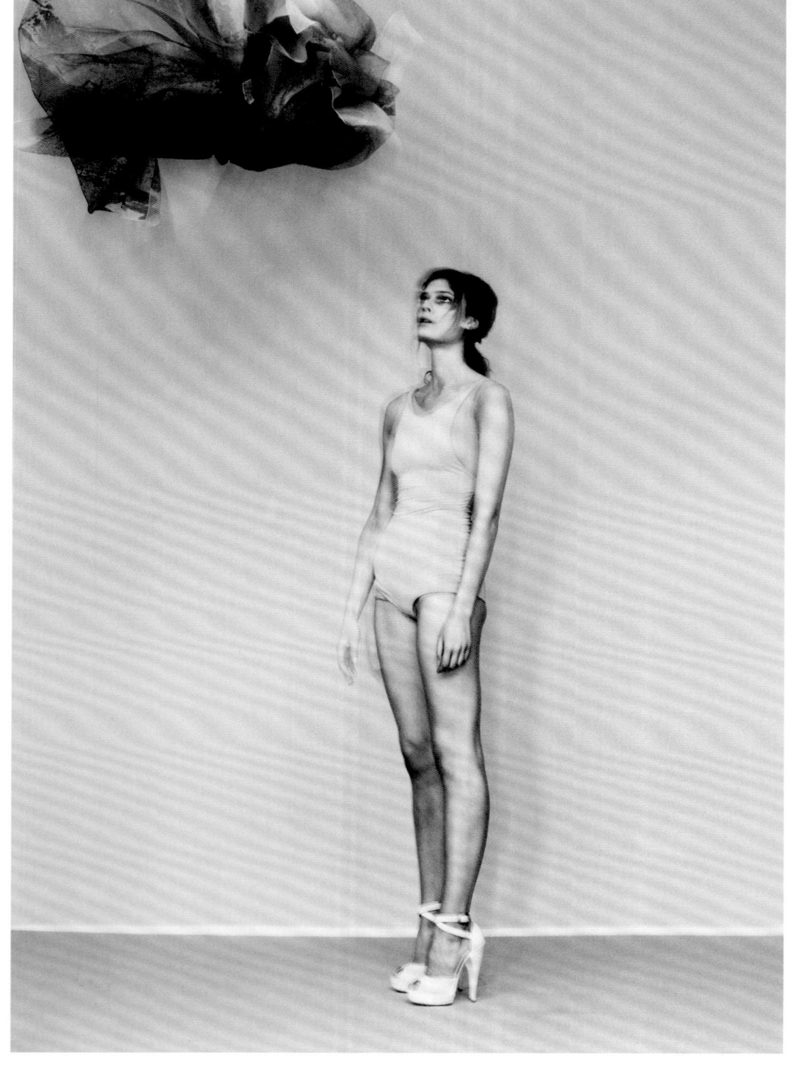

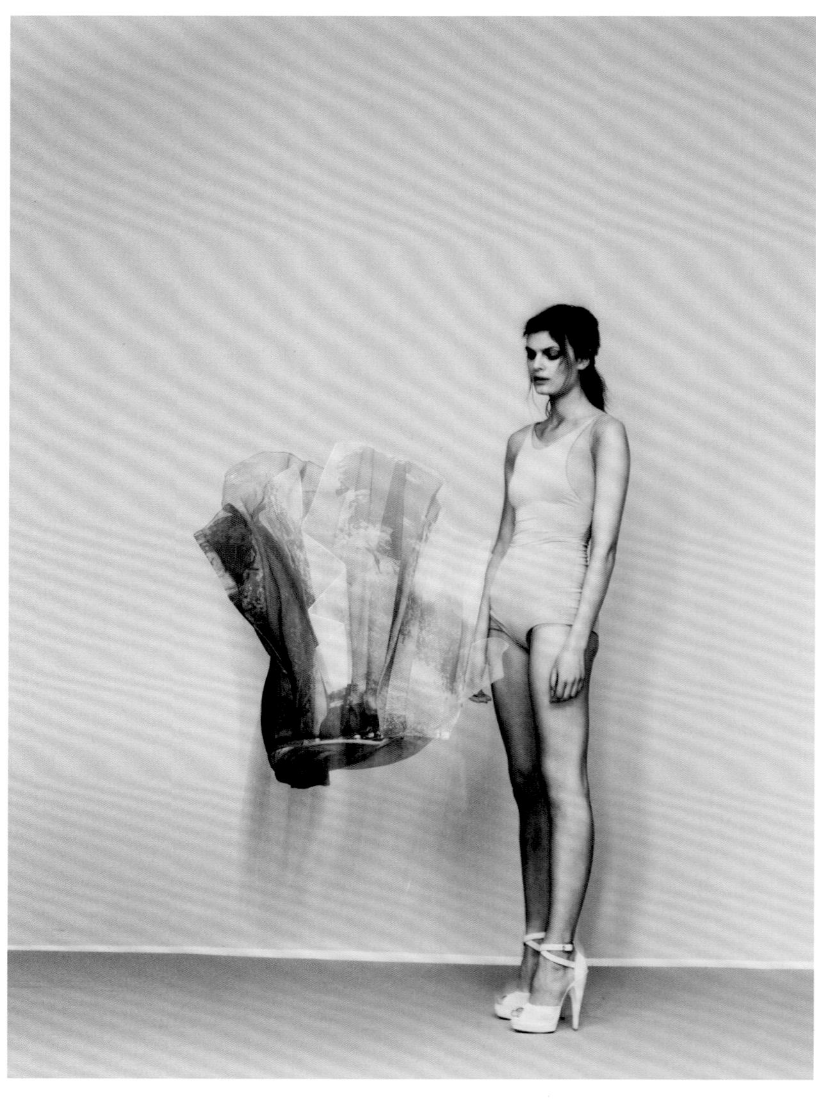

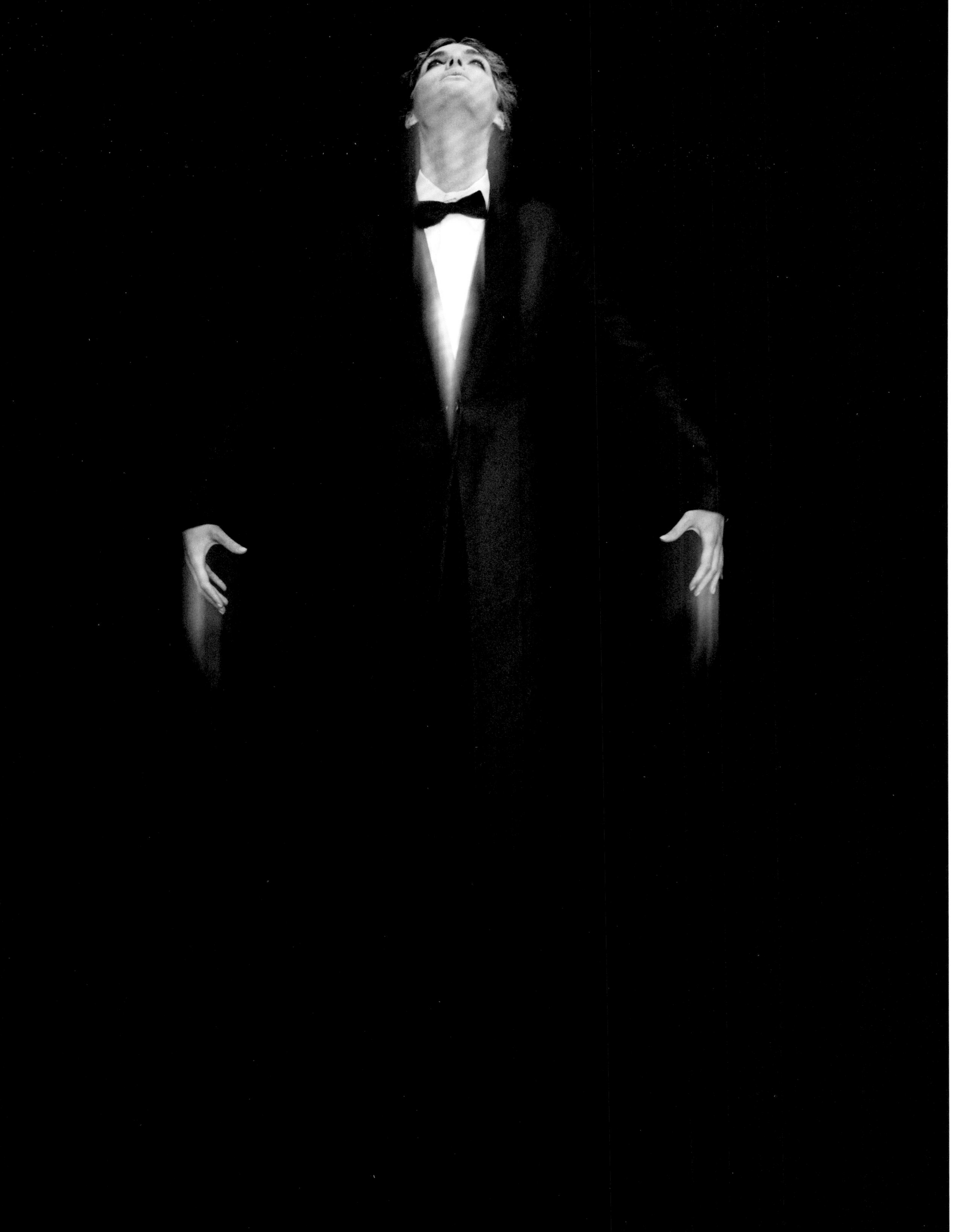

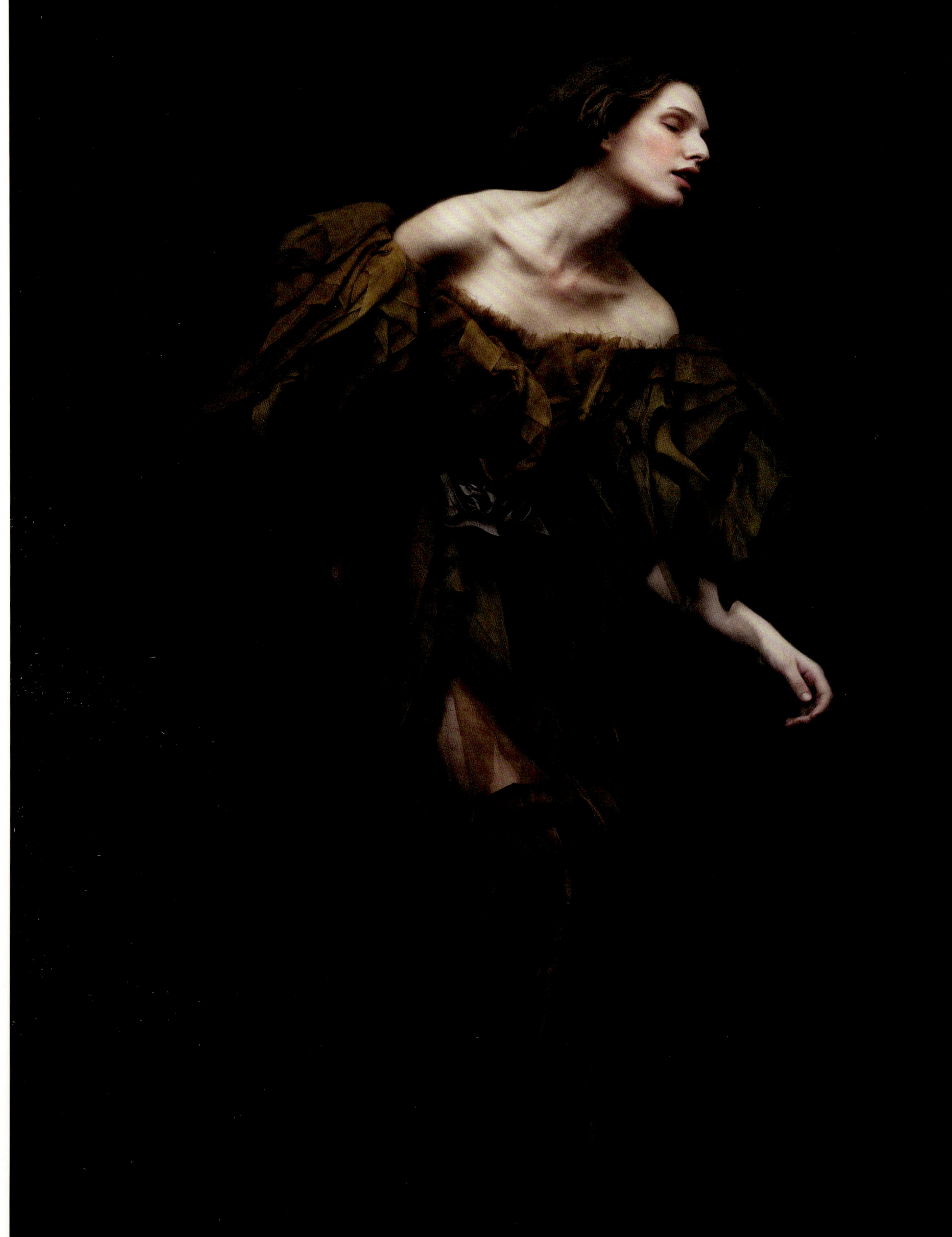

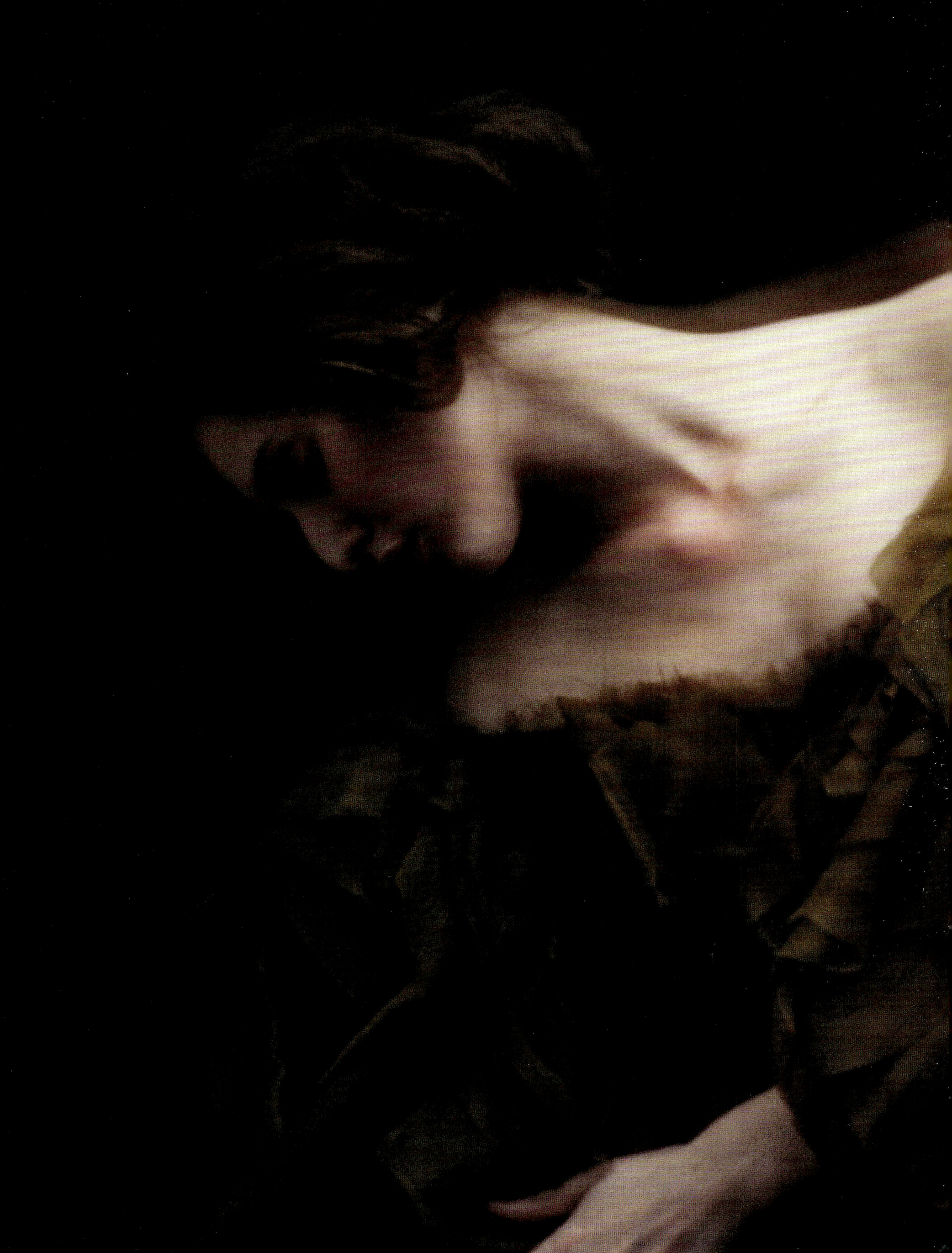

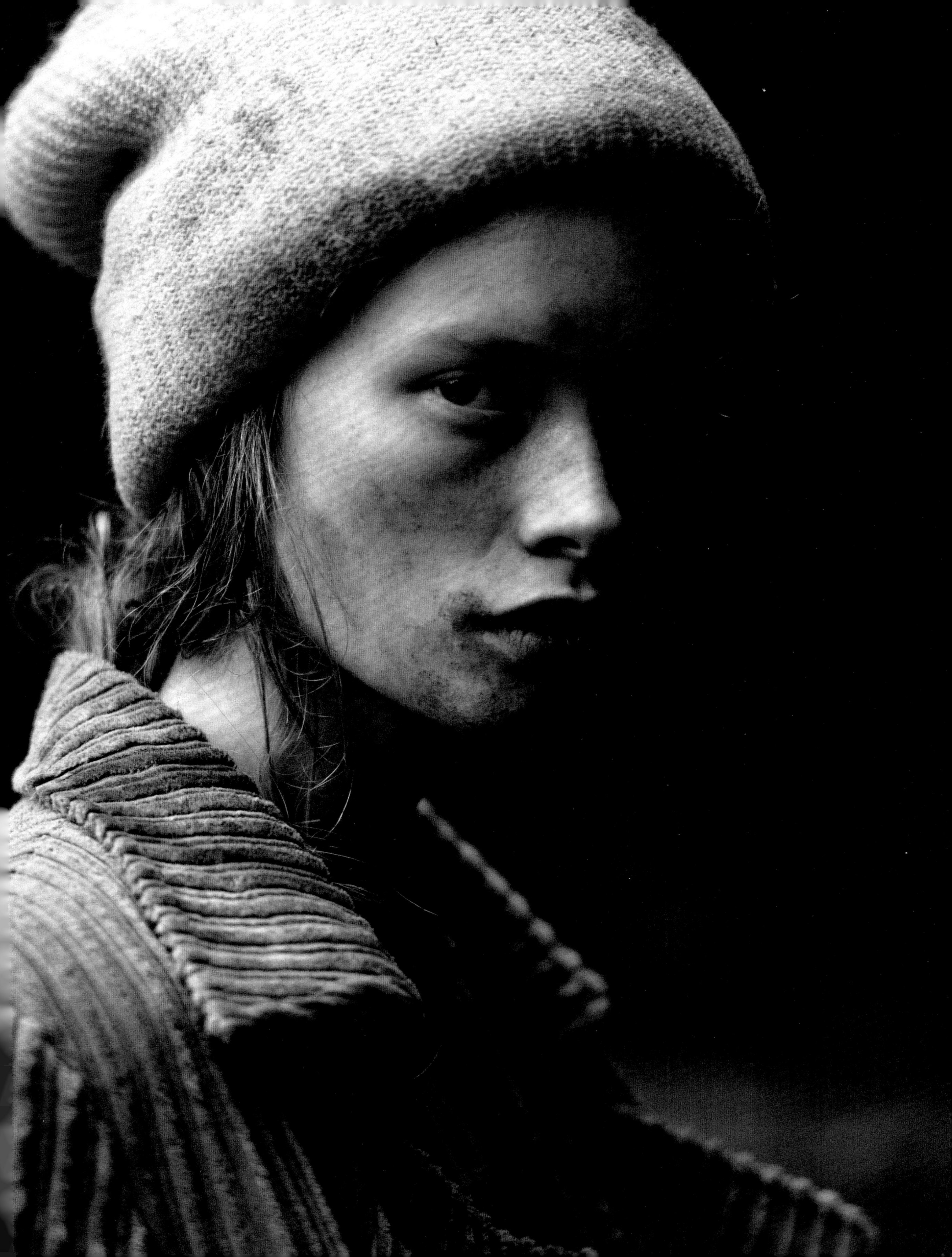

'Spring Forward'
for British *Vogue*, 2012
photography by Daniel Jackson
courtesy M.A.P.

In New York-based photographer Daniel Jackson's imagery, all the energies of fashion and art collide. Taking in the emotion and physicality inherent in the pursuit of looking good, Jackson does not disguise the less savoury aspects that simmer beneath the surface. Instead, these contrary forces explode out onto the page: sudden violence, sexual repression and the competitive jealousy of beautiful individuals in close proximity rip through photographs that otherwise have all the poise and restraint of Old Master paintings.

Amidst subdued tones sensitive to the subtleties of texture, light and shade, a sudden movement upsets a formal composition. Working with stylist Mattias Karlsson for the 2011 editorial 'Twilight of the Idols' for *AnOther Man*, the strained composure of a society banquet is pushed to breaking point (pages 134–35). The title of the shoot, riffing on Friedrich Nietzsche's philosophical diatribe of power and superiority of the same name, is suggestive of what follows – a sudden outburst over a society dining table. Force-feeding rubs up against gluttony in a scene that takes a Dickensian attitude towards the themes of food, society, repression and sexuality; Jackson's steady camera gorges on its visual symbolism. This sense of Victorian repression let loose is even more explicitly felt in the shoot 'It's My Party' for *Acne Paper* in 2010, where models pose and preen like peacocks, when their company allows (pages 132–33). But in this competitive environment, fights break out.

Jackson's women wrestle and tug at each other as they seek the spotlight. And, once they achieve it, the poses they adopt are not so much ones of dignified modesty as superior self-satisfaction.

The explicit energy of these shoots contrasts with a photographic style that seems best suited to a more classical form of portraiture, and it is this dichotomy that brings vitality to his less narrative-based work. When he is engaging directly with his subject and not satirising the effort of looking beautiful he is the master of this frozen moment, recapturing the timeless elegance of traditional portraiture through photography that focuses on the form of the body. The strength of Jackson's style ultimately lies in his aesthetic tendency towards subtle colours and texture reminiscent of paint on canvas. In a Winter 2008 shoot, also for *Acne Paper*, he imagines Guinevere Van Seenus as a model from the seventeenth-century Dutch Golden Age. In this classic composition, though, the humble serenity of her hunched pose belies the dangerous energy of her gaze. Even in these portraits, Jackson laces his images with the urgent force of the human condition, presenting a cool hand documenting a storm.

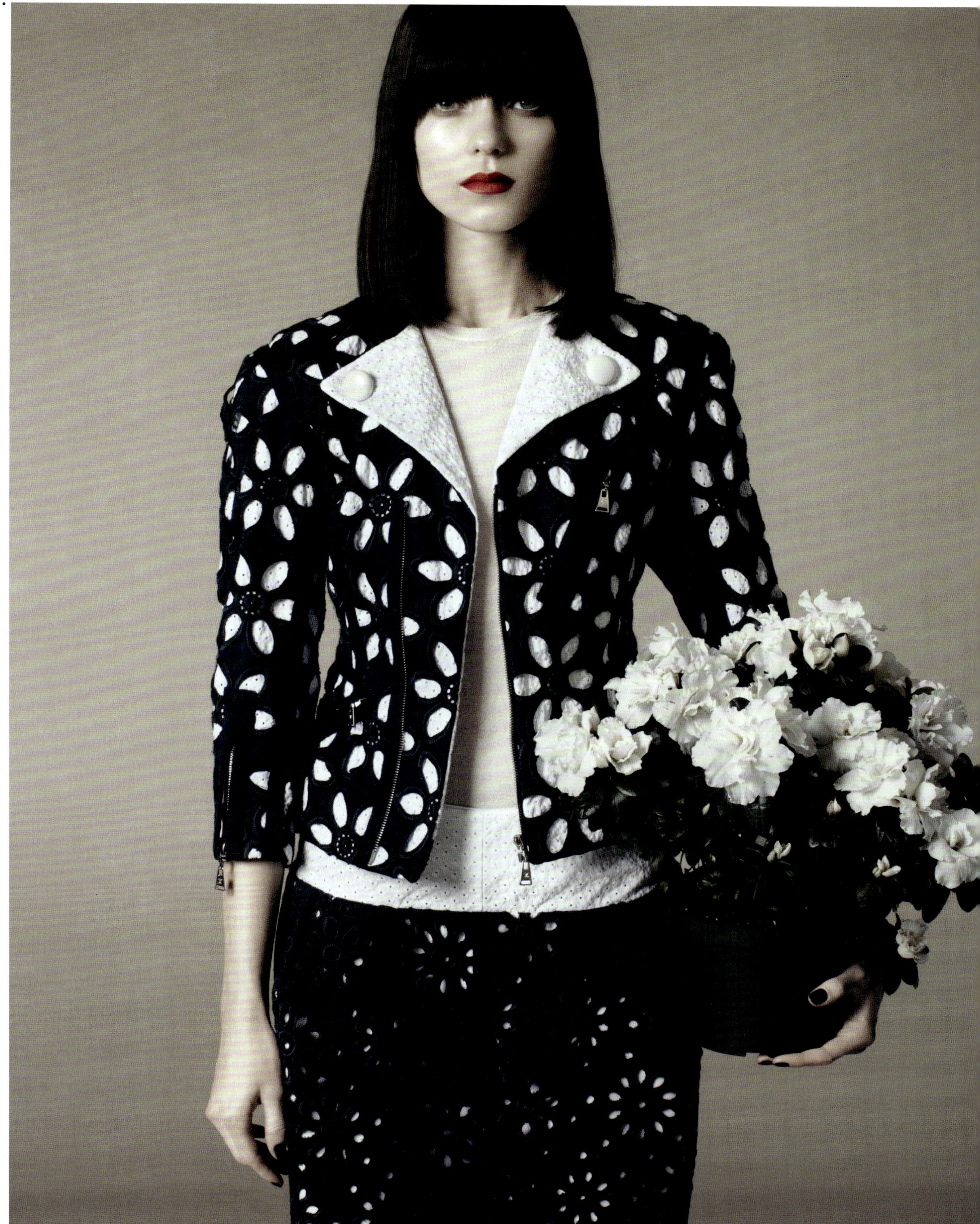

DANIEL JACKSON

'It's My Party' for *Acne Paper*, 2010
photography by Daniel Jackson
courtesy M.A.P.
styling by Mattias Karlsson

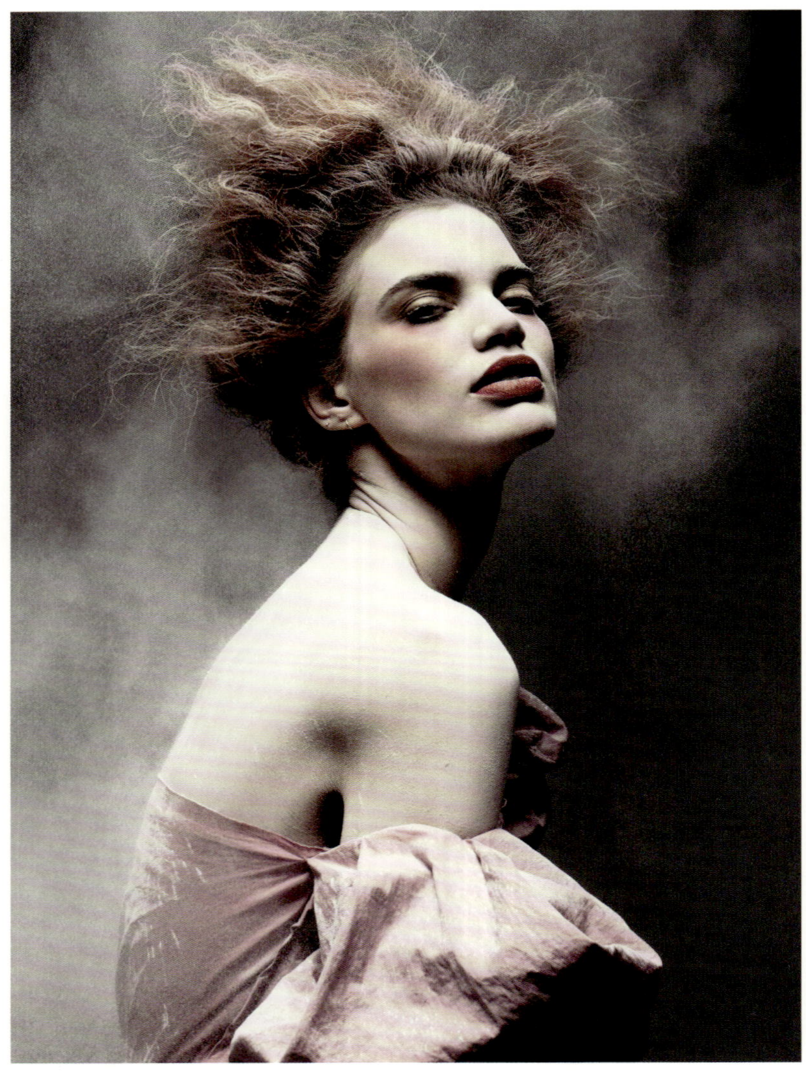 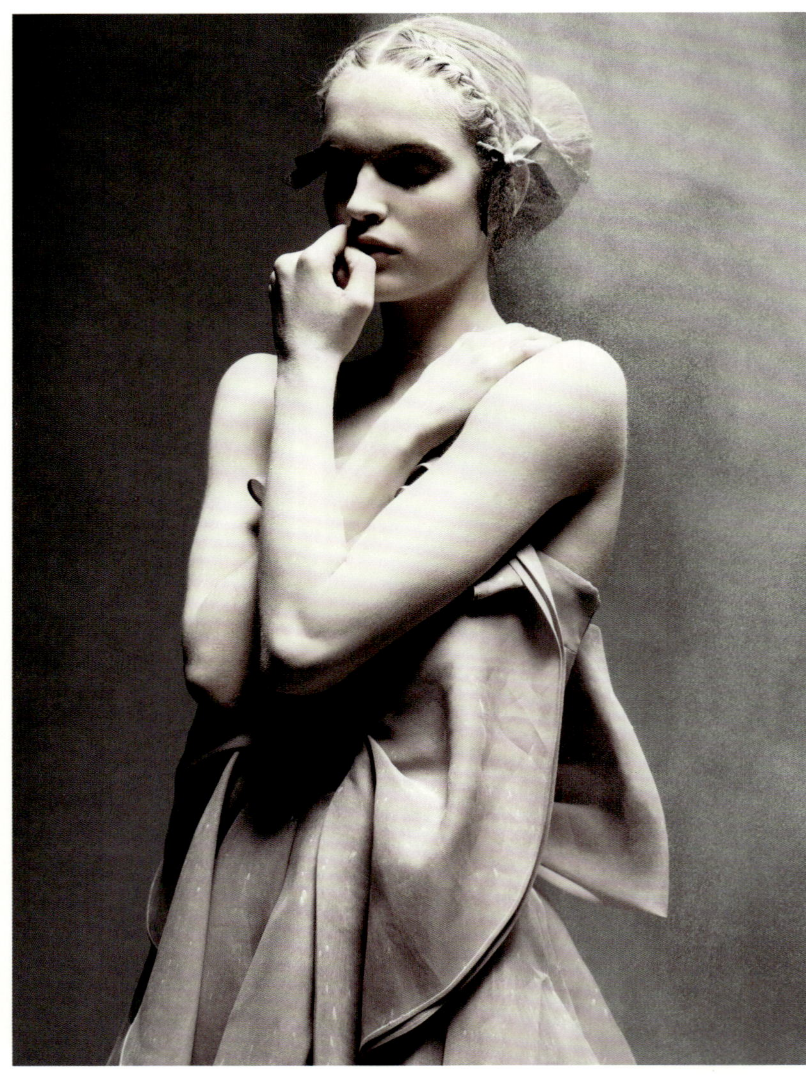

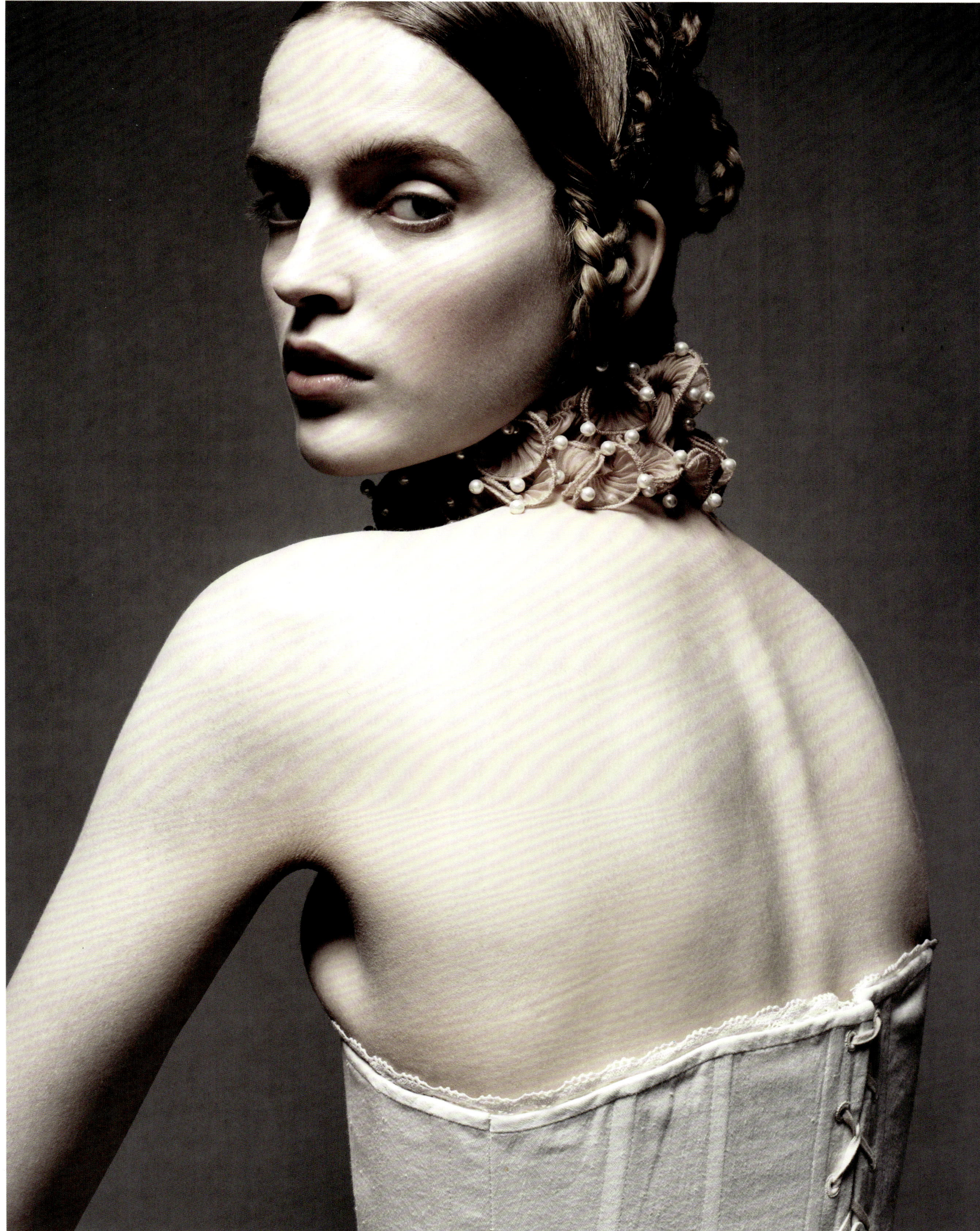

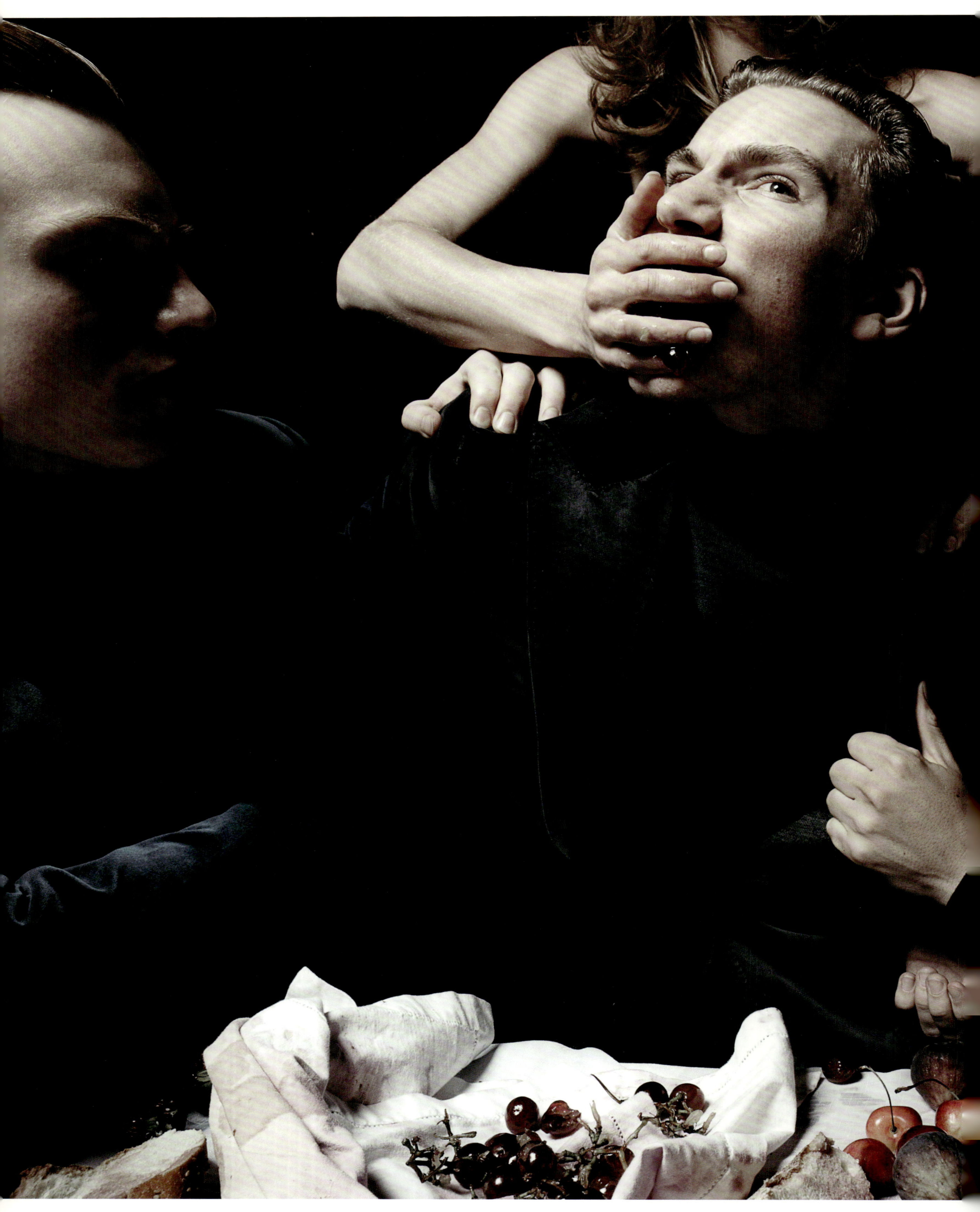

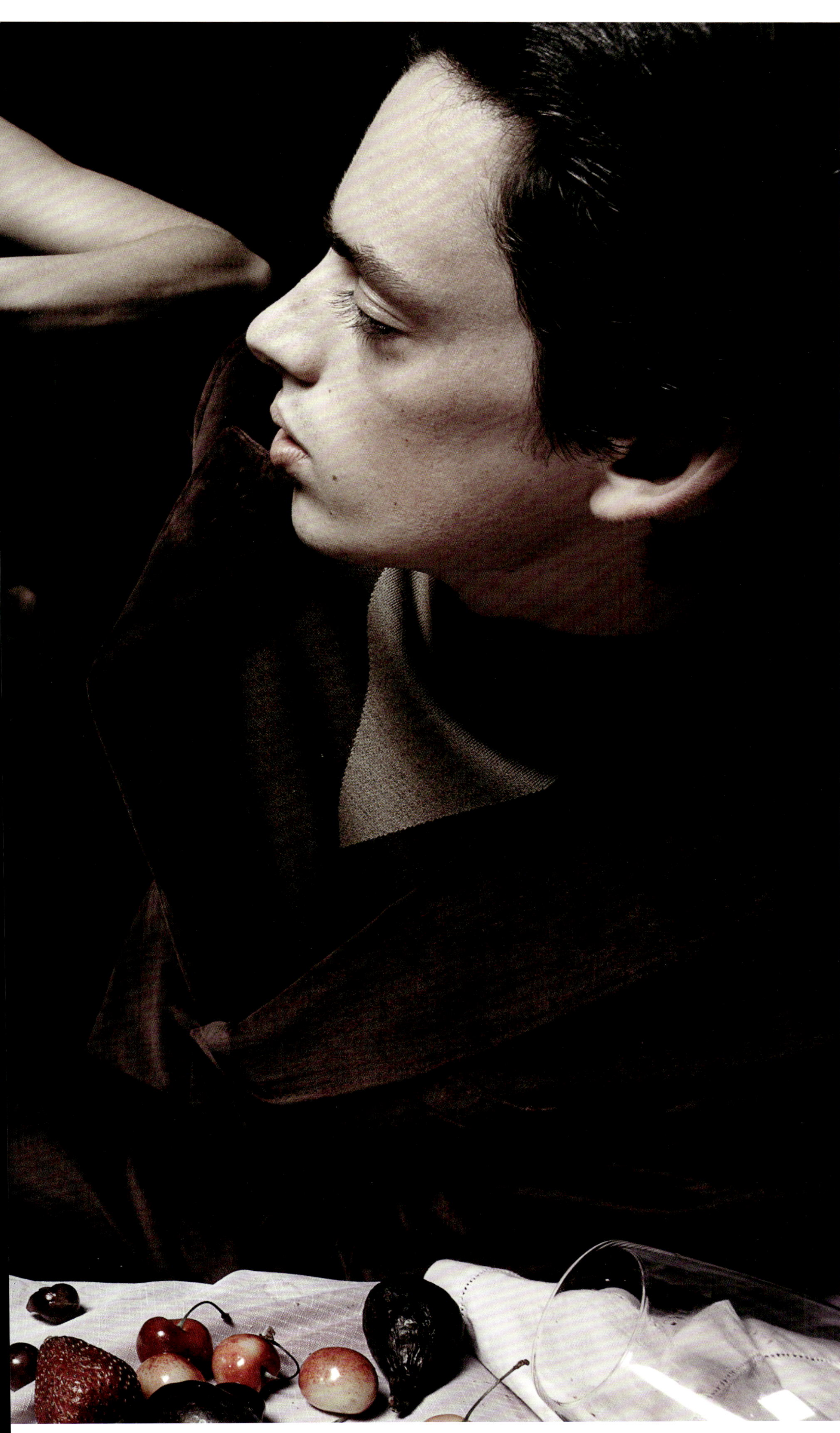

DANIEL JACKSON

'Twilight of the Idols'
for *An.Other Man*, 2011
photography by Daniel Jackson
styling by Mattias Karlsson
courtesy M.A.P.

WING SHYA

from *BIBA*, 2008
photography by Wing Shya
courtesy Wing Shya
styling by Kanako Bouelle

Hong Kong photographer and designer Wing Shya has created an imagined world that is fuelled by forbidden romance, his protagonists caught in cycles of fulfilment and desire. Shya's tonal range feeds on this subject matter – his camera moves in close on private encounters that burn red in darkened corners, or draws back to depict the lonely ambience of men and women amongst the neon-lit buildings of forgotten side streets. Applied to the work of fashion designers such as Rodarte, this approach breathes life into fragile forms, the deconstructed fabrics appearing almost as living extensions of the subjects themselves.

The depiction of urban souls trapped in narratives of longing allows Shya's images to extend beyond their own boundaries. In 'Pearls of the Orient' for *Time*, the enigma of the image suggests what might have existed in the past and what might occur in the future, implying a relationship or interaction much larger than the moment it presents (pages 138–39). Although the story remains untold and lives only in the mind of the viewer, the emotions are immediate and real. Again, Shya's understanding of dress enhances the reading: identities are written in garments that work as uniforms, serving to reveal an interior world enhanced by the relationships between the protagonists and their physical context. This approach is innately cinematic. Shya, who turned to fashion photography in 1997 after realising its potential during his work with filmmaker Wong Kar-wai, uses the techniques of film and photography interchangeably. When working with film, he imposes on it the timeless composure of his still imagery. His art direction

for Wong Kar-wai's *In the Mood for Love* in 2000 represents the approach at its most refined, playing out as a perfectly arranged photographic tableaux through which the director's characters move in a seductive dance of slow-burning eroticism.

With an eye informed by his simultaneous graphic design practice, Shya's images effortlessly embody the emotive qualities of colour, light and shadow. This awareness leads to experiments with technique that do not conform to convention – shooting for the YDC Hong Kong Young Fashion Designer's Contest in 2012, Shya substitutes professional lighting for low-budget Christmas lights to create a cruder, more convincing effect. The decision to use 'found' equipment in place of a more technical setup is indicative of an approach that is intuitive and responsive rather than calculated, a by-product of a temperament that Shya locates in his art school education, which causes him to look for beauty in deliberately contrary places. This experimental journey also comes through in his relationships with the people he shoots. His work with Maggie Cheung, a model who has evolved alongside his aesthetic, demonstrates this essential interaction. Over many years, each portrait of Cheung is new and distinct, as if she is reborn again and again through the photographer's lens. This is a perpetual revelation of a multi-faceted concept of personal identity, representative of the constant mutation of ideas that embodies the artist's search itself.

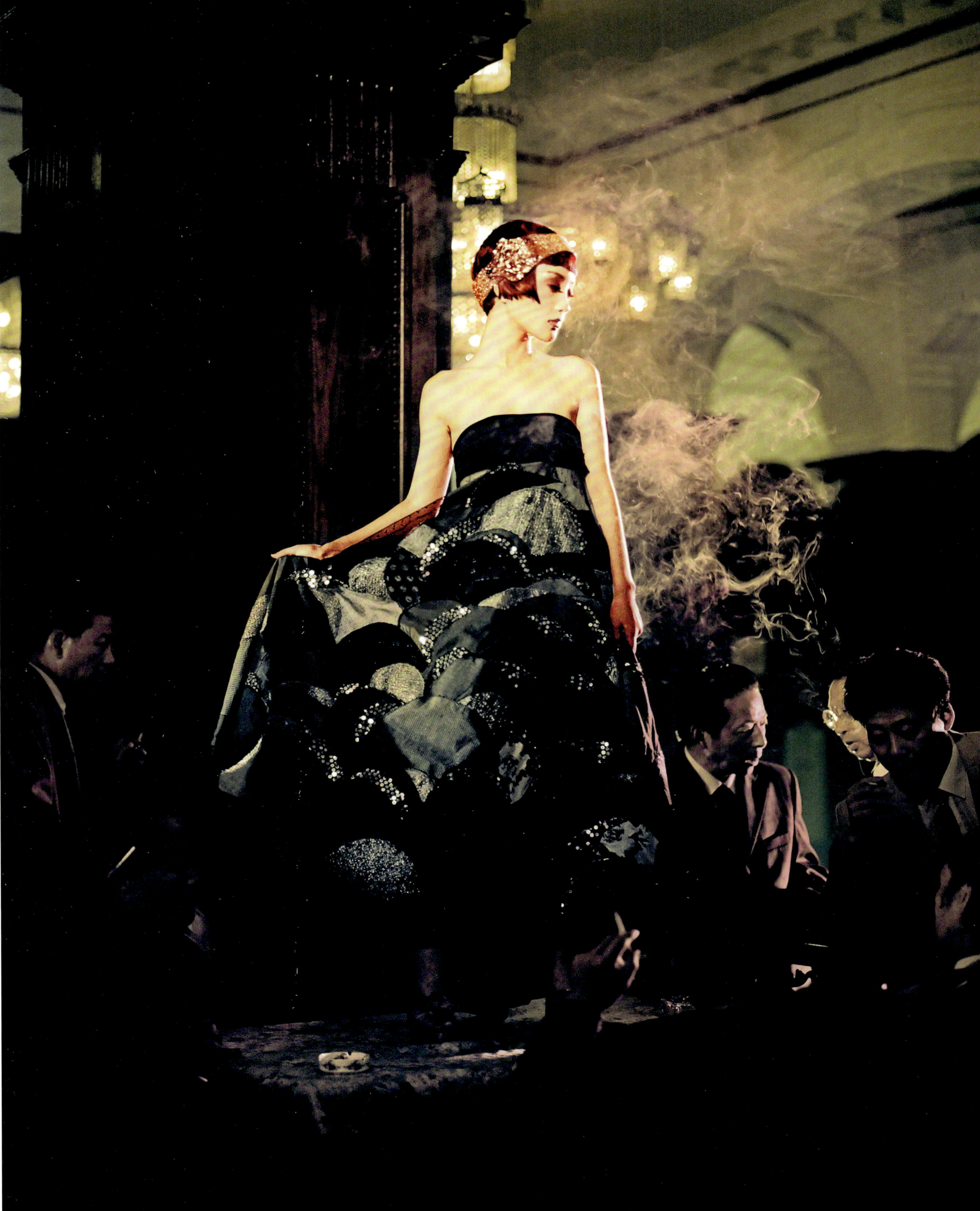

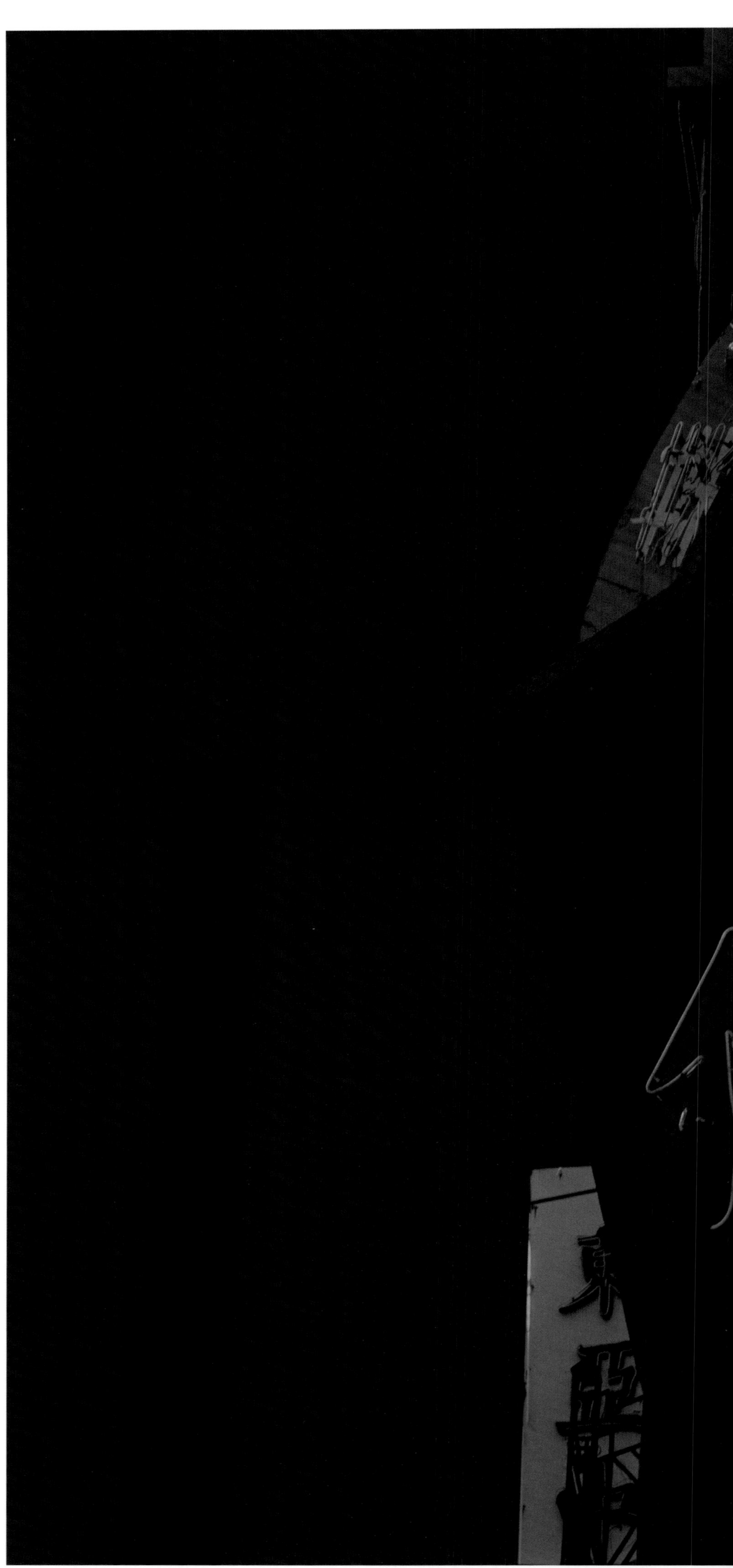

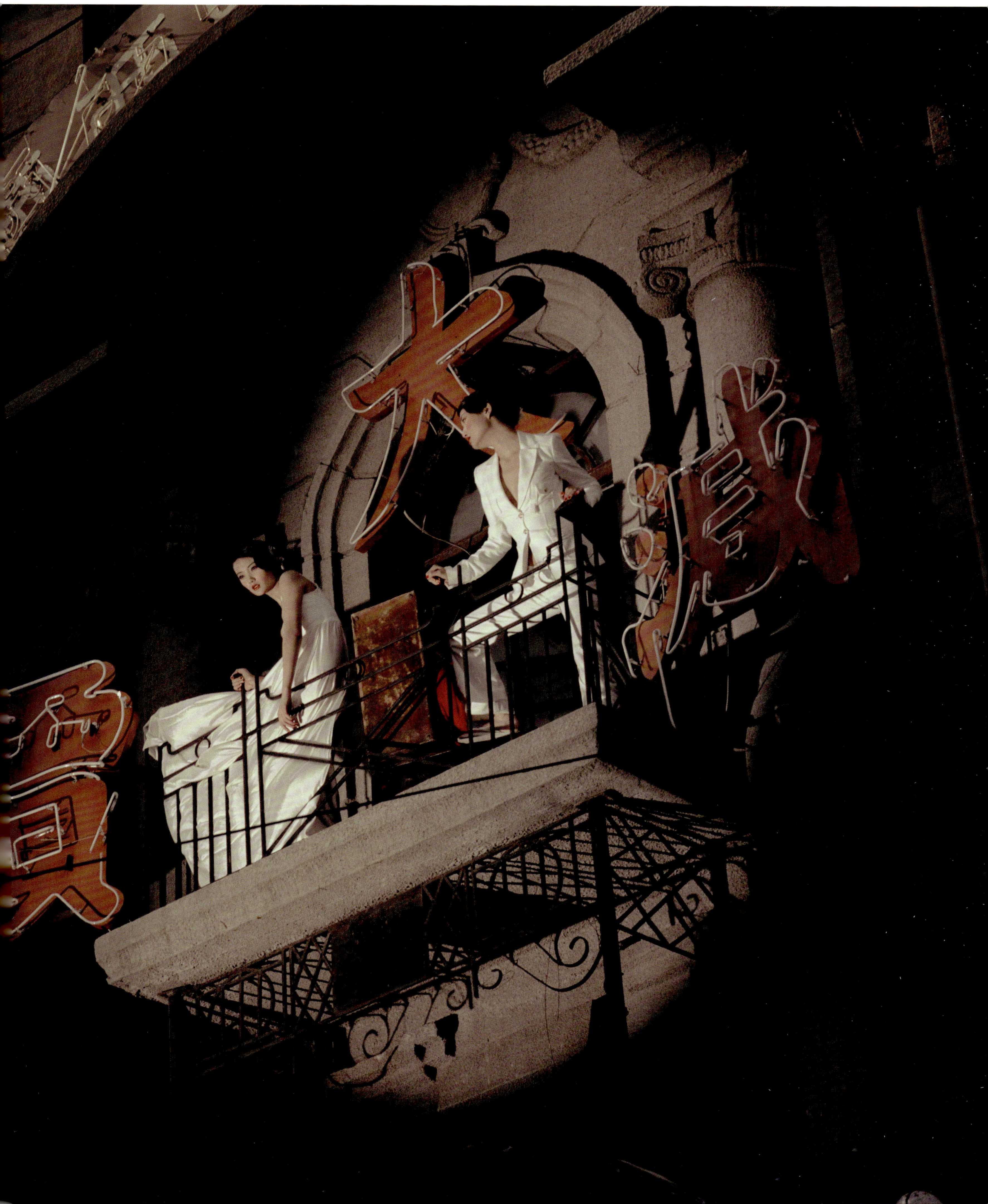

大
飯
店

WING SHYA

Shu Qi and Daniel for *i-D*, 2002
The Independent Issue
photography by Wing Shya
courtesy Wing Shya
styling by Kanako B Koga

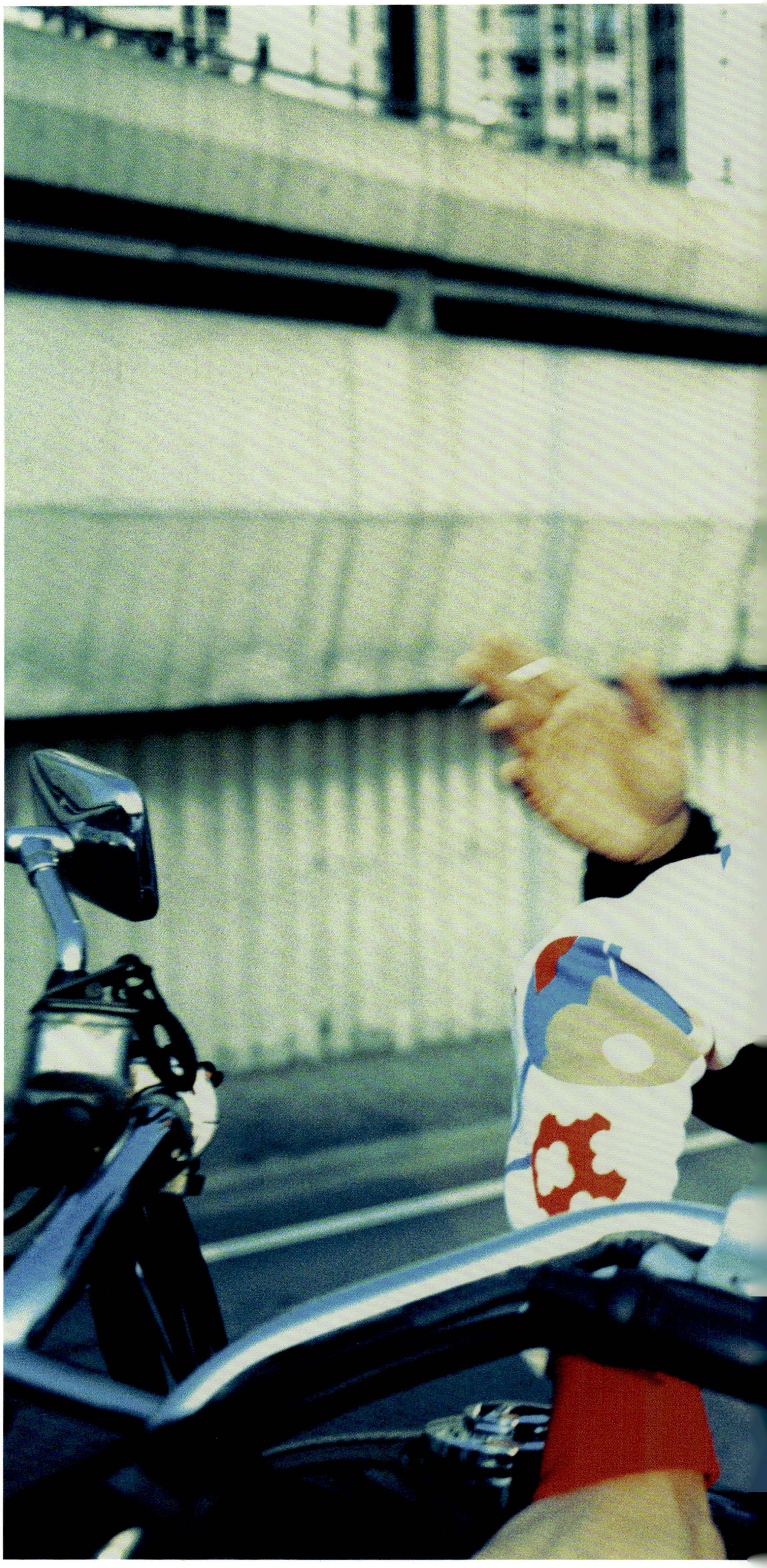

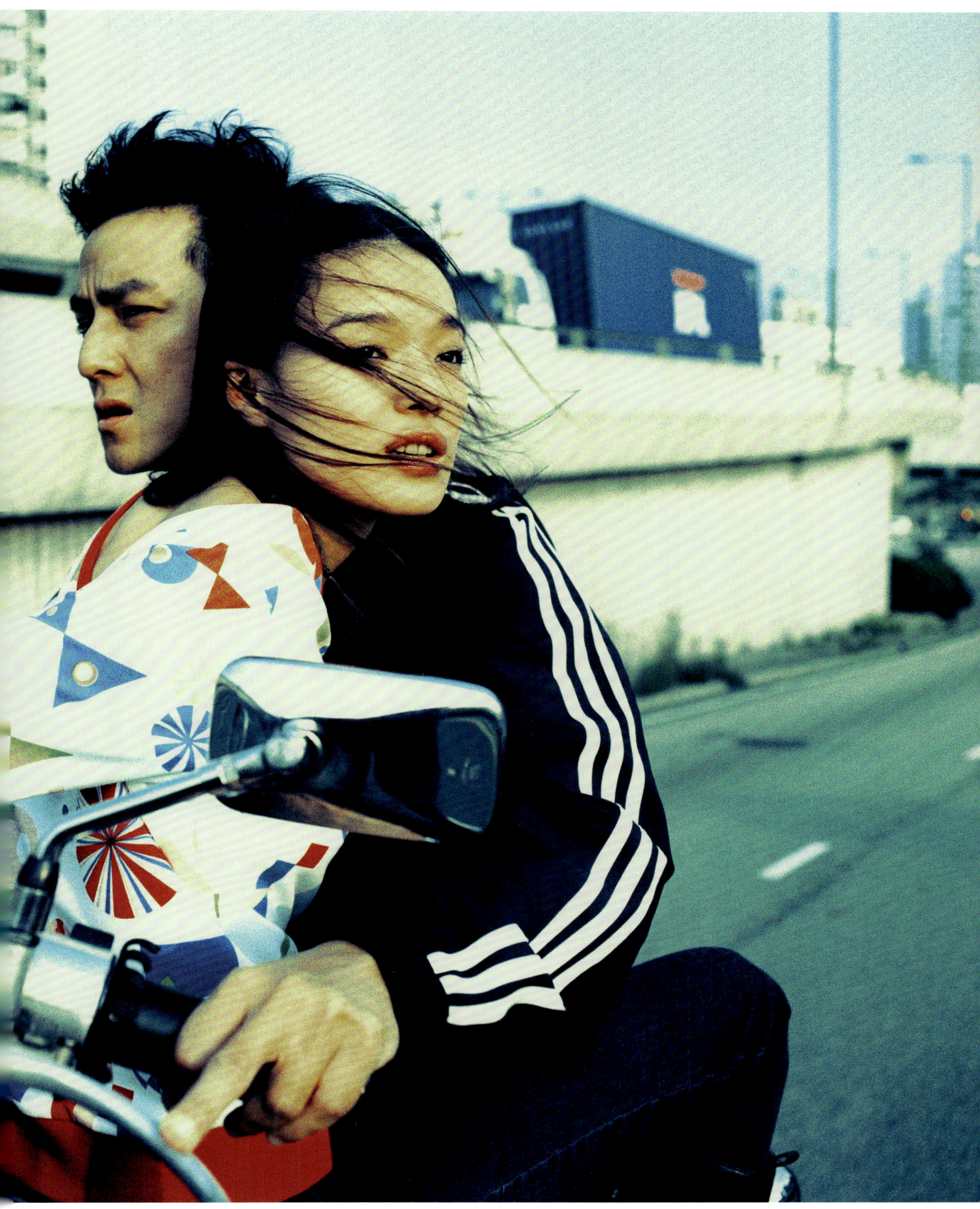

from 'Bonnie and Clyde' for *LoveCat*, 2010
photography by Aram Bedrossian
courtesy Aram Bedrossian
styling by Carissa Cirino

San Francisco's Aram Bedrossian has a talent for narrative and he weaves it effortlessly into nostalgic shoots that echo vintage cinema. From the direct referencing of cult film scenes to the more indirect exploitation of the language and symbolism of genre fiction, Bedrossian's world is one of seductive women playing dangerous games in a romanticised world of intrigue.

Bedrossian's love affair with the visual sensibility of film takes diverse forms. Motivated by a belief that new ideas grow out of a revisionist approach to old, he bathes his breakthrough 2010 shoot 'Bonnie and Clyde' for *LoveCat* in the bleached-out bliss of a sun-drenched America (pages 143–47). Deploying the imagery of retro diners and classic cars he casts the pair as the beguiling anti-heroes first conceived in Arthur Penn's definitive movie. This is fashion as unashamed escapism and a perfect vehicle for the Paul Smith and Ralph Lauren designs worn by his models. In 'Body Double', also for *LoveCat*, the atmosphere is darker and more intense, tapping into the world of the suspense thriller. Bedrossian's tendency towards guns and glamour here is more reminiscent of an eroticised Ian Fleming novel than a Hollywood film reel.

Alongside these narrative-driven shoots Bedrossian experiments with a more direct form of portraiture that brims with ferocious potential. Whether it is Nicole Trunfio gnawing at a sawn-off rabbit's foot or Camilla Hansen appearing in extreme close-up with a bullet between her teeth, Bedrossian brings out an unrestrained sensual energy in his models as he once again dresses them in symbolism from his cineaste imagination. His style, rooted in early experiences working under director Taj Stansberry, may seek beauty through escapist fantasy, but it is directed by an eye that is drawn towards authenticity in image-making. His shots feel like private photographs, their analogue finish a result of a conscious decision to shoot medium-format film. Using a Hasselblad 500 c/m and Mamiya RZ67 Pro II in resistance to digital, Bedrossian sees the traditional process of shooting and developing film as a curb on excessive retouching and a gateway to a more convincing reflection of the exact moment. It works as a dynamic counterpoint to the magical otherworldliness of shoots such as 'We Were Once a Fairytale', enhancing their romanticism. In these, he responds intuitively to a perceptive awareness of his surroundings, keeping his photographs loose and not too wedded to the sense of narrative they embrace. Bedrossian's style may exhibit an infatuation with the compelling illusions of pulp cinema but it is always anchored by a sensitivity to the personality of his models and to the environments in which he shoots.

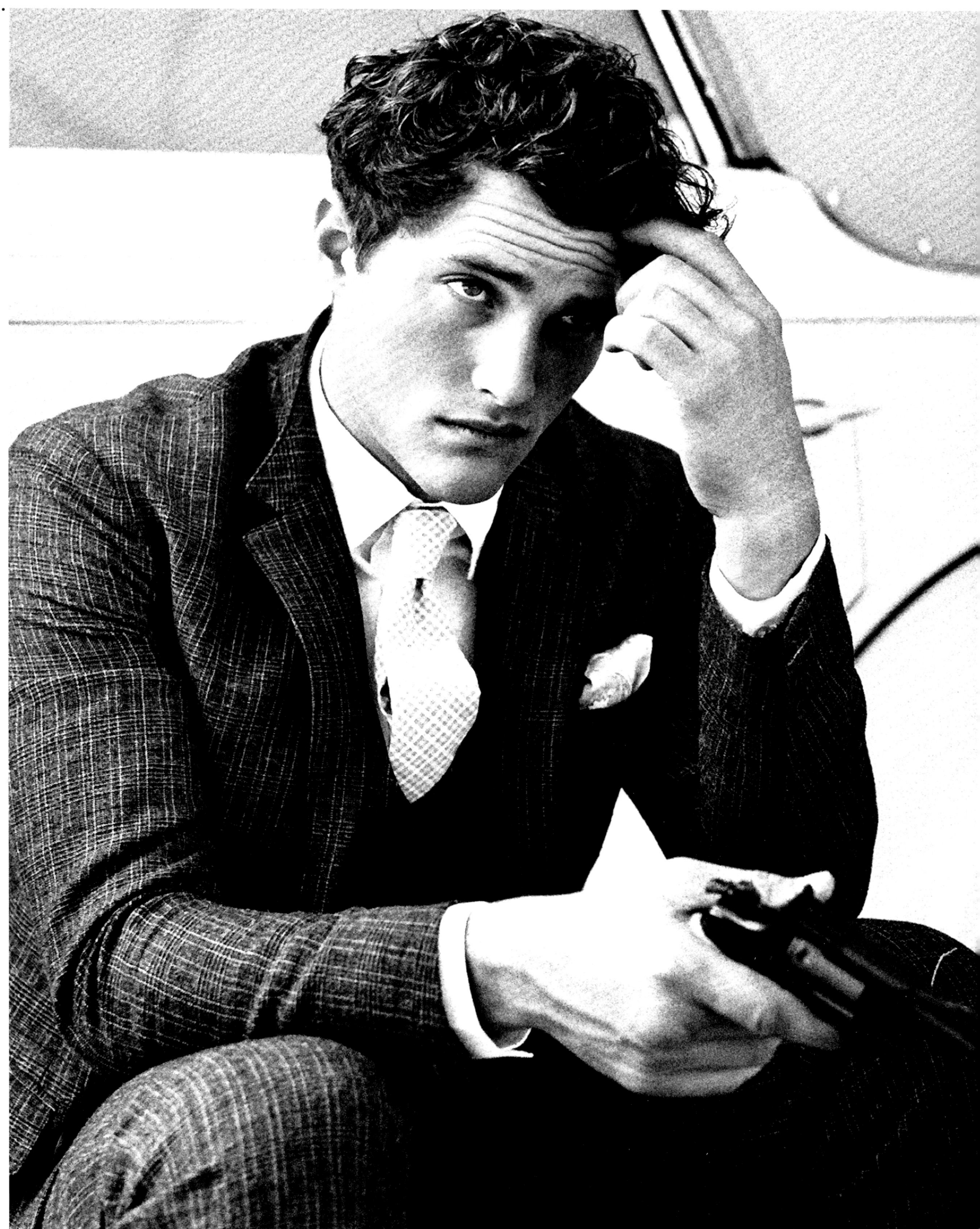

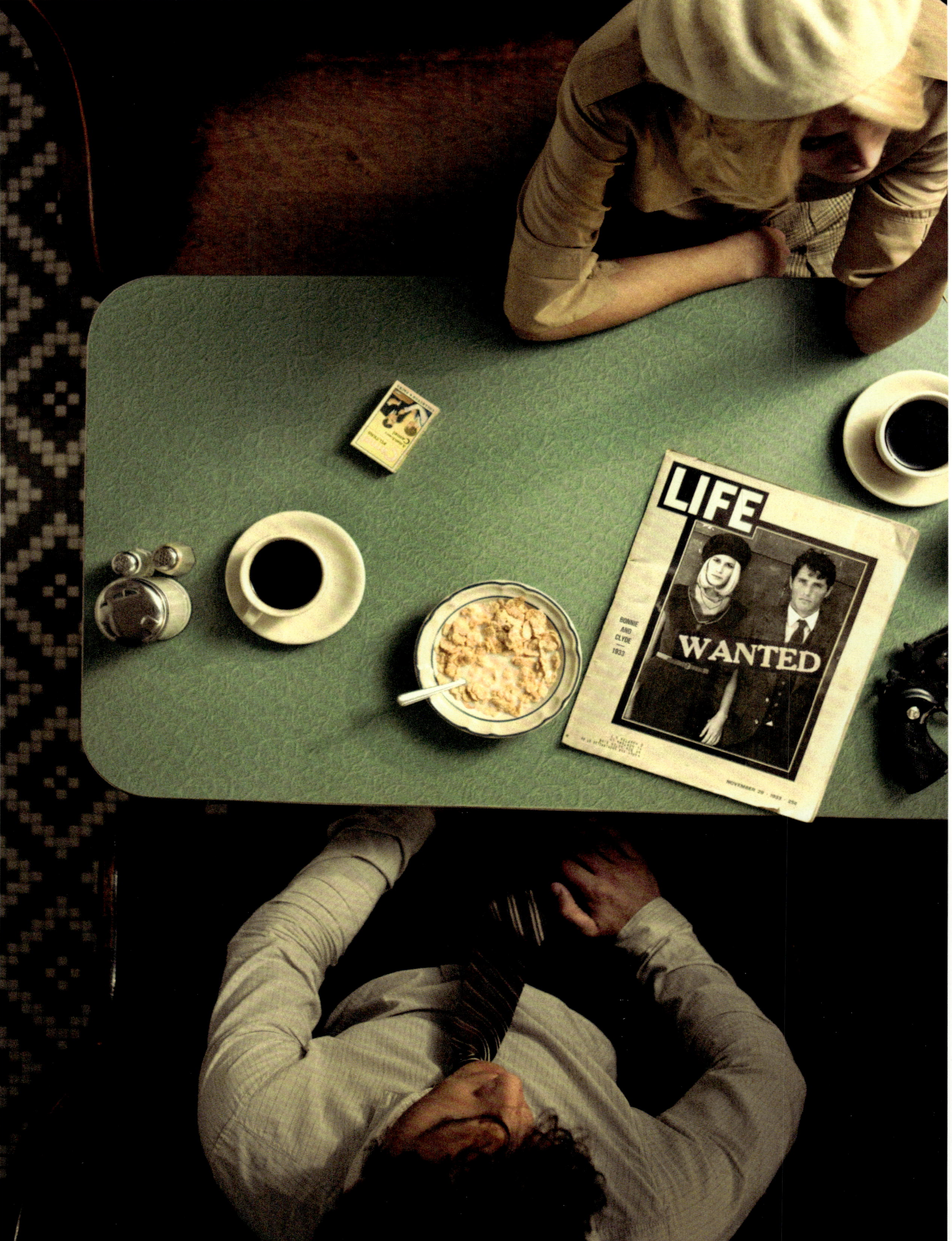
LIFE
BONNIE
AND
CLYDE
1933
WANTED
NOVEMBER 28 · 1933 · 25¢

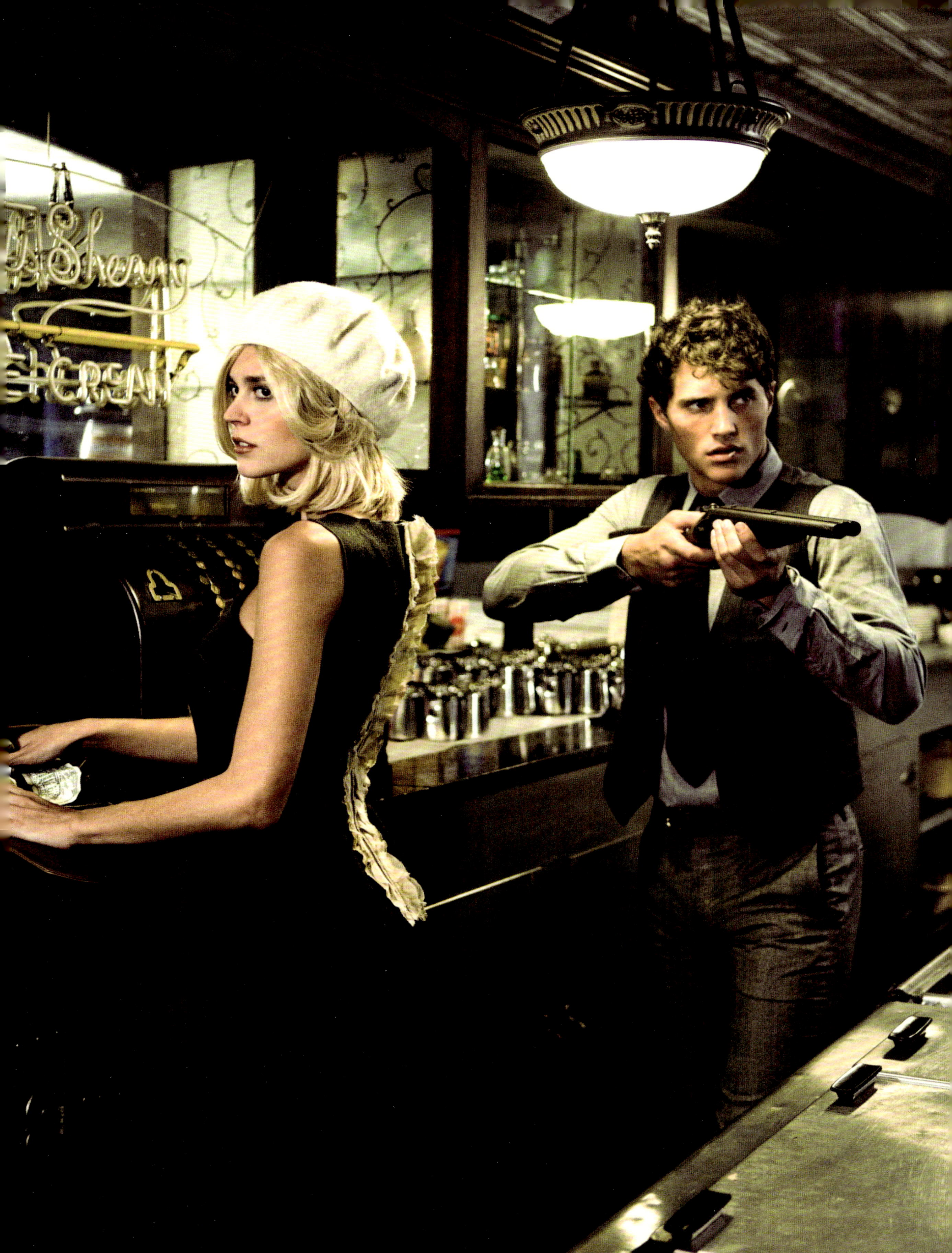
Fresh
Cream

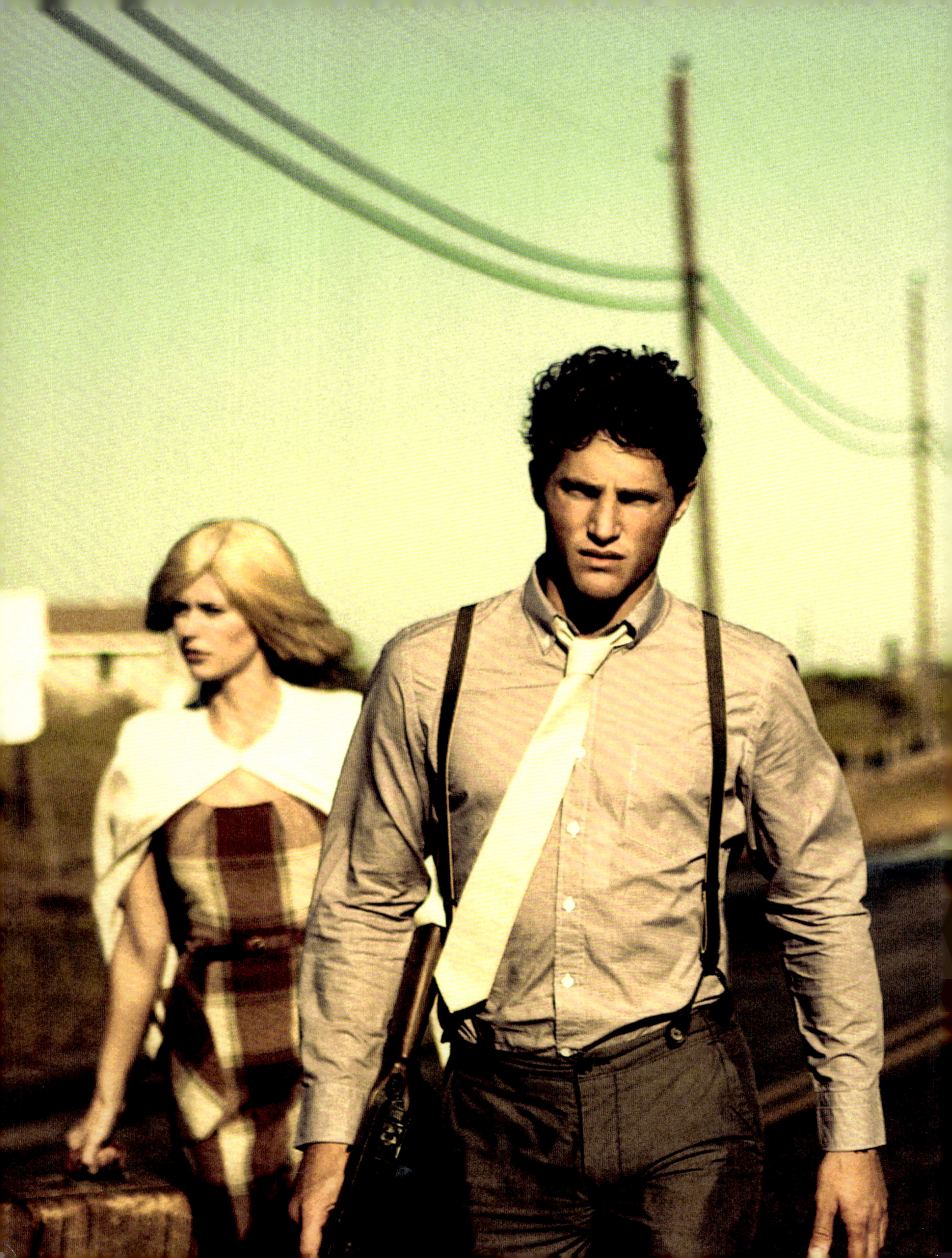

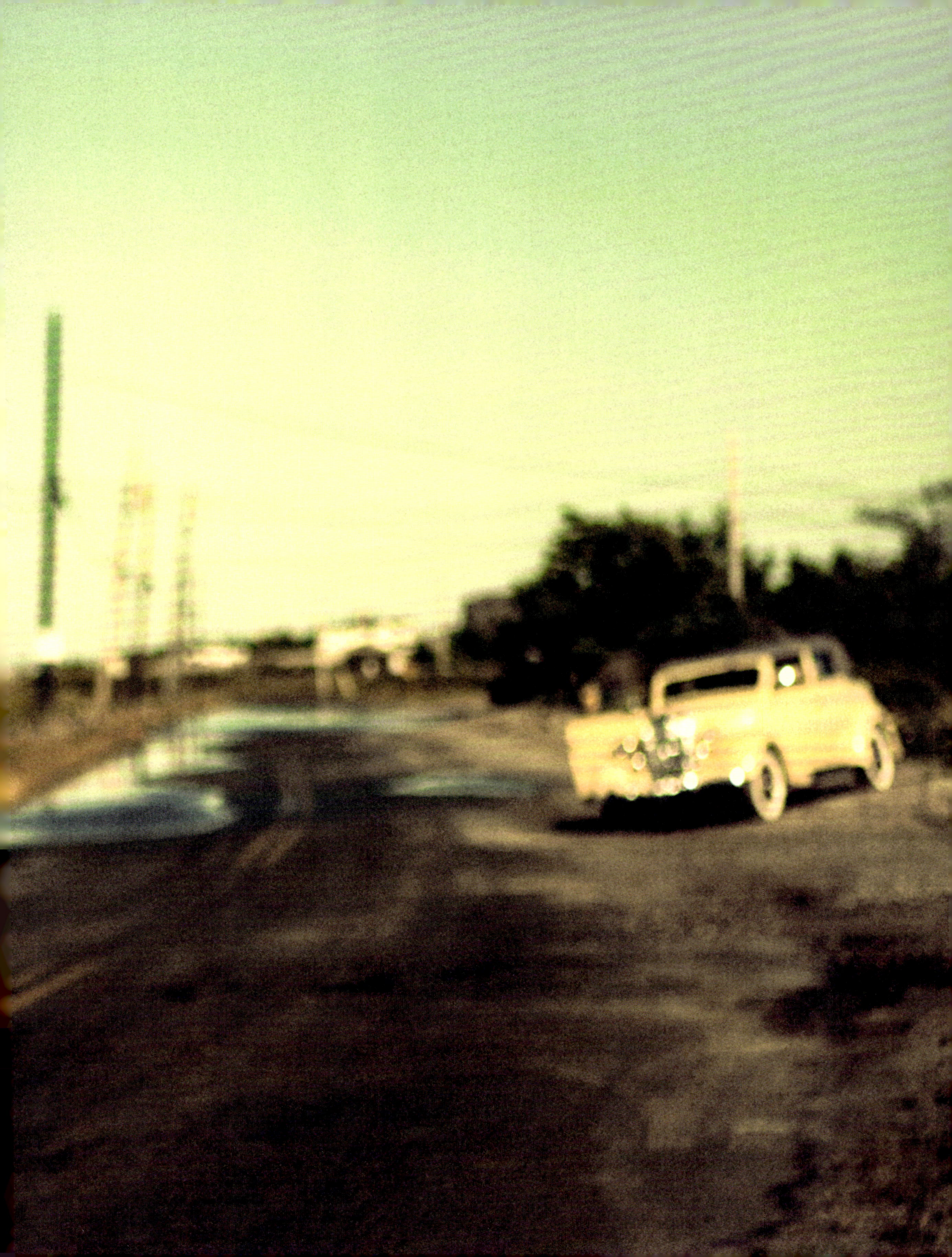

TAKAHIRO OGAWA

RJ King for *WestEast*, 2012
photography by Takahiro Ogawa
courtesy Takahiro Ogawa
styling by Takayuki Sekiya

pages 150–51:
for Asia Beauty Expo, 2010
photography by Takahiro Ogawa
courtesy Takahiro Ogawa
hair by Peter Gray and Masa Honda
styling by Nicola Formichetti
Katie Shillingford and Robbie Spencer

pages 152–53:
'I Don't Know How I am' for *Metal*, 2010
photography by Takahiro Ogawa
courtesy Takahiro Ogawa

The style of Takahiro Ogawa has a stripped-back clarity that suggests a love for the construction and formal aspects of well-executed fashion. Ogawa's shoots accentuate the structure and shape of garments and bring out their mood through an attention to the transcendent elements of their design. At the same time there is a freshness to his images; they are never too clean, never too composed, and have a lightness of touch that works in harmony with what is predominantly a minimalist aesthetic.

At its most stripped down, Ogawa's style brings out form as abstract architecture. In the shoot 'Hiding Theme' for the magazine *And*, he captures the fashion of Yohji Yamamoto, Rick Owens and Anne Demeulemeester, distilling his images down to the fundamentals of the designers' edge and line, while exploiting the starkness of black and white to create a strong sense of atmosphere from the simplest of elements. At the same time his grasp of pose and composition has the capacity to realise these as moments of theatre. Collaborating with art director Kazuya Goan and stylists Nicola Formichetti and Katie Shillingford to show off a display of extreme hair by Peter Gray and Masa Honda at Asia Beauty Expo in 2010, Ogawa captures the drama of fashion in artfully rendered scenes reminiscent of a Surrealist stage set (pages 150–51).

Ogawa's taste for the theatrical crosses over into punk attitude in his shoot of Harry Wakefield for the series 'I Don't Know How I Am' for *Metal* magazine, in which hair and facial adornment once again are the focus of attention (pages 152–53). Here the face is obscured by rough-cut hair, and despite the simplicity of the images Ogawa ensures that they maintain a coarse physicality. The process is exposed too: flecks of cut hair lie untidily on the model's shoulders, introducing a vitality to these otherwise careful compositions.

Born in Sendai and graduating from Tohoku University of Art and Design in Japan, Ogawa's design background comes through in the clean lines and sense of definition that make up his arrangements. He has mastered photography through restraint. His shots are reduced to their most essential elements and, although there is a self-assured energy at work, it is unpretentious and engaging. The images are not over-processed and looking at them conveys a sense of liberation and excitement. There is a sense that fashion can be all about the beauty of fabric and form, free from the negative forces of an unattainable philosophy of aspiration.

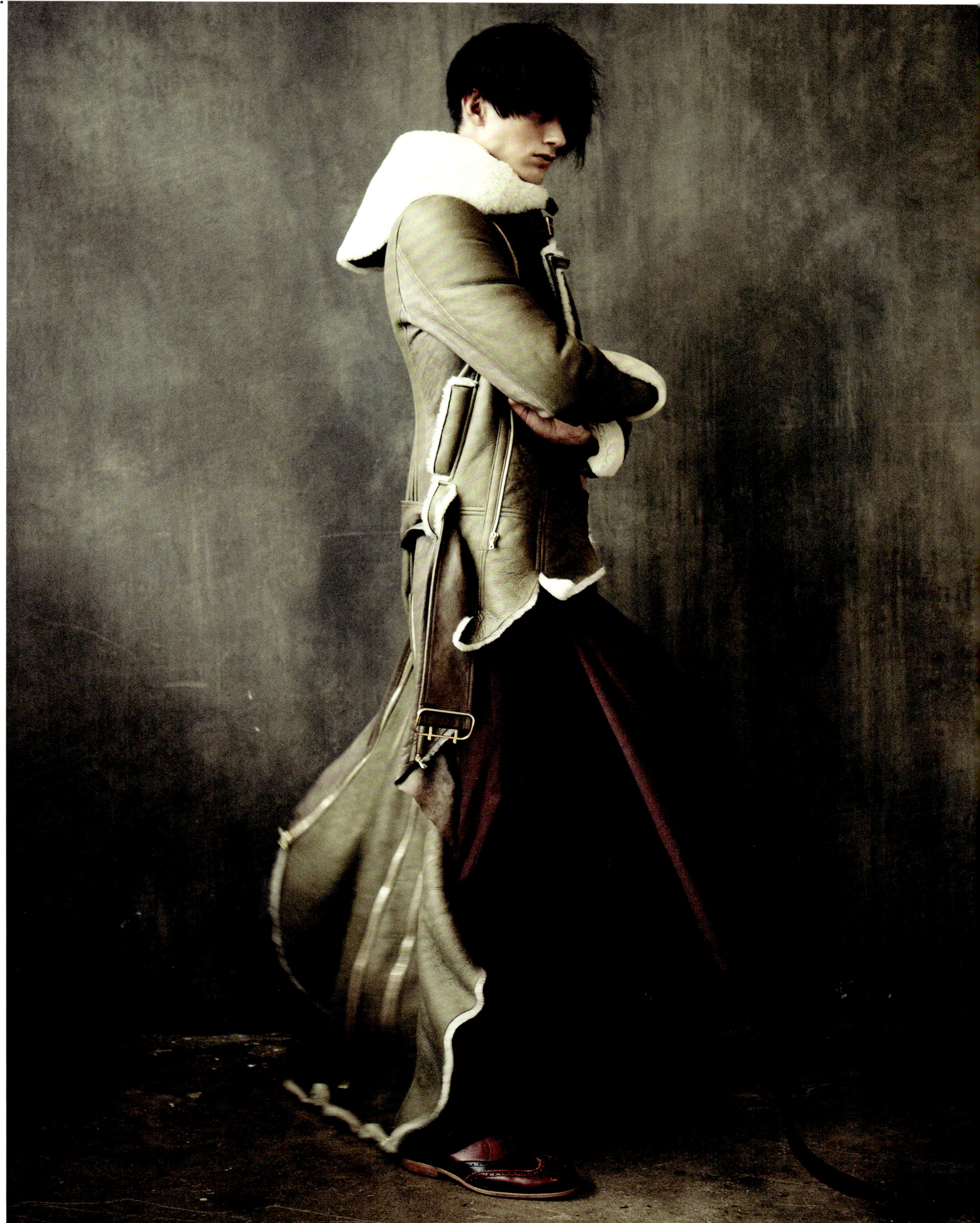

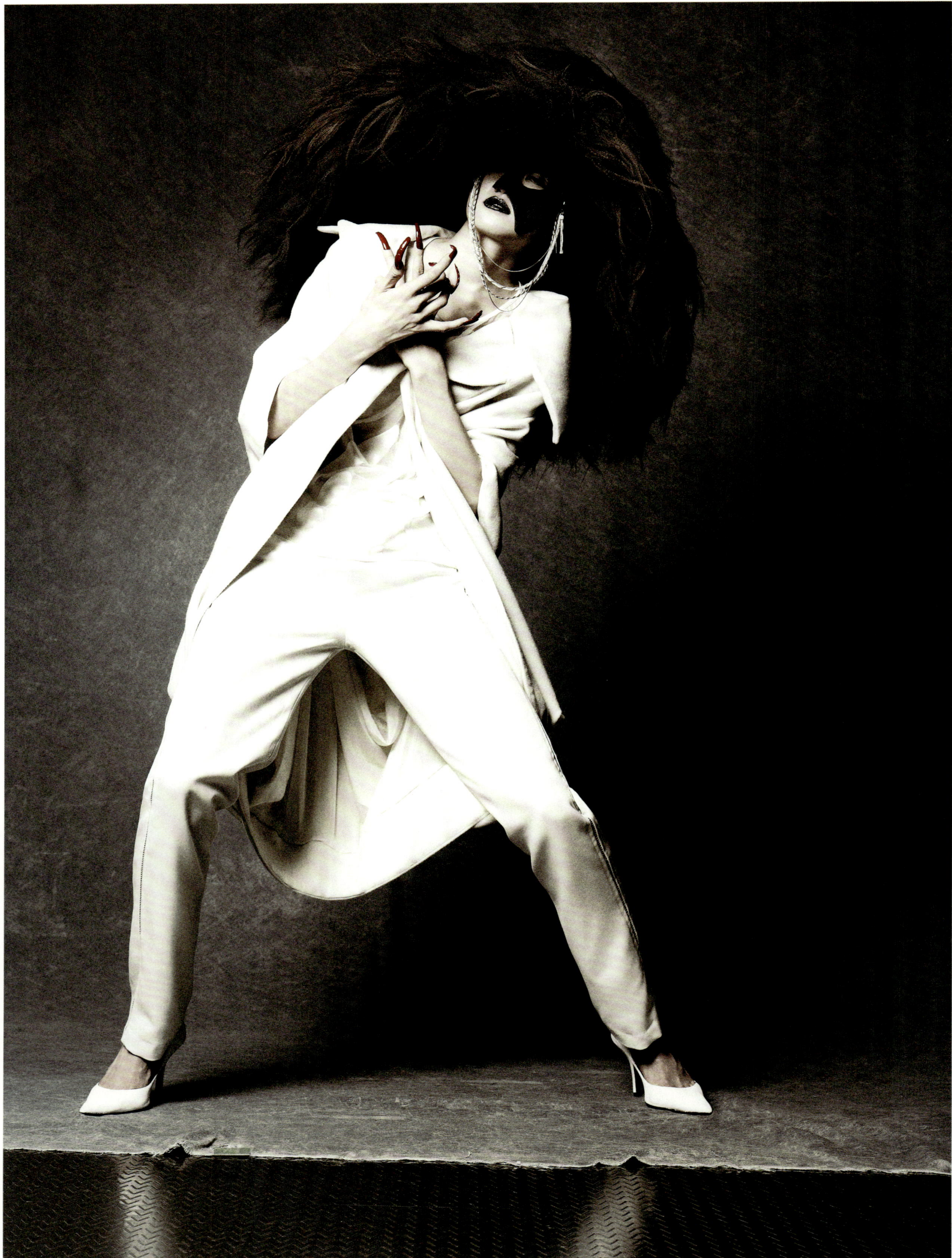

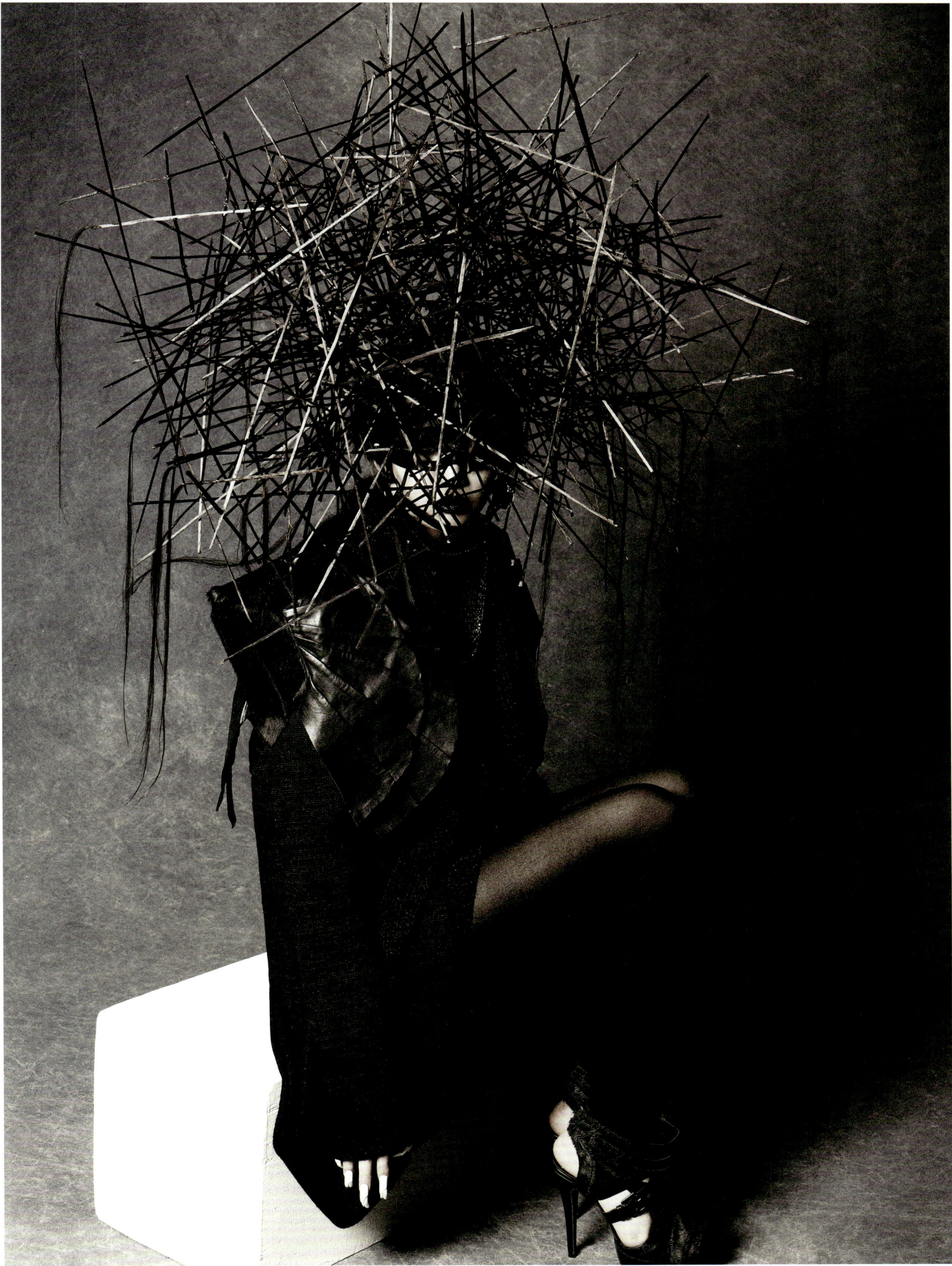

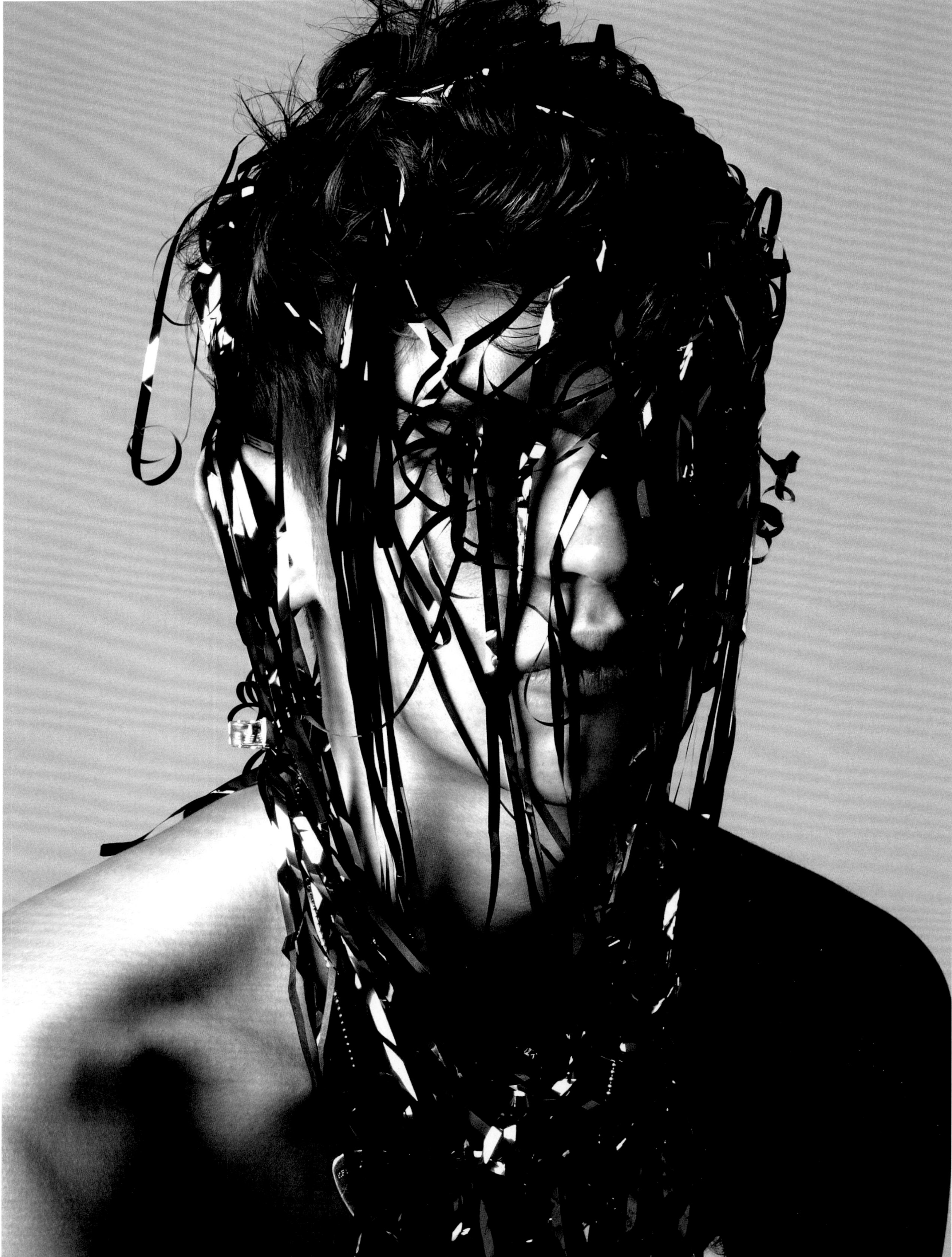

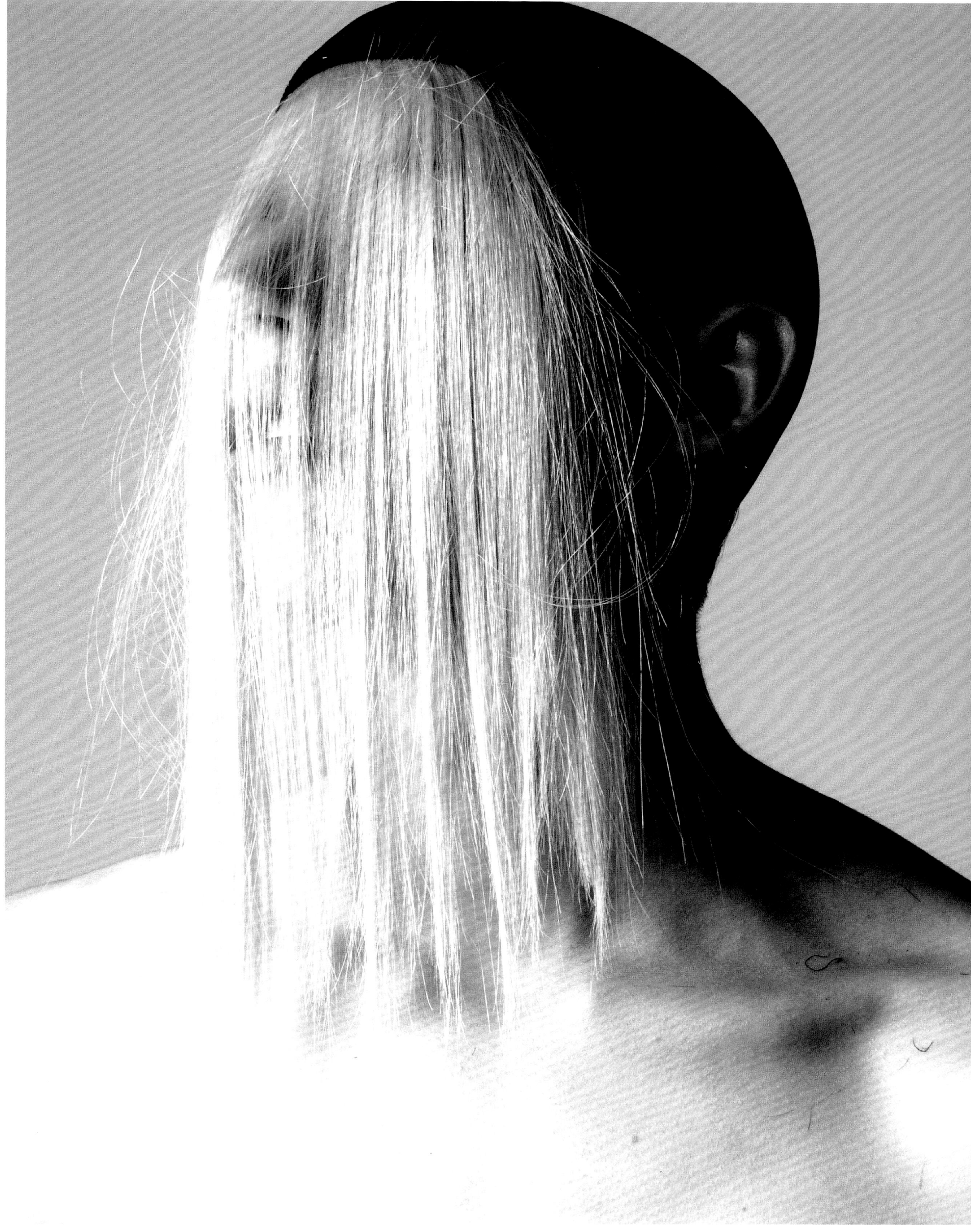

SEAN ELLIS

For *i-D*, 2005
photography by Sean Ellis
courtesy Sean Ellis

Traversing two disciplines, the fashion world of UK photographer-turned-filmmaker Sean Ellis is charged with the drama of his cinematography. Pioneering an early trend for the macabre in the pages of *The Face* during the 1990s, Ellis's favoured subject matter is often dangerous. Sex and war, performance and voyeurism: there is always an attitude to his photography that gravitates towards the forces of lust and conflict, either through epic intensity or claustrophobic intimacy.

Drawn to subjects such as cult Japanese director Takeshi Kitano and shooting fashion for *Harper's Bazaar* in collaboration with auteur David Lynch, Ellis's early photographic work anticipates his subsequent sidestep into film. Debuting with the psychological horror *Left Turn* in 2001 and following up with the Oscar-nominated *Cashback* in 2006, cinema has in turn informed his fashion photography in the twenty-first century. The potential energy that loads his imagery comes from the moment in film that precedes an explosive event. In the moving image, a pregnant sense of anticipation winds up over a period of time, but in Ellis's photography this moment is compressed into a single frozen frame, the threat or promise of what is to come dictating its emotional immediacy. The 2010 *GQ* shoot 'Paths of Glory' takes this cinematic starting point in a more literal direction, aping authentic footage from the frontline of war in a glamourising series set on a contemporary battlefield (pages 156–57). Capturing his subject in blurred snapshots through the detritus of an urban battleground, the energy of warfare and its associations are revisited as Ellis draws upon a theme he first explored a decade earlier.

Testing the boundaries of fashion taste in the 1990s, Ellis enjoyed a collaborative period with Isabella Blow that culminated in his epic 1998 set piece in which a medieval Alexander McQueen appears bruised and bloodied on the field of battle. Another breakthrough shoot, 'A Taste of Arsenic', also for *The Face*, displays a similar fearlessness in its desire to harness unexpected threat. Stalked by autonomous children darkly clad in Victorian attire, the provocative shoot gives power to those it depicts as they express themselves outside adult intervention. The dark shadows and bursts of light that give drama to these photographs owe a debt to Ellis's training as a still-life photographer in Brighton in his early twenties. Experimental editorials such as his psychedelic 2003 series for *Surface* explore the potential of colour and light further, utilising the effects of coloured fluid to mutate the form of the body (pages 160–61). The editorial has a graphic clarity that at first glance appears to be the result of digital post-production, but the process is more manual than that, the artificial effects owing as much to considered illumination and a hands-on cut-and-paste approach that leaves a raw finish to the surface.

Ellis's approach is not always dark and combative. Offsetting it is a more sensitive, personal photography visible in his two books, *365* and, more recently, *Kubrick the Dog*, of 2011. A series of photographs depicting the glamorous lifestyle of Ellis's pet as it interacts with the people in his life, *Kubrick the Dog* offers an alternative biography of the photographer himself through the eyes of his former canine companion.

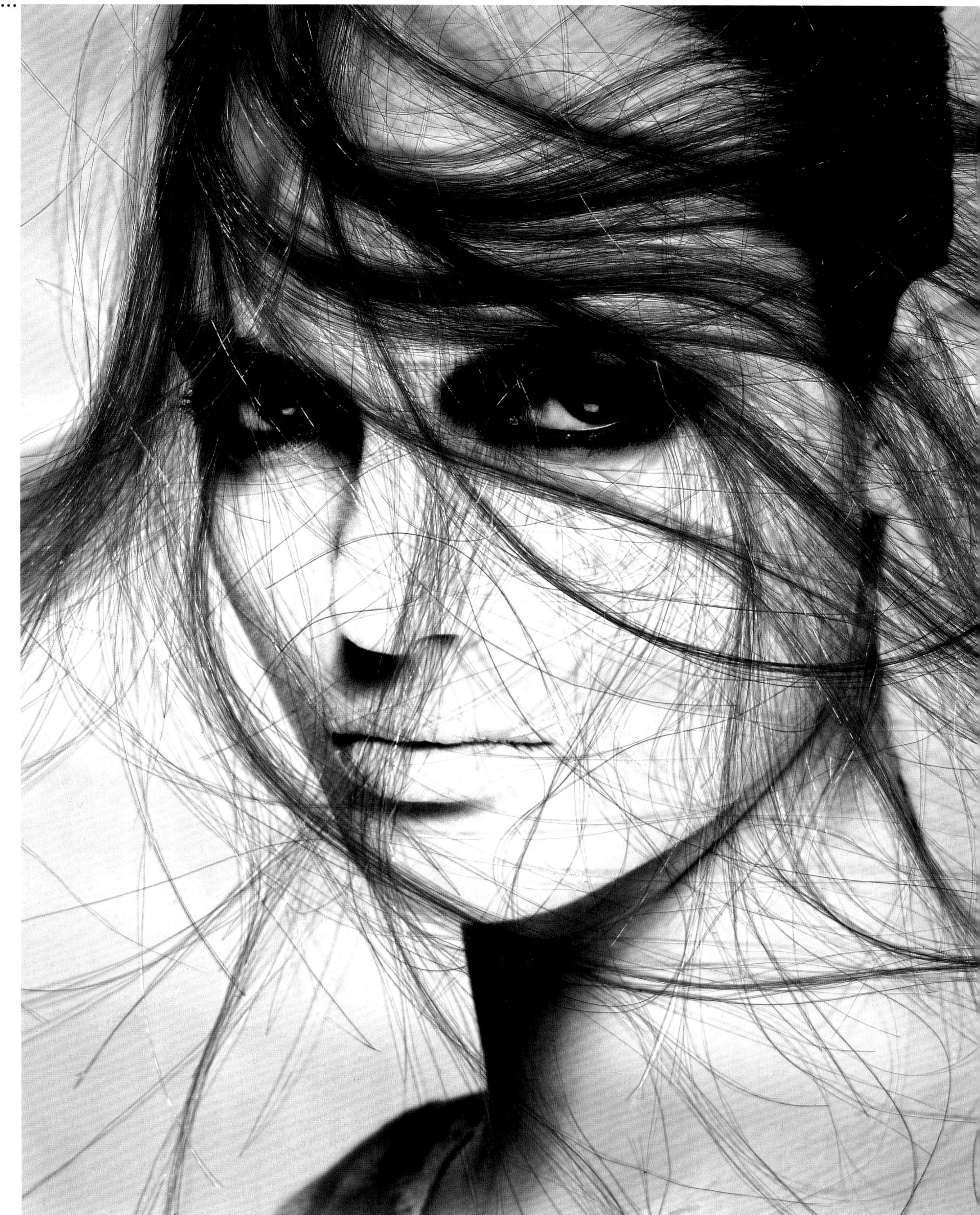

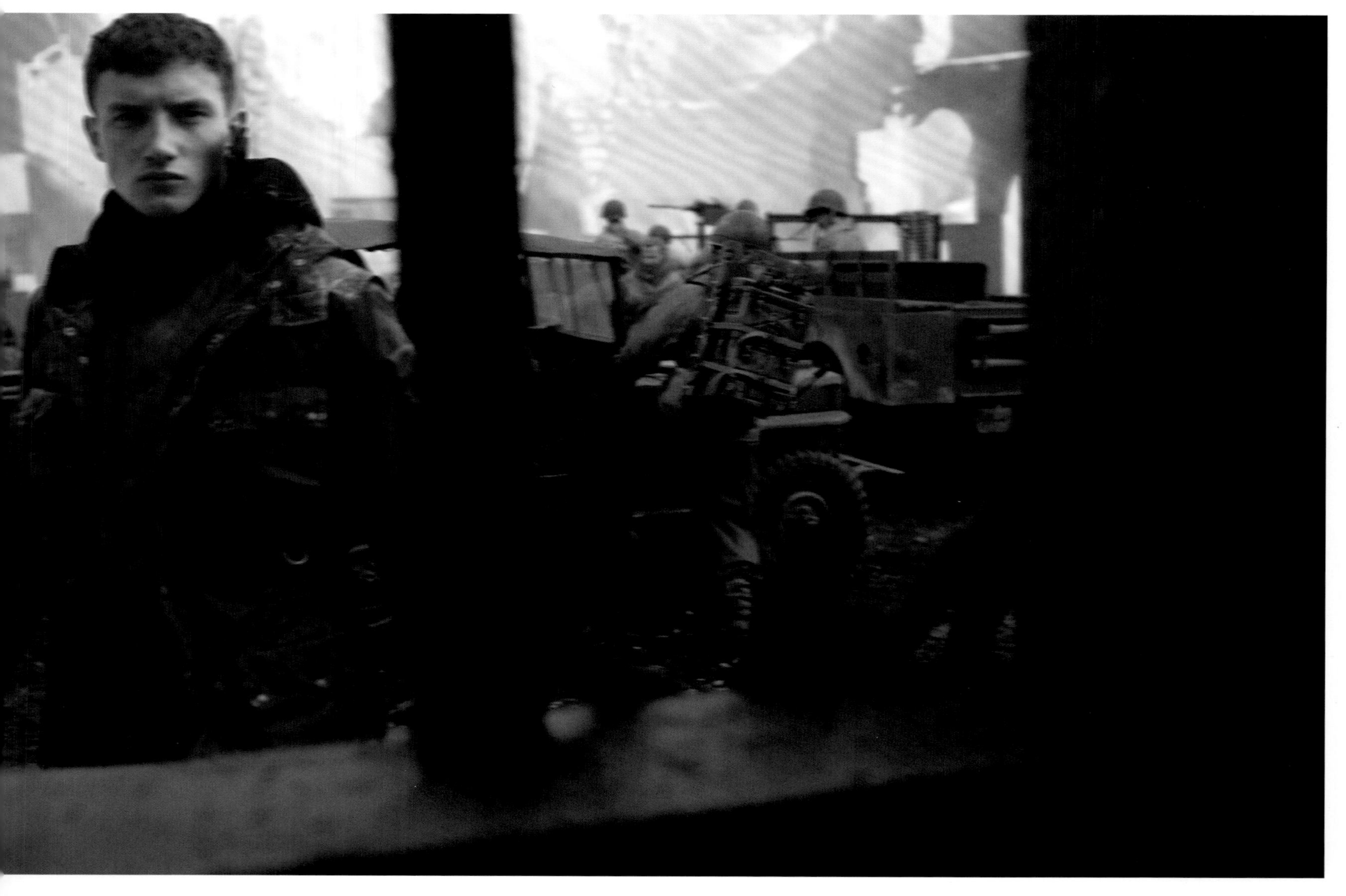

SEAN ELLIS

from 'Paths of Glory'
for *GQ Style*, 2010
photography by Sean Ellis
courtesy Sean Ellis
styled by David Lamb

pages 156–57:
Anne Watanabe
for *Numéro Tokyo*, 2008
photography by Sean Ellis
courtesy Sean Ellis

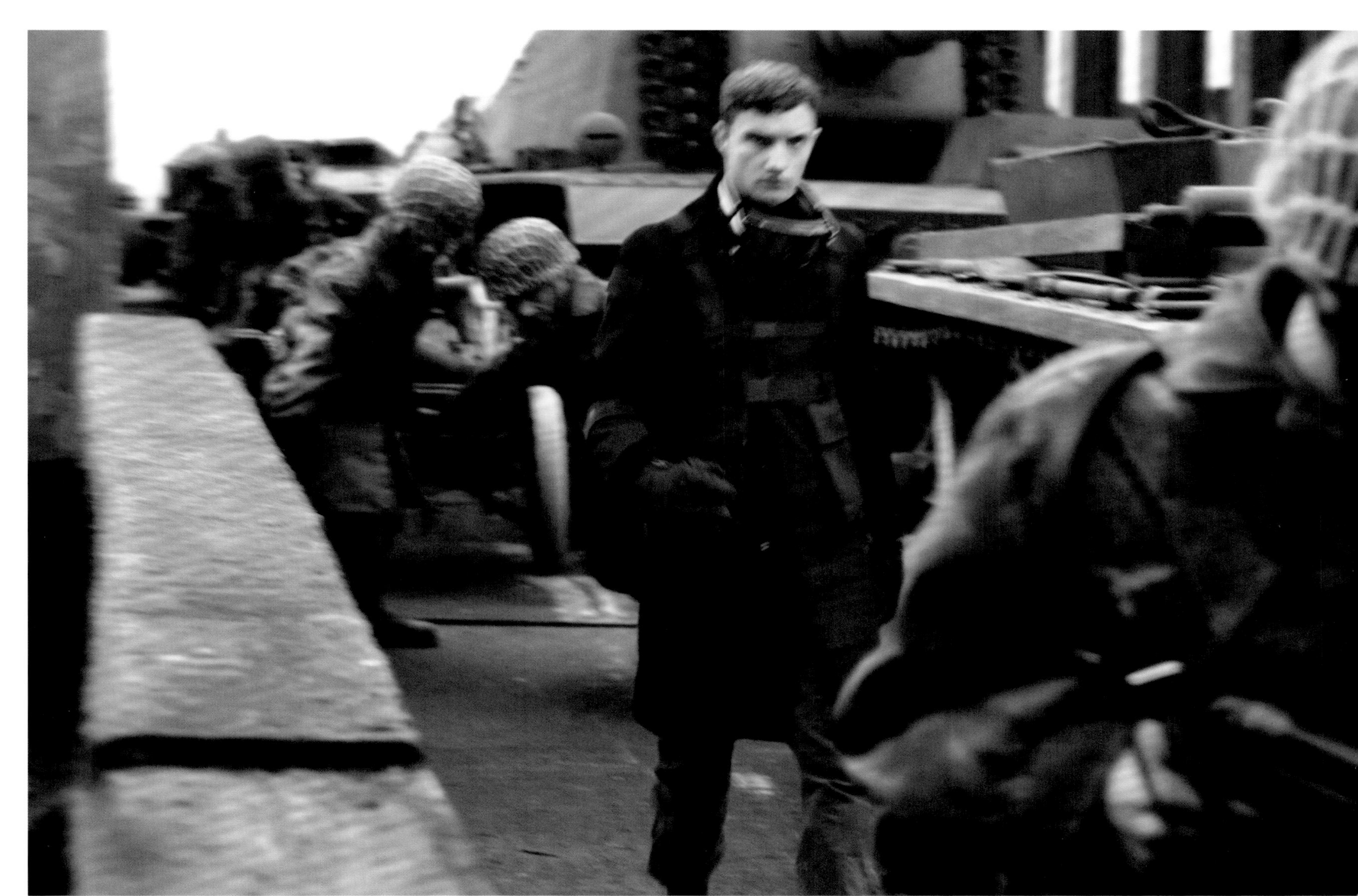

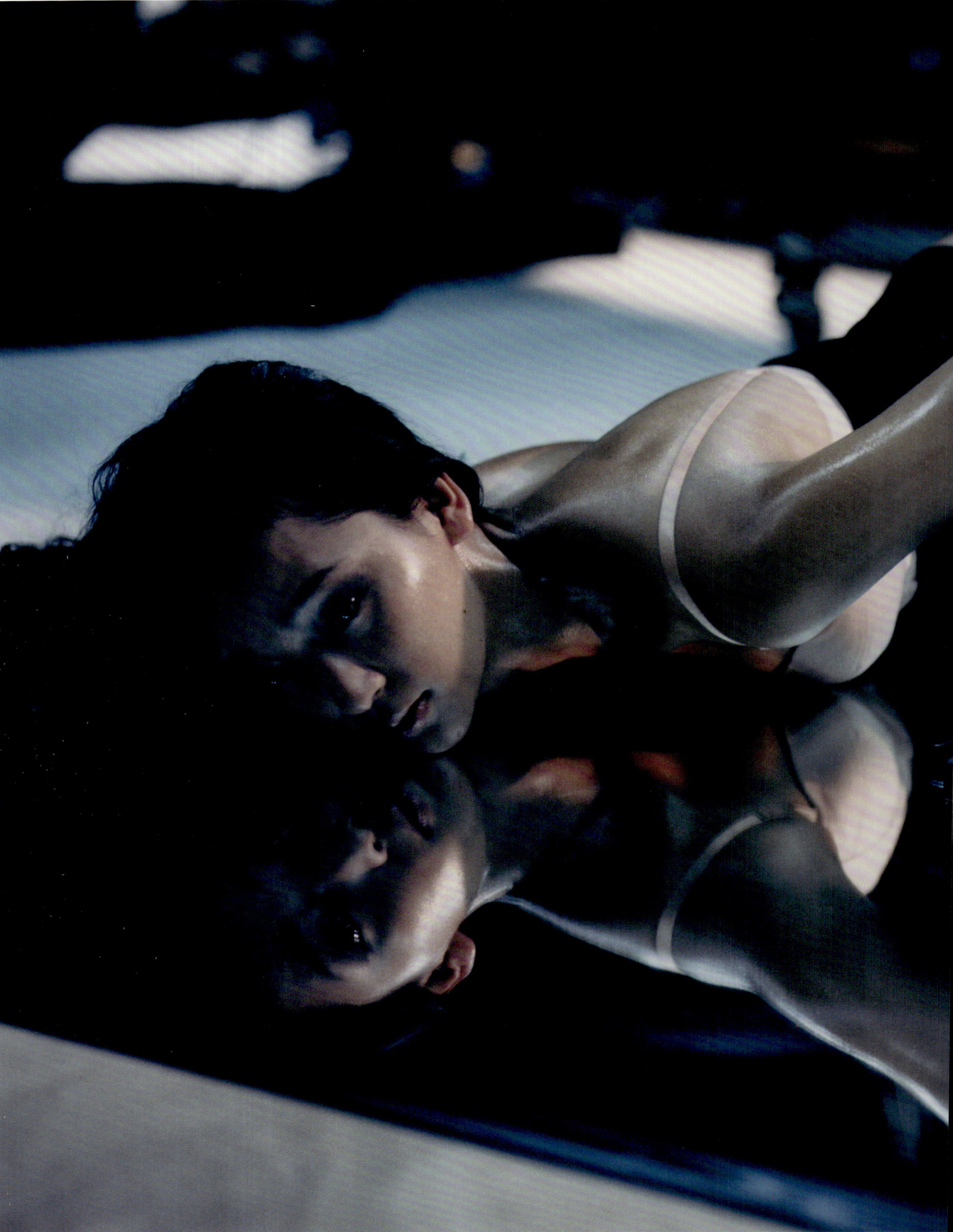

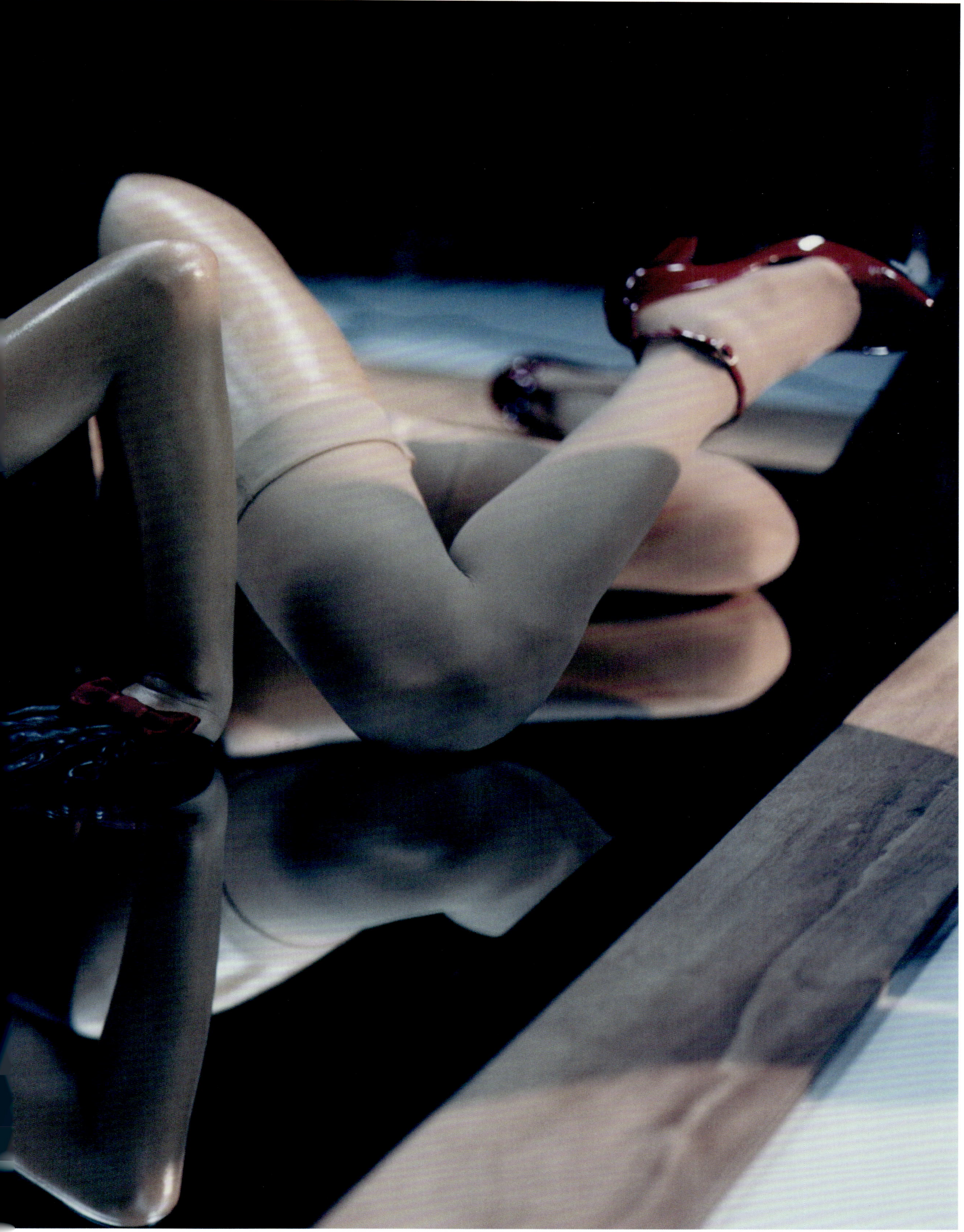

S E A N   E L L I S

for *Surface*, 2003
photography by Sean Ellis
courtesy Sean Ellis

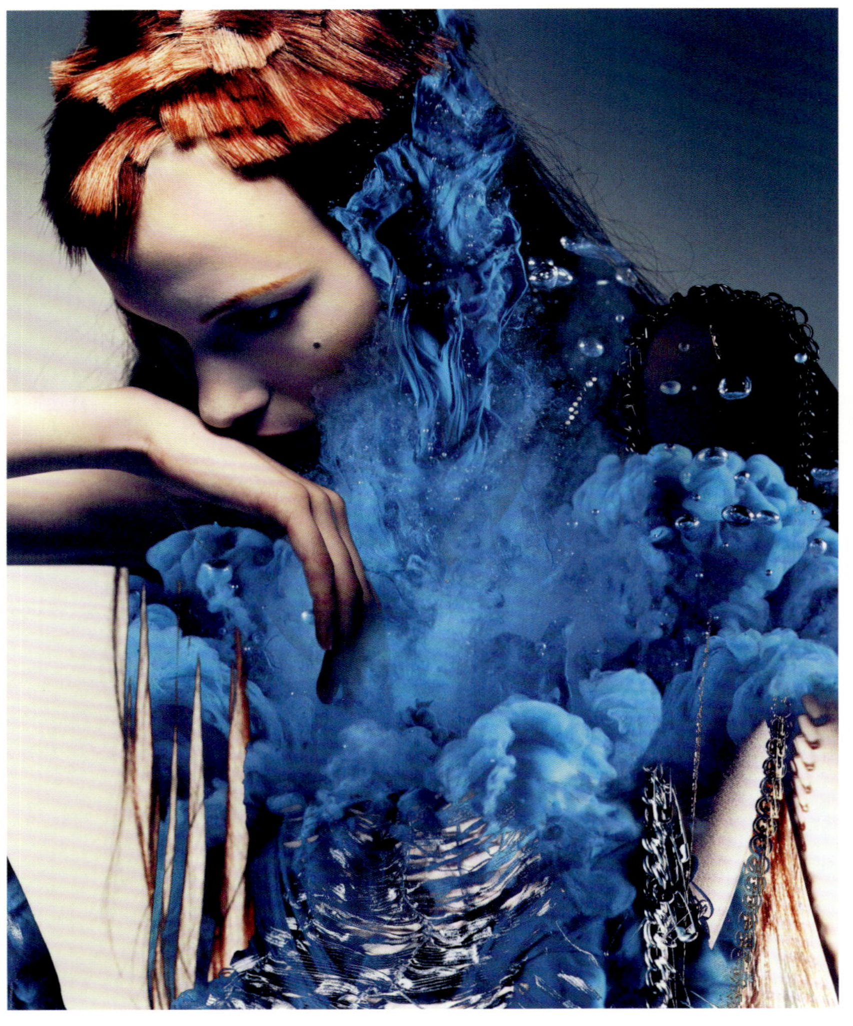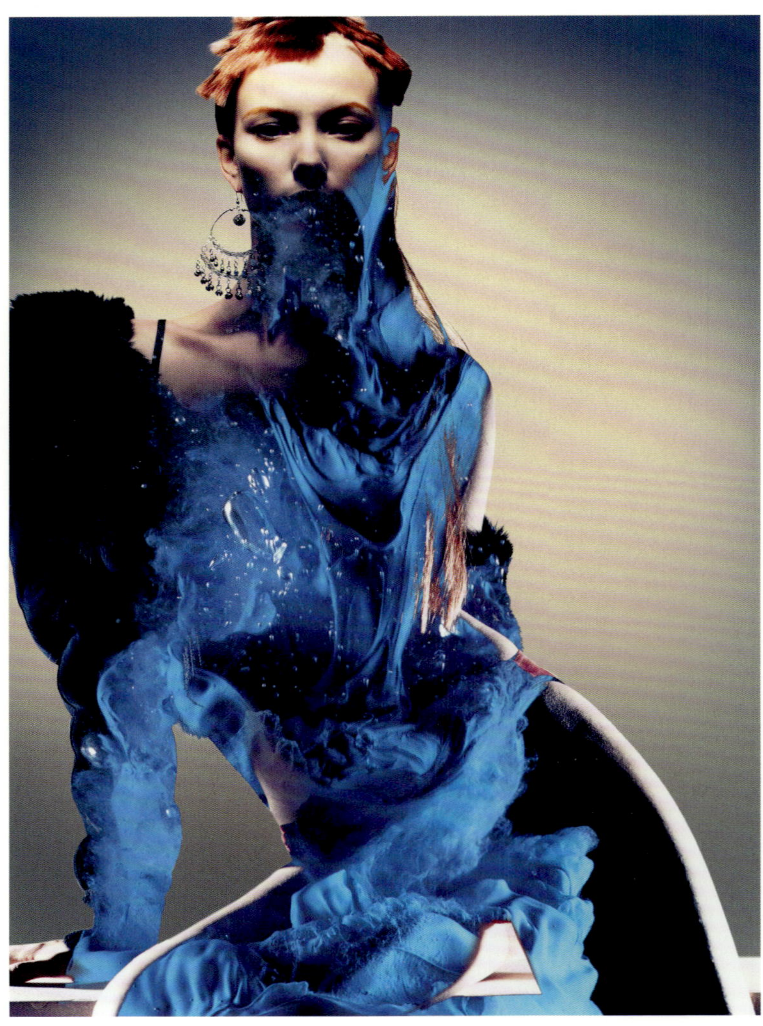

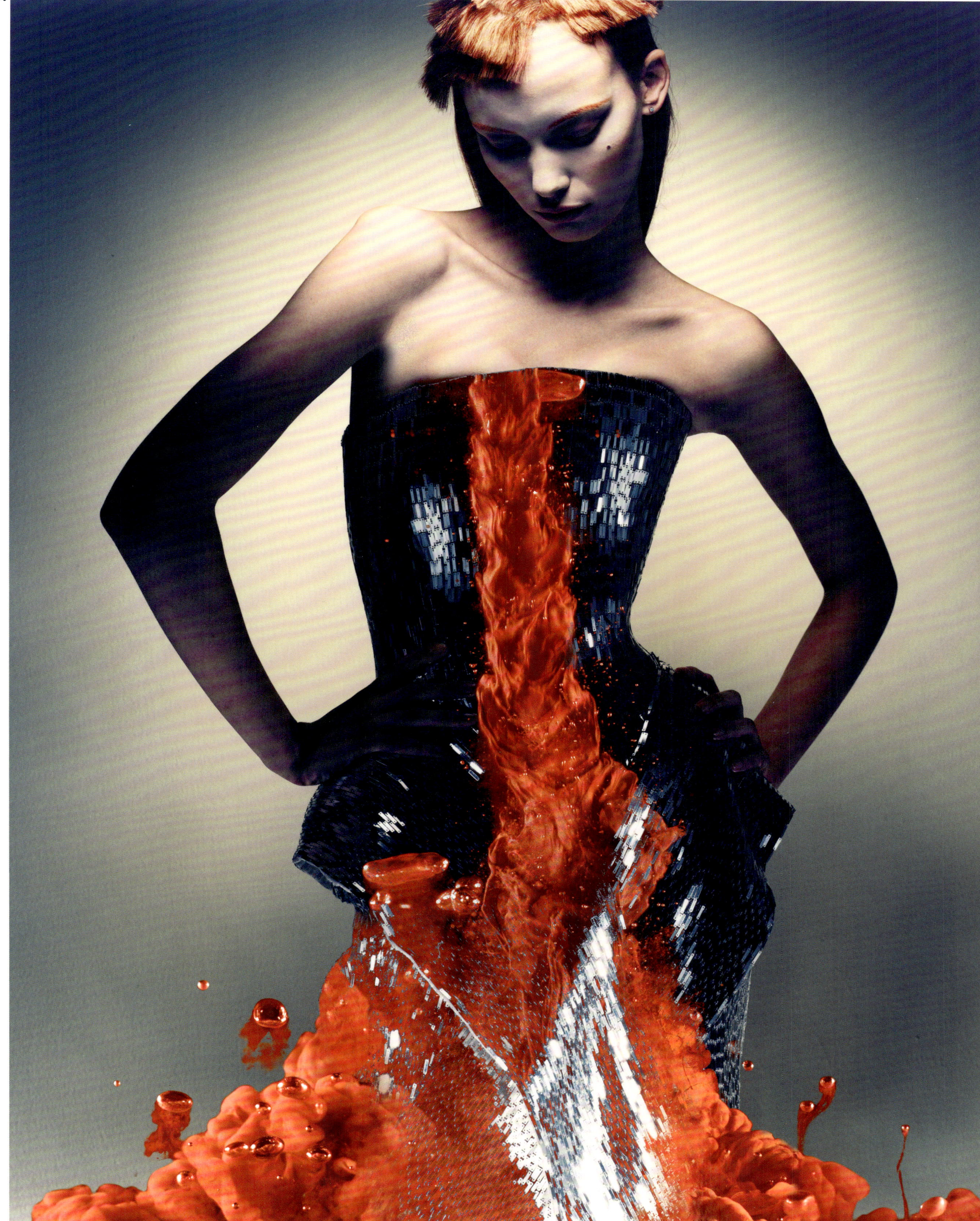

Nataša Vojnović for *AnOther* magazine, 2008
photography by Serge Leblon
courtesy Management Artists
editor Cathy Edwards

pages 164–65:
Barbara Palvin for *Numéro*, 2012
photography by Serge Leblon
courtesy Management Artists
editor Sheila Single

pages 166–67:
Baptiste Radufe in 'New Romantics'
for *Mister Muse*, 2012
photography by Serge Leblon
courtesy Management Artists
editor Tom Van Dorpe

_|

The soft-focus romanticism of Belgian-born Serge Leblon's fashion photography appears to belie his past as a war photographer. Look closer though and the implications of his earlier employment live on in subtle traces. Leblon, who cut his teeth on the frontline of Middle-Eastern conflict in and around Lebanon, allows his warm imagery both to acknowledge the scars and provide an antidote to this history. An unashamed indulgence in the pleasure of being alive rubs up against moments of pensive melancholy or sorrow. Underpinning these intuitive visualisations of human consciousness is a humility that brings Leblon's subjects down to earth and invites empathy.

Making the transition from reportage to fashion via a commission for *The Face* in the 1990s, Leblon has gravitated towards similar publications to develop his dream-like style, delivering editorials for *Dazed & Confused* and *AnOther* magazine, for which he shot Nataša Vojnović in 2008 (page 163). The pleasure of life is felt through the spontaneous physicality of this shoot, Vojnović responding intuitively to the potential of the present moment. Her body contorts in obedience to an inner energy as she moves to her own rhythm, as if possessed, before his lens. Colour works as an emotional indicator, washes of blue pushing the images further into the vagueness of dreams to express what Leblon describes as a quality of 'evanescence' — or transience. The inner music and organic movement inherent in such a shoot perhaps explains Leblon's subsequent appeal to musicians such as Goldfrapp, his

transient photographic quality finding a mutual pairing in the soft-edged wistfulness of the pagan-inspired album *Seventh Tree*.

For all the vitality that Leblon communicates, melancholy is a consistent theme. Shooting actress Julianne Moore for *BlackBook* in 2010, Leblon sidesteps the aggrandizing qualities typical of celebrity portraiture to indulge instead in a brooding introversion more reminiscent of her casting in fashion designer Tom Ford's 2009 film *A Single Man*. Carefully controlled lens flare hints at a visualisation of Leblon's emotional layers, a technique applied in different ways across his work. Yet, even as melancholy makes its presence felt through colour and light, the photographs are not sad. Rather, they have an enriching character that Belgian fashion designer Veronique Branquinho describes as the 'charisma of French avant-garde movies'. There is a nostalgic escapism about them, a quality effectively encapsulated in the aged over-exposure of the Polaroid depictions of Baptiste Radufe for Leblon's *Mister Muse* editorial, 'New Romantics', in 2012 (pages 166–67). It is perhaps the sense of wilful abandonment in such shoots, lost amidst memories of the past while simultaneously maintaining an intuitive lust for the present, that really resonates throughout his work.

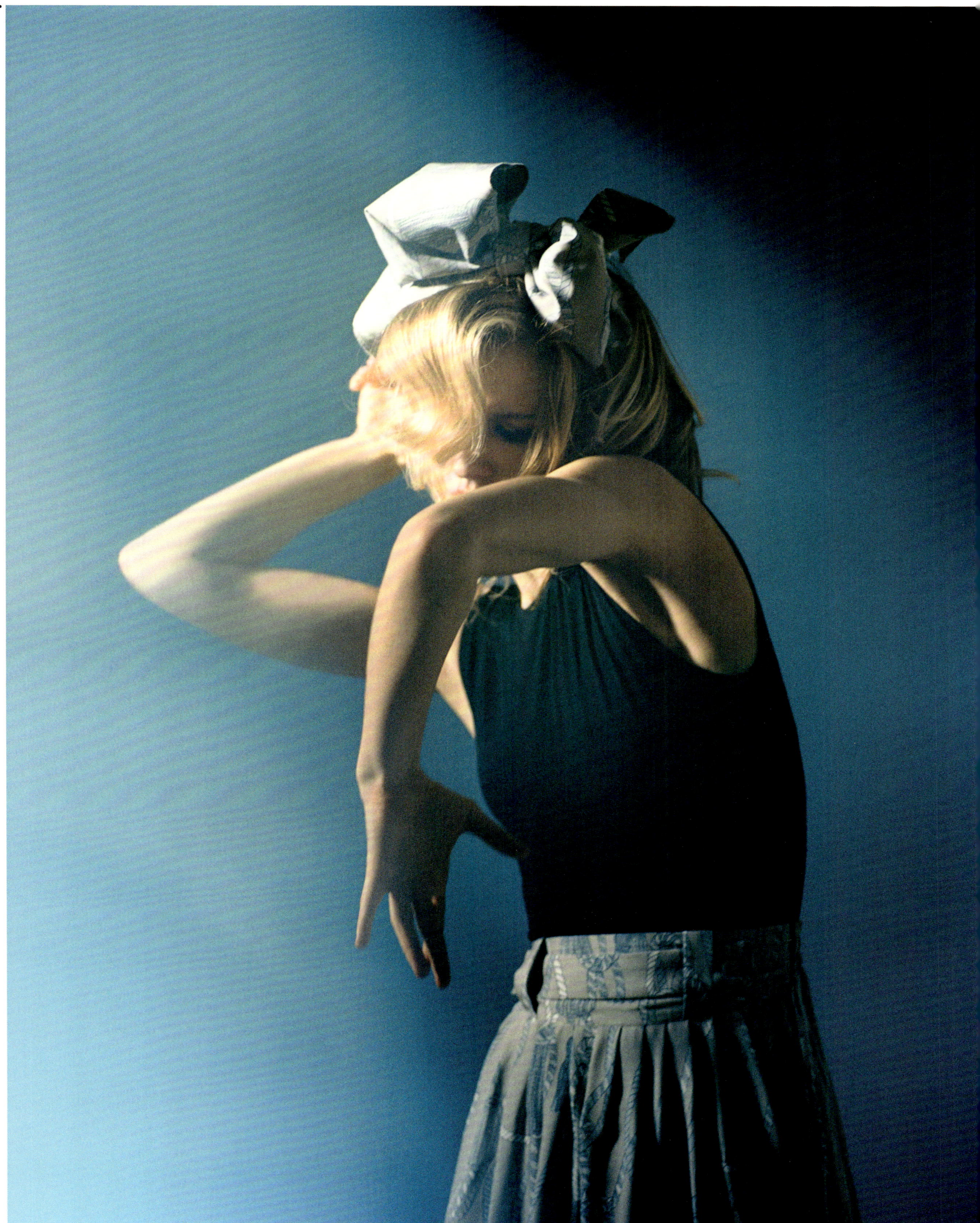

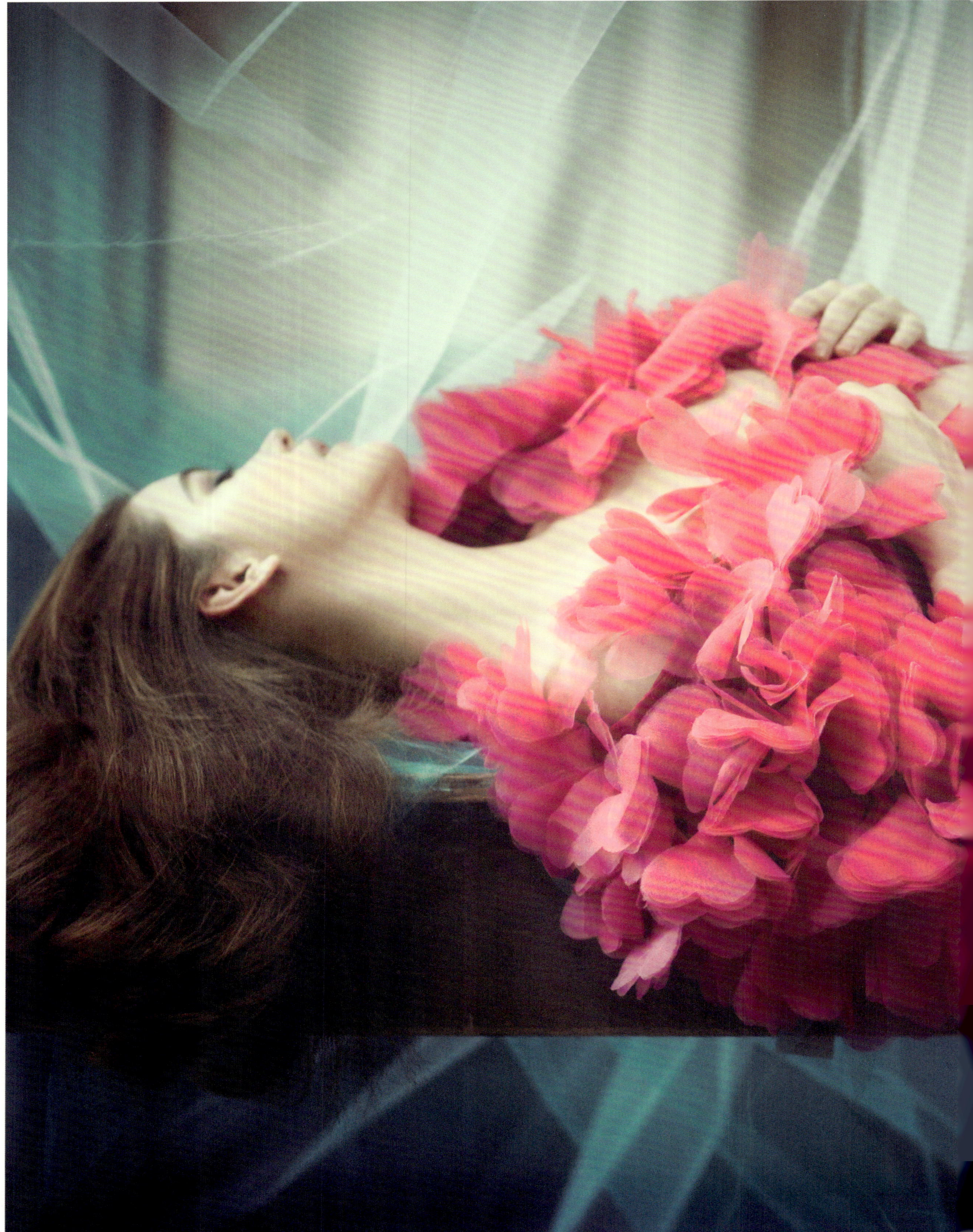

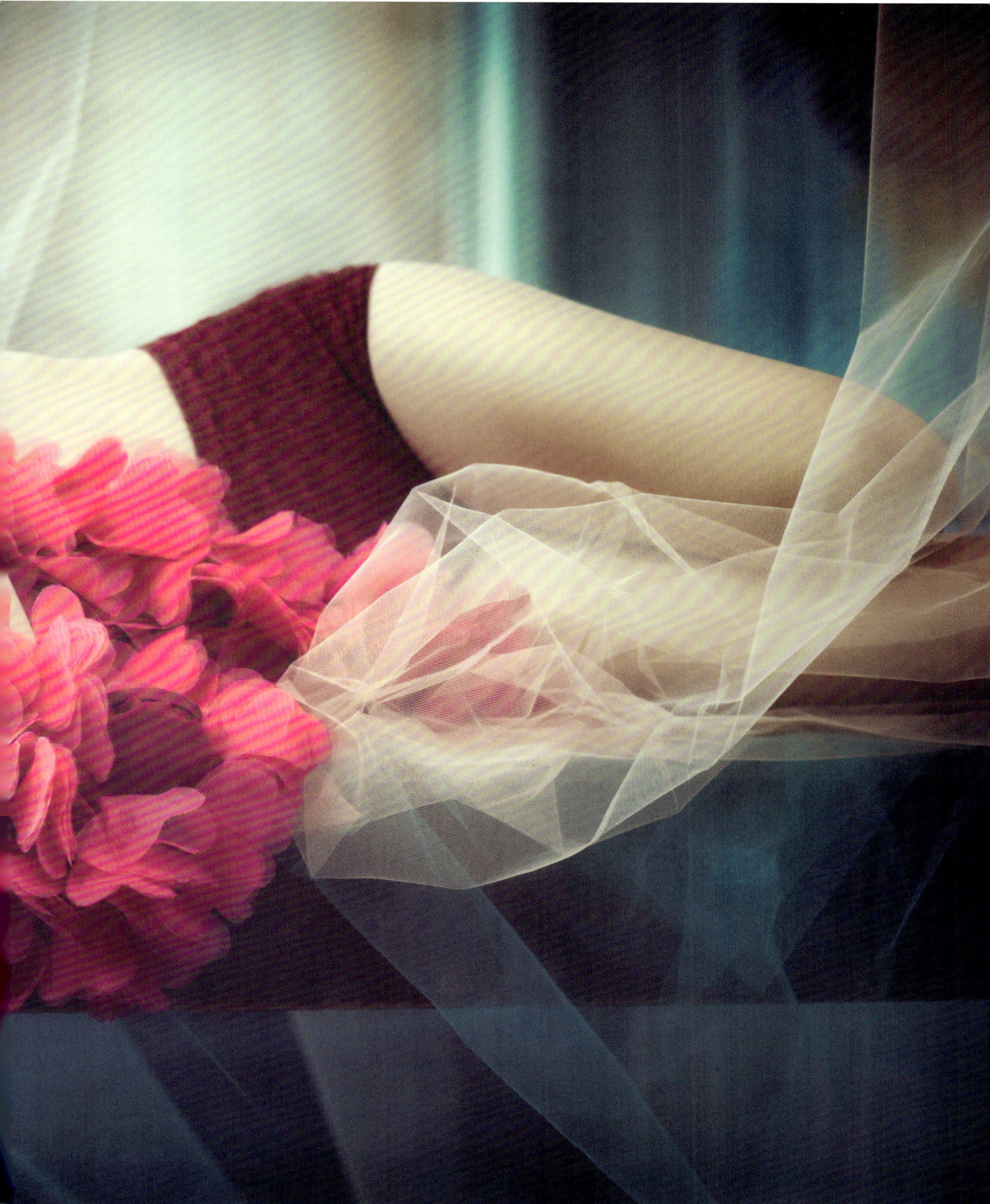

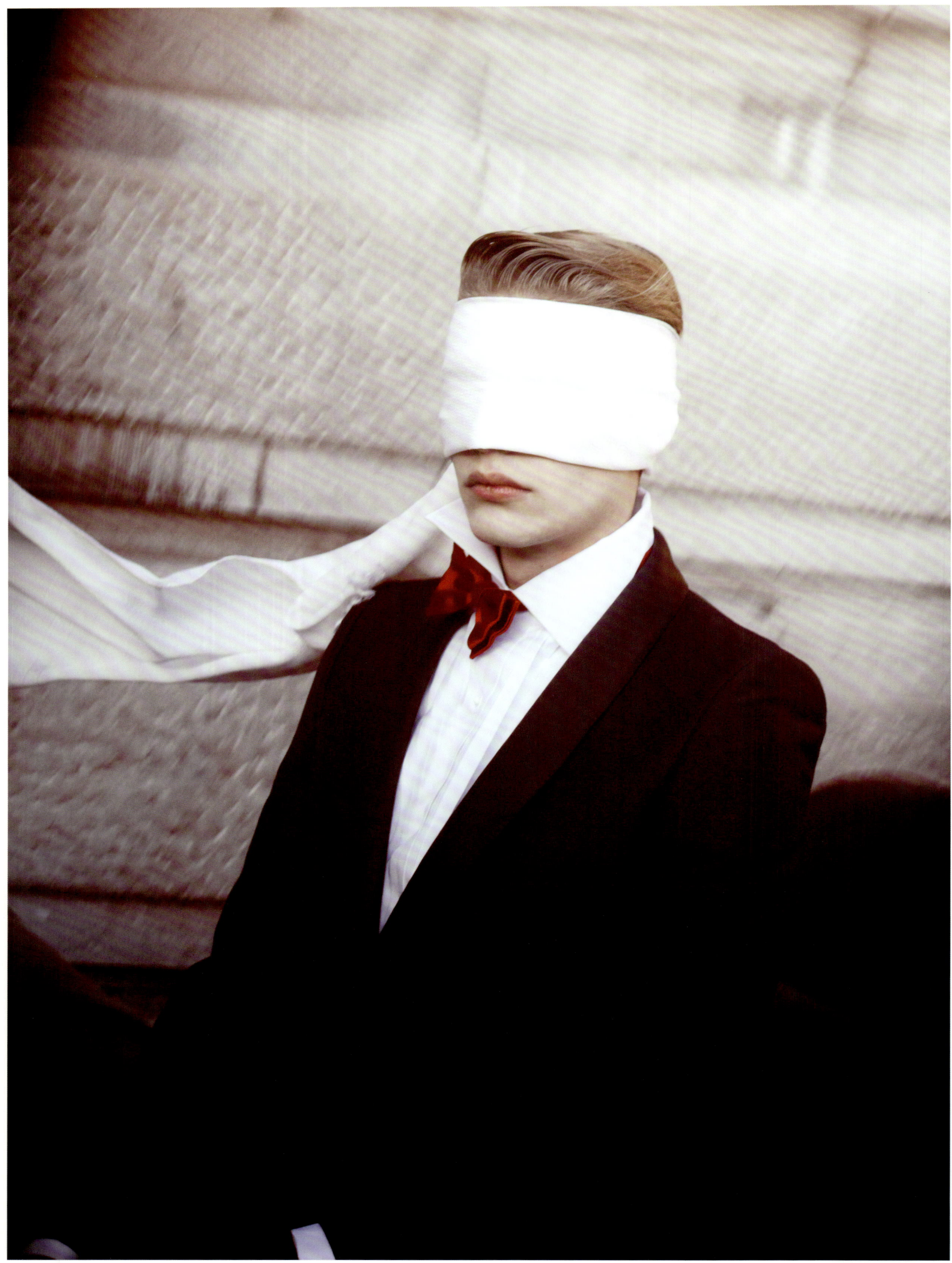

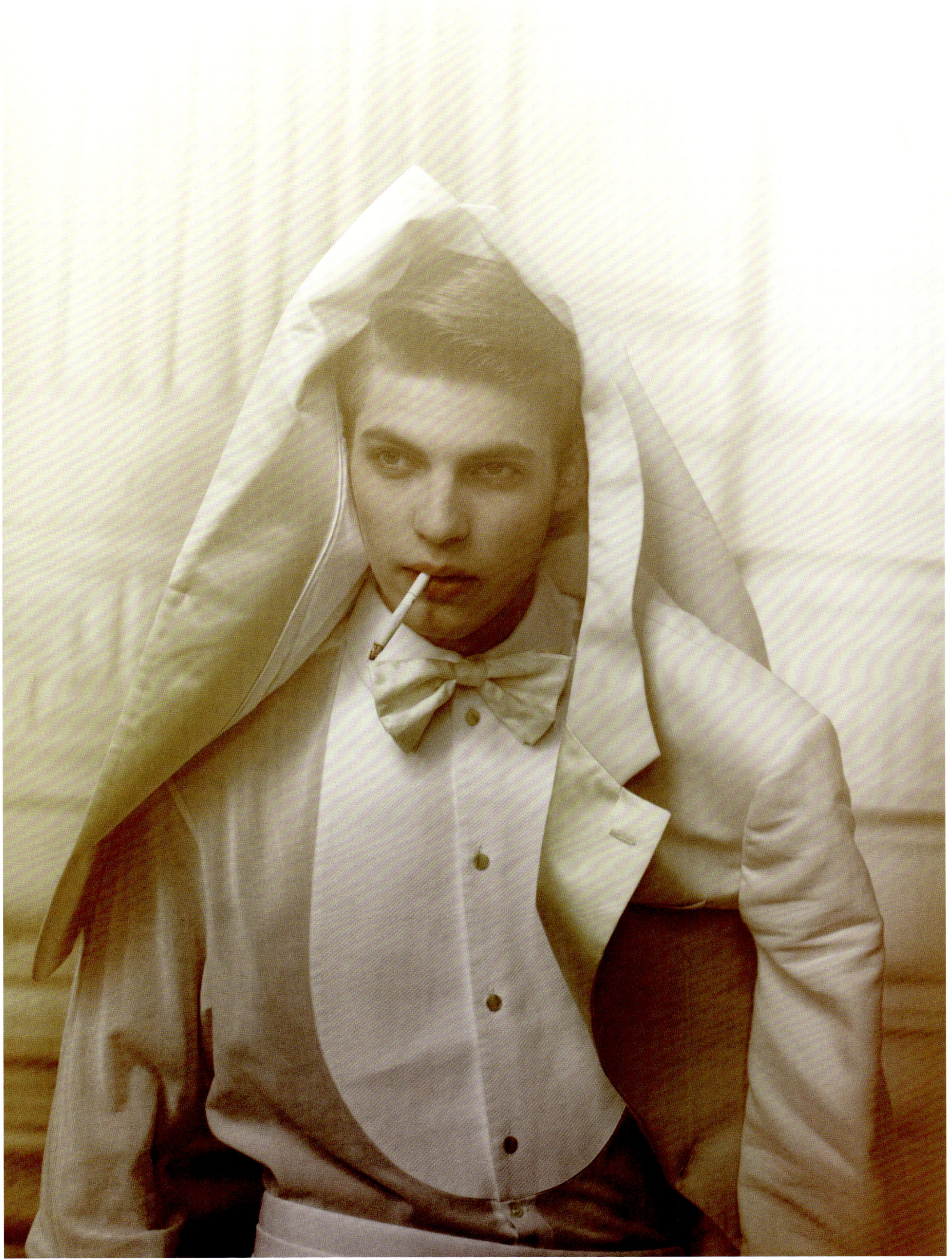

pages 169–71:
from 'Art', 2011
photography by Bruno Dayan
courtesy Bruno Dayan

Warmly ethereal and touched with sensuality, the photographs of French-Canadian Bruno Dayan are suggestive of a narcotic trance. Experimental lighting, rich use of iridescent colour and long shutter speeds are combined with subtle digital manipulation to create an ambience that unites both beauty and fashion with the less tangible sphere of the subconscious. His understanding of movement is informed by his work with film and in his photographs he places blurred moments that upset the equilibrium of the still frame.

In his 2011 series 'Art', Dayan is haunted by ghost-like phantoms and tormented faces from Caravaggio-esque paintings (pages 169–71). The deep-set eyes of his protagonist are immersed in a shadowy blackness as colour bursts out from the environment around her. It is as if we are being invited into a sub-sensory space where the activities of the mind are brought to life. Though depicting a version of the present, these are photographs that owe much to the past. Recalling the eighteenth-century Romantic Gothicism of Henry Fuseli in their composition and symbolic associations, they hover somewhere between a nightmare and an erotic reverie.

The polychromatic colouration of Dayan's series 'Dreams' has a similar feel but draws on a more recent era, its hallucinatory sequences located in rooms that are sparsely populated with domestic relics from the twentieth century (pages 172–73). Amongst faded mattresses, patterned wallpaper and cathode-ray TVs, a jaded version of seventies psychedelia plays out. Spectral bursts radiate from subjects as if capturing a moment of intoxication, while careful manipulation of underwater photography once again invokes the gravity-free world of the imagination. Digital alteration is integral yet subtle enough to effectively immerse the viewer in these supernatural interior sequences.

The trajectory of Dayan's career has seen him move back and forth between photography and cinema. While studying Fine Arts and Film in Canada at the beginning of his career, Dayan produced the film *Vie d'eau*, which went on to make the selection for the Cannes International Film Festival that year. Later, he spent a decade in Tokyo working on projects that utilised both print and the moving image before moving to France, where he now resides. Dayan's focus on photography followed a major shoot, 'The Seven Deadly Sins', for Louis Vuitton in 1997, after which he embarked on a series of campaigns for labels including Moschino, Yves Saint Laurent, and magazines such as *Numéro* and *Vogue*. Yet his reputation, much like his work, maintains an elusive air.

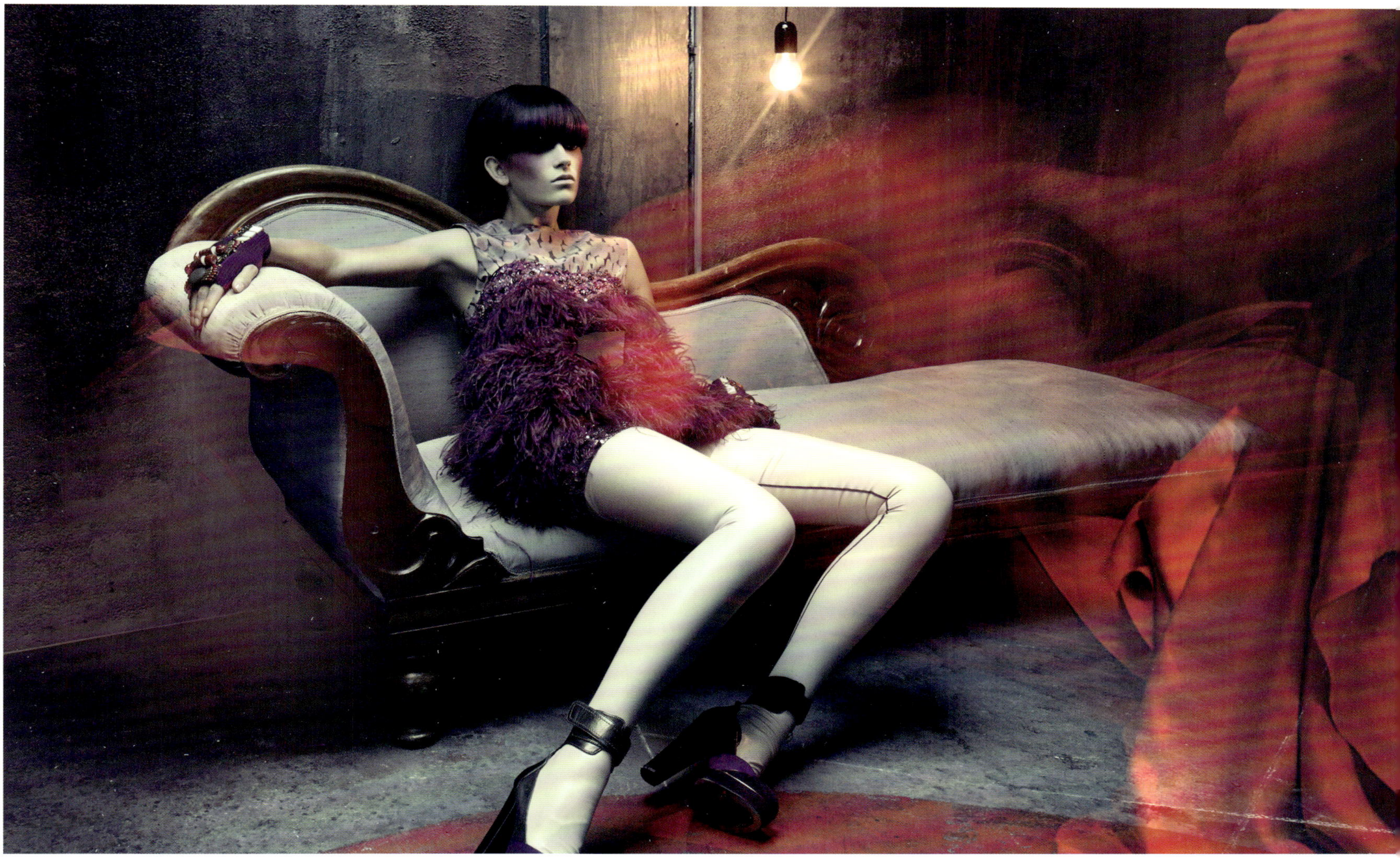

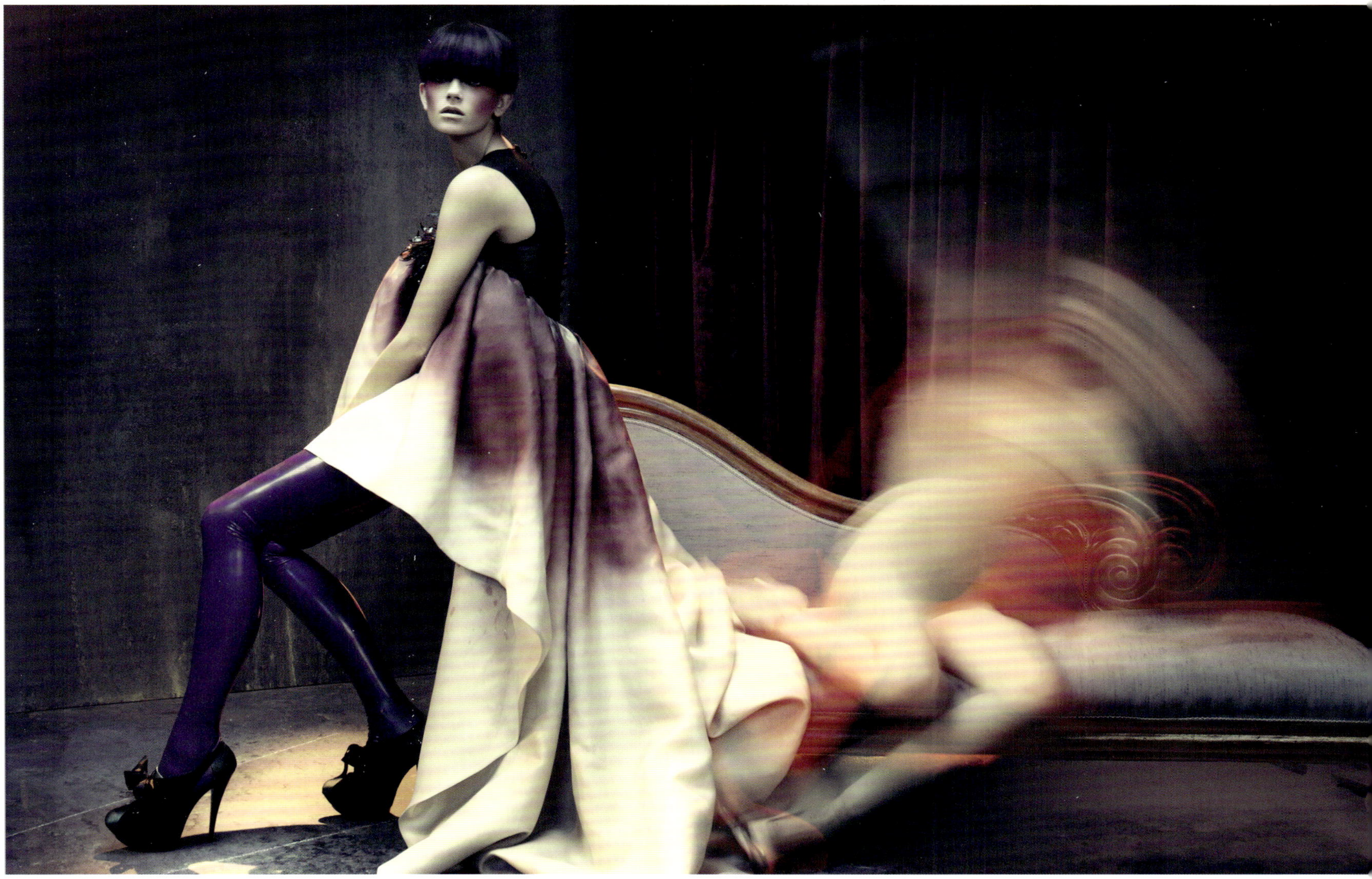

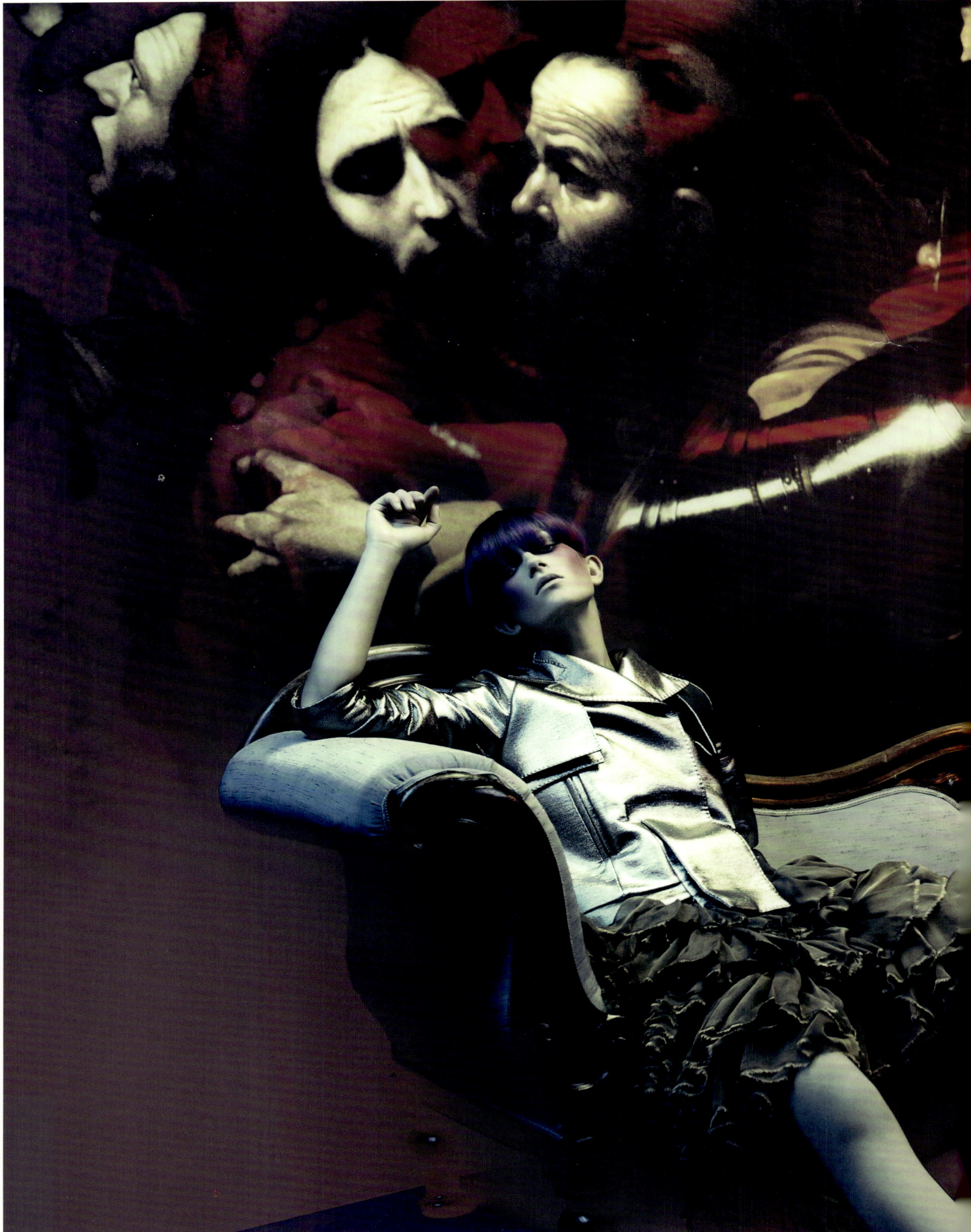

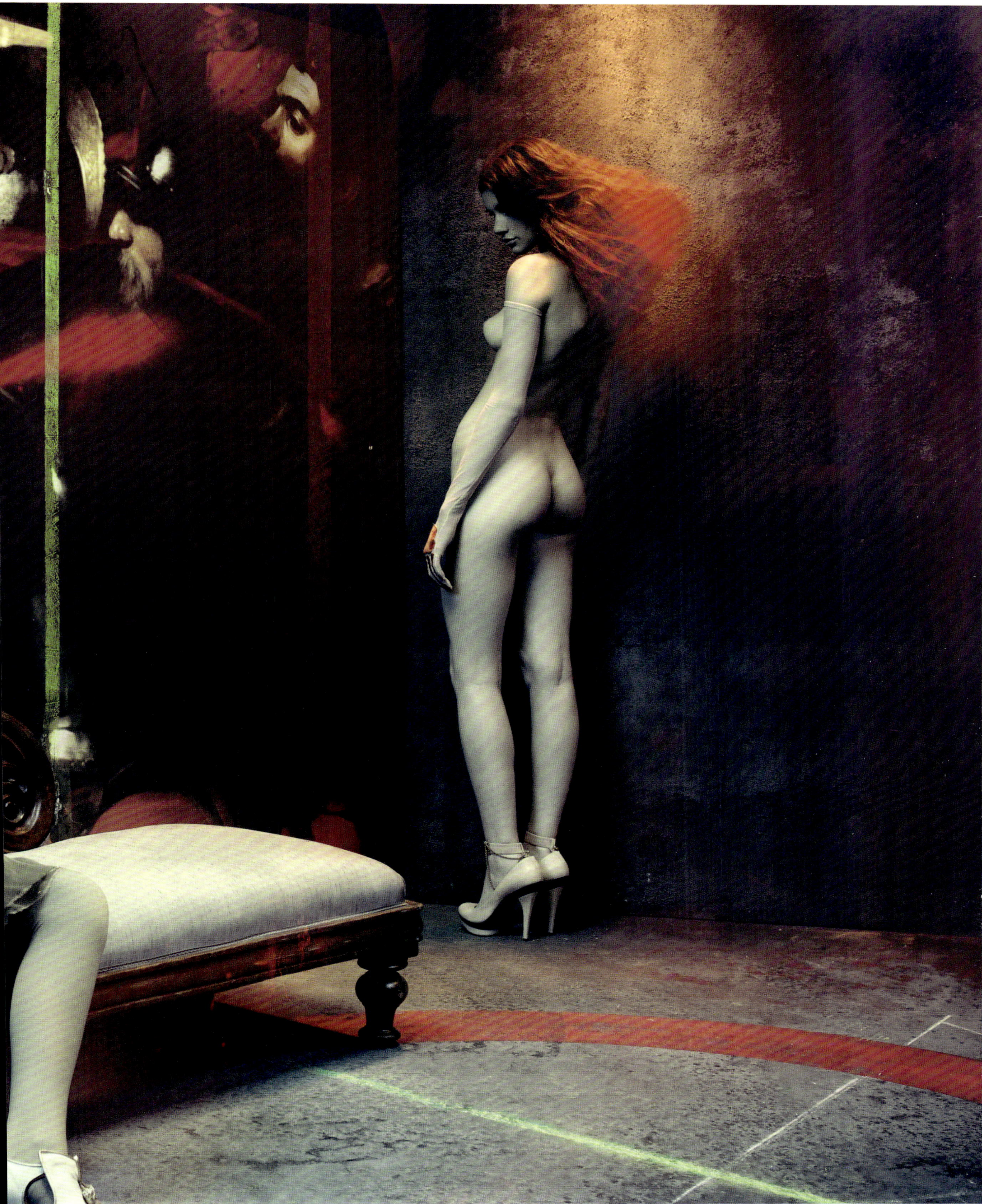

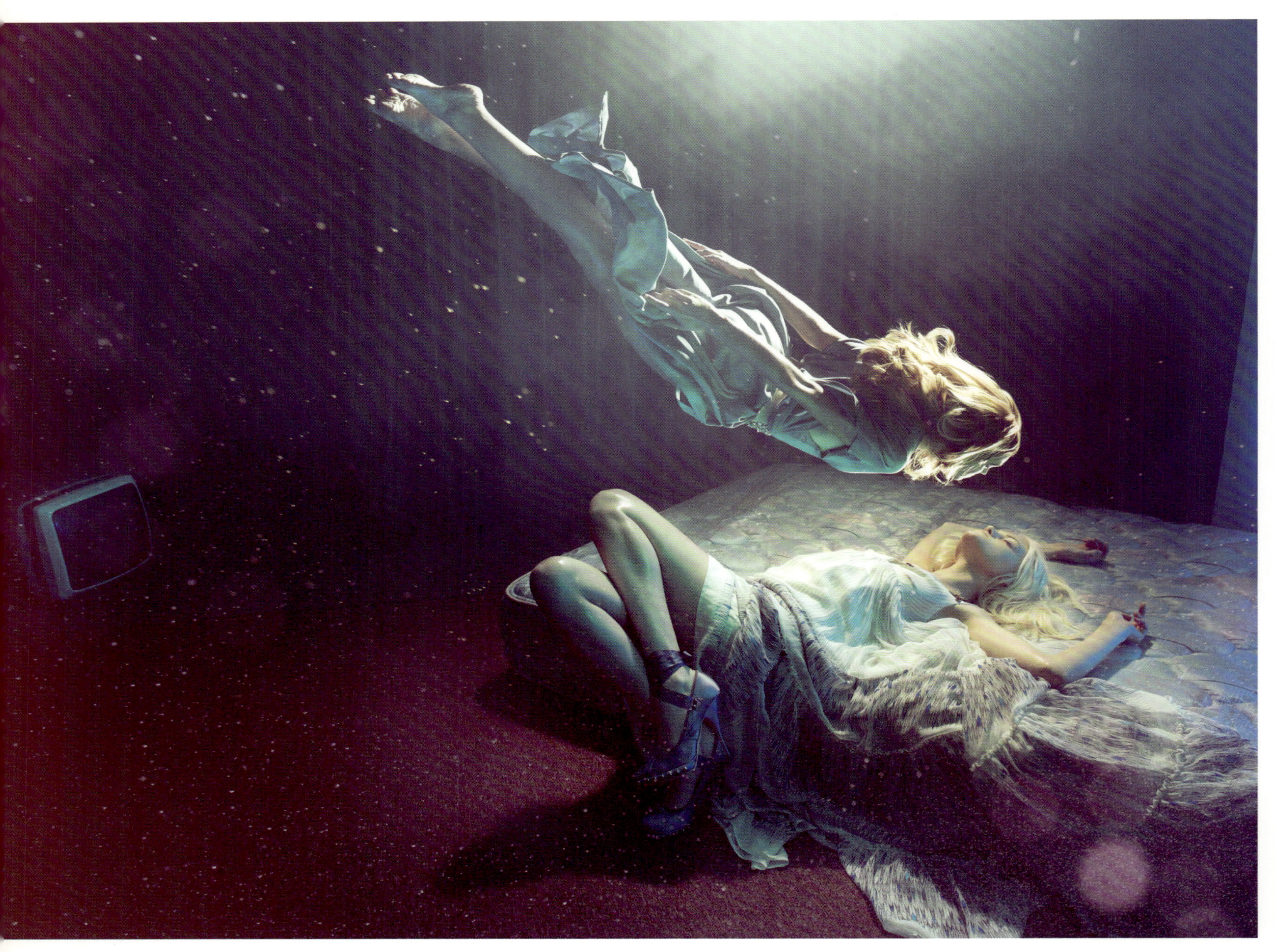

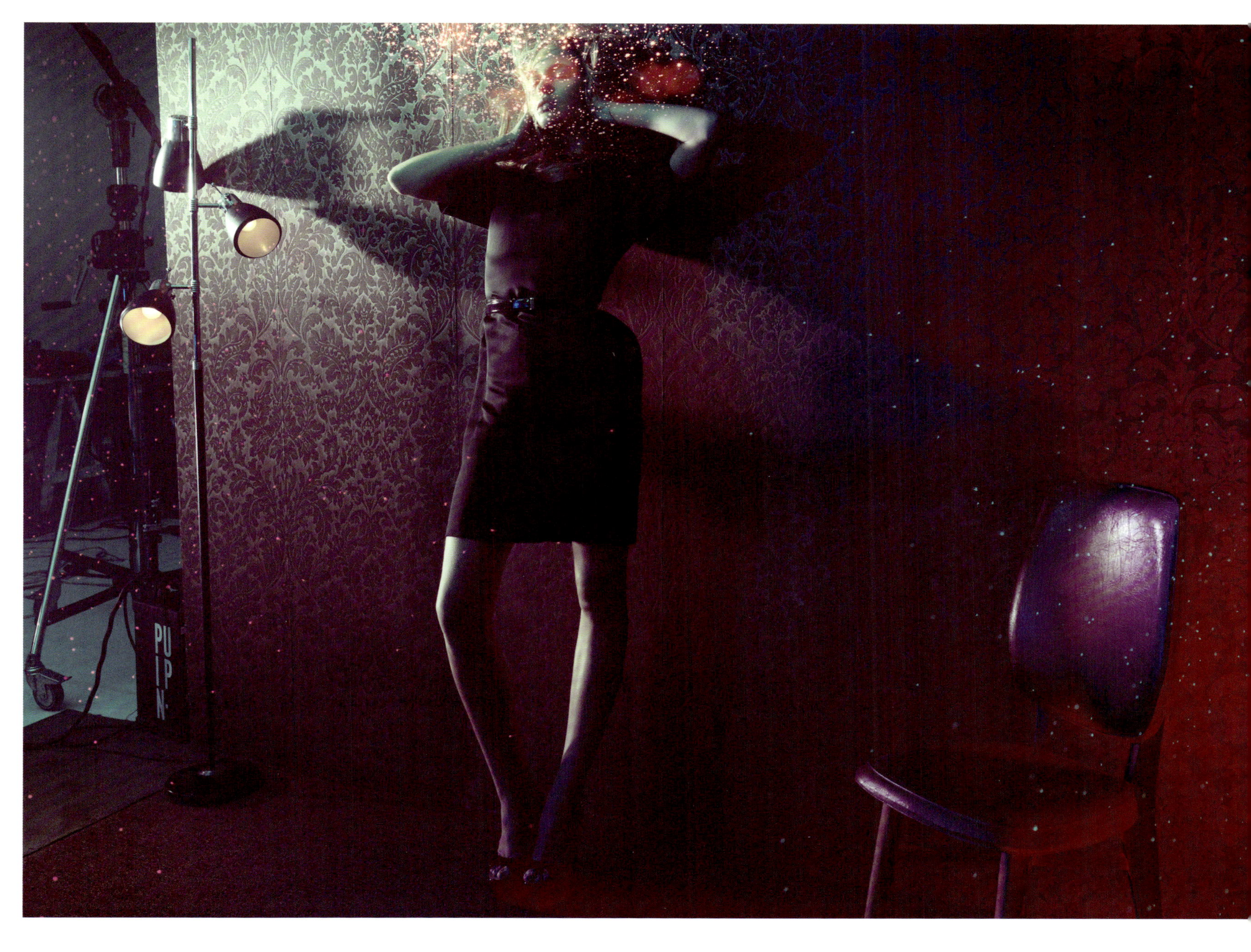

BRUNO DAYAN

from 'Dreams', 2011
photography by Bruno Dayan
courtesy Bruno Dayan

Swiss-born René Habermacher oscillates between fashion and conceptualism, expressing human emotion through the vocabulary of theatre in his photographic stage sets. For Habermacher, fashion works not in isolation but through a continuous cyclical engagement between creator, wearer, stylist and photographer. It is the potential of this complex collaboration to express something deeper about the human condition that dictates the wide scope of his projects and draws him towards work that is characterised by creative dialogue.

Habermacher's trajectory has shifted from his early interpretation of fashion as an abstract form divorced from reality to something increasingly intimate. Initial forays into fashion imagery walked a line between photography and illustration, utilising a hyperreal airbrushed style that he described as 'iconographic', a technique that he would revisit in a project with makeup artist Pat McGrath for *V* in 2010. Increasingly moving away from illustration techniques and towards conceptualism, however, Habermacher has worked with stage director Dimitris Papaioannou to cross photography with theatre, and with film director Antoine Asseraf to integrate conceptualism with the moving image. Working on a short with Asseraf for *Vogue* Italia's 'One-Minute Light' series of fashion films led to the inevitably ghostly *Spectre* in 2010. Stills depict the superimposition of moving limbs and abstract objects inspired by the 1929 Man Ray film *Les Mystères du Château de Dé*. Set in the Villa Noailles, a location haunted by its rich avant-garde past as a residence for artists, *Spectre* is a vehicle for a visual exploration of the creative history that haunts the place.

Working with Papaioannou on the theatrical project *Medea(2)* for the 2008 Athens–Epidaurus Festival, Habermacher exercises a similar sensitivity to the ghosts of transient moments in the abstract motion of performance, although this time the action is jarring and energised. Such instances of media cross-pollination reflect back onto his photographic style. In an echo of *Medea(2)*, the 2011 shoot 'Metaphysica' with Dimitris Alexandrou subverts expectations through more static arrangements (pages 178–79). Dissonant visual associations reflect the work of René Magritte and other Surrealists: a doorway appears pregnant with gravity-defying water in one shot while a lightbulb hangs incongruously from the sky in another. This appetite for visual props allows Habermacher to populate his imagery with symbolism: in an editorial for *POP* in 2012, Habermacher visualises Serbian performance artist Marina Abramović's exploration of identity and the self through her interaction with a puppet alter ego. Another 2008 shoot pairing the cult figure François Sagat with an apple explicitly references the Swiss story of William Tell to cast the muscle-bound adult actor as a provocative new role model for masculinity (page 181).

Habermacher's collaborations are charged with a passionate energy that comes from an understanding of the role of fashion as, in his own words, 'an expression of momentum'. More than just fabric, fashion operates as a mirror to the issues of the individual in contemporary society, while photographers and stylists interact with it to build a mutual creative discourse. These are the essential ingredients that hold together a complex blend of abstract theatre, conceptualism and beauty.

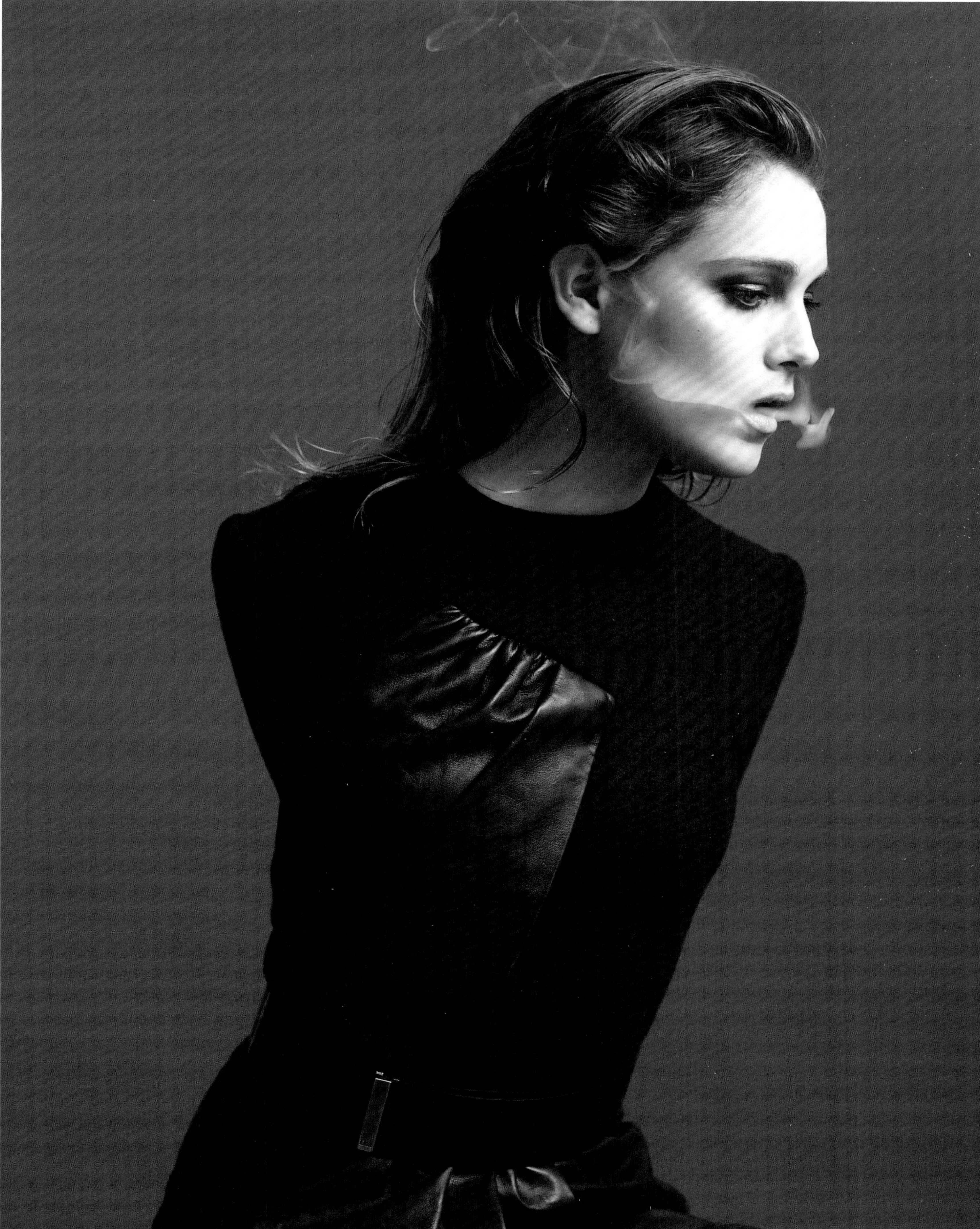

RENÉ HABERMACHER

'Swings' featuring Ymre Stiekema for *POP*, 2011
collaboration with Efi Spyrou
photography by René Habermacher
courtesy René Habermacher

pages 178–79:
'Metaphysica' featuring Dimitris Alexandrou
for *Trendsétera*, Mexico City, 2011
photography by René Habermacher
courtesy René Habermacher

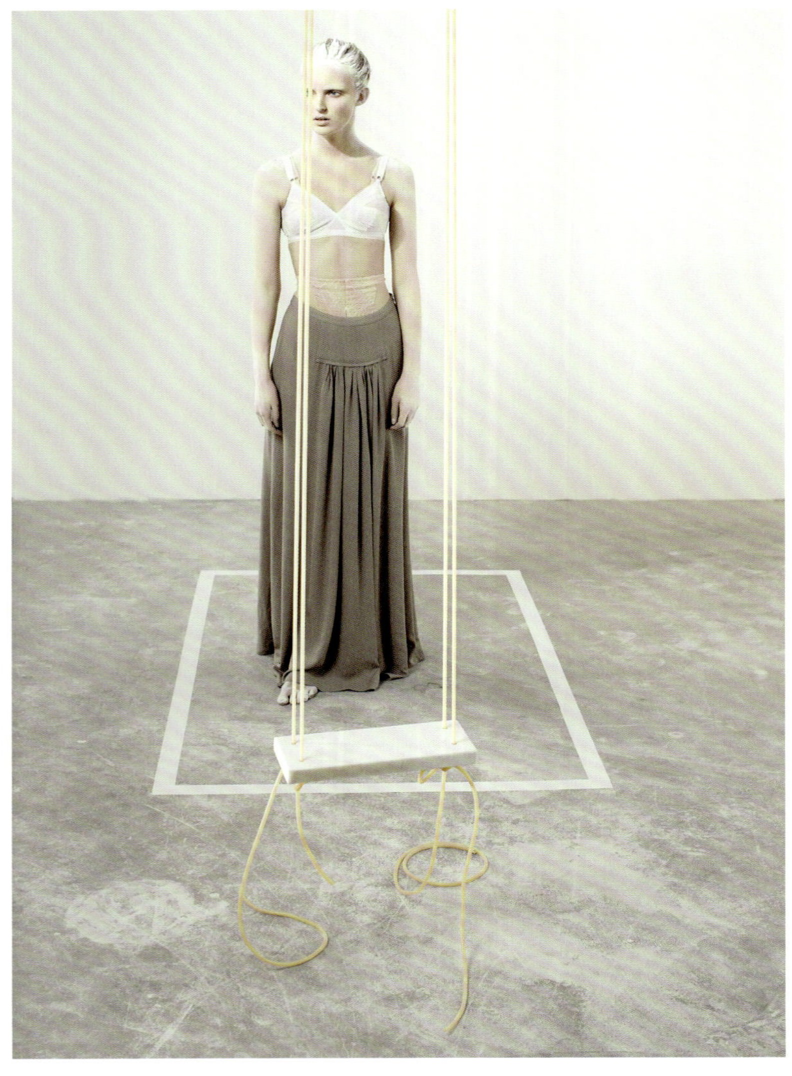

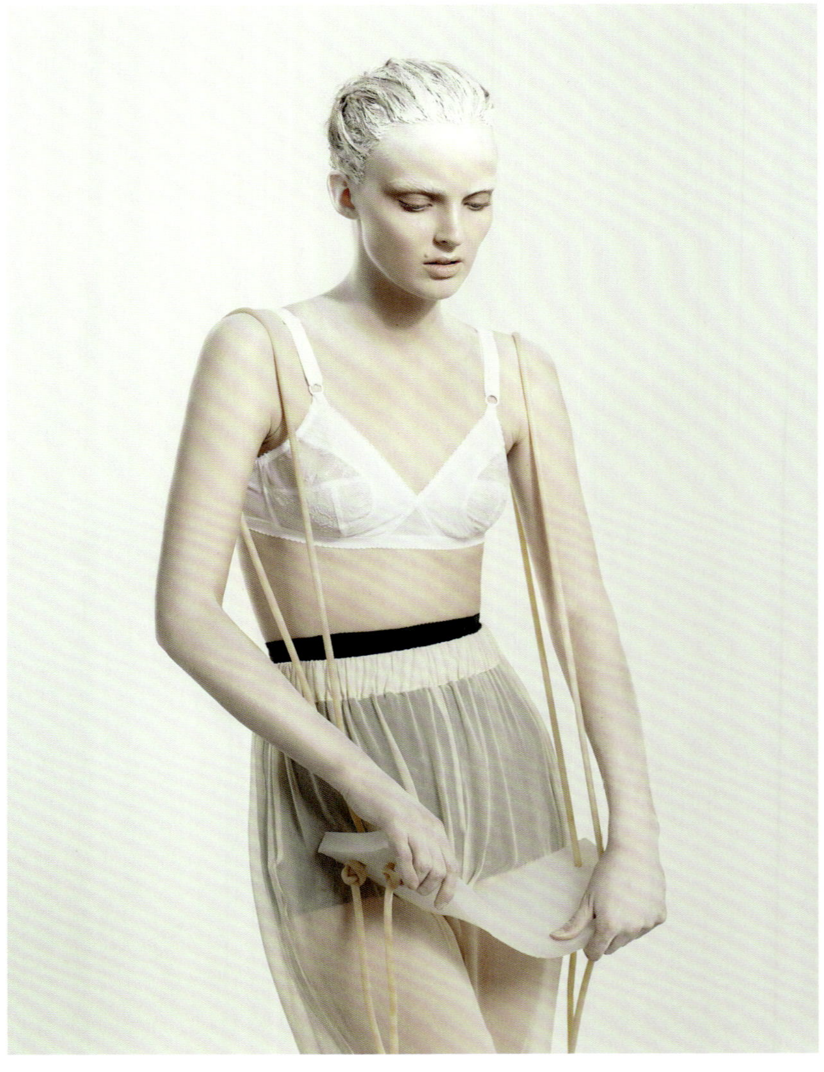

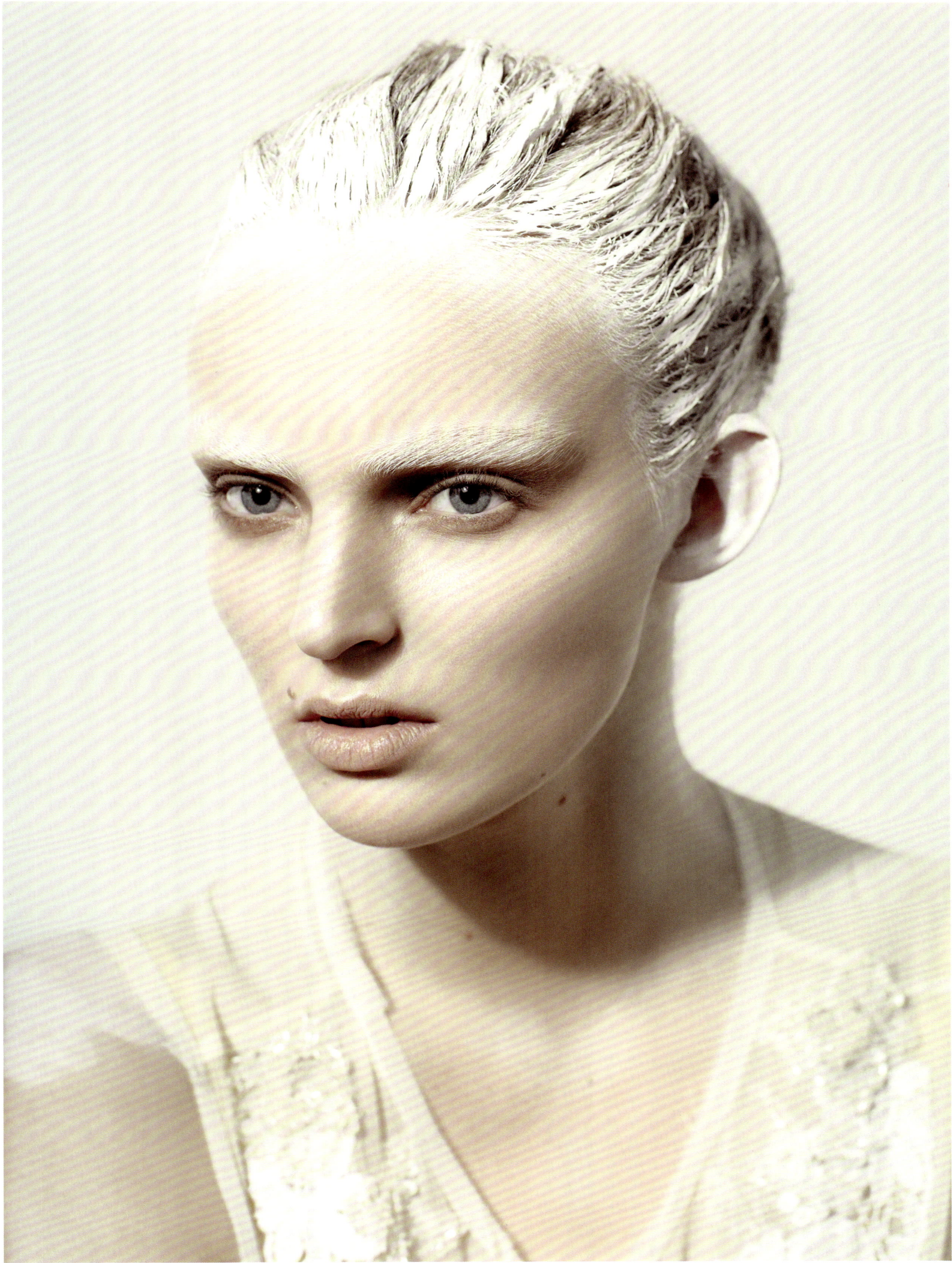

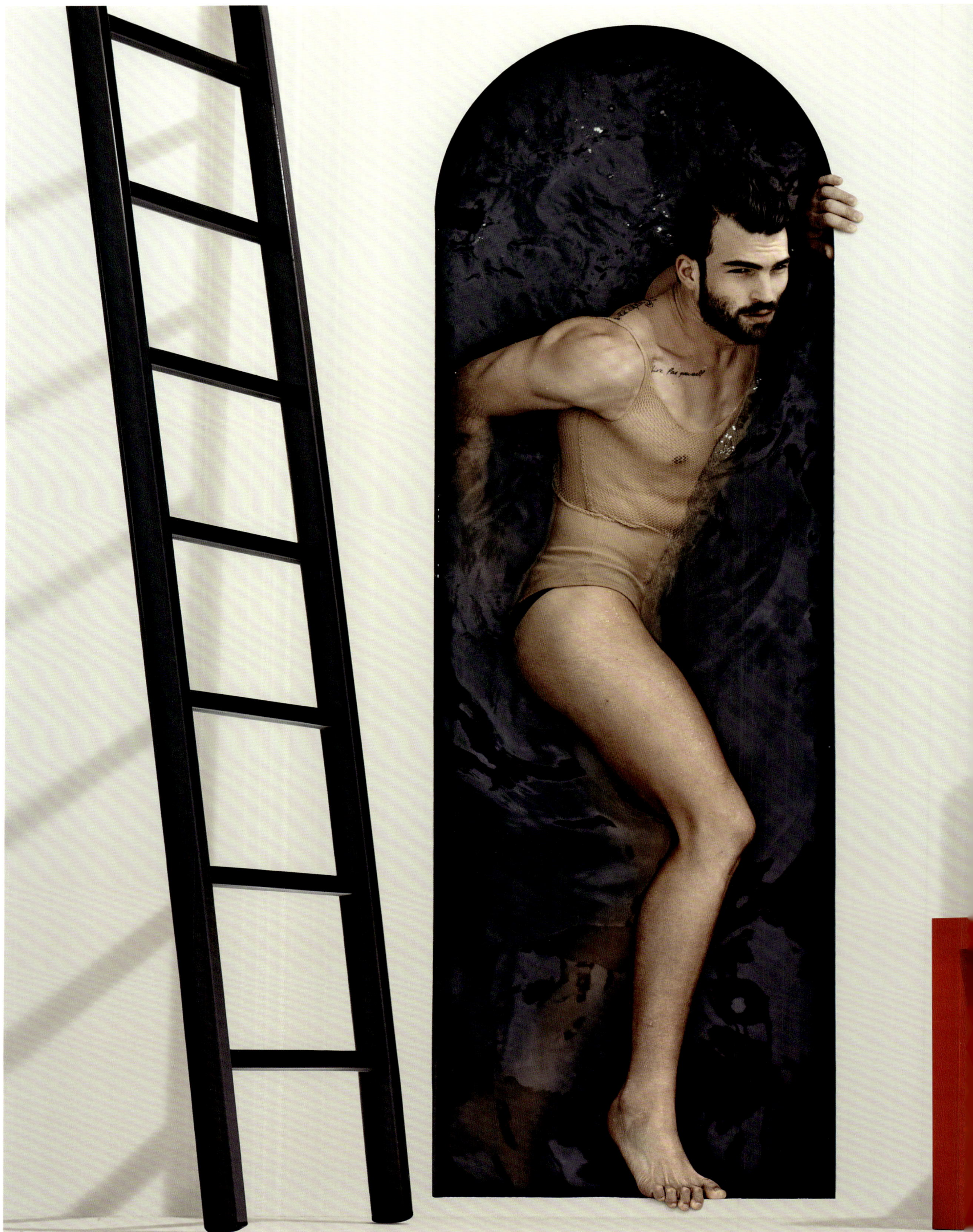

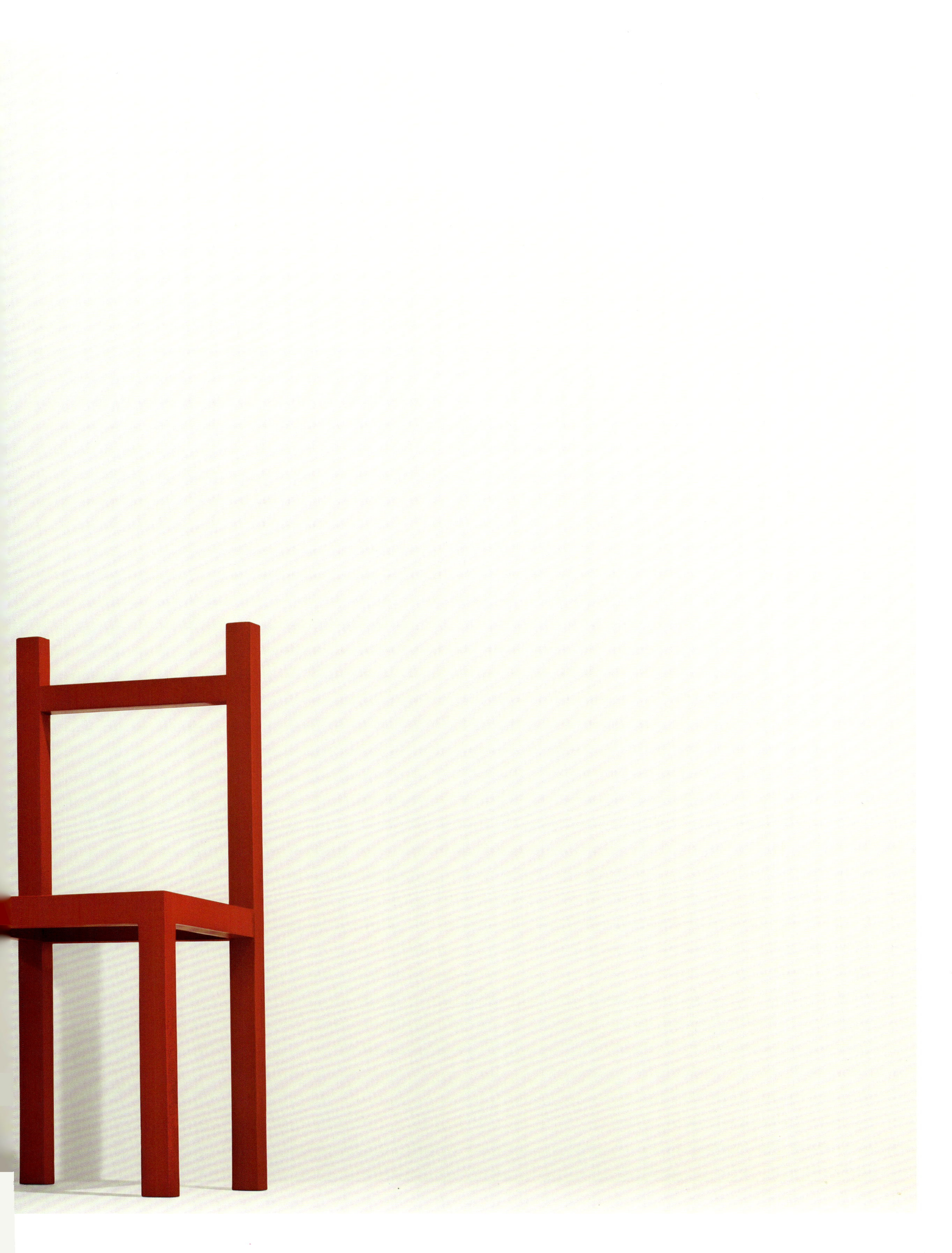

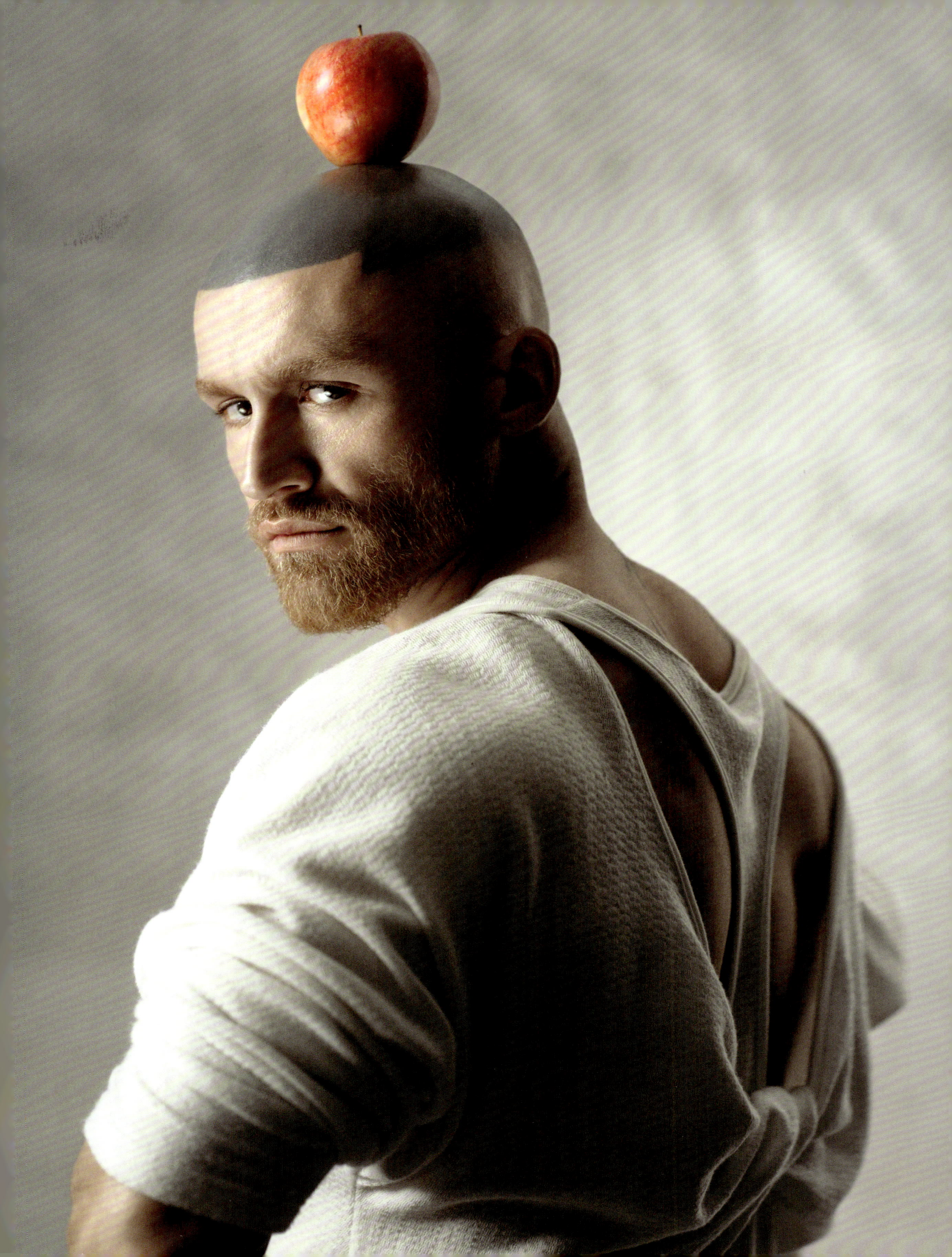

from 'Mental States'
for *Dazed & Confused*, 2011
photography by Pierre Debusschere
courtesy 254FOREST
and Pierre Debusschere

page 182:
Caleb Trent, *CT RE 8 NF PD*, 2012
photography by Pierre Debusschere
courtesy 254FOREST
and Pierre Debusschere
styling by Nicola Formichetti

page 183:
Dorian Jespers, *DJ RE 15 PD*, 2012
photography by Pierre Debusschere
courtesy 254FOREST
and Pierre Debusschere

pages 184–85:
from 'The Day the World Went Away'
for *Under/Current*, 2012
photography by Pierre Debusschere
courtesy 254FOREST
and Pierre Debusschere

Belgian-born experimental photographer and film director Pierre Debusschere deploys the diverse tools of digital photography as weapons with which to attack and remake his own work. A photograph in his hands is unlikely to escape unscathed: wild digital brush strokes swipe at his subjects, obscuring, warping and reforming the face and body to create something new and unfamiliar. Images are superimposed and double-exposed; on-screen, looped sequences create split-second animations as hypnotising, schizophrenic portraits.

Within all this frenzied, dazzling activity, Debusschere maintains control with a keen sense of composure. Compositional conventions are adhered to, if only to present an opportunity to abuse them. Within this framework, moments of high drama occur. In his series 'The Day The World Went Away' for the March 2012 edition of independent fashion magazine *Under/Current*, scenes of natural disaster, countdown clocks and seismograph readings are overlaid onto subjects that sit in serene, almost traditional poses (pages 186–87). The noise of fashion, news and pop media clash in what feels like a representation of a doomsday prophecy. The conflation is dynamic and controversial yet effective. Debusschere's taste for this kind of trance-like shifting also applies itself to his experiments in fashion film. In *The Lake*, French actress Isild Le Besco is submerged in a liquid that mutates from water to crystal. Again a timer counts down to the end of the footage, escalating the tension as the kinetic energy of the imagery is let loose.

In a field increasingly dominated by the technical potential of photography captured in pixels rather than photographic emulsion, Debusschere makes bold use of its side-effects. In his February 2012 series 'Mental States' for *Dazed & Confused*, supported by Katie Shillingford's wardrobe of vivid neon, Debusschere defaces model Marte Mei Van Haaster to create an aesthetic that celebrates the un-brush-like effect of digital retouching (page 183). The jarring animation of a GIF or the artificial feathering of a software brush, the seamless synthesising of multiple images and the blending of illustration into the real takes fashion photography into new territory that mirrors the relentless technical shifts of contemporary media.

Debusschere's style seems to buzz around so fast it is hard to pin down, and ultimately this is its driving force. Perhaps more than anything else, this high-octane approach is a simultaneous exploitation and satirisation of the overwhelming glare of fashion in a new media age.

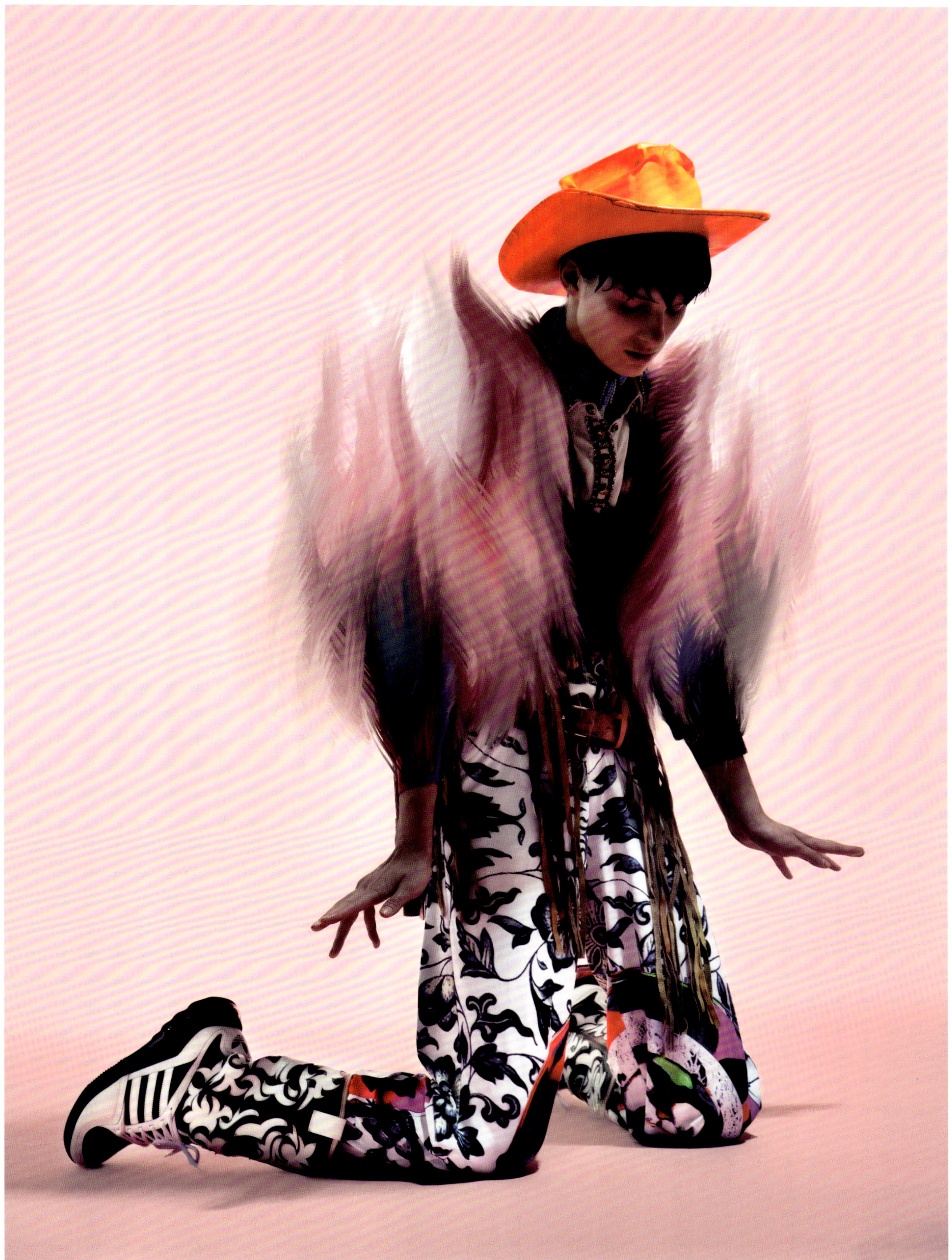

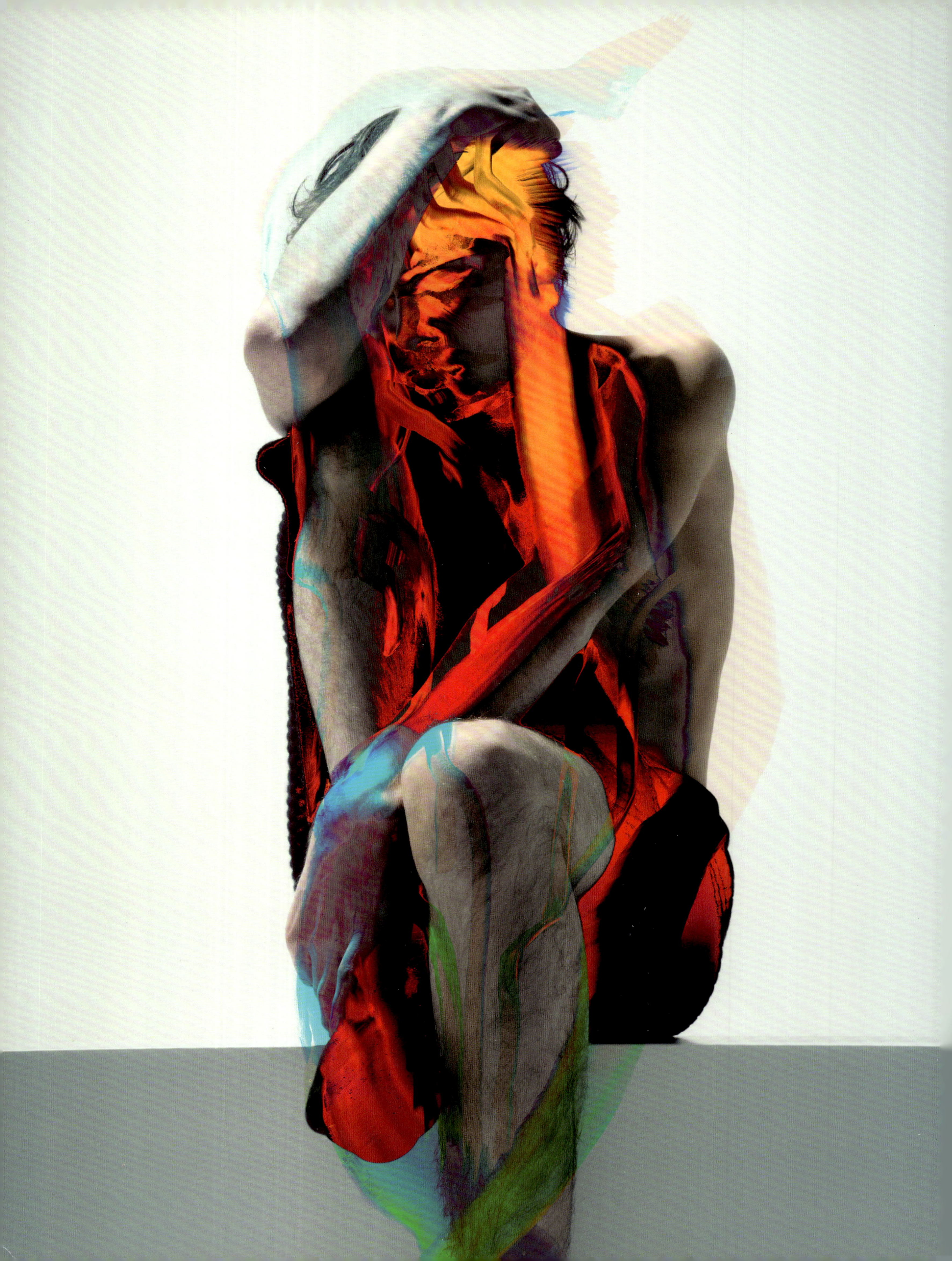

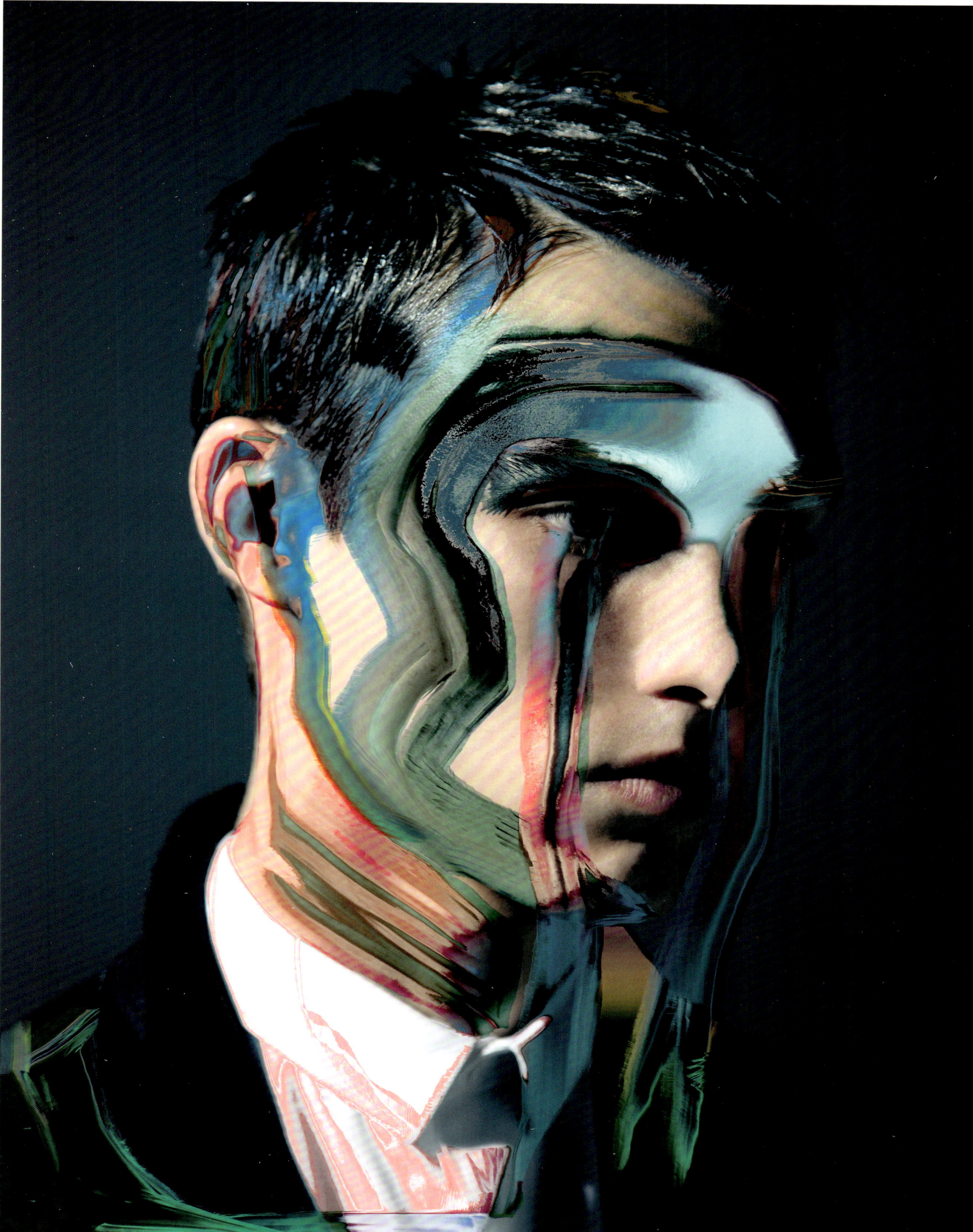

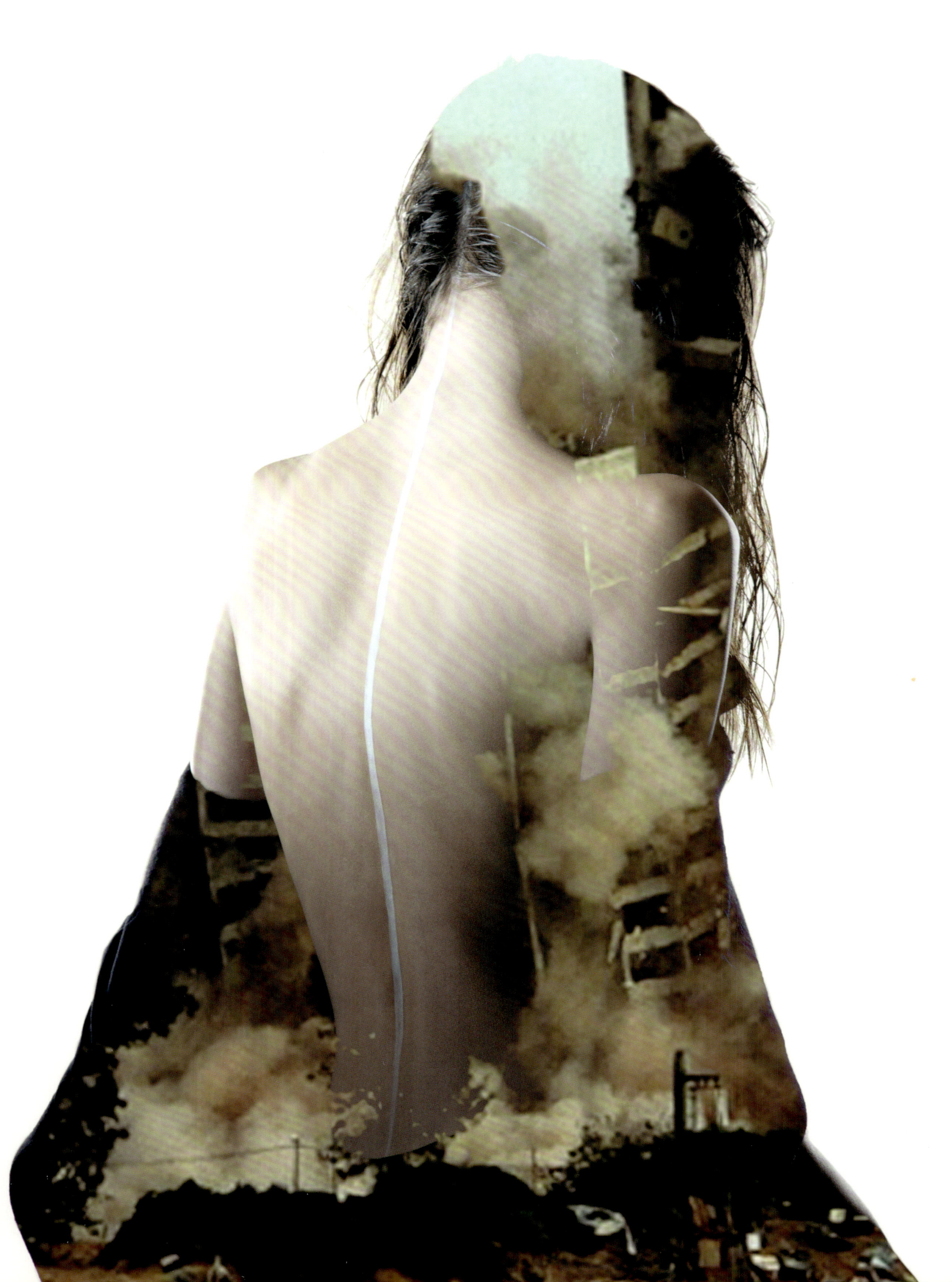

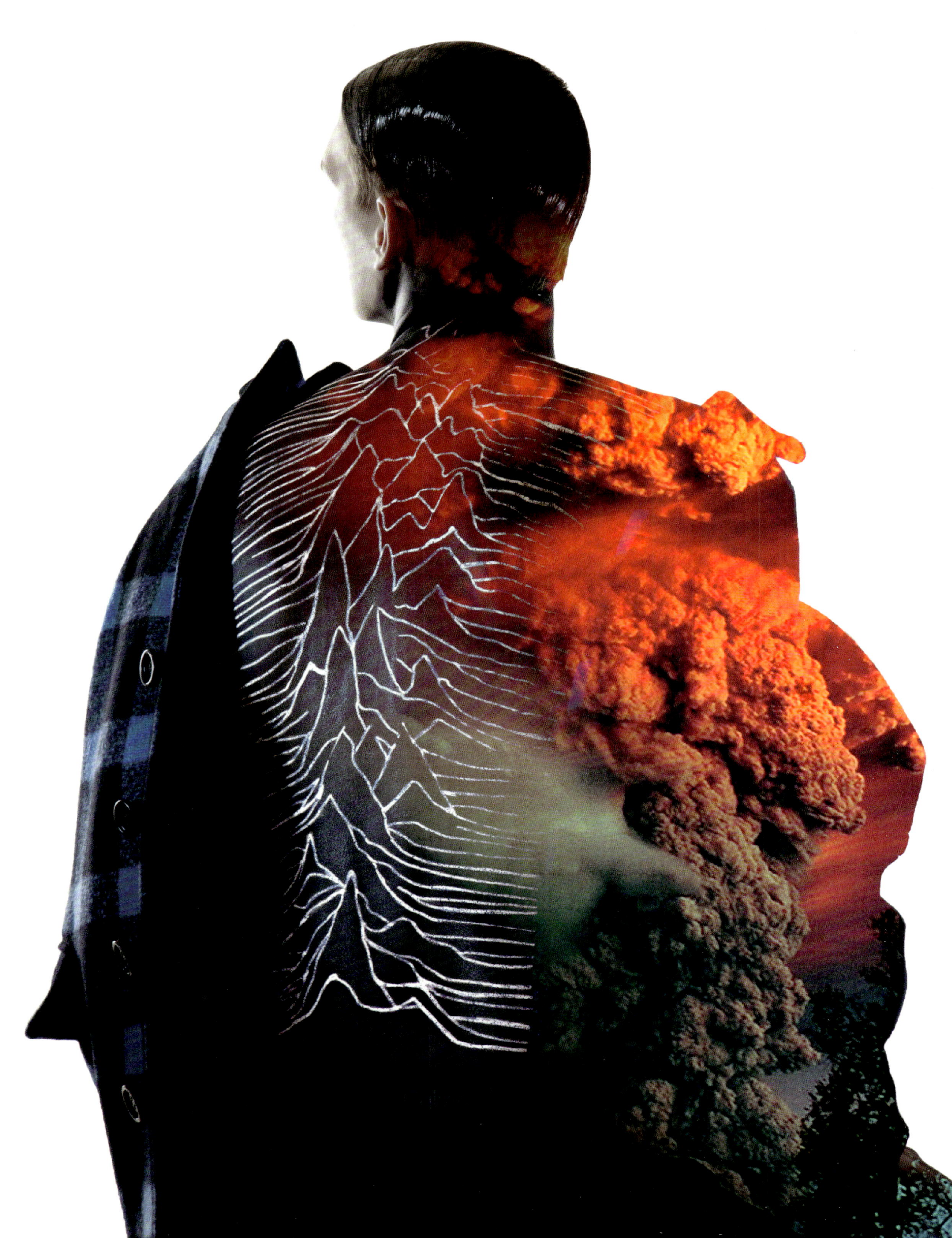

TIM RICHARDSON

'These Synthetic Moments'
for *Commons & Sense Man*
photography by Tim Richardson
courtesy Tim Richardson
styling by Shun Watanabe

pages 190–91:
'One Impression of Francis Bacon'
for *Vogue Hommes* Japan, 2012
photography by Tim Richardson
courtesy Tim Richardson
styling by Nicola Formichetti

pages 192–3:
'Collections' for *Dazed & Confused*, 2009
fashion by Tommy Hilfiger and Givenchy/Riccardo Tisci
photography by Tim Richardson
courtesy Tim Richardson
styling by Robbie Spencer

_|

Director and photographer Tim Richardson dissects the relationship between movement and the body through the filter of technology. Compressing sequential events into single images, he ruptures form through the fusion of time. These visual deconstructions splinter the image, creating an explosive transformation of the relationship between performance, fashion and the individual.

Richardson's grasp of the fluidity of movement places his work in a state of perpetual evolution. Still moments emerge out of motion and reform into a dynamic assemblage. The techniques of Richardson's experimental film *Physical Frequencies* inform the 2009 *Dazed & Confused* shoot 'Transition', in which pixel noise borrowed from compressed digital footage disrupts the image. In 2010, an editorial for Diesel styled by Shun Watanabe rarifies this image adulteration further to produce a pair of portraits that reemerge as neo-Cubist figures (pages 6–7). This process of perpetual reconstruction echoes the cycle of fashion as it revisits history, re-applying styles of the past in an ongoing socio-cultural dialogue.

From the angular macro-blocking of digital film footage to the soft blur of a slow shutter, technology defines the image, but concept dictates the technology. Richardson's process moves between photography, high-definition video and 3D scanning – the medium selected for its ability to translate the idea, in a call–response relationship between photographer, stylist and subject.

Contemporary art critic Russell Storer describes the audio-visual noise of Richardson's work as like the 'skull-cracking, nihilistic rhythms of industrial music, expressionist painting and punk rock,' spliced with 'a certain romanticism.' Richardson's engagement with change is not always angular and jarring. A connection with a softer-focus past is made in 'One Impression of Francis Bacon' for *Vogue Hommes* Japan in 2012 (pages 190–91). The origins of Bacon's images are the frenzied convulsions of a body in thrall to an internalised primal scream, but the colour, execution and finish of his paintwork lends romance to this physical surrendering. Acknowledging the fluidity of the artist's grasp of the body in transitional states, in one of many collaborations with stylist Nicola Formichetti, Richardson's homage captures the liquid flow of sinewy bodies as they break out of a three-dimensional frame reminiscent of the loose lines that hover around Bacon's own portraits.

Richardson's focus on the synthesis of ideas lifted from a world in flux finds a perfect partner in the performing arts. The energy of *6 Breaths*, a 2010 music and dance piece by Italian composer Ezio Bosso and Spanish choreographer Rafael Bonachela, is translated by Richardson into a reverse fracturing of a head and torso, shattered remnants streaming together to create a united whole. In these collaborations, in Richardson's own words, 'a visual friction with tradition leads to a digital clash between classical and contemporary visualizations of the figure'. Exposing moments that escape the eye but are revealed by technology, Richardson's language is ultimately the fragmented visualisation of time itself.

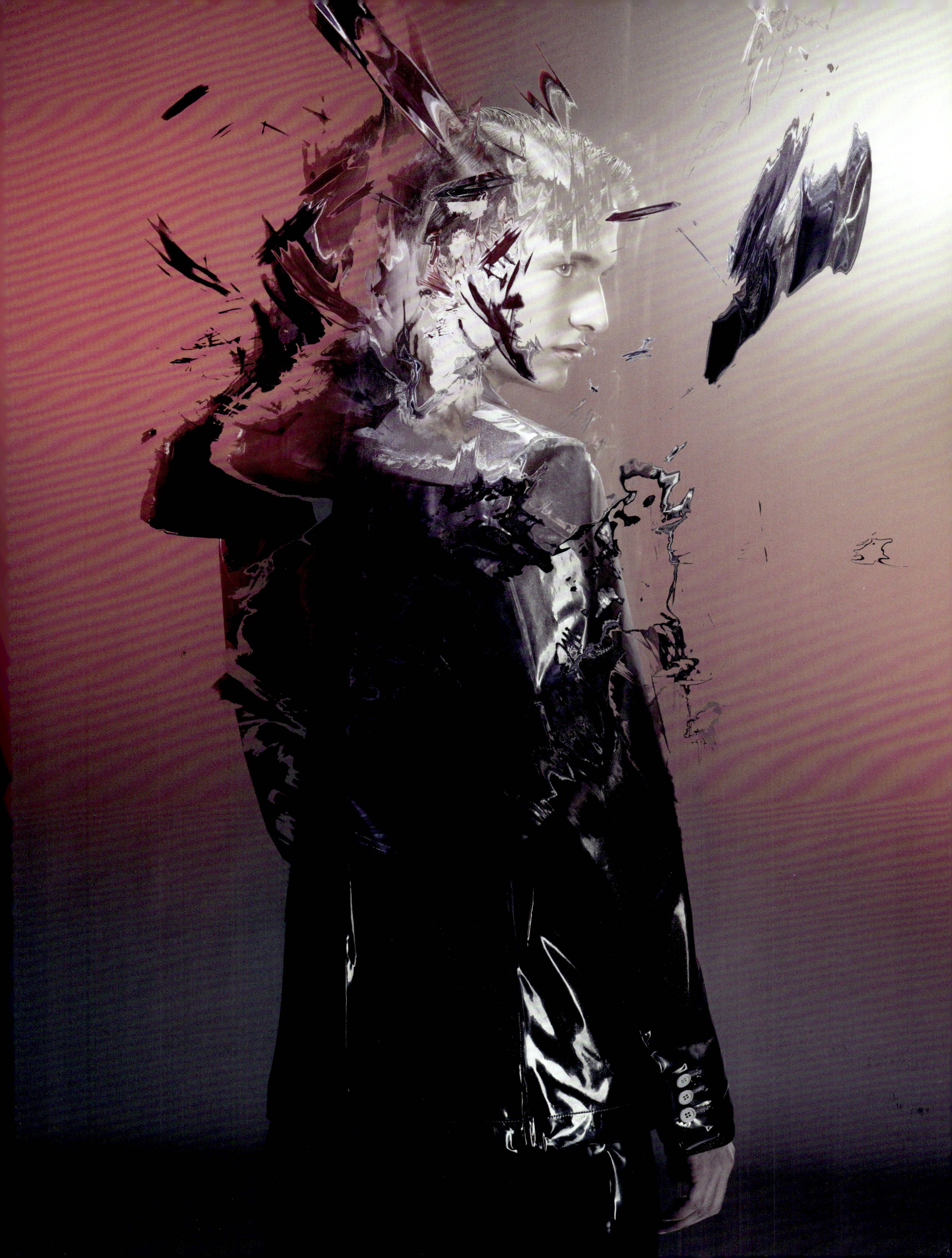

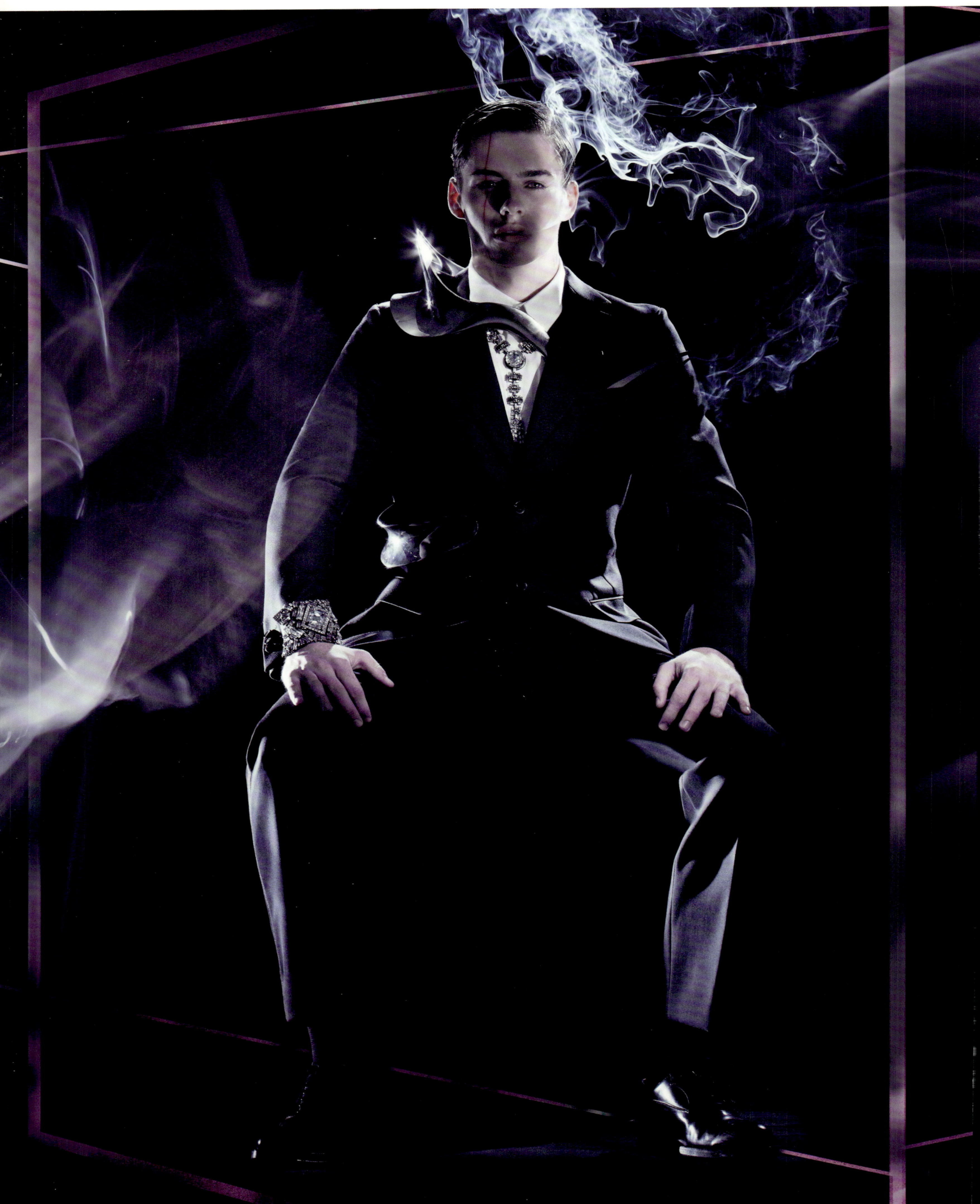

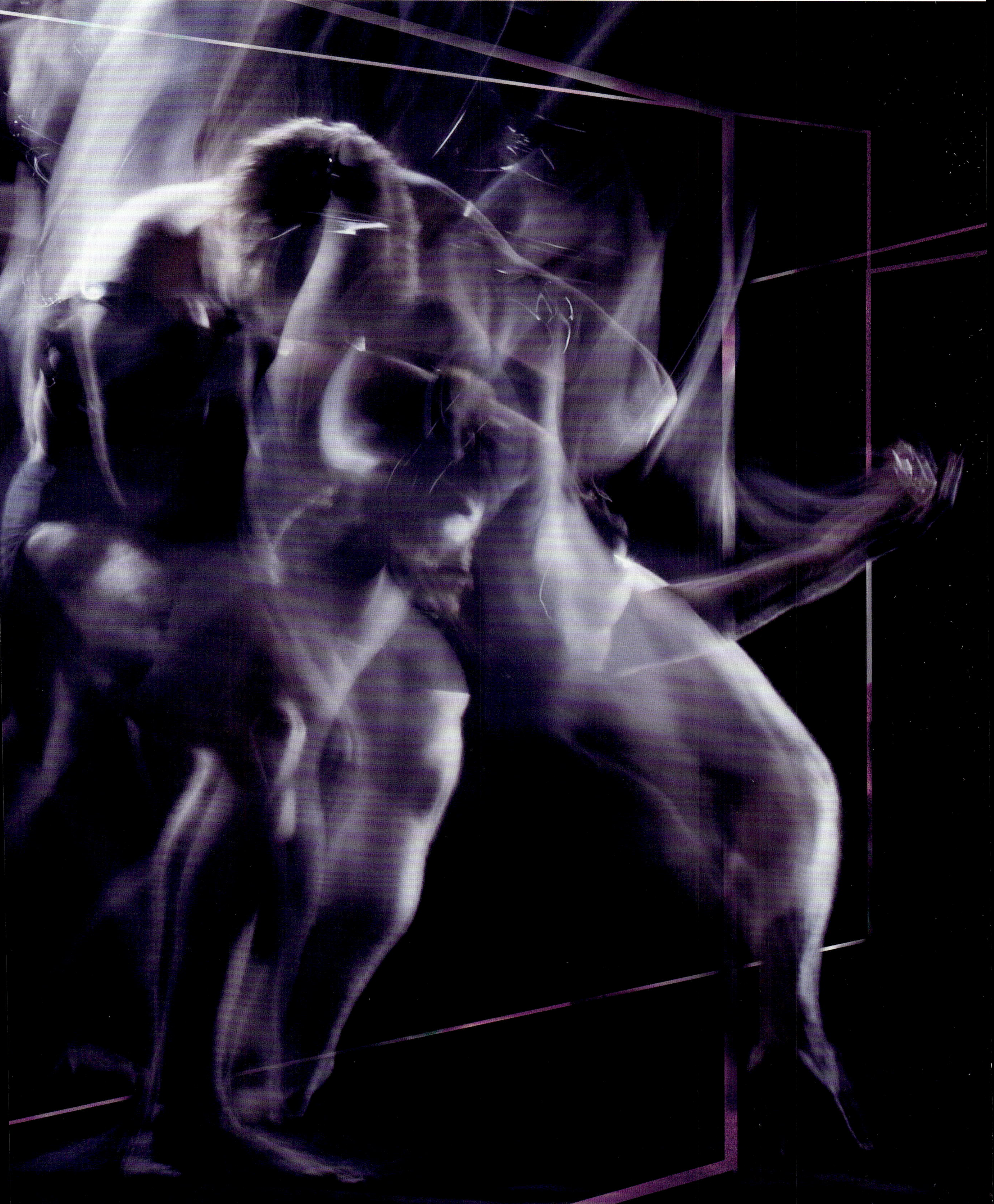

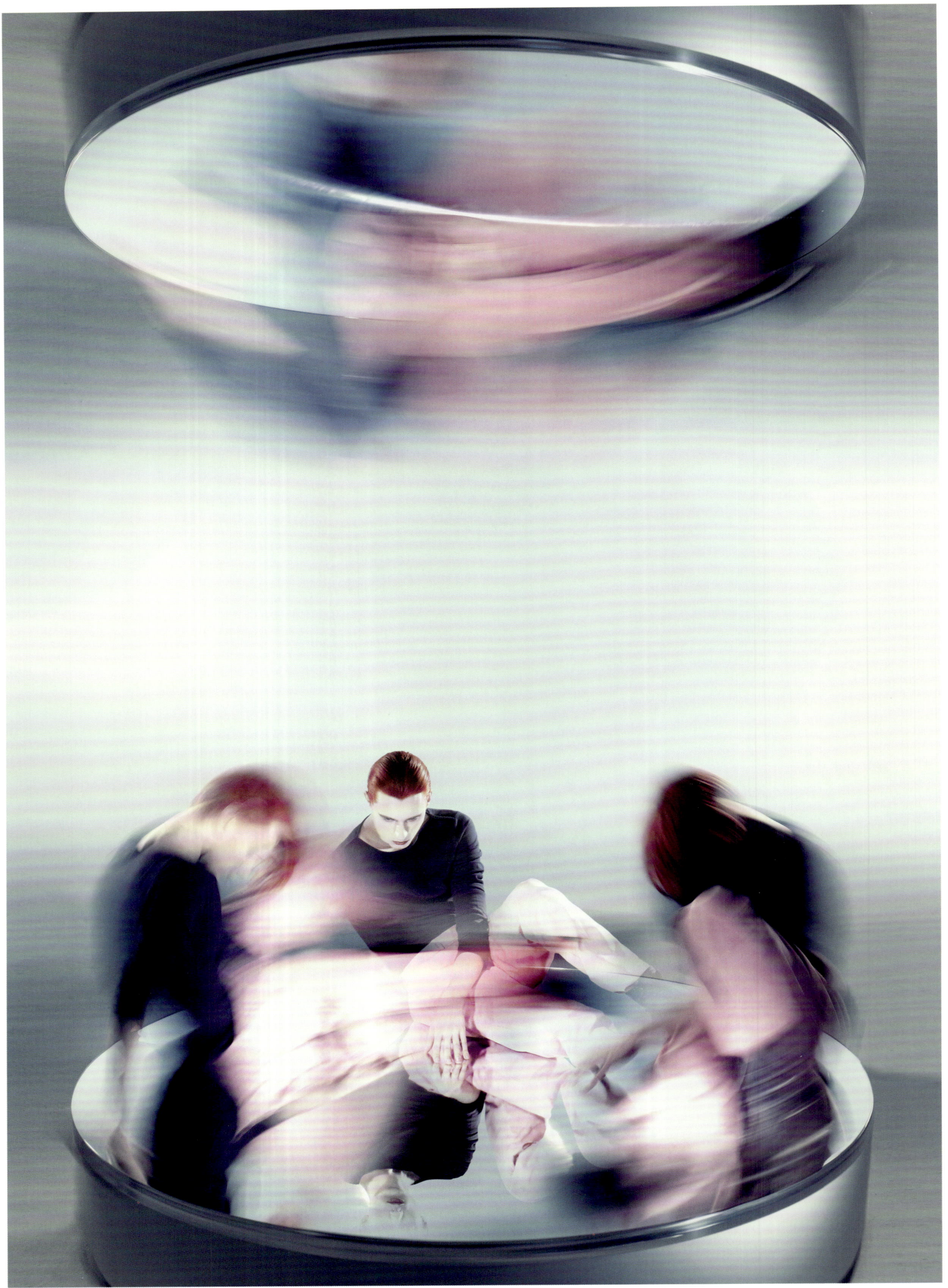

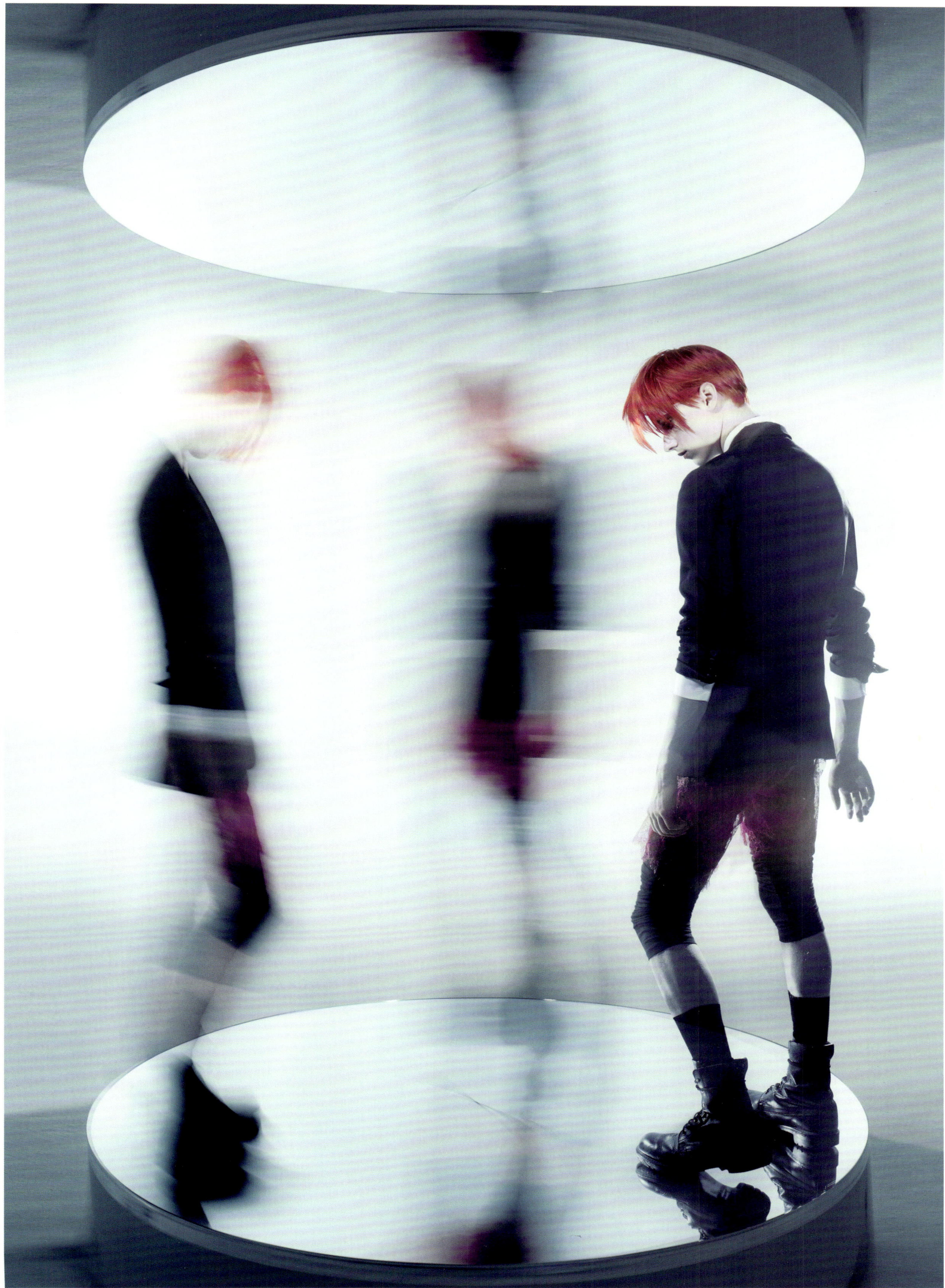

'Nonsense in the Dark', 2009
photography by Paco Peregrín
courtesy Paco Peregrín
styling by Kattaca

Spanish photographer Paco Peregrín combines avant-garde futurism with otherworldly beauty. Using a technique that distinguishes itself by its clean lines and rich contrasts, Peregrín's images of contemporary fashion recreate the familiar as Arcadian elegance. At the same time there is a persistent sense that something sinister is lurking beneath the surface, an effect achieved through disconcerting interventions on the face and body.

The alien aspect of Peregrín's work is achieved through a theatrical use of makeup and a dedication to digital post-production, techniques rooted in his multidisciplinary background in theatre and design. His vivid exploration of colour dictates the tone of each series he creates, the consistency throughout his work found not so much in the colours themselves as the attitude he takes towards them. Whether relishing in the cool austerity of a restricted palette for his 2009 editorial 'Nonsense in the Dark', or indulging in all-out kaleidoscopic arrangements for his 2011 solo exhibition *Beautiful Monster*, this vibrant fusion is exercised at both extremes but delivered with a consistent finish.

The fashion depicted in 'Nonsense in the Dark' is firmly focused in fantasy (pages 195–97) . An air of disquiet is created through a futuristic take on tribal dress that is elevated by cosmetic enhancement, deployed either to wash out features or to pick out details in black. The clothes disfigure the body and exaggerate the hair, the figures themselves set within cool, concrete settings that border on the abstract. There is something pensive and uncertain about this series; we are being invited to look upon a future world that seems to have developed out of science fiction, but it is unclear whether it is a utopia or dystopia.

Peregrín's portraits for *Beautiful Monster* epitomise the double-edged nature of his art. The photographs glimmer with the beauty of the people they depict, but the faces themselves have been subjected to such intrusive over-adornment that the line between seduction and horror has become blurred. Each image involves refiguring of the face, perhaps the most immediately vulnerable part of the body. One woman leans forward suggestively, but her eyes are hidden by a circle of diamonds. The diamonds spread out across her features and push out from between her lips, creating a mask that draws out the structure of her skull. In another portrait, a head is bound in muslin and makeup leaks unsettlingly out from beneath (pages 198–99). Another is entirely obscured as her own hair takes over. Despite this monstrous undertone, however, it is a curious beauty that dominates. In finding this beauty in uncertain places, Peregrín's work creates a platform from which to raise questions about the presentation of the human form as a canvas for fashion.

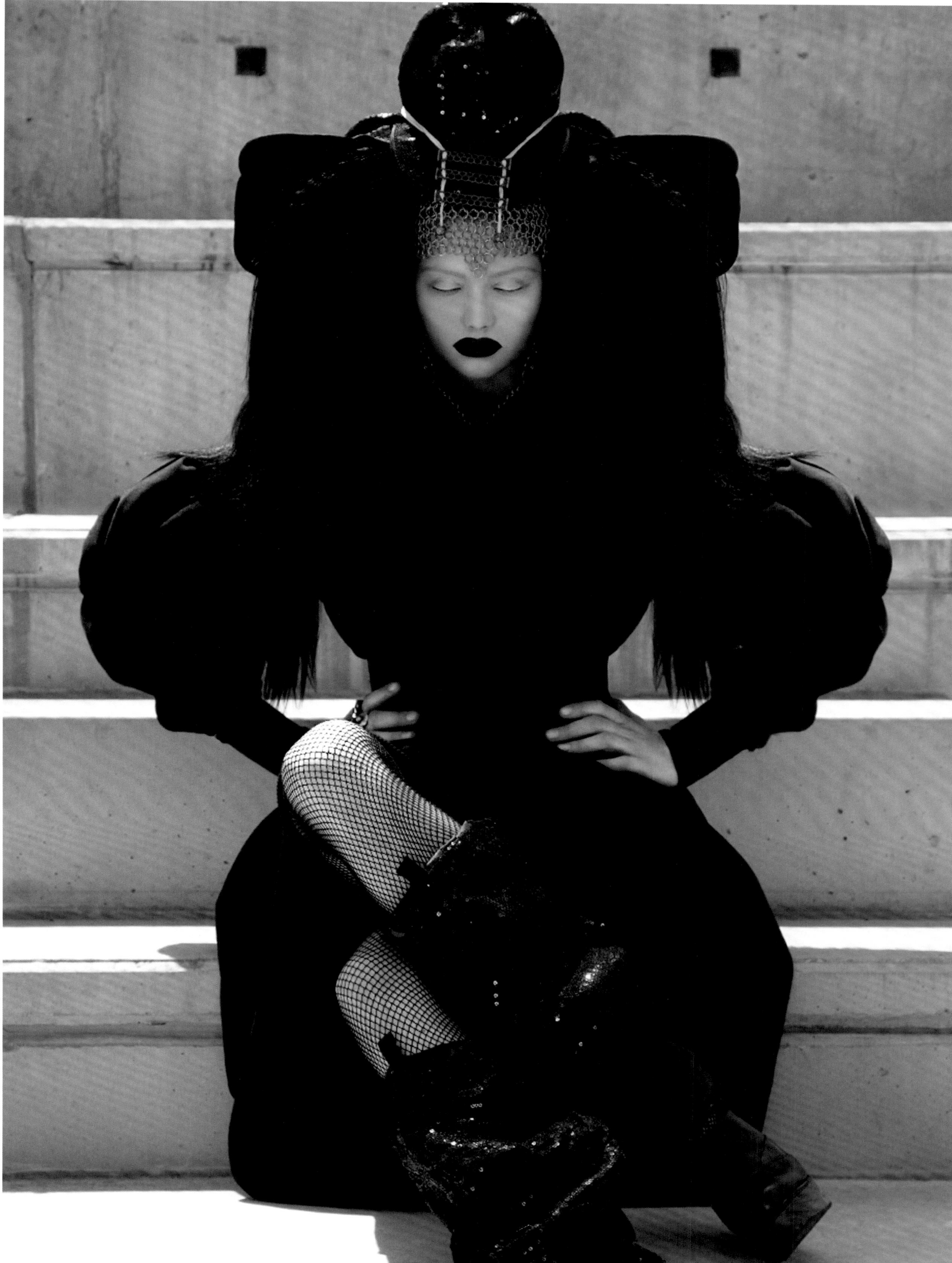

PACO PEREGRÍN

from 'Nonsense in the Dark', 2009
photography by Paco Peregrín
courtesy Paco Peregrín
styling by Kattaca

pages 198–99:
from *Beautiful Monster*, 2011/12
exhibited at Visionairs Gallery,
Paris and Vered Art Gallery, New York
photography by Paco Peregrín
courtesy Paco Peregrín

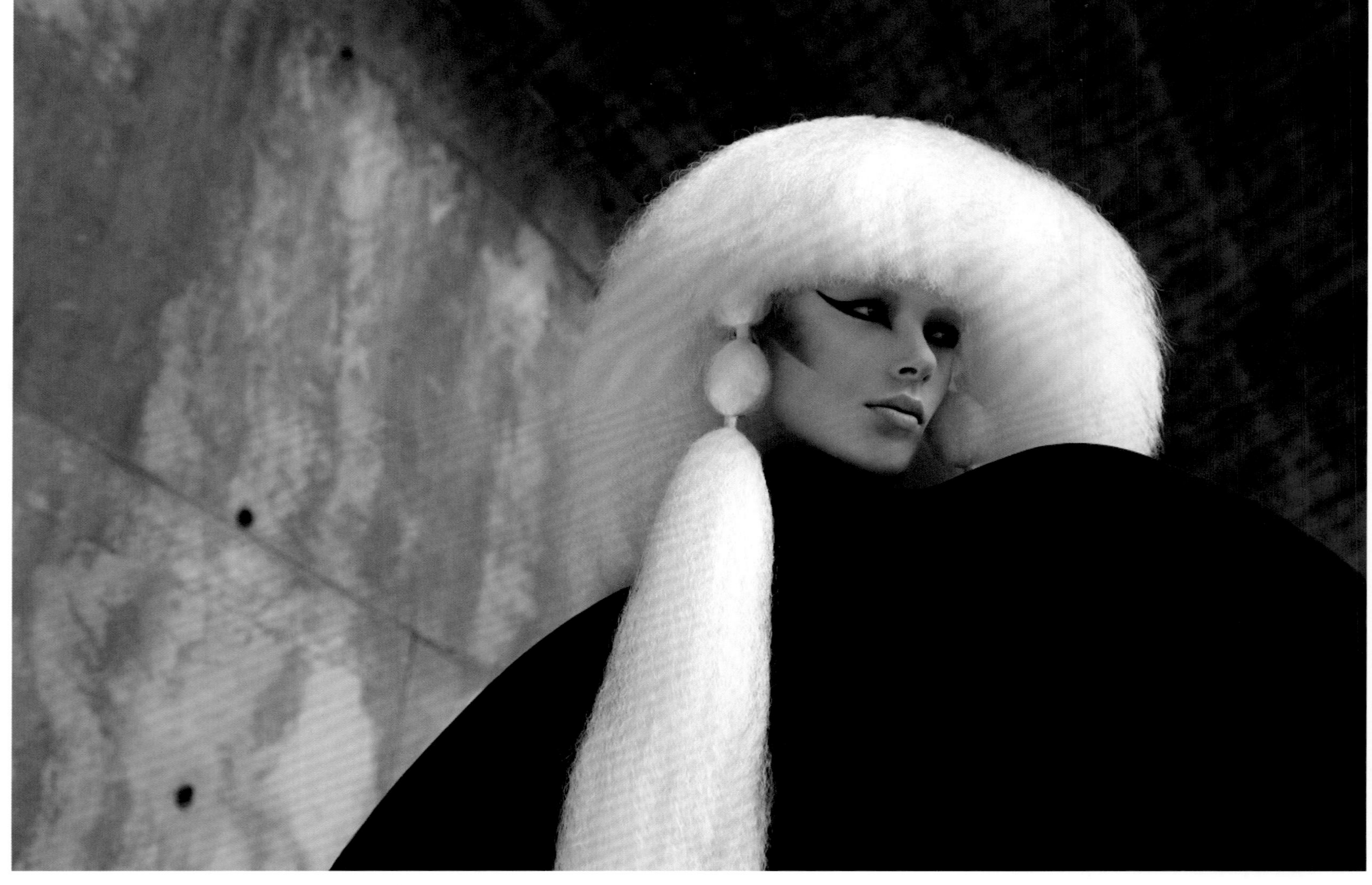

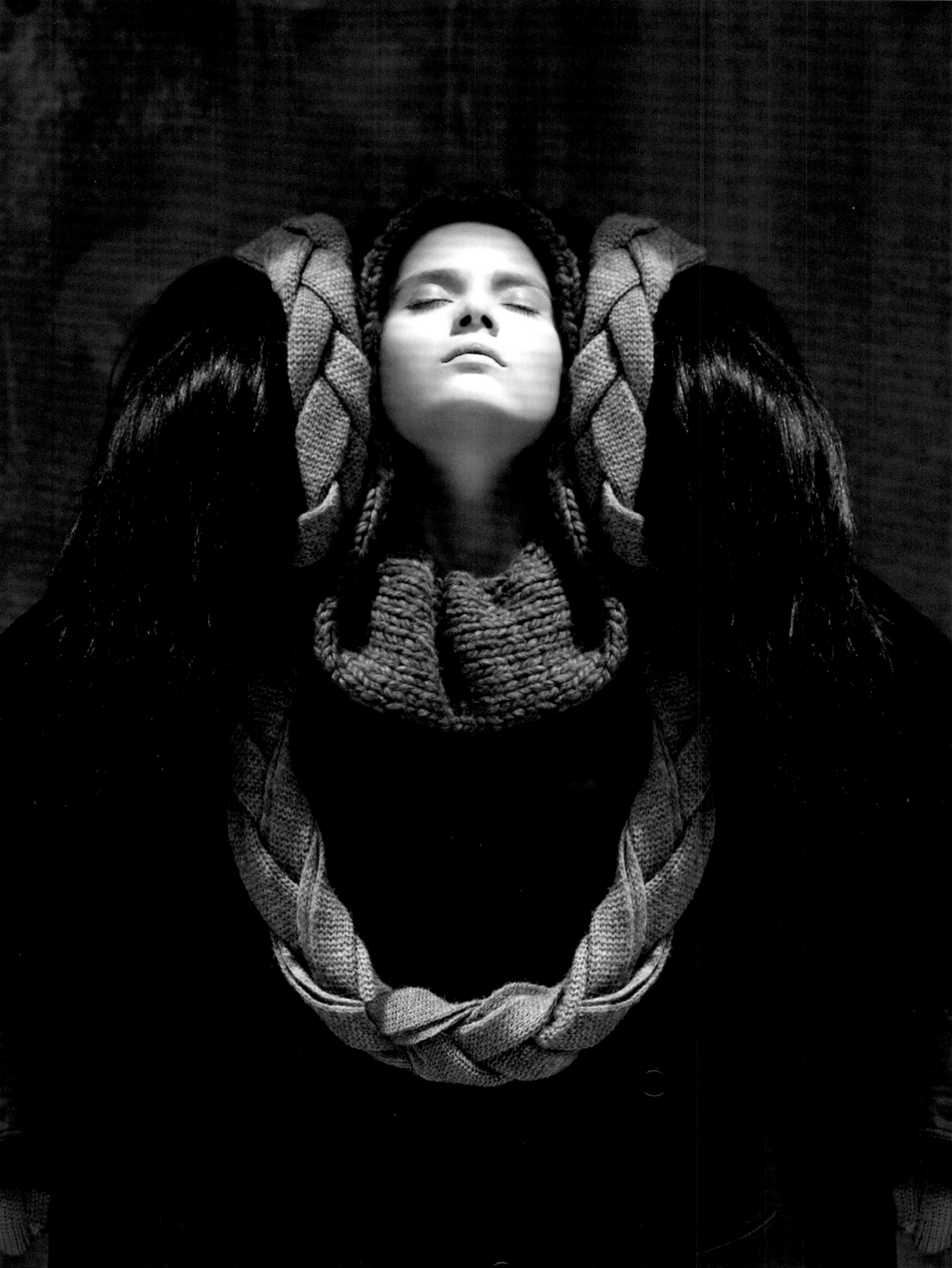

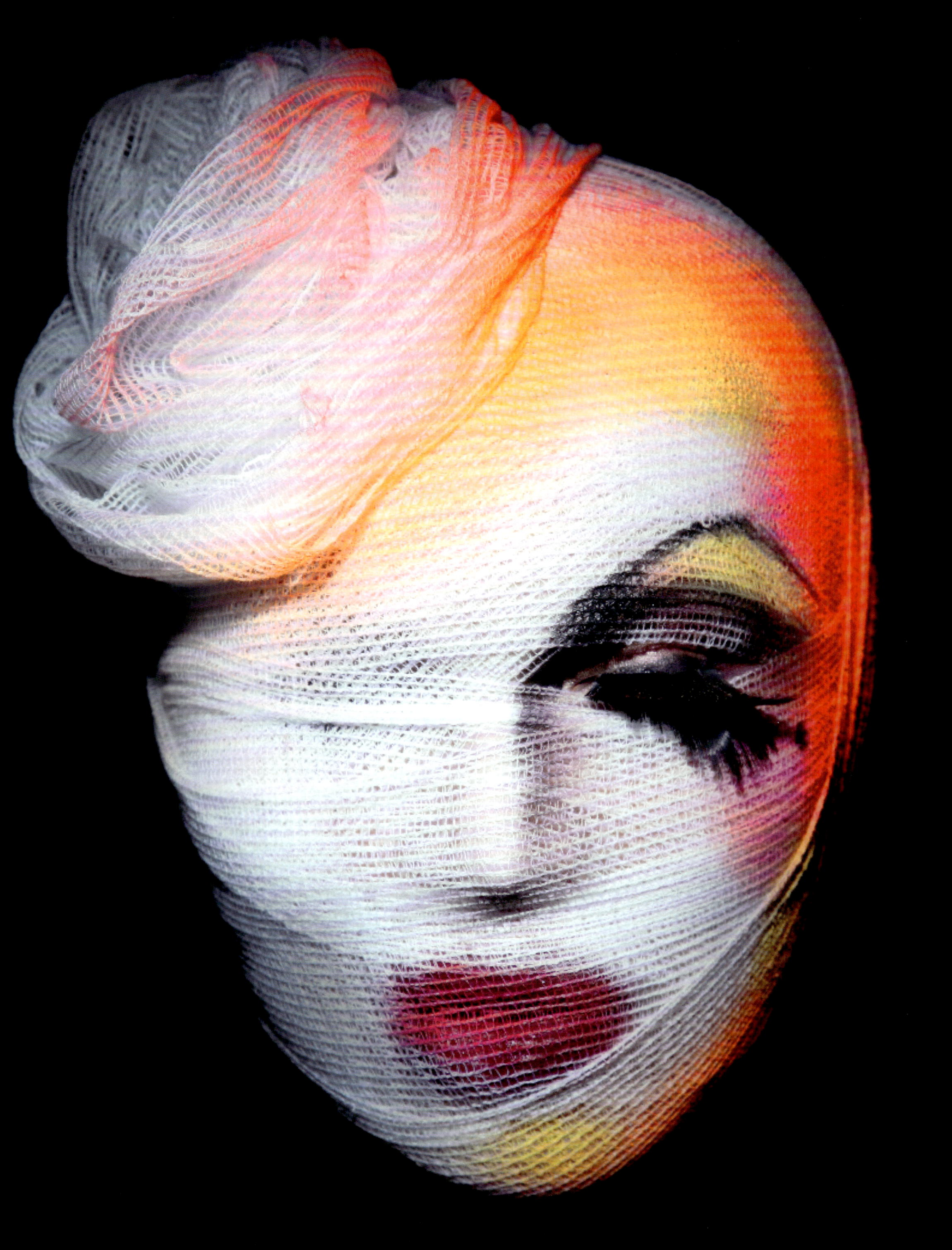

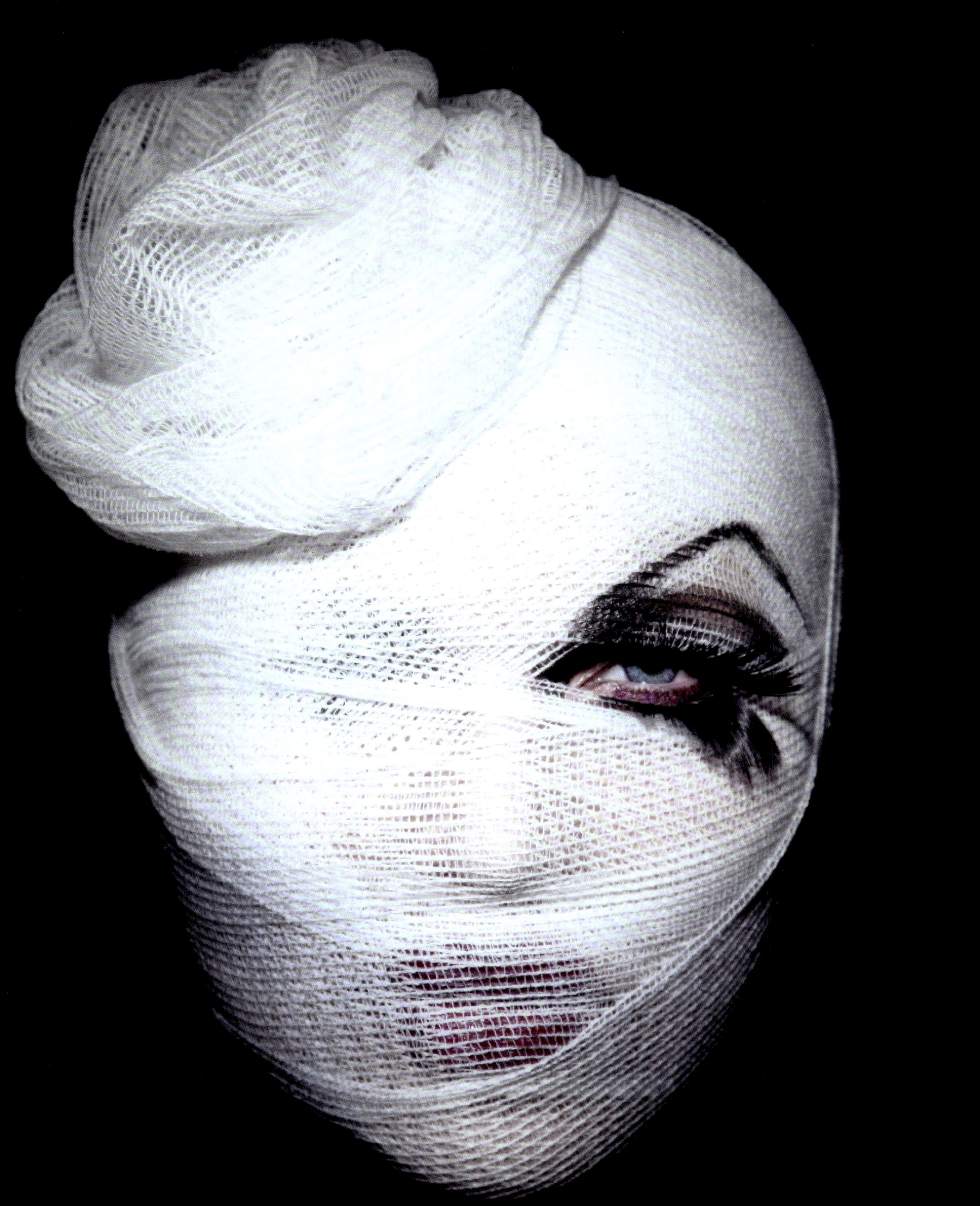

Antonia Wesseloh for *Vision* China, 2012
photography by Yasunari Kikuma
courtesy Yasunari Kikuma
styling by Kamo

pages 202–5:
Untitled + 0, 2010
photography by Yasunari Kikuma
courtesy Yasunari Kikuma
fashion director Robbie Spencer
featuring fashion from graduates
of Central St Martins London

Japanese photographer Yasunari Kikuma looks at couture through a purist lens, turning to future fashions for inspiration and producing photographs that embrace the avant-garde in design. Clean portraits, free from props and distractions, express the interaction between extraordinary fashion and the individual, allowing dress to become an outward extension of character and disposition.

Kikuma experiments with moments in transition in his 2012 collaboration with fashion director Robbie Spencer, using the experimental fashions of recent graduates of Central St Martins College of Art and Design in London (pages 202–5). Models wear deconstructed fabrics and fibreglass armatures that, as college experiments, exist outside the confines of the market. Kikuma's staggered double-exposures create a disruption that mirrors the disruptive thrill of the work on display. The effect makes translucent costumes from polygonal matrices hover, seemingly gravity-free, around undressed models in a visualisation of the blurred boundary between physical and digital worlds (page 202).

Kikuma's interaction with dress amounts to a filtered reinterpretation of the designer's vision. In one portrait, slabs of colour slapped onto sheets of fabric with thick paint wrap around a model. It is a powerful expressive moment, but the image takes things further by painting the strips of colour across the wearer's face, so that the dress and the individual become one. This intimate interaction is reminiscent of the working relationship between the fashion of Issey Miyake and the lens of Irving Penn. Just as Penn reworked Miyake's collections and in doing so creatively sparred with the designer, so Kikuma's photographs give new life to clothes and adornment, allowing them to speak through a non-invasive approach to photographic technique.

In a 2012 editorial for *Vision* China, Kikuma collaborates with hair artist Kamo to produce a series of futurist masks that compliment Kikuma's grasp of shape through fragmented forms. Reflective shards cling to the eyes and metal visors wrap around the face to create avatars to a parallel universe. A mask made of polygonal shapes (page 201) is suggestive of a model plugged into a digitised alternative reality; others propose a new armour for an imagined future.

Originally from Shizuoka in Japan, Kikuma began photography during a two-year period in Paris. Returning to Japan he embarked on a career that has since included shooting portraits of Penélope Cruz, Dita Von Teese, Jane Birkin and Kate Moss. Drawing on a style that he explicitly locates in the cultural aesthetic of Japan, his focus on fashion that exposes construction, geometry and technique echoes the deconstructed approach of Japanese designers such as Junya Watanabe, Rei Kawakubo and Yohji Yamamoto.

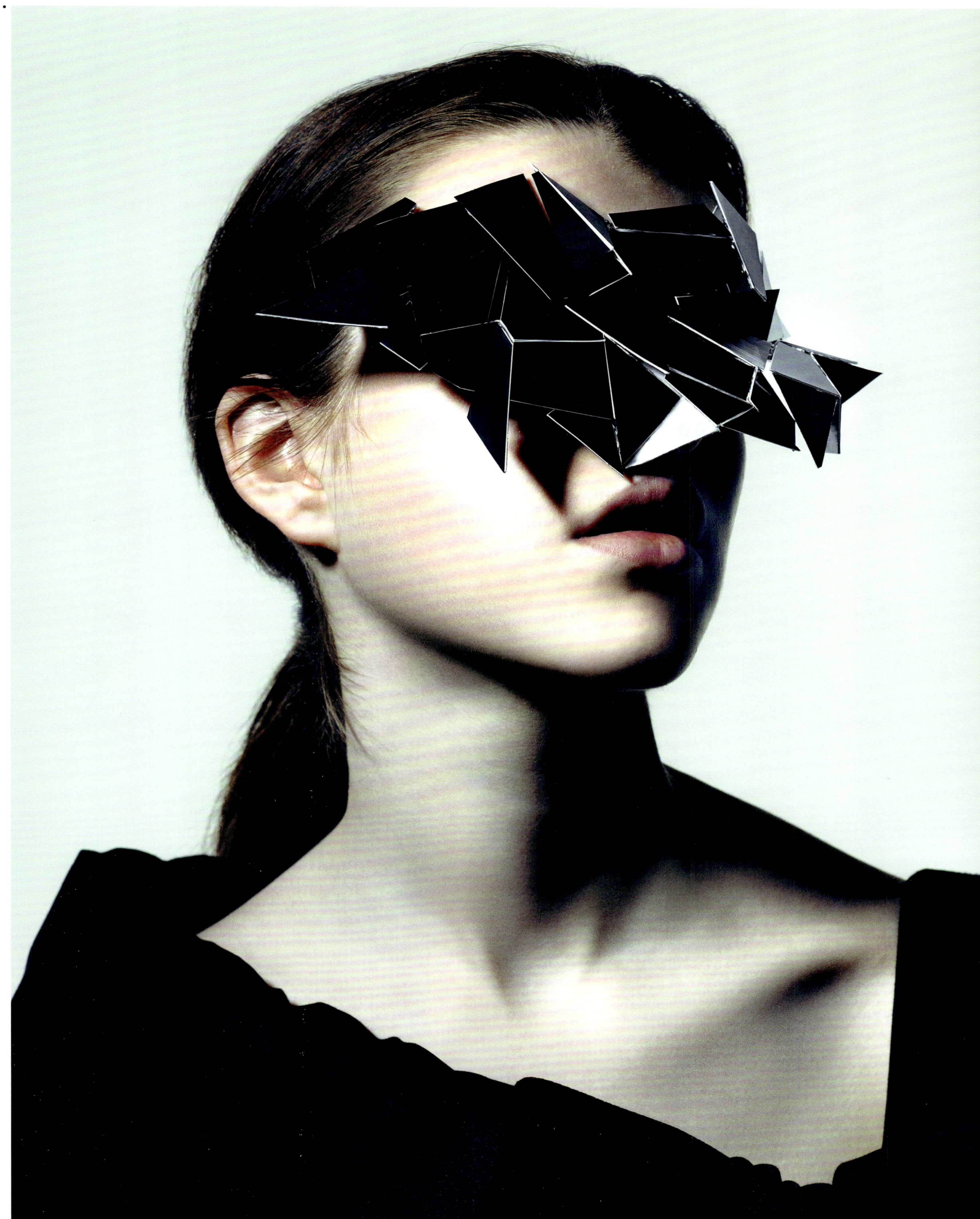

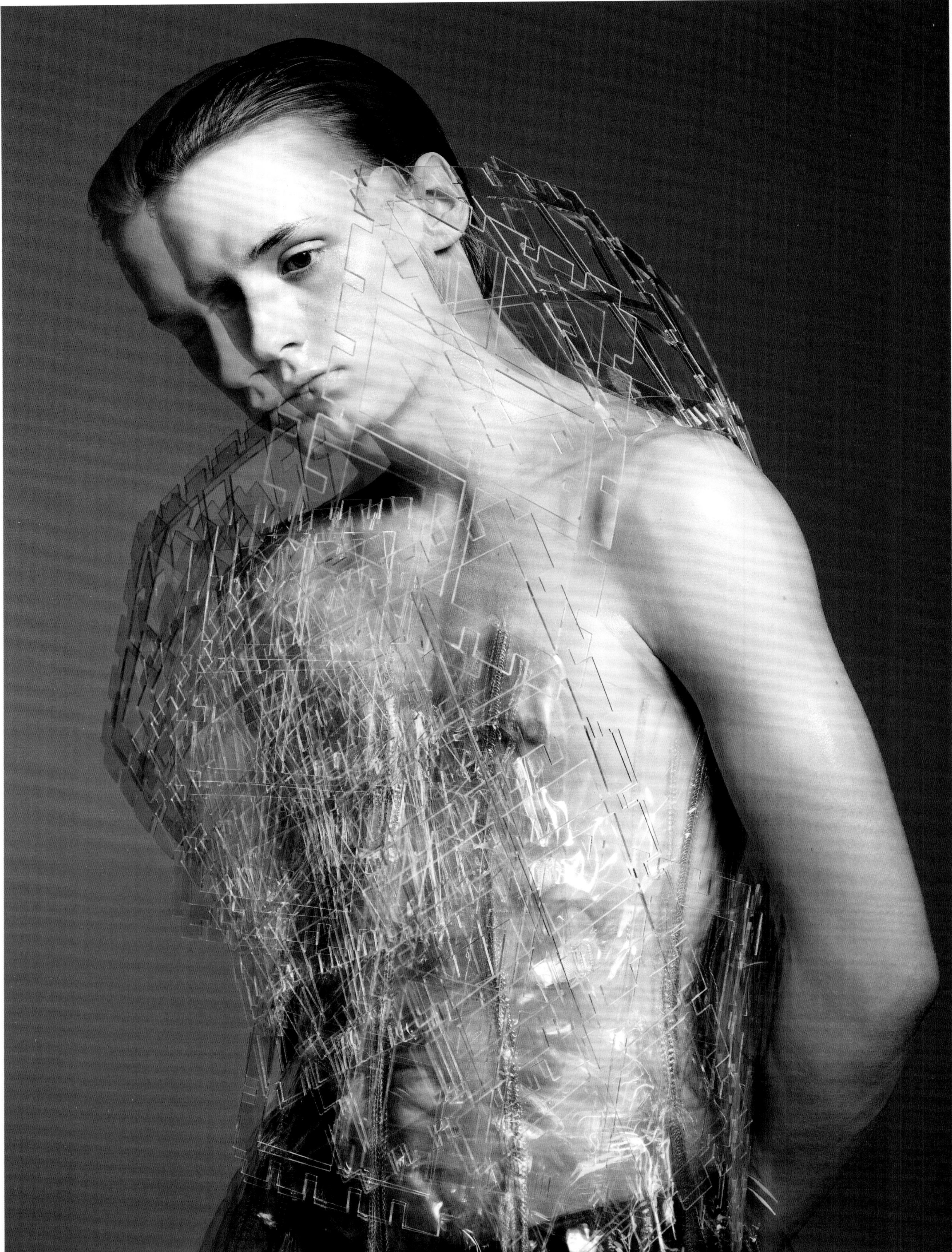

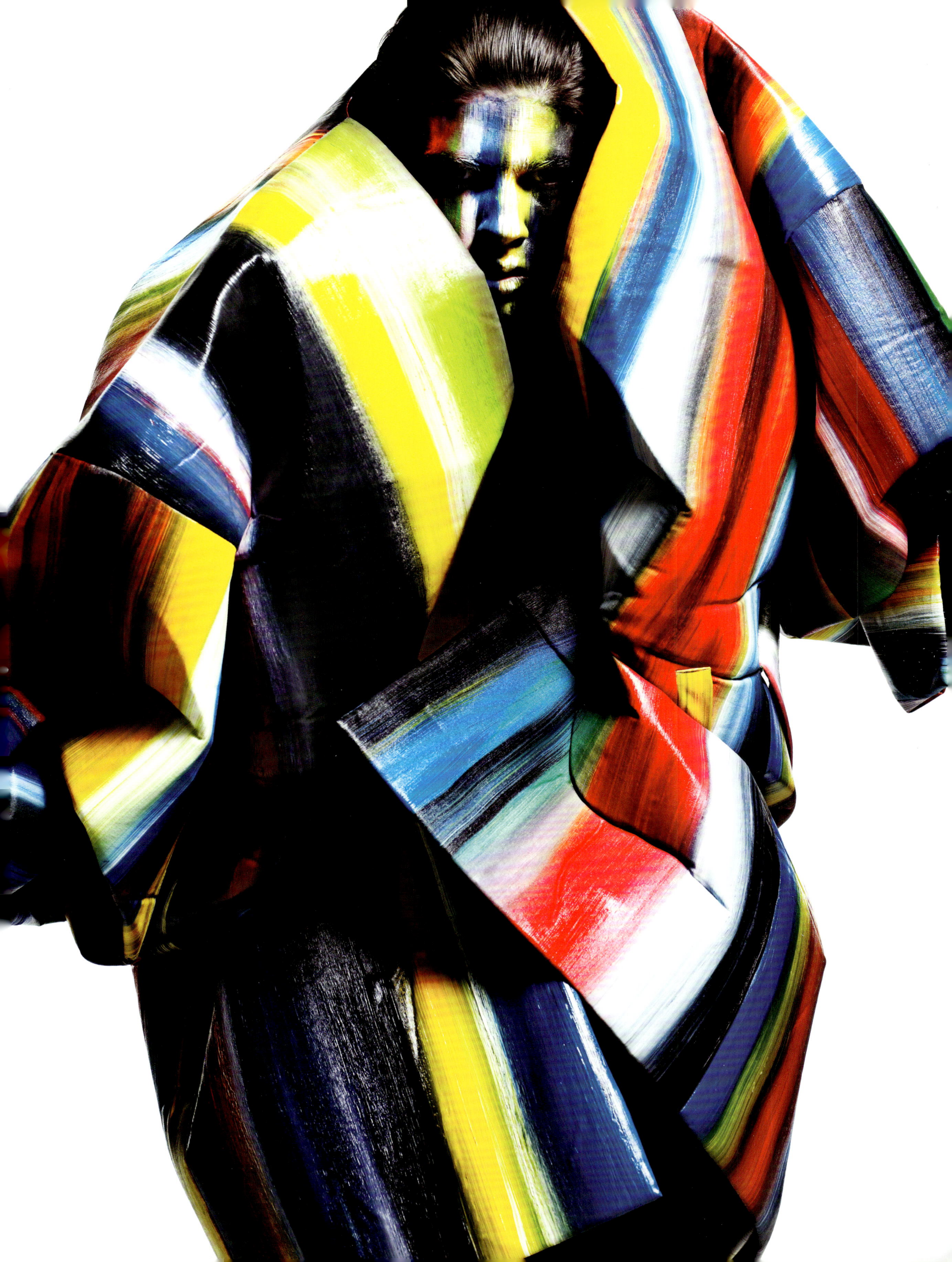

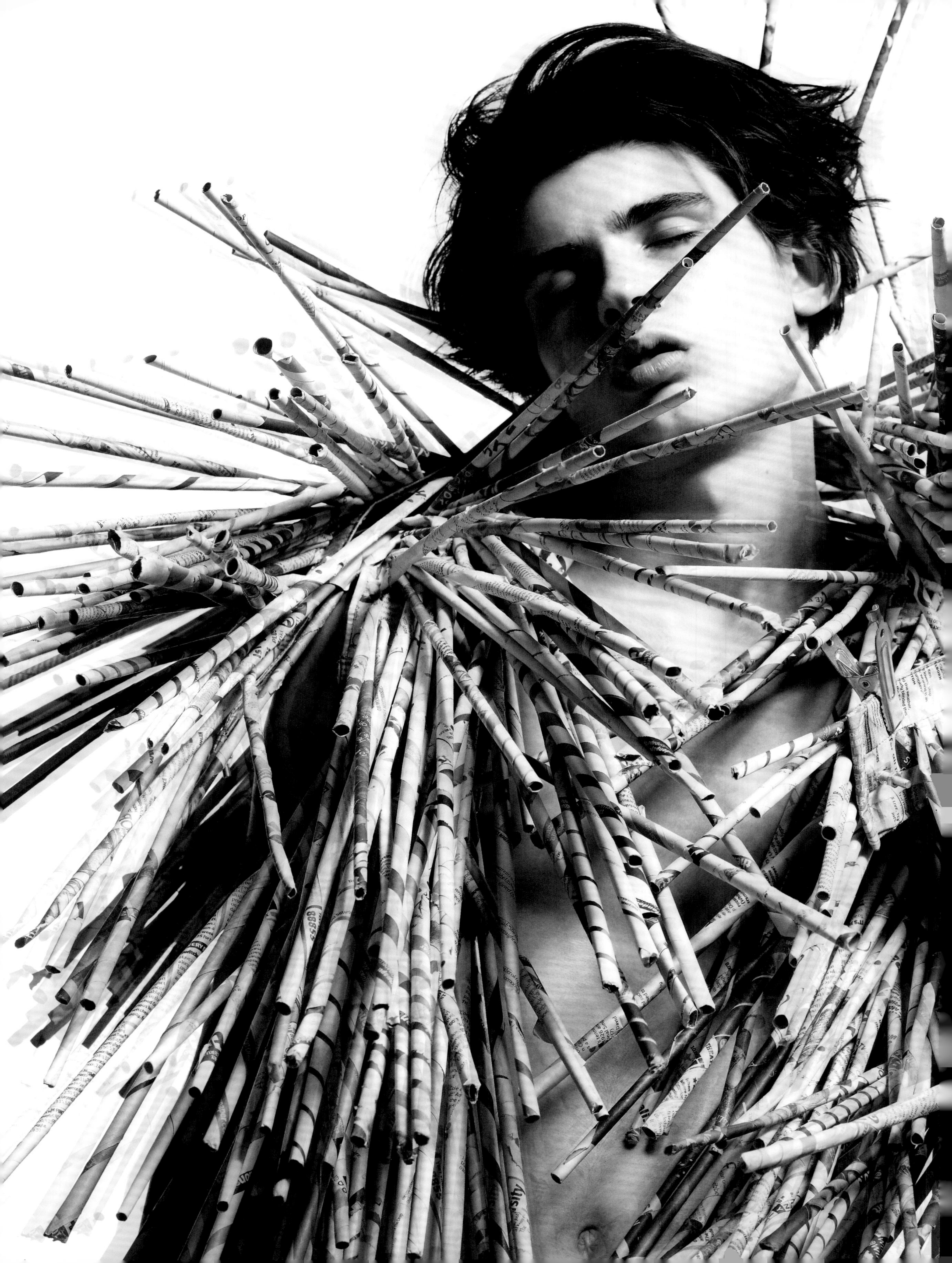

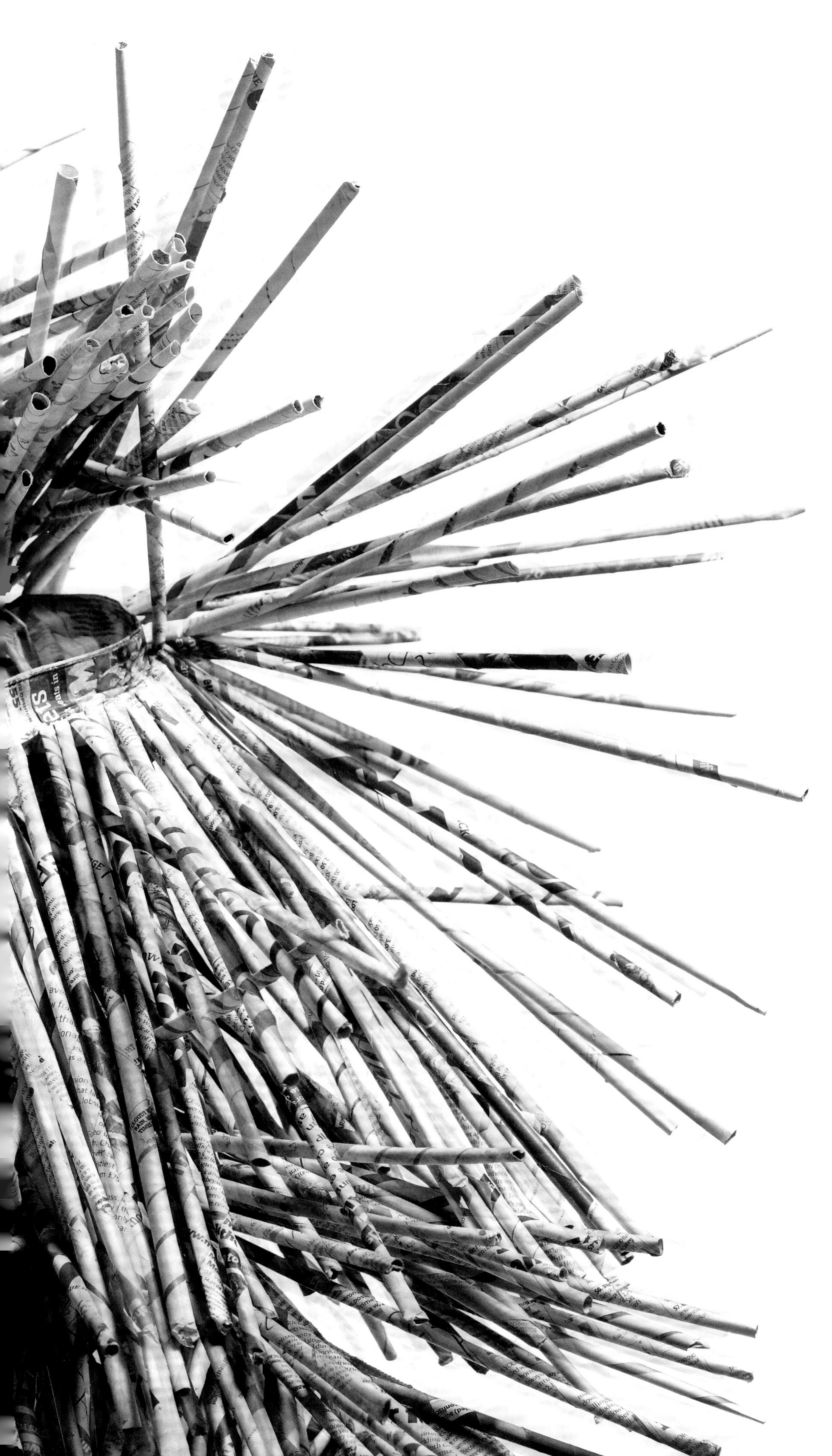

RUVEN AFANADOR
Alongside editorials for magazines such as *Vogue* Paris, *Harper's Bazaar*, *Elle*, *LA Times*, and *Yo Doña*, Ruven Afanador has published the collectible photography series *Torero*, *Mil Besos* and *Sombra*. His work has featured in the book *Isabel Toledo* and in the exhibition *Beyond Words: Photography in The New Yorker* at Howard Greenberg Gallery in New York in 2011. Solo exhibitions include *Seven* at the Forma Photography Centre in Milan, Italy, in 2006, *and Mil Besos/Torero* at the Fahey/Klein Gallery in Los Angeles in 2011.

MILES ALDRIDGE
Miles Aldridge has shot covers and editorials for American *Vogue*, *Vogue* Italia, *Numéro*, the *New York Times* and *Paradis*, amongst others, alongside campaigns for Lavazza and Angelo Marani. His work has appeared in *Weird Beauty* at the International Center of Photography in New York and his 2009 exhibition *Doll Face* at Hamiltons Gallery in London accompanied the launch of his book *Miles Aldridge: Pictures for Photographs*. His work also resides in the collections of the Victoria & Albert Museum and the National Portrait Gallery in London.

ARAM BEDROSSIAN
Since pursuing fashion photography professionally in 2010, Aram Bedrossian has shot editorials for *LoveCat* and *Avenue*, and has shot campaigns for Dannijo, Selima NY, True and Coach. He has also directed the latest film for fashion designer-turned rapper Dominic Lord's 2012 release 'Pierce' from his EP *Fashion Show*.

DANIELE + IANGO
Daniele + Iango have shot regularly for *i-D* , including covers for the thirtieth-anniversary edition in 2010. Their work has also regularly been published in *D la Repubblica* since 2001, as well as *Vogue*, *Interview*, *W*, *Visionaire*, *Dazed & Confused* and *AnOther* magazine. They have shot campaigns for Givenchy, Versus, Plein Sud, and Addiction. A collection of their personal work was exhibited as *The Modern Muses* at Colette in Paris in 2011 and appeared in the Ron Arad spring collection in the Arums Galerie in Paris in 2009.

BRUNO DAYAN
Bruno Dayan has shot major campaigns for Moschino, Louis Vuitton, Yves Saint Lauren and Dior. His work has been published in *Vogue*, *Numéro*, *Flair*, *Harper's Bazaar*, *D la Repubblica*, *Dansk* and *125*, amongst others. His short film *Vie d'eau* was selected at Cannes International Film Festival. He has also worked for Hennessy, Net-A-Porter and Swarovski.

PIERRE DEBUSSCHERE
Pierre Debusschere has photographed for *Vogue Hommes* Japan and produced a moving-image editorial for the first iPad edition of *Vogue Hommes* Japan Digital in collaboration with Nicola Formichetti. He has also produced editorials for *Citizen K*, *Dazed & Confused*, and *Under/Current*. He has produced campaigns for Raf Simons, for whom he is Online Art Director.

SEAN ELLIS
Regularly published in *The Face* in the 1990s, Sean Ellis has since directed several films including the Oscar-nominated *Cashback* and *The Broken*. His work has also appeared in *GQ*, *i-D*, *Numéro*, *Visionaire*, *Arena*, *Surface*, and he has shot campaigns for John Galliano, Kenneth Cole, Hugo Boss, Davidoff and Pirelli, amongst others. He has collaborated with David Lynch for *Harper's Bazaar*, and has released two books, *365* and *Kubrick the Dog*.

RENÉ HABERMACHER
René Habermacher has shot covers and editorials for *POP*, British *Vogue*, *Rolling Stone*, *Stern*, *Harper's Bazaar*, *V*, *L'Officiel* and *Numéro*, for whom he has also produced illustration work. He has worked on campaigns for Bulgari and Nieman Marcus amongst others. His film work has been commissioned for *Vogue* Italia's 2010 'One-Minute Light' series, and he has worked for theatre productions including *Medea(2)* for the 2008 Athens–Epidaurus Festival. He is associate editor of online creative community The Stimuleye.

ALICE HAWKINS
Having begun her career as party photographer for *i-D*, Alice Hawkins has shot for *Love*, *AnOther* magazine, *POP*, and *The Sunday Times Magazine*. She has shot portraits of Donatella Versace, Roberto Cavalli, Marilyn Manson and Keith Richards, has produced campaigns for Versace and Agent Provocateur and has collaborated with Nick Knight for SHOWstudio.

DANIEL JACKSON
Daniel Jackson has regularly shot covers for *Acne Paper* and *i-D*, and has shot for *Love*, *The Last Magazine* and *Self-Service*, as well as British *Vogue*, *Vogue* Germany, *Harper's Bazaar* and *The Wall Street Journal Magazine*, amongst others He has also shot film for *Love*, and campaigns for Calvin Klein, J.Mendel, Jil Sander and Alexander Wang.

YASUNARI KIKUMA
Working for *Vogue* Japan, Yasunari Kikuma has photographed Kate Moss, Dita Von Teese and Penelope Cruz, amongst others. He has also been published in *Schön*, *Dazed & Confused* Japan, *Vision* China and *Elle* Japan, and has shot for Fumihiro Hayashi's cult Japanese magazine *Dune*. Based in Tokyo, he also works regularly in New York.

NICK KNIGHT
Nick Knight is the founder and Director of SHOWstudio, an interactive web-based archive of contemporary art and fashion practice based around collaboration. He has worked for magazines including *Vogue*, *W*, *i-D*, *Dazed & Confused*, *AnOther* magazine and *AnOther Man*, has shot campaigns for Levi Strauss, Yves Saint Lauren and Calvin Klein, and has collaborated with Yohji Yamamoto and Alexander McQueen. The monograph *Nick Knight* was published in 2009. His work has been exhibited in The Victoria & Albert Museum, Saatchi Gallery and Hayward Gallery amongst others.

PAOLA KUDACKI
Paola Kudacki has produced editorials for *Hercules*, *i-D*, *GQ*, *Vogue* Japan, *Vogue* España, *Vogue* Paris, *Harper's Bazaar*, *25*, and *The Last Magazine*, amongst others. She also shoots a regular online fashion/travel diary and has produced campaigns for Louis Vuitton, J. Crew, Elisabetta Franchi Celyn, Massimo Dutti and Gas Jeans amongst others. In 2010 she won the Marie Claire Prix d'Excellence de la Mode for photographer of the year, and appeared in the *Vanity Fair* Hall of Fame exhibition at Barcelona Fashion Week in 2012.

LAROACHE BROTHERS
LaRoache Brothers have appeared in *Wig*, *Schön*, *Esquire*, *Interview*, *125* and *Dazed & Confused*. They have shot campaigns for Toni & Guy and Adidas, and portraits of Pete Doherty, Mickey Rourke and Willem Dafoe, amongst others. They have worked on the other side of the camera for Irving Penn.

SERGE LEBLON
Following a career as a war photographer Serge Leblon turned to fashion and has been published in *Grey*, *The Face*, *Dazed & Confused*, *AnOther Man*, *Vogue* China, *Vogue* Japan, *Vogue* Russia and *Elle*. He has worked on campaigns for Swarovski, Azzaro and Kate Spade. The collectible book *Serge Leblon* was released in 2010.

MARKUS + INDRANI
Markus Klinko and Indrani Pal-Chaudhuri have photographed album covers for Beyoncé, Mariah Carey and Mary J. Blige, and have shot for *Flaunt*, *Interview*, *Rolling Stone*, *V*, and *Vogue*. They have collaborated with iconic fashion figures David Bowie, Daphne Guinness and Dita Von Teese, and have worked on charitable projects including SEEschool and the Cannes Gold Lion award-winning *Buy Life/Digital Death* project for Keep a Child Alive. They are the subjects of the TV show *Double Exposure*.

TAKAHIRO OGAWA
Takahiro Ogawa regularly shoots for *Elle* Mexico, and has also been published in *WestEast*, *Metal* and *Vision*. His collaborative work with stylists Nicola Formichetti, Katie Shillingford and Robbie Spencer appeared as part of the 2010 Asia Beauty Expo.

PACO PEREGRÍN
Paco Peregrín has shot for *Harper's Bazaar*, *Elle* Mexico, *Schön*, *Vision*, *Vogue* Italia, and regularly for *Neo2* and *White*. He has worked on campaigns for Diesel, Nike, Levi's and EMI Music. He received a Gold Lux Award in 2008 for his shoot 'In My Room' for *Neo2*, and his work has been exhibited in solo shows at Visionairs Gallery, Paris, and Vered Art Gallery, New York.

RANKIN
Rankin co-founded *Dazed & Confused* in 1990, *AnOther* magazine in 2000, *AnOther Man* in 2005 and *The Hunger* in 2010. His work has also appeared in *Rolling Stone* and *Wonderland*, and he has shot covers for *Esquire*, *GQ* and German *Vogue*. He has published many books of photography including *Destroy/Rankin* in 2009, *Portraits* in 2010, *Myths, Monsters and Legends* in 2011 and *Open Rankin* in 2012. He has worked in collaboration with Damien Hirst, Ayami Nishimura, Caroline Saulnier, Alex Box and many others, and has worked with charities including Breakthrough Breast Cancer, Women's Aid, End of the Line and Oxfam.

EUGENIO RECUENCO
Eugenio Recuenco has shot editorials for Spanish *Vogue*, *V*, *Madame Figaro* and *Yo Dona*, and produced campaigns for Lavazza, Diesel, Nina Ricci and Loewe. His work has appeared in *Gothic: Dark Glamour* in 2008. In 2005 he picked up a Cannes Golden Lion Award for a photograph for TBWA/PlayStation, and his work has been featured in many galleries including El Matadero in Madrid, Spain, as part of Madridfoto 2012.

TIM RICHARDSON
Director and photographer Tim Richardson is a regular contributor to *Dazed & Confused*, *V*, *Elle* and *Interview*. He has worked on campaigns for Levi's, Sony, Nike and Diesel amongst others, and has shot portraits for Rinko Kikuchi, Spike Lee, Nicola Formichetti, and LCD Soundsystem. He directed the Lady Gaga film *Gaga Constellation* in 2012, and has also directed commercial fashion projects for Thierry Mugler and Givenchy. In 2010 choreographer Rafael Bonachela commissioned Richardson to direct *6 Breaths*, a video installation shown as part of the Venice Dance Biennale.

KOURTNEY ROY
Kourtney Roy has been published in *WestEast*, *Sex Mode & Digestion* and *Soup*. Her work has appeared in exhibitions at Les Rencontres d'Arles in France in 2008, and as part of the Dior multimedia exhibit alongside Peter Lindbergh in Shanghai in 2011. She won the Grand Prize at Diane Pernet's A Shaded View on Fashion Film Festival (ASVOFF) in Milan in 2012.

SANCHEZ AND MONGIELLO
Sofia Sanchez and Mauro Mongiello have regularly photographed for *Numéro*, and also shoot for *Vogue* Nippon, *L'Uomo Vogue*, *Interview*, *Garage*, *TAR* and *10 Magazine*. They have produced campaigns for Armani and Jeanne Lanvin Couture, and held their first solo exhibition, *La Niña Santa*, at La Toute Petite Agence in Paris in 2011.

DANIEL SANNWALD
Daniel Sannwald's work has appeared in *Arena Homme +*, *10 Men*, *i-D*, *Dazed & Confused*, *POP*, *V*, *032C*, and *Vogue Homme* Japan. His work has been exhibited at Issey Miyake's 2121 Design Sight in Tokyo in 2009, the Hyères Festival in France and the Cristóbal Balenciaga Museum in Spain in 2011, and at quartier21 in Austria in 2012. His book *Pluto and Charon* was published in 2011.

SEAN AND SENG
Sean and Seng have shot covers and editorials for *Interview* and *Dazed & Confused*, and their work has also appeared in *i-D*, *032c*, *Numéro*, *Le Portrait*, *Qvest*, Turkish *Vogue* and *Harper's Bazaar*. They have collaborated with stylists such as Ayami Nishimura and Isabella Blow, shot campaigns for L'Oreal and Vivienne Westwood, and in 2012 shot the short film *Temptation* for Dazed Digital, featuring Sam Riley and Joan Smalls.

WING SHYA
Wing Shya has worked as Art Director for Wong Kar-wai's multiple award-winning 2000 film *In the Mood for Love* and the follow-up, *2046* in 2004, as well as *Eros* and *Happy Together*, and is the Director of the 2010 film *Hot Summer Days*. He has been regularly published in *i-D*, *Visionaire* and *Tank*, amongst others. He is the founder of art and design agency Shya-La-La Workshop, based in Hong Kong.

CHADWICK TYLER
Chadwick Tyler has shot covers for *Grey*, and editorails for *Dazed & Confused*, *V* and *AnOther* magazine, amongst others. He has worked with designers Alexander Wang and Rad Hourani, and for Mercedes Benz. His work featured in a solo show, *Tiberius*, at the Honey Space Gallery in New York in 2009/10.

YELENA YEMCHUK
The multi-disciplinary illustrator, director and photographer Yelena Yemchuk has worked as Art Director for The Smashing Pumpkins albums *Adore* and *Machina/The Machines of God*, has exhibited her illustrations at the Dactyl Foundation in New York, and at the Brachfield Gallery in Paris in 2012 under the title *Beware My Lovely*. She has shot editorials and covers for *Dazed & Confused*, *Numéro*, *AnOther* magazine, *Muse*, *Vogue* Italia, *Vogue* Nippon and *Le Monde*, among others.

New Fashion Photography was produced by Paul Sloman with Tim Blanks, Natasha Isaacs, Marcelo dos Santos Pereira, Christine Antaya, Ali Gitlow, and with the generous cooperation and contributions of the photographers.

Special thanks also to the following people for their support and assistance: Justin Rose at Trunk Archive, Amy Poole at Rankin Photography Ltd, Marìlu Menendez at Marìlu Menendez Communications, Robin Jaffee at Streeters, Sabrina Mansouri at Marek and Associates, Martin Weston at Patricia McMahon, Gianfranco Meza and Valeria Gentile at Gianfranco Meza, Thuy Tran at 2b Management, Julie Brown at M.A.P., Justinian Kfoury at TotalWorld, Nicholas Hardy at Factory 311, Valerio Cordioli at Aura Photo Agency, all at 254FOREST, Paz at Studio Eugenio Recuenco, Angela de Bona Photo Agency, Sebastian at Daniel Sannwald Studio, and Fanni Szokoli at Management Artists.

Thanks also to Jasmine Vega at DMGLA, Anne Nelson at IMGworld, ML McCarthy at Urban Productions Ltd, Velvet d'Amour, Sarah at Next Models, Muse NYC, John Gnerre at Women Management, Claudia Midolo at ModelWerks, Bryna Rifkin, Mark at Altaimage and Laura Cuccoli at Conti Tipocolor.

Thanks finally to Andrew Hansen and Ali Gitlow for making it happen.

Dedicated to Ron Sloman, a little-known pioneer of dye-transfer colour photography in the early twentieth century.